On the Reproduction of Capitalism

On the Reproduction of Capitalism

Ideology and Ideological State Apparatuses

LOUIS ALTHUSSER

PREFACE BY ETIENNE BALIBAR

INTRODUCTION BY JACQUES BIDET

TRANSLATED BY G. M. GOSHGARIAN

VERSO

London • New York

This English-language edition published by Verso 2014
Translation © G. M. Goshgarian 2014
First published as *Sur la reproduction*
© Presses Universitaires de France 1995
Preface © Etienne Balibar 2014
Introduction © Jacques Bidet 2014

'Ideology and Ideological State Apparatuses' first appeared in Louis Althusser, *Lenin and Philosophy and Other Essays*, trans. Ben Brewster, London, New Left Books, 1971. The translation has been modified.

'Ideology and Ideological State Apparatuses,' translation
© Ben Brewster 1971, 1994, 2014

7 9 10 8 6

Verso
UK: 6 Meard Street, London W1F 0EG
US: 20 Jay Street, Suite 1010, Brooklyn, NY 11201
www.versobooks.com

Verso is the imprint of New Left Books

ISBN-13: 978-1-78168-164-0 (PBK)
ISBN-13: 978-1-78168-165-7 (HBK)
eISBN-13: 978-1-78168-215-9 (US)
eISBN-13: 978-1-78168-524-2 (UK)

British Library Cataloguing in Publication Data

A catalogue record for this book is available from the British Library.

Library of Congress Cataloging-in-Publication Data
Althusser, Louis, 1918-1990.
[Sur la reproduction. English]
On the reproduction of capitalism : ideology and ideological state apparatuses / Louis Althusser ; preface by Etienne Balibar ; introduction by Jacques Bidet ; translated by G.M. Goshgarian.
pages cm
"First published as Sur la reproduction, [copyright] Presses Universitaires de France 1995."
Includes index.
ISBN 978-1-78168-164-0 (pbk. : alk. paper) – ISBN 978-1-78168-165-7 (hardback : alk. paper)
1. Production (Economic theory) 2. Marxian economics. 3. Capitalism. 4. State, The. 5. Social conflict. I. Title.
HB241.A5613 2013
335.4'12–dc23
2013033117

Typeset in Bembo by Hewer Text UK Ltd, Edinburgh, Scotland
Printed and bound by CPI Group (UK) Ltd, Croydon, CR0 4YY

Contents

FOREWORD

Althusser and the 'Ideological State Apparatuses'

Etienne Balibar

Jacques Bidet and the Presses Universitaires de France have invited me to contribute an additional introduction to the second edition of Althusser's posthumously published book Sur la reproduction, *which they first published in 1995. Since then, there has been steady demand for the book. I am touched and honoured by their invitation, and am very happy that they have accepted, by way of a contribution to their enterprise, a text that is not absolutely new, because it was written some time ago and has already been published, albeit not in French. It is the preface that I wrote for Ariella Azoulay's Hebrew translation of the chapter from Althusser's text entitled 'On Ideology'.[1] I do not wish to modify it. The reason is that I was already trying to formulate the questions that I myself have about the construction and implications of an ensemble the most striking part of which is, like it or not, the discussion of the 'Ideological State Apparatuses', even as I was doing my best to recall and reconstruct the circumstances of the text's composition and partial publication; for it so happens that I was rather closely associated with both. I also welcome the opportunity to associate our readings of Althusser with a colleague whose own work (which bears, in particular, on the 'mode of production' of the visual arts) holds an important place in the field of contemporary 'theory', and whose fight for justice at the side of the Palestinian people, oppressed by the state of Israel, is in my view quite admirable. That certain of Althusser's works, produced in a very different context that is, by now, forty years behind us, should seem to people here and in other places across the globe to be an intellectual, moral and political resource is, I think, a lovely lesson of history, truly.[2]*

---

1   Tel Aviv, Resling, 2003.
2   See esp., by Ariella Azoulay, *The Civil Contract of Photography*, New York, Zone Books, 2008; *Atto di Stato. Palestina-Israele, 1967–2007: Storia fotografica dell'occupazione*, Milan, Bruno Mondadori Editore, 2008; and the poem 'Nous sommes tous des palestiniens' [We are all Palestinians], written when Israel invaded Gaza in 2008–9, available at mediapart. fr/club/blog/ariella-azoulay.

In the present brief preface, I do not want to make a detailed commentary on Althusser's text about Ideological State Apparatuses [ISAs], now translated into Hebrew for the first time. In response to a request from Ariella Azoulay, whom I very warmly thank for soliciting a contribution from me and then waiting patiently for it, I would simply like to offer a few remarks about the text's status and the conditions under which it was produced.

I believe it can be said that this text has become, and will remain, one of its author's major works. It is one of those that serve as a reference point when it is a question of characterizing his thought; one mobilizing concepts that bear his 'personal signature' and are immediately recognizable as his (here, 'Ideological State Apparatuses' and 'ideological interpellation'; elsewhere, 'the epistemological break', 'symptomatic reading', and so on); finally, one that contemporary philosophy in the structuralist or post-structuralist line continues to work on.[3] Yet its status – even when it is considered in the context of a fragmentary, unfinished and largely posthumous text – is altogether paradoxical.

To begin with, which text are we talking about? Given the modalities of its release and re-release, it is impossible to assign it a unique identity today or to trace its boundaries with certainty. On the contrary: we have to recall its history and inscribe it in various, partially competing ensembles so as to understand how it is that the commentaries it has elicited, which today accompany it or prescribe the way it is read, can be so divergent. The text translated into Hebrew comprises Chapter 12, titled 'On Ideology', of the posthumous volume that Jacques Bidet edited and issued in 1995, five years after Althusser's death. This is a reasonable choice, since it gives the reader access to a version, both coherent and complete, of Althusser's autonomous discussion of, specifically, ideology. Yet it was not at all in this form that the text was initially released before being reprinted, translated into various languages, and read and discussed. The first edition, which initially appeared as a contribution to the journal *La Pensée* (no. 151, June 1970) and then as a chapter in the book *Positions* (Paris, Editions Sociales, 1976), under the title 'Idéologie et appareils idéologiques d'Etat (Notes pour une recherche)', was both longer, inasmuch as it prefaced the theory of the 'mechanism of ideology' with an argument about 'the reproduction of the conditions of production', and, at the same time, an abridged version of its own argument. It was presented as 'made up of two extracts from an ongoing study' that were

---

3   See, for example, Judith Butler, *The Psychic Life of Power: Theories in Subjection*, New York, Routledge, 1997.

being submitted to others for discussion. Since the ongoing study was never finished and was not published in its author's lifetime, while the debate occasioned by the extracts was very lively and substantial in a number of different countries, it is safe to assume that most commentators will continue to refer to this 'historic' version. I shall, therefore, say something about the circumstances and causes of this imbroglio.

Jacques Bidet, in his critical and philological introduction, says that there exist two versions of the complete manuscript of 'De la superstructure' from which these extracts were taken. Both are unfinished. The first, approximately 150 pages long, was written in March–April 1969. The second, some 200 pages long, is undated; it revises and augments the first. The 1970 *Pensée* piece, made up of extracts from Chapter 3 ('The Reproduction of the Conditions of Production'), Chapter 4 ('Base and Superstructure'), Chapter 6 ('The State'), Chapter 9 ('The Reproduction of the Relations of Production') and Chapter 12 ('On Ideology'), lies, Bidet surmises, 'somewhere between the two versions', independently of the cuts, condensations and addenda that mark it. All this is incomprehensible if we do not explain what led Althusser to release such a partial montage rather than a text that was 'complete', but unfinished – and, in fact, unfinishable.

To explain that, we have to go back to the way Althusser's illness (which the psychiatrists called a 'manic-depressive psychosis') was bound up with the political circumstances of the day. In May–June 1968, at the time of the 'events' that Althusser himself described, after the fact, as an 'ideological revolt of the masses of young people in the school system'),[4] he found himself, doubtless not by accident, in a clinic in a Paris suburb, where he was undergoing treatment for a depressive episode. During the treatment, he was cut off from the world outside. In the months that followed, after taking the measure of the significant changes in the social situation and political atmosphere in France and abroad, and trying to interpret their meaning in the course of sometimes difficult discussions with a number of his friends and students, some of whom had taken a more or less active part in the movement, Althusser proposed to make a contribution of his own to a work then in progress by returning to questions of Marxist theory bearing on the relations between 'base and

---

4 Louis Althusser, 'A propos de l'article de Michel Verret sur Mai étudiant', *La Pensée*, no. 145, June 1969. See also Althusser's letters to Maria-Antonietta Macchiocchi, which Macchiocchi published in *Lettere dall'interno del PCI a Louis Althusser*, Rome, Feltrinelli, 1969. These letters were not reproduced in the French or English editions of the same work.

superstructure'. A group to which I, too, belonged (along with Pierre Macherey, Roger Establet, Christian Baudelot, and Michel Tort) had, setting out from notes and public interventions from the preceding period, undertaken to produce a collective work (according to the plan, it was to be voluminous) on the theory of the school system in capitalist society (the capitalist 'mode of production'). In particular, we had decided to use a terminology that included the notions of 'scholastic form' (patterned after 'commodity form' in the first part of *Capital*) and 'scholastic apparatus' (patterned after 'state apparatus' in Marx's *Eighteenth Brumaire of Louis Bonaparte* and his other 'political works'). It was agreed that these two elaborations (ours and Althusser's) would be confronted. A common doctrine was supposed to emerge from the confrontation. It was our sense that we comprised something like an original school of thought within 'Western' Marxism. The strikes and the mass social movements of 1968 and the following months had spread the idea on the Marxist Left that we were entering a new revolutionary cycle that could bring on fundamental changes. When compared with the classical models, however, a certain number of differences leapt to the eye. (They put 'orthodox' Marxists such as Althusser, convinced of the primacy of class struggle and the polit- ically organized workers' movement, in a ticklish situation.) Not only were the 1968 struggles affecting the countries of the 'socialist camp' and the 'capitalist camp' alike, from China through Czechoslovakia, France, Germany and Italy to Poland, from the United States to Brazil; they also assigned or, at least, seemed to assign, a leading role to 'new social move- ments', including the student movement (even secondary school students had mobilized), in relation with the overt crisis of major 'authoritarian' institutions such as the schools and the family. From his first widely debated essays on,[5] Althusser had attached great importance to developing the 'Marxist' theory of ideology or even producing a theory from scratch, with a view to refounding or reconstructing historical materialism. This, to be sure, gave him the impression that he could account for the novelty of the political phenomena of his day. At the same time, however, it presented him (and us as well) with a challenge it was not easy to take up in an intellectual environment increasingly strained by the proliferating division into irreconcilable tendencies of political organizations all claim- ing to be Marxist, at a time when many 'critical' theorists were increasingly taking their distance from references to Marx.[6]

---

5   Above all, *For Marx* (London, Allen Lane, 1969), a collection of essays written from 1961 to 1965 that was first published in book form in French in 1965.

6   Michel Foucault's evolution is typical in this regard. It had brought him to

None of these plans was to be realized as originally envisaged. Althusser, working in a state of great excitement, as he always did after a depressive phase, had in a few weeks produced a manuscript which, albeit incomplete, already took the form of a book. He sent it to the 'group working on the schools', which had set to work earlier than he had and independently of him, but was progressing more slowly, amid critical readings of Bourdieu, Durkheim, Freinet and Krupskaya, as well as statistical tables on the primary and secondary school experiences of bourgeois and working-class children. The question at this point was how to make the 'suture' between the analyses of the scholastic apparatus that we had arrived at, for our part, and the general idea, elaborated by Althusser, of 'Ideological State Apparatuses' and their function in reproducing capitalist relations of production. Despite the similarity of our ideas and terminologies, we were unable to reach agreement. The result was general paralysis. It was exacerbated by political tensions which originated in the fact that some of us felt closer to Maoist groups (the Union des Jeunesses communistes Marxistes-Léninistes and, subsequently, the Gauche Prolétarienne), whereas others, including Althusser himself, deemed it necessary to stay 'inside the Party' (that is, the official Communist Party).[7] The 'autonomy of theory' was falling to pieces . . . Althusser, for his part, soon fell ill again. This was perhaps not just a reaction to these tensions and, more generally, the ordeal to which he was subjected because of his attachment to the party (which charged him with being the master thinker behind the radical leftists, at a time when many of his close disciples had become dissidents and demanded that he join them, before going on to accuse him of revisionism and treason). It was also due to a general weakening of his physical state that had deep roots and only got

---

unequivocally anti-Marxist formulations by the 1970s. See, for example, his 1976 *History of Sexuality, Vol. 1: The Will to Knowledge*, trans. Robert Hurley, New York, Random House, 1978, as well as the course he gave the same year, now available as *Society Must Be Defended: Lectures at the Collège de France, 1975–76*, trans. David Macey, Harmondsworth, Penguin, 2003, which contains a transparent critique of the notions of ideology, apparatus, and ideological apparatus). Today, however, it is possible, not to relativize, but to situate the question of Foucault's relation to Marxism in a longer, more complex evolution. His relationship with Althusser, at once personal, intellectual and institutional, did not by itself determine this evolution, but certainly helped determine it from first to last.

7 Althusser, in his 1984 'autobiography', published posthumously in 1992 (*The Future Lasts a Long Time*, in '*The Future Lasts a Long Time' and 'The Facts'*, trans. Richard Veasey, London, Chatto and Windus, 1993), puts a conspiratorial face on this 'tactic'. I do not subscribe to his presentation of things, but it is certain that it eventually proved impossible to maintain the cohesion of a working group which, because it was made up of intellectuals loyal to rival organizations, had to remain secret. (In retrospect, I find this ridiculous.)

worse as the years wore on. The upshot was that all the work all of us had done was broken off and never finished.[8] Althusser's manuscript *Sur la reproduction* ended up joining a series of other texts in various states of completion that he turned out between 1968 and 1980. These often took the form of 'treatises' or 'popularized' essays written on the model of the classical Marxist introductions to historical materialism; he worked on them when his illness was in remission and left them unfinished. Some have now been published in collections of his posthumous works.

In 1970, however, when Althusser returned to active life, friends of his, notably Marcel Cornu, editor of the review *La Pensée*, invited him to share some of his work in progress with the public. It now seemed to Althusser that an elaboration of his views on ideology could spark another round in a discussion that, he hoped, would help him get back to work. This is what motivated the 'montage' of extracts that he published under the title 'Idéologie et appareils idéologiques d'Etat' [Ideology and Ideological State Apparatuses]. Destiny was to convert this stopgap solution into something with definitive or, at any rate, long-term status. For it was on the faith of impressions spawned by the conjunction of two fundamentally discontinuous series of arguments – one centred on the question of the 'reproduction of the relations of production', the other on the 'ideological' mechanism of interpellation, recognition and guarantee – that the commentaries, utilizations and critiques were to be based. At the point of aporetic encounter between the two lay the notion, or cabbalistic expression, 'ISAs'.[9]

In the original edition (by which I mean the 1970 piece), dotted lines were inserted between the extracts after they had been reworked. These lines, especially those separating two major developments, have taken on

---

8 In the following period, Christian Baudelot and Roger Establet 'salvaged' part of the collective manuscript on the schools, completed it in line with their own views, and released it as a book: *L'Ecole capitaliste en France*, Paris, Maspero, 1971. Michel Tort published, in counterpoint, *Le Q.I.* [The intellectual quotient], Paris, Maspero, 1974.

9 This rapid presentation may give the impression that this period in Althusser's career was a totally sombre one, marked only by intellectual crises and abortive projects. To put things back in proper perspective, we should point out that, in the same years, Althusser was working on another project, in some sense 'private', the very admirable result of which we now know, but of which most of his collaborators were unaware at the time: a projected book on Machiavelli (and, via this detour, on the very concept of the political). See *Machiavelli and Us*, trans. Gregory Elliott, London, Verso, 1999. This essay on Machiavelli has been translated into a number of languages, including Italian. It was published in French in *Ecrits philosophiques et politiques*, ed. François Matheron and Olivier Corpet, Paris, Stock/ Imec, vol. 2, 1995, and reissued in a paperback edition in 2009 together with two essays by Matheron (*Machiavel et nous*, Paris, Tallandier, 2009, preface by Etienne Balibar).

an unforeseen function: they materialize an absence (a 'void', to use a word highlighted by one of Althusser's best commentators and editors, François Matheron, who thus puts one of the philosopher's favourite expressions in play and *en abîme*)[10] that is also the site of very important, very forbidding problems. I have always felt that the fecundity of Althusser's text has, precisely, to do with this suspension of the argument in the vicinity of the decisive articulation – signposted and simultaneously spirited away – which is materialized by the dotted line. Readers were led to look for the 'solution' to the problem themselves, either because they imagined that Althusser himself was in possession of it but, for some mysterious reason, would not or could not reveal it, or because they had understood that he was not, in fact, in possession of it, and so tried to find a way to develop and transform each available sketch of a solution in hopes of coming up with one themselves. What they could not have known, obviously, and what publication of the manuscript in its entirety shows us today, is that which forms the 'missing link' in Althusser's text. Essentially, it is a discussion of *law* and of *revolution*, separated by a suggestion to 'extend' the 'classical' Marxist concept of the 'state'.

In his discussion of law, Althusser sets out from theses that are basically quite close to those of the positive law tradition (and, underlying it, the Kantian definition of law and its difference from morality), in order to insist on the 'repressive' nature of the law. His conclusion is that law is by itself incapable of guaranteeing the reproduction or stabilization of the dominant social relations; whence, he says, the 'functional' necessity of an ideological supplement of effectivity. In his discussion of the state, he endeavours to explain (while sounding cautionary notes in profusion) how one can simultaneously think the perpetuation of the conditions of exploitation and the necessity of their interruption. This is the usual crux in Marxist attempts to articulate theory and practice. The most interesting aspect of Althusser's text is doubtless its reconsideration of his earlier discussion of the *difference in the temporalities* of the political struggle: a 'short' temporality, that of the class struggles that unfold in the public sphere, with, as their stakes, possession of state power; and a 'long' temporality, that of the class struggles which, riding roughshod over the border between public and private, unfold in the *materiality of ideology*.[11] This

---

10 François Matheron, 'The Recurrence of the Void in Louis Althusser', trans. Erin A. Post, *Rethinking Marxism*, Vol. 10, No. 3 (Fall 1998), pp. 22–37. See also Matheron, *Machiavel et nous*.

11 Here Althusser falls back on the eighteenth-century French philosophers whom he knew well, Montesquieu and Rousseau, in order to suggest that we read this materiality, or the 'practical' nature of ideology (formalized by the 'Ideological State Apparatuses'), as an

sketch of a solution, however, merely highlights (by way of the embar-
rassment betrayed in the writing itself) the aporia that Althusser encounters:
the 'ideological class struggle' on which the effectivity of the political
struggle itself depends, since it prepares the conditions for the political
struggle and mobilizes its bearers (the 'revolutionary class'), cannot itself
be the historical 'last instance' of the political. Its own effectivity is referred
back to the enigmatic short circuit of two heterogeneous 'materialities'.[12]
'It is the infrastructure that is determinant in the last instance.' Thus the
fact that contemporary readers now have access to Althusser's intervening
arguments will by no means diminish their perplexity. On the other
hand, it will paralyze their theoretical imaginations by replacing a glaring
void with an apparent fullness. That is why, notwithstanding the depress-
ing and even – in the end – tragic consequences to which it is due, I
consider it an extraordinary 'objective fluke' that Althusser was forced to
publish his essay in the form, not of a (pseudo-)treatise on historical materialism, but, rather, as a collage of two heterogeneous propositions 'open'
to the unknown.

It remains to ask, before leaving the readers to confront Althusser's
words on their own, how we are to think the effects of that heterogene-
ity today. It seems to me that one can advance two hypotheses here. First,
history (political, social, intellectual) has completely shattered the unity,
even the problematic unity, of the two discourses that Althusser's 'structural Marxism' sought to combine in such a way that each would help
sustain the other; it has relegated them to contexts that hardly communi-
cate now. This is not to say that history thereby flags the absurdity of the
attempt: for that attempt has a great deal to teach us about the theoretical
demands of its day, and testifies to a remarkable seriousness (or 'sense of
responsibility for the consequences of one's discourse') whose lesson has
not been lost. Second, the divorce between the contexts in question

---

equivalent of the classical theory of 'custom' [*mœurs*], in opposition to an 'idealist' theory of
ideology as the reign of ideas or opinion.

12   To be honest, the aporia in question merely reproduces one that is constant in
Marx, especially in the famous Preface to *A Contribution to the Critique of Political Economy*
(1859), with the difference that Marx speaks of the 'encounter', in the revolutionary
conjuncture, of the materiality of the 'productive forces' and the ideality of the 'forms of
social consciousness'. In insisting on the fact that ideology itself is material and – for the
most part – unconscious, Althusser attempts to displace this classical philosophical difficulty,
without really managing to explain how the same formal concept of the 'class struggle'
applies from one end of historical materiality to the other. He broaches the same problem
in 'Note on the ISAs', a text he appended in December 1976 to the German and Spanish
translations of his essay. I shall return to the 'Note', which Jacques Bidet has included as an
appendix to the present volume.

testifies, in its fashion, to the omnipresence of a multiform question: that of the subject and, indissolubly bound up with it, that of political 'subjectivation', which, clearly, always has its place within several different intellectual horizons at the same time.

Althusser's discussions of the 'reproduction of the relations of production' are based on a concept of structure which, it has been said, is essentially 'functionalist'; he had constantly to defend himself against that charge.[13] But it is a question, rather, of inscribing the possibility or even necessity of a *break* with the dominant capitalist system at the precise point of this system's constitutional 'fragility' (that is, in a sense, its point of 'contingency', as Althusser would later put it). The Althusserian reading of Marx's texts suggests that we should identify this point with an extended conception of social 'reproduction'. In these discussions, which all remain more or less unfinished and are all heavily marked by the traditional terminology of 'historical materialism', Althusser accordingly endeavours strategically to bring to bear on this one point all the elements of the structure's *retroactive action* on itself, in order to make them the privileged sites and objects of the class struggle. We might say that his inspiration is ultra-Leninist, in the sense that he does not content himself with defining the objective of the organized class struggle as 'state power' and the 'state apparatus', but redoubles the latter notion in such a way as to be able to include in it both 'ideological domination' and the latent centralization of ideological practices and representations on the basis of a 'State Ideology' (which, in the bourgeois epoch, is probably *legal* ideology in his view). Thus it is as if Althusser were trying to *reinforce* and accentuate the 'totalitarian' image of bourgeois domination and the obscure power of the state, in order ultimately to arrive, by an oxymoron, at the possibility of overthrowing it. The 'strongest link' is also, potentially, 'the weakest'. This also grounds his disagreement with Gramsci: it is crystallized in Althusser's rejection of the Gramscian notion of 'hegemony' and in his insistence on the *exteriority* of the revolutionary *party* (or movement) to the whole system of bourgeois 'superstructures', the correlative of its interiority or critical immanence to the practices of the

---

13 Notably in the aforementioned 'Note on the ISAs'. The 'Note' ends with a long discussion of the status of the 'revolutionary party', which is at once essentially 'outside the state' by virtue of its class base and historical objectives, yet structurally 'subjected' to the dominant class by way of the Ideological State Apparatuses. This text contains recurrent allusions to the practice of the European (French and Italian) Communist Parties of its day, which had set out on the 'Eurocommunist' parliamentary path in the name of a Gramscian 'war of position'. It affirms, in transparent fashion, the necessity of 'breaking' with this political logic.

popular masses and the working class. But this merely displaces the problem. And the idea of an organization external to ideological forms of organization, which are obviously apparatus-forms in their turn, is, it will be agreed, quite enigmatic.[14]

The other aspect of Althusser's work on ideology in fact belongs to a completely different context. The idea that ideology has a 'structure in general' is not only not traceable to the Marxist tradition, even if Althusser demonstrates its kinship with certain remarks by Marx, particularly in *The German Ideology* ('ideology has no history of its own'), which he read 'symptomatically'. (This simply proves that Marx and Marxism are not the same thing.) That idea in fact refers us to a different concept of 'structure'. In question here, as far as Althusser's own work is concerned, is a series of texts stretching from the 1964 essay 'Freud and Lacan' (republished in *Positions* in 1976) through, notably, two essays collected in *For Marx* ('The "Piccolo Teatro": Bertolazzi and Brecht' [1962] and 'Marxism and Humanism' [1963]) to the 1976 or 1977 text 'On Marx and Freud' (published in the *Proceedings of the Psychoanalytic Congress of Tbilisi*).[15] In these writings, Althusser pursues a study of the *imaginary constitution of the subject* as the fundamental 'ideological effect', or, better, as an *effect of the structure of ideology*. (Obviously, however, there is an element of circularity here, for the effect of the structure of ideology par excellence is, precisely, to constitute 'subjects' – to which we may add that, if the essential goal of the structuralist movement, in which Althusser participated in his way,[16] was to conceptualize the *constitution of the subject* in place of 'the constitutive subject' of the classic transcendental philosophies, ideology here becomes simply another name for structure.) Althusser develops his study (as appears, in particular, at the moment of the transition from the first to the second and third moments of the 'constitution of the subject': hailing, recognition, guarantee) by working

---

14   This idea does not differ much from the Leninist idea of a 'state' that is a 'non-state' (in *State and Revolution*). In other words, it names the *transition*, anticipating it or 'putting it back before' the seizure of power; and it constitutes something like its condition.

15   Louis Althusser, 'Freud and Lacan', in *Writings on Psychoanalysis: Freud and Lacan*, trans. Jeffrey Mehlman, ed. François Matheron and Olivier Corpet, New York, Columbia University Press, 1996, pp. 7–32; 'The "Piccolo Teatro": Bertolazzi and Brecht – Notes on a Materialist Theatre', in *For Marx*, trans. Ben Brewster, London, Allen Lane, 1969, pp. 129–51; 'Marxism and Humanism', in *For Marx*, pp. 219–41; 'On Marx and Freud', in *Writings on Psychoanalysis*, pp. 105–24.

16   Like so many others, Althusser moved alternately back and forth between recognizing and repudiating structuralism, approaching it and distancing himself from it. All the structuralists, or almost all of them (Lévi-Strauss is the exception), said, at one moment or another, 'I am not a structuralist', or even 'I am anything but a structuralist.'

on theoretical models borrowed from Hegel, Freud, Feuerbach and Spinoza (under the general aegis of Spinoza, credited with having inaugurated a critical philosophy of the imaginary and its social effectivity). It is certainly not a 'complete' theory (but does it make any sense to demand that a theory be complete?). One of the keys to its interpretation (which one may consider extrinsic, but which does also point to the circulation of problems and concepts in the conjuncture of the period) resides, manifestly, in a latent controversy with Lacan (a controversy about which students today are often curious) around the question of the 'symbolic'. Althusser basically takes the signifiers of the symbolic from the discourse of monotheism, especially with his two references to its Mosaic refoundation ('I am your servant Moses') and its repetition/transformation in the New Testament ('Thou art Peter'). In this connection, we may say that Althusser very unceremoniously pulls the Lacanian symbolic back into the field of the imaginary and the speculary relation characteristic of it, in order to make it a 'function' internal to the imaginary. By the same token, obviously, he implicitly asks how we should think the 'real', which, in the well-known Lacanian scheme, forms the third pillar of the explanation of the unconscious. All indications would seem to be that Althusser refuses to identify the 'real', as Lacan does, with the *negative* function of an impossible or a traumatic event that is unrepresentable because it cannot be symbolized: in short, a transcendental 'thing-in-itself'. What, then, constitutes the *positivity* of the real, the correlate of the *materiality* of the imaginary? The suggestion is made on the text's horizon, but, here too, in very enigmatic fashion, that this question can probably not be divorced from the question of the 'bad subject', the one who does not manage to 'go all by herself' or who resists interpellation. We might also say that it is a question of the subject's *excessive power*, the result of her very *weakness*, with respect to the circuit of interpellation, which, nevertheless, constitutes her or confers her 'form' on her. Yet one notes (this has often been noted) something of a strange reservation on Althusser's part here. It has, moreover, often been interpreted as a form of resistance or denial . . .

I cannot, obviously, pursue an introduction and a discussion that would, if taken any further, sow the illusion of accomplished knowledge. I prefer to leave the reader with questions; it will be understood that they were not really posed for the first time today. However, when I look back on this presentation of the materiality characteristic of Althusser's writing, which I have just attempted to make at Ariella's invitation, I see that I have voluntarily or involuntarily suggested, after all, that the two divorced 'halves' whose combination I have described have the same vanishing point: let us call it the question of practice, a possible common name for the idea of an 'organization without organization' that would make the revolution conceivable; and also for the idea of a 'counter-interpellation of the subject' capable of manifesting, in the very forms of the imaginary, the externality (or positivity) with which it finds itself in a constitutive relationship unawares. To be honest, this suggestion smacks of the impenitent 'May 68er' I have certainly continued to be; and, as it does no more than name something, it resolves nothing. One can only wish that contemporary readers of Althusser's text, in one or another of its configurations, will find other keys capable of investing it with meaning.

INTRODUCTION

An Invitation to Reread Althusser

Jacques Bidet

The present volume contains, at last available to the public, 'The Reproduction of the Relations of Production'.[1] This is the manuscript from which Althusser extracted his famous text 'Ideology and Ideological State Apparatuses', first published in 1970 in the review *La Pensée*.

Althusser here explains, in systematic fashion, his conception of historical materialism, the conditions for the reproduction of capitalist society, and the revolutionary struggle that seeks to put an end to it. His propositions about ideology and the 'apparatuses', put back in the overall framework of his project and the context of his political thought, reveal their object and presuppositions.

This text may seem to be coming back to haunt us from another day and age. It does indeed bear witness, in part, to opinions that have become impossible to maintain today. Yet it continues to have, twenty-five years after it was written, a singular capacity for theoretical provocation. It confronts us with a question that is today less than ever possible to dismiss as obsolete: under what conditions, in a society that proclaims its devotion to the ideals of freedom and equality, is the domination of some people over others endlessly reproduced?

At first sight, Althusser's manuscript presents itself as a didactic, militant text, and it is, at the same time, the best of introductions to his thought. As it unfolds, however, it gradually reveals that it also contains an original conceptual elaboration. Thus it calls for a reading at several levels: it is a political text that bears witness to its period; an introduction to the Althusserian categories for the analysis of capitalism; and a (novel) theory of the 'Ideological State Apparatuses' and ideological 'interpellation'.

---

1 Bidet gives the original title of Althusser's manuscript, which went unpublished in the author's lifetime. When the manuscript finally appeared, the French publisher retitled it *Sur la reproduction*, and the two French titles have been conflated for the English edition.

POLITICAL TEXT, THEORETICAL TEXT

The spirit of May 1968 runs through the entire text, that of a May that was as much the workers' as the students', a May that witnessed the biggest strike in French history. Communist memory was reinvigorated by the prospect of the radical changes that now seemed to be on the agenda. Althusser passionately embraced this moment and assigned it its place in the long-term course of the socialist revolution. His field of vision, in this text, encompasses 'a century of class struggle by the workers' movement across the face of the earth' ('hundreds of thousands of anonymous worker militants', and so on, p. 135). It also encompasses an indubitable future: 'We are entering an age that will see the triumph of socialism across the globe . . . *the Revolution is already on the agenda. One hundred years from now*, perhaps only fifty years from now, the face of the world will have changed: the Revolution will have carried the day from one end of the earth to the other' (p. 6). Althusser has his eye on 'the many young militants who have flocked or will flock' to the political struggle (p. 133). Indirectly, he is addressing them.

This will not fail to surprise readers who know only Althusser's philosophical texts. The essential reference, in the conception of the trade union and political struggle under capitalism, the schema for the conquest of power by the 'proletariat and its allies', and the conception of the dictatorship of the proletariat, is to Leninism, 'the Leninism of Maurice Thorez' (p. 133). The reference to Leninism finds expression in a return to the vocabulary of the Bolshevik Revolution and the Third International: 'the masses', 'organized in the trade union', must be 'led towards truly revolutionary objectives' by 'the party of the vanguard of the proletariat' (p. 134). Althusser expressly places himself in the line of what he calls the 'classics of Marxism'. 'Here we shall be advancing cautiously on a terrain on which Marx, Lenin, Stalin and Mao have long since preceded us, but without systematizing, in theoretical form, the decisive progress that their experiences [*expériences*, which also means 'experiments'] and procedures implied. Why? Because these experiences and procedures were essentially confined *to the terrain of political practice*' (p. 74). 'Stalin neglected these questions' (p. 92). One rubs one's eyes in disbelief. Stalin's name disappears from the piece published in *La Pensée*. The fact remains that there is something surrealistic in this imaginary repetition of Leninism in an altogether different place and time – in a time, notably, in which the party that Althusser called his was proposing, as if its validity were self-evident, an utterly different strategy, founded on the idea of a march towards socialism by way of a gradual, legal process of public appropriation of the major means of production.

Yet the political pathos, and the accompanying strain of exaltation, declarations of fidelity or ostentatious allegiance, and defiance of realism, should not prevent us from making our way through the book and noticing that it is also the vehicle of a theoretical investigation of great importance. That is not to say that there is not a close relation between this particular vision of history and the set of concepts it offers for an understanding of the structure and social essence of capitalism. In any case, whatever we make of the emphatic reference to 'Marxist-Leninist philosophy' (p. 2), 'our philosophy' (p. 4), it soon becomes clear that, although what is in question here is indeed Marxism and Leninism, Althusser's thought can by no means be classified as 'Marxism-Leninism' in the ordinary sense of an orthodoxy. It is equally clear that it deserves to be revalued today as an autonomous source of intellectual stimulation.

The great importance of the theoretical intervention makes itself felt every time that Althusser underscores the merely 'descriptive' nature of traditional theory: the topography of base and superstructure (p. 54–5); the correspondence between productive forces and relations of production (p. 20, p. 163); or the Marxist 'theory' of the state (p. 70), law (p. 164), or ideology (pp. 155–6). On all these subjects, which is to say, the doctrine as a whole, Althusser proposes to go beyond the form of 'description' (pp. 53–4), a form by nature 'unstable', and move towards 'theory in the full sense' (pp. 72–3, p. 166). Behind the show of modesty – the author offers us 'unprecedented clarifications', but only of 'certain limited points' (p. 8) – it is a question, ultimately, of producing, where we have nothing more than description, a theory in the true sense of the word.

FOR A REREADING OF THE THEORY OF THE ISAS

The first chapter introduces Althusser's thesis about philosophy as a form that presupposes social conflict and scientific work, and about the history of philosophy as a sequence of conjunctures in which novelty arises at the conjunction of decisive 'political–economic and scientific' 'events' (p. 16). It situates Marx's contribution in the 'scientific' realm: the discovery of the 'continent of history' (p. 7) and the invention of a theory capable of providing a basis for diverse social sciences.

The following chapters provide – even if they offer, to a certain extent, nothing more than a reprise of 'classical theses' (p. 19) – an articulated presentation of the major categories commanding Althusser's interpretation of historical materialism. Every 'social formation' is characterized by a 'dominant mode of production' (p. 19). In the relationship between the relations of production and the productive forces that comprise the base, the former play the determinant role (Althusser develops this point in Appendix 1). In the model as a whole, the base, not the superstructure ('Law, State, Ideologies'), is 'determinant in the last instance' (p. 21).

The specific contribution that this manuscript makes resides, of course, in the argument about 'Ideological State Apparatuses' and 'ideology' developed in Chapters 5 to 12.

Publication of the present volume should offer an occasion to revisit these themes, and also, no doubt, to re-evaluate them. For putting the fragments included in the text published in *La Pensée* back into Althusser's discourse as a whole brings out the close connection between his thesis on ideology (and its materialization in apparatuses) and his conception of the course of modern history. In and of itself, this is a matter of strict logic. A theory of structural reproduction has, as its corollary, a theory of the transformation of the structure: it tends to show the constant conditions in which variation occurs, and eventually puts an end to those constant conditions. Althusser's conception of ongoing variation, like his conception of the transition to socialism, shapes, in its turn, his conception of the conditions for the reproduction of capitalism as well as his idea of the structural constant. Ultimately, it is a question of a single theory, but a theory with double entries: reproduction and revolution. Hence the new light shed by the previously unpublished sections.

It seems to me important to grasp that the pivot of the theoretical dispositive is the question of law, the subject of Chapters 5 and 11, and its presumed disappearance, the correlative of the disappearance of commodity relations in the course of the socialist revolution. I would like to suggest that the questions that Althusser has brought out have lost nothing of their contemporary relevance, and have yet to find pertinent answers at the level at which he poses them.

LAW AND THE PREDICTION THAT IT WILL WITHER AWAY

The idea of law, introduced before that of the state, is nevertheless dependent on the theory of the state as an instrument of the dominant class's domination. The state apparatus, far from being 'traversed by the class struggle', is, Althusser repeats, an apparatus of domination in its entirety. What holds for the pre-capitalist modes of production holds for capitalism as well: here, too, power is exercised by the dominant class. The struggle of the dominated class has, to be sure, an impact on society. Only the dominant class, however, exercises 'power'. Power is to be understood – as Althusser was to write a little later – as the 'excess' of this class's force over that of the dominated class: 'class domination does indeed find itself sanctioned in and by the state, in that *only the Force of the dominant class enters into it and is recognized there.* What is more, this Force is the sole "motor" of the state, the only energy to be trans-formed into power, right, laws and norms in the state'.[2] Law, far from countering domination, is simply a moment of domination. This is the radical thesis commanding the problematic of the ideological appara-tuses: law is produced by the conversion of violence into power in the state machine.

Chapter 5, 'Law', none of which Althusser included in the text he published in *La Pensée,* makes two statements. One is rather classical, but Althusser formulates it with remarkable clarity. It is the idea that the rela-tions of production comprise the law's (absent) content. Yet law, which exists only as a function of class relations, recognizes only individuals (p. 59). The relations of production are therefore not legal relations; they are not defined by the mode of 'ownership'. The revolution, for its part, is not a modification of legal relations, a transition from private to collective ownership of the means of production. It consists in a practical, common 'appropriation' by freely associated men and women. This, however, leads Althusser to make a more problematic statement, according to which this revolution signifies, simultaneously, but in a single process, the disappearance of law and the disappearance of commodity exchange: 'The withering away of law can only mean the withering away of *commod-ity* exchanges, exchanges of goods in the form of commodities . . . and their replacement by *non-commodity* exchanges' (p. 62).

Here Althusser inscribes himself in the tradition of the communism associated with the Second and Third Internationals, expressing it in all its coherence. To be sure, he rejects the notion that planning can provide an alternative to the market. Rather, he attempts to define a third term, an external term that appears, notably, in the form of 'the intervention of the masses'; planning is only a 'subordinate means' to that end (p. 63 n. 10). He translates 'the Soviets plus electrification' as political intervention plus the planning of the productive forces (ibid.). He fails to take into account, it seems to me, that the planned social order, inasmuch as it opens the way, specifically, to appropriation from the centre, is irreduc-ible to a determination of the 'productive forces' (or of technological rationality), but itself constitutes, like the social order based on

---

2 Louis Althusser, 'Marx in His Limits', in *Philosophy of the Encounter: Later Writings, 1978–1987,* trans. G. M. Goshgarian, London, Verso, 2006, p. 109.

commodity exchange, a configuration of the 'relations of production', that is, potentially, of class relations.

Here certain ambiguities of Marx's resurface; they have to do with the relation between the question of law and that of the market. One cannot, Althusser writes (the passage has, admittedly, been crossed out; but that is only further evidence of its author's uncertainty, p. 60 n.3), speak of socialist law, for 'the law that subsists . . . is still *bourgeois law, for the only law as such is based on commodity relations and is thus bourgeois law.* The socialist mode of production will *abolish* all law. Marx understood this perfectly' (p. 60 n.3). It seems that Althusser here even goes beyond Marx. For he presents the law as, purely and simply, a condition of domination, inasmuch as it puts class relations into play. Similarly, bourgeois democracy is, in his view, merely 'the dictatorship of the bourgeoisie in the form of a parliamentary or presidential democratic apparatus' (p. 104), with the result that 'the class struggle . . . basically unfolds outside these legal, bourgeois–democratic forms' (p. 105).

IDEOLOGY AS APPARATUS AND THE MACHINERY OF THE STATE

A central theme of this text is that the topography, the metaphor of base and superstructure, is insufficient and deceptive. For this metaphor suggests that the economic base determines everything else, whereas, in Althusser's view, it is the social relations of production which characterize a mode of production in the last instance; their reproduction is ensured by the ensemble Repressive State Apparatus plus Ideological State Apparatuses.

The power of the thesis about the Ideological State Apparatuses is due, first of all, to the fact that it flows from an interpretation of society as penetrated or saturated by class relations and subject to a class power that is exercised through the whole set of institutions. This power is not exercised by way of state institutions alone, according to a schema in which those institutions would configure a public sphere that could then be opposed to the private sphere, the place where encounters between private individuals occur. It is exercised quite as fully by private institutions, such as churches, parties, trade unions, the family, private schools, cultural associations, and so on. Althusser's 1970 text made no small contribution to creating a new (and ephemeral) awareness of the fact that the major social institutions are part and parcel of the relations of class domination.

It is well known that Althusser drew part of his inspiration from Gramsci, who uses the term 'civil society' – as opposed to 'political society', that is, the state organs in the strict sense – to designate the whole set of institutions, private and public, by means of which the pre-eminence of the ruling classes' ideology, their 'hegemony', is realized. However, Gramsci, who assigns this notion of ideology the broad sense of a world-view, knowledge, culture and ethics, contends that civil society also provides the terrain on which the progressive struggle of the ascendant class, the proletariat, is played out, and, therefore, the terrain on which is played out the revolutionary process itself, which he assimilates to the conquest of hegemony. Althusser turns this conception of things around by presenting the ensemble of institutions as elements of the state machinery thanks to which the bourgeoisie secures its domination.

Obviously, Althusser is not unaware of the emancipatory potential associated with bourgeois law and bourgeois democracy. The references to Kant and Hegel that open the chapter on law (p. 57) bear the most conspicuous witness to this. Nor is he unaware of the socialist movement's democratic impact on society as a whole (as is well known, he summons his readers to make a political commitment on the terrain of established institutions). However, he suspends this consideration, as it were, and endeavours, in a discussion marked by extreme tension, to formulate a fact that comes into view only when one thinks at the extreme: public institutions are the organs of a 'class struggle' in which one class subjugates the other and ensures that this domination will be reproduced. This is very close to Hobbes, with the difference – a major difference, it is true – that, for Hobbes, the state realizes the real pacification of society, putting an end to violence conceived as the war of all against all, whereas, for Althusser, it ensures, precisely, the exercise of social violence, conceived as the war one class wages on another.

Thus we have a war for the subjection [*assujettissement*] of one class to another, by way of a mobilization of commodity relations and law, which 'sanctions' these relations (p. 165). This is not, however, a functionalist thesis, as Althusser emphasizes in the 'Note on the ISAs' to be found near the end of the present volume. For the apparatuses are merely instruments of class struggle; the class struggle, accordingly, has primacy over the dominant ideology, over the apparatuses. Of course, 'the state's politics is ultimately determined by the dominant classes's interests in the class struggle' (p. 223). However, 'the class struggle never ends'. There is no confining it to apparatuses that reproduce domination. The class struggle is bigger than they are.

Althusser adds that the law falls back on repression only in the last resort, and that, as a general rule, norms are internalized. In the form of moral ideology, norms present themselves by way of an (interior) voice that interpellates me – as, precisely, a subject.

INTERPELLATING INTERPELLATION

Althusser significantly subverts the traditional Marxist problematic by inviting his readers to reconsider the classic way of talking about ideology alongside other elements of the superstructure, and by integrating ideology into the state as the State Ideology. The great interest of his analysis resides in the fact that it confers a status of materialist realism and social ontology on ideology, at the same time as it poses it as an 'interpellation' by means of which everyone is summoned and constituted socially as a subject. In other words, he proposes these two theses: 1) ideology does not have 'an ideal, idea-dependent, or spiritual existence, but a material one', for 'an ideology always exists in an apparatus' (p. 184), and Ideological State Apparatuses are the site of a 'realization' of ideology (p. 184); and 2) 'every ideology has the function (which defines it) of "constituting" [concrete individuals as] subjects' (p. 188).

I would here like to suggest, while referring the reader to texts in which I expound my views at greater length,[3] that this is a theoretical contribution of fundamental importance, even if it calls, as I see it, for an immense conceptual reworking. I would further suggest that Althusser's contribution has to do, very precisely, with the close relationship between the two theses just cited.

The reader will perhaps allow me to prolong Althusser's discourse, subvert it once again, and suggest that it leads somewhere other than to the place to which he would take us.

For it is not an 'inner voice', the voice of conscience, that interpellates me. It is a public voice. That voice declares that I am a free subject. This discourse is precisely that of the modern constitution, of its necessary preamble: the declaration of the rights of man, which posits that everyone is 'free-and-equal' [*librégal*], declares that the subject is sovereign and that the sovereign is a subject, and adds that I myself am subject to myself as sovereign. The material existence of this interpellating discourse does not find its measure in the event that, historically, brought it into existence, or in the form in which it finds itself transcribed, or, again, in the locus in which it has been provisionally situated. Its ontological status, in the sense of social being, is defined by the institutional forms that it commands, the practices that are at one with those institutional forms, and, *on the same grounds*, the class struggle that is constitutive of modernity, for which

---

3 Jacques Bidet, *Théorie générale*, Paris, PUF, 1999; *Explication et reconstruction du Capital*, Paris, PUF, 2007; *L'Etat-monde*, Paris, PUF, 2011.

the declaration of freedom-and-equality comprises the essential reference. This reference to interpellation is in fact recalled at every moment in the class struggle; the class struggle expressly appeals to it as a promise which, as such, should be kept.

Ideology and interpellation are 'eternal', in the sense in which Althusser intends that word: that is, they are constitutive of humanity. They display, however, diverse historical forms, in line with the historical diversity of the forms in which subjectivity has been constituted. And we must take the full measure of 'modern' interpellation.

As human interpellation, a merely human proclamation, it is merely a promise, a promise that everyone makes to everyone, a promise that each of us makes her own insofar as she recognizes herself as a citizen. It is a pact, nothing more than a pact.

The fact that this pact is not respected is what has generally escaped the attention of contract theorists of the state. Marx provides the dialectical formulation of this failure: the contractual relationship free-and-equal 'is transformed into its opposite' insofar as, realizing itself in the form of the market, it confers on the dominant, notably by virtue of their ownership of the means of production, the ability to dispose of those who dispose only of their labour-power or of insufficient means of production. Interpellation of free human beings, free to present themselves on the market, (always already) becomes a lure, an injunction to conform to the social order based on commodity exchange, to the legal forms that rule it, the representations that justify it, and the practices that they call for.

The promise, however, remains: the interpellation of the dominated subject as free, as a partner in the pact of freedom-and-equality [*libertégalité*]. It is an injunction to obey the natural, and therefore legitimate, order of the market; but it affirms, at the same time, that this liberty of the market-based order is, precisely, the liberty of the citizen. This also implies, in contradictory fashion, that the citizens together dispose freely of the social order and are therefore also summoned – in this mutual and yet 'univocal' interpellation that is *interpellation* – freely to create the world in the image of their freedom. Those who have risked the adventure, since, notably, 1917, have encountered the other limit: the public speech of freedom, as soon as it ceases to be cast in the form of the contractual and the social rationality of the market, lurches radically towards the other form, which initially presents itself as the general will, discovered at last, but which, with that as its justification, also runs the risk of translation into the terms of the social rationality of administered and planned reason, with other effects of subjection.

The grand forms of the 'class' relation in the modern age – of the class relation which, as Althusser clearly shows, constitutes for law, which does not talk about it, its very object in the last instance – can therefore only be interpreted if we set out from interpellation. A merely human interpellation, and thus a pact that has, in the institutional forms in which it is cast, a social-ontological status comparable to that of the class relations in which it 'is transformed into its opposite'.

A strange paradox: today, one cannot talk about exploitation or mass poverty, the enslavement of the peripheral zones, or the extermination of peoples, without setting out from what claims to be the interpellation of freedom and equality. It should be noted that that is precisely what Marx does in *Capital*, which begins – not to didactic ends, but in conformity with a requirement for 'thinking' the modern world – by positing the Eden of commodity exchange, in which individuals recognize one another as free-and-equal.

That, however, means that they are also not subjected to that order. That is why this seeming 'paradox' is also the one thanks to which the perspective of emancipation remains open – yawning, unfathomable – that of the realization of the promise.[4]

---

4   [Note to the 2011 second edition of *Sur la reproduction*] I suggest a later interpretation of Althusser's thesis about 'interpellation' in a book in progress: *Althusser et Foucault, révolution et résistance, interpellation et biopolitique*.

Editorial Note

Jacques Bidet

1) The manuscript 'On the Reproduction of the Apparatuses of Production' is the one from which Althusser extracted the fragments that together make up his famous essay 'Ideology and Ideological State Apparatuses', first released in June 1970 in the review *La Pensée* (no. 151, pp. 3–38). The text that Althusser planned to publish was initially to be titled 'What is Marxist-Leninist Philosophy?'. The title was later changed to 'On the Superstructure'. The book was to be included in the series called 'Théorie' published by the left-wing Parisian publisher François Maspero. The change in the title indicates how the nature of the project changed as it proceeded. Ultimately, Althusser hoped to develop a theory of the reproduction of capitalist society in his text.

2) There exist two successive versions of this manuscript, which may be consulted at the Institut Mémoires de l'Edition Contemporaine (IMEC) in St Germain la Blanche Herbe, just outside Caen, France. The first is a 150-page typed text dated March–April 1969. The second, the basis for the French edition, bears a set of corrections and addenda that increase the length of the first typescript by about one-third. Chapter 2, notably, was completely rewritten. Althusser did not, however, finish revising his text. Down to Chapter 6, he incorporated his modifications in the margins and between the lines of a photocopy of the first version, or on intercalated pages. He then introduced an additional chapter, Chapter 7 ('Brief Remarks on the Political and Associative ISAs of the French Capitalist Social Formation'). For the next chapter, Chapter 8, he wrote a new first section, which replaced Sections 1 and 2 of the former Chapter 7. The rest of the manuscript was not substantially modified. Since he inserted a new Chapter 7, we have of course changed the chapter numbers from Chapter 8 on: Chapters 8, 9, 10 and 11 of the manuscript in the state in which Althusser left it have been renumbered, respectively, 9, 10, 11 and 12.

Plainly, Althusser never made all the revisions to the manuscript that he originally intended to. However, aside from indispensable emendations of obvious grammatical mistakes, missing words, and inexact textual references (of all of which there are, to be honest, quite a few), we have scrupulously respected his text, retaining even the imperfections due to the fact that it was left unfinished.[1] We have also respected the text's graphic particularities, notably the abundant recourse to capitalization, which, as a rule, sets off terms used in a technical sense.[2]

3) The piece that Althusser published in *La Pensée* lies somewhere between the two manuscript versions, while partially overlapping with the second version. It does not incorporate all the modifications made to the second manuscript version, which would thus appear to have been revised after the *Pensée* piece appeared. On the other hand, it is marked by stylistic improvements, significant omissions (of historical references and political allusions), and, above all, modifications of which there is no trace in the manuscript, notably to Section 3 of Chapter 6 and Sections 1 and 7 of Chapter 12.

The most important point, however, and the justification for the present publication, is the fragmentary nature of the *Pensée* piece in comparison with the text from which it was extracted, which comprises the immediate context for interpreting it. The extract Althusser published in 1970 reproduces only Chapters 3, 4, and 9 of the manuscript in their entirety, and parts of only two more, Chapters 6 and 12. Thus it leaves out the section here entitled 'To My Readers', in which he explicitly states his aims; Chapter 1, about philosophy; Chapter 2, which discusses the concept of the mode of production; Chapters 5 and 11, on law; Chapters 7 and 8, which take up the question of proletarian trade unions and parties as Ideological State Apparatuses; Chapter 10, on reproduction and revolution; and parts of Chapter 6 (Sections 1 and 2) and Chapter 12 (Section 3), which have to do with ideology and ideological apparatuses.

4) It should be noted that the projected book's second volume, which Althusser announces on the very first page of his note, 'To My Readers,' and again at the end of the manuscript, remained a project; it was never written.

---

1 [TN: For a list of the major transcription errors in the second French edition, contact Verso Books.]

2 [TN: In the present translation, capitalization has been standardized.]

5) The present volume, for which we have chosen the title *Sur la reproduction*, contains the second version of the manuscript in its entirety. It includes sometimes lengthy footnotes that are not to be found in the *Pensée* publication, as well as an appendix announced in the manuscript proper. The volume also includes 'Ideology and Ideological State Apparatuses (Notes towards an Investigation)' and a later text, entitled 'Note on the ISAs', in which Althusser returns to the debate sparked by the *Pensée* piece. Dated December 1976, the 'Note' was first published in French in the 1995 first edition of *Sur la reproduction*. It had been previously issued in German and Spanish collections of Althusser's writings (trans. Peter Schöttler, in *Ideologie und ideologische Staatsapparate*, Hamburg and Berlin, VSA, 1977, pp. 154–173; trans. Albert Roies Qui, *Nuevos Escritos*, Barcelona, LAIA, 1978).

6) Althusser's manuscript may be profitably compared with other of his texts of the period, likewise marked by the intense theoretical and political turbulence of the day. There is, first, 'Philosophy as a Revolutionary Weapon', an interview that he gave *L'Unità* in February 1968, and second, 'How to Read Marx's "Capital"', which appeared in *L'Humanité* on 21 March 1969; this is an extract from a longer manuscript, also available at the IMEC, on the basis of which Althusser once planned to write a book entitled 'A Revolutionary Science'. Third, there is 'Marxism and Class Struggle', dated January 1970, a text that served as the preface to Martha Harnecker's *Los conceptos elementales del materialismo histórico* (Mexico City and Buenos Aires, Siglo XXI, 1971). All three texts were collected in *Positions* (Paris, Editions Sociales, 1976).[3]

7) It should also be pointed out that Althusser was, at the time, working closely with a group of graduates of the Ecole normale supérieure in Paris, notably Etienne Balibar, Pierre Macherey, Michel Tort, Christian Baudelot and Roger Establet. They were collaborating on a project on the French school system (in which Renée Balibar also took part) that is mentioned at several points in the manuscript. As Althusser saw it, the conclusions he reached in this text, which he transmitted to the group in the form of propositions, represented, in some sense, a theorization of their research. That research was supposed to issue in a collective book,

---

3 [TN: English translations of these texts are available in, respectively: Louis Althusser, *Lenin and Philosophy and Other Essays*, London, New Left Books, 1971, pp. 13–25; *Marxism Today*, 1969, pp. 302–5; and the Oxford journal *Radical*, no. 1, November 1985, pp. 12–13.]

of which there exist very substantial drafts by, notably, Etienne Balibar and Pierre Macherey, that are available at the IMEC. The group eventually disintegrated and the projected book was never finished. However, Christian Baudelot and Roger Establet's *L'Ecole capitaliste en France*, published in 1971, materialized in the context of this collective undertaking. Althusser attentively followed the writing of the planned book and contemplated contributing a preface to it.

The subject of 'reproduction' was, at the time, at the centre of debates in the critical sociology of Marxist inspiration. In the 1960s, Althusser had invited Pierre Bourdieu and Jean-Claude Passeron, who published *La Reproduction* in 1971, to participate in seminars at the Ecole normale supérieure. Their approach was thus familiar to his students and collaborators, who envisaged, precisely, working out an alternative formulation in phase with the Althusserian problematic.

The work of other writers with whom Althusser kept up a correspondence (see his letters of the period, also available at the IMEC) likewise belongs to this context. Their names appear in *Sur la reproduction*. Let us single out those of Emmanuel Terray, Nicos Poulantzas and Charles Bettelheim.

8) I thank François Boddaert and Olivier Corpet, the head of the IMEC, who authorized publication of this manuscript by the Presses Universitaires de France in the series *Actuel Marx Confrontation*.

My special thanks go to François Matheron, responsible for the Fonds Louis Althusser and the editor of Althusser's *Ecrits philosophiques et politiques* (Stock/IMEC, 1994), who attentively followed my work and provided me very helpful advice.

I also thank Sonia Feltesse, who vigilantly decrypted Althusser's manuscripts and prepared them for publication.

Translator's Note

G. M. Goshgarian

The present book contains translations of all the texts by Althusser that Jacques Bidet assembled, edited and published in French under the title *Sur la reproduction* (Paris, Presses Universitaires de France, 1995, 2nd ed. 2011). It also contains a translation of Bidet's introduction to the 1995 edition of *Sur la reproduction*, reproduced virtually unchanged in the second edition, as well as a translation of Etienne Balibar's preface to the second edition. Written in French, Balibar's text initially appeared in Hebrew as the preface to a Hebrew translation (trans. Ariella Azoulay, Tel Aviv, Resling, 2003) of an extract from the text that Althusser published in *La Pensée* in 1970. Althusser's 1970 piece first appeared in English in a collection of his writings, *Lenin and Philosophy and Other Essays* (London, New Left Books, 1971, pp. 121–73) translated by Ben Brewster. Titled 'Ideology and Ideological State Apparatuses (Notes Towards an Investigation)', Brewster's translation has been republished a number of times since, in reprints of *Lenin and Philosophy* and also in *Essays on Ideology* (London, Verso, 1984). It has been reprinted in the present book as well. The 1976 'Note sur les AIE' first saw the light in Peter Schöttler's 1977 German translation and first appeared in English in 1983 ('Extracts from Althusser's "Note on the ISAs"', trans. Jeremy Leaman, *Economy and Society*, vol. 12, no. 4, pp. 455–65) as the appendix to an essay by Mike Gane. Leaman's translation omits only a short passage at the beginning of the 'Note'.

Balibar's Foreword, Bidet's Introduction, and all the other material collected in *Sur la reproduction*, with the exception of the 'Note' and the 'ISAs Essay', are here published in English for the first time.

My translation is based on the second French edition of *Sur la reproduction*, which I have compared throughout with Althusser's manuscript at the Institut Mémoires de l'édition contemporaine (IMEC) in Saint Germain la Blanche Herbe, near Caen. I have also profited from reading

Frieder Otto Wolf's German translation and his notes to it (*Über die Reproduktion*, 2 vols., Hamburg, VSA, 2011–12).

At the publisher's request, Althusser's idiosyncratic capitalization and italicization have been standardized throughout. Specifically, Althusser, like many French writers, tends to capitalize only the first word in a compound term used in a technical sense, but sometimes capitalizes both (or all three: *Appareil Idéologique d'Etat*). I have capitalized every word in such terms of the author's own coinage, even when Althusser capitalizes only one. Thus *Appareil répressif d'Etat* becomes 'Repressive State Apparatus'. I have not capitalized other terms, such as Productive Forces or State, that Althusser generally tends to capitalize.

Leaman's English translation of 'Note on the ISAs' was based on Schöttler's German translation. I have made a new, rather different, translation of the 'Note' based on the French. There are also disparities between Ben Brewster's elegant and, with rare exceptions, accurate English translation of the 'ISAs Essay' and my translation of the corresponding passages in Althusser's manuscript. Some of them reflect differences between the 1970 *La Pensée* text and the hastily composed manuscript. Others are due to choices for which I bear the sole responsibility.

To My Readers

I

I would like to call readers' attention to certain features of a book that may, in many respects, surprise and disconcert them.

1) This short book is the first volume of a work that is to comprise two volumes. Volume 1 is about the reproduction of capitalist relations of production. Volume 2 will be about the class struggle in capitalist social formations.

For reasons of theoretical and political urgency obvious to everyone, I have decided to publish the present volume, Volume 1, without delay. In a certain way, it forms a whole that can stand on its own (aside from the liminal chapter on philosophy). While the theoretical basis for this volume has not been improvised, I have had to write the 200 pages it contains very quickly so that the text could appear rapidly.

I thought it might be useful to recall the basic principles of Marxist-Leninist theory concerning the nature of capitalist exploitation, repression and ideologization. Above all, it seemed to me imperative to show clearly what sort of system ensures the reproduction of the conditions of capitalist production – production being nothing but a means to the end of capitalist exploitation, since, under the capitalist regime, the production of consumer goods obeys the law of profit alone, and thus the law of exploitation.

A full discussion would consider 1) the reproduction of the productive forces and 2) the reproduction of the relations of production.

Since Marx discusses the reproduction of the productive forces at length in *Capital* Volume 1 (the theory of wages: reproduction of labour-power) and *Capital* Volume 2 (the theory of the reproduction of the means of production), I have treated this question cursorily. On the other hand, I have discussed *the reproduction of the relations of production* at length. Marx has left us important pointers on this subject, but they are unsystematic.

The system that ensures the reproduction of the relations of production is the system of state apparatuses: the repressive apparatus and the ideological apparatuses. That explains the title of Volume 1: *The Reproduction of Capitalist Relations of Production* (exploitation, repression, ideology).[1]

As the reader will see, I have taken the considerable risk of putting forward theses on these two points which, while they are in perfect conformity with the theory and practice of the Marxist-Leninist workers' movement, had not yet been stated in systematic theoretical form. Thus I have sketched a theory of what I call the *Ideological State Apparatuses* and also of the functioning of *ideology in general*.

Since the analyses in Volume 1 depend, in certain cases, on principles to be worked out in Volume 2, I ask readers to grant me a kind of theoretical and political 'credit'. I shall try to honour the obligation thus incurred in Volume 2, in which I shall broach the problems of the *class struggle in capitalist social formations*.

2) The present volume, Volume 1, begins with a chapter that will seem surprising: it is about the 'nature' of philosophy. It will seem the more surprising in that, after marking off the terrain with a few signposts, I leave the question of philosophy in abeyance and make a very long detour in order to discuss the question of the reproduction of the capitalist relations of production.

Why have I begun with this first chapter on philosophy when I could simply have begun with Chapter 2, on the mode of production? I do so for reasons that are very important both theoretically and politically. They will appear at the end of Volume 2, when we will be in a position to answer the questions: What is Marxist-Leninist philosophy?[2] In what does its originality consist? Why is it a revolutionary weapon?

The present account of the reproduction of capitalist relations of production has not been placed under the aegis of the question of philosophy simply to facilitate the exposition. The fact is that we cannot say what Marxist-Leninist philosophy is without making the long detour through Volume 1 (Reproduction of the Relations of Production) and Volume 2 (The Class Struggle).

But why foreground the question of Marxist-Leninist philosophy this way, as well as the logically prior question of philosophy *tout court* (Volume 1, Chapter 1)?

---

1   [TN: Elsewhere, Althusser refers to the manuscript as "The Reproduction of the Relations of Production".]

2   [EN: Footnote crossed out in the manuscript: 'I am deliberately using, for the time being, the term "Marxist-Leninist philosophy". I shall propose another, more accurate term at the end of the present essay.']

I have not chosen to proceed in this fashion because I am, academically speaking, a philosopher – that is, because I am a specialist eager to talk about a subject I know a little about or because I want to 'praise my wares'. I have done so for political and theoretical reasons, as a communist. Here are those reasons, in brief.

Everything that falls within the purview of the science founded by Marx (especially, in this volume, the theory of the reproduction of the relations of production) depends on a revolutionary science that Marx was only able to found *on the basis of* what the Marxist tradition calls the philosophy of dialectical materialism – very precisely, as we shall point out and also prove, on the basis of a proletarian class position in philosophy. It is, consequently, impossible – Lenin admirably understood and showed this – to grasp or, *a fortiori*, expound and develop Marxist theory, even on a single, limited point, without adopting proletarian class positions in the realm of theory. The characteristic task of each and every philosophy is to represent, in theory, a given class position. The characteristic task of Marxist philosophy is to represent, in theory, the proletarian class position.

Whence the primordial importance, for every exposition and every development of Marxist theory, of dialectical materialist philosophy – that is, the proletarian class viewpoint in philosophy. We shall show in Volume 2 that the role of Marxist-Leninist philosophy is not only vital for the development of Marxist science and the 'concrete analyses of concrete situations' (Lenin) which alone makes Marxist science possible, but that it is also vital for the political practice of the class struggle.

If this is so, it is no wonder that our first volume begins by asking 'What is philosophy?' or that our second volume should culminate in a definition of the revolutionary nature of the Marxist-Leninist conception of philosophy and its role in scientific and political practice. When we have reached that point, we will understand why and how philosophy is, in a concrete sense, a revolutionary weapon.

II

While my communist comrades, at least, will be willing to grant me, at the outset, what I have just said about the importance of Marxist-Leninist philosophy in scientific practice (above all in the theory of history founded by Marx, but in the other sciences as well) and also in the communist practice of the class struggle, an objection can nevertheless be raised against it, even from a Marxist standpoint. It may be objected that others have long since said and written what needs to be said about

Marxist-Leninist philosophy, called, in the classical tradition, dialectical materialism. For everyone knows that there are many celebrated texts on the philosophy founded by Marx and his successors. For example, the *Theses on Feuerbach* (1845) and the afterword to the second German edition of *Capital* [(1873)]; for example, Engels' *Anti-Dühring* (1877) and *Ludwig Feuerbach* (1888); for example, Lenin's *Materialism and Empirio-Criticism* (1908) *and Philosophical Notebooks* (1914–15); for example, Stalin's essay 'Dialectical and Historical Materialism' (1938); for example, Mao's *On Practice* and *On Contradiction* (1937), and *Where Do Correct Ideas Come From?* [(1963)].

Why, under these circumstances, should we raise the question of Marxist-Leninist philosophy again?

1) Let us say: in order to take stock of things, but also in order to spell out certain crucially important points, while throwing the political and theoretical character of our class practice in philosophy into sharper relief.

2) We cannot, however, stick to this still speculative expository standpoint. It is not just a question of making the reader 'see and understand' the specificity and novelty of our philosophy. It will also be a question, from now on, of putting that philosophy to work in a practical way – in short, of 'putting it to work' on scientific problems.

It will appear in short order, beginning with our simple analysis of the unity comprised by a mode of production (the unity between productive forces/relations of production) but also in all that follows, that we are absolutely incapable of clearly perceiving these scientific questions and thus advancing the state of our knowledge unless we bring our philosophy directly into play.

That is why we affirm – for all the historical, theoretical and practical reasons just stated – that the time is ripe and that the moment is propitious, at least in our country, for taking critical stock of the state of Marxist-Leninist philosophy, demonstrating its revolutionary nature, refining certain aspects of it, and 'putting it to work' without delay on various scientific problems, some of which have a direct bearing on the class struggle today.

1. *The time is ripe* because we need to take stock of things and are capable of taking stock of things.

We have learned a great many new things since Marx and Engels and even since Lenin's *Materialism and Empirio-Criticism*. Today, we have at our disposal the extraordinary experiences of the Soviet Revolution and the Chinese Revolution; the lessons offered by the various forms of the construction of socialism and their diverse results; the lessons of all the working-class struggles against the capitalist bourgeoisie, and all the popular mass struggles as well (the struggle against fascism, the liberation movements of the 'Third World' countries, the Vietnamese people's victorious struggle against French and then American imperialism, the struggle of Black Americans, student revolts, and so on).

We have not only the experience of the great victories of the workers' movement at our disposal, we also have that of its defeats and crises.[3] Lenin told us twenty times over that when we succeed in thoroughly analyzing the causes of a failure in order to draw its lessons, it always has more to teach us than a victory, since its consequences force us to go *to the bottom of things*. This holds *a fortiori* for a serious crisis.

When we consider the lessons that Marx drew from the initiatives of the popular masses under the Commune and from an analysis of the reasons for its failure or the lessons that Lenin drew from the popular masses' invention of the Soviets during the 1905 revolution and the failure of this 'dress rehearsal', we can only say: *What about us?* What lessons are we to draw from all the unprecedented experiences, all the defeats, failures and victories we now have 'at our disposal', and from the crisis we are living through today?

Can all this stupendous experience leave philosophy indifferent? Should it not, rather, guide, nourish and enrich the revolutionary philosophy that the Marxist workers' movement has handed down to us?

2. We also think that *the moment is propitious* for taking stock of the present state of Marxist-Leninist philosophy.

The moment is propitious because it is urgent to invest or reinvest Marxist-Leninist philosophy with all its revolutionary force, so that it can fulfil its ideological and political function as *a revolutionary weapon*, in the crisis that we are currently living through, as at other times. For the crisis we are living through should not be allowed to mask another that is infinitely more important.

Let there be no mistake: we need only become aware of the unprecedented crisis into which imperialism, beleaguered by its contradictions and its victims and assailed by the peoples, has now

---

3 The present crisis is dominated by two events of crucial importance: 1) the Twentieth Congress and its consequences, which called aspects of Stalin's politics from the 1930s on into question; and 2) the split in the international communist movement, which called the political line that emerged from the Twentieth Congress into question.

plunged, in order to conclude that it will not survive it. We are entering an age that will see the triumph of socialism across the globe. We need only take note of the irresistible course of popular struggles in order to conclude that in a relatively near future, despite all the possible twists and turns, the very serious crisis of the international communist movement included, *the revolution is already on the agenda. One hundred years from now*, perhaps only fifty years from now, the face of the world will have changed: the revolution will have carried the day from one end of the earth to the other.

That is why it is urgent to provide all those who are finding their way to communism – and more and more people are, especially among young men and women in the factories, the fields and the schools – with the means they need to arm themselves with Marxist-Leninist theory and the experience of the class struggle. The philosophy of Marxism-Leninism is one of these means, for it is a revolutionary philosophy: it is the *only* revolutionary philosophy.

To put it very simply, taking stock of the current state of Marxist-Leninist philosophy means understanding clearly, and as profoundly as possible, what this philosophy is, how it produces its effects, and how it must be utilized so as to serve, in Marx's phrase, not to 'interpret the world' but to 'change' it.

Taking stock of the current state of Marxist-Leninist philosophy also means recalling, in order to explain and understand that philosophy, the basic acquisitions of the new science founded by Marx, historical materialism, *without which Marxist-Leninist philosophy would not exist.* Again, it means recalling that if Marx had not adopted a proletarian (dialectical-materialist) class position in philosophy, the science that he founded, historical materialism, would not exist. It follows that we have to 'put this philosophy to work' in order to refine and advance the state of our knowledge in Marxist science, so that we can more lucidly analyze the current concrete situation.

To make our exposé clearer, let us indicate the structure of what follows.

To grasp the sense in which Marxist-Leninist philosophy is revolutionary, we have to know what distinguishes it from earlier philosophies. In order to be able to make this distinction, we have first to know what philosophy in general is. Hence the order of our questions. First question: What is philosophy? Second question: What is Marxist-Leninist philosophy?

It appears at a glance that it is imperative to ask these two questions in the order just indicated. Yet they do not define *the structure* of our study.

Why not? Because, as we shall see in a moment, it is impossible to answer the second question – What is Marxist-Leninist philosophy? – without making *a very long detour,* that is, without proceeding by way of an exposition of the basic results of the Marxist science of history, of which historical materialism is the general theory.

As a matter of fact, contrary to what all philosophers, including many Marxist philosophers, spontaneously think, the question 'what is philosophy?' *does not fall under the jurisdiction of philosophy, even Marxist-Leninist philosophy.* If it did, this would mean that it is philosophy's task to define philosophy.

This is what philosophy has thought and done throughout its past history, constantly, *with a few rare exceptions.* This is what makes it fundamentally *idealist,* for to maintain that it is, in the last instance, the duty and right of philosophy and philosophy alone *to define itself* is to assume that it *can know itself,* that it is Self-Knowledge, that is, Absolute Knowledge, whether it uses this term overtly (as Hegel does) or practices the concept shamefacedly, without saying so (as all philosophy did before Hegel, with a few rare exceptions).

Thus it is no wonder that, if we want to propose a definition of philosophy that does not merely repeat philosophy's purely subjective, hence idealist, hence non-scientific 'self-consciousness', but, rather, comprises objective knowledge of philosophy, we have to turn to *something other than philosophy itself:* namely, the theoretical principles of the science or sciences capable of providing us with the scientific knowledge of philosophy in general that we are looking for. As will appear, we shall have to refine some of these principles and advance the state of our knowledge in some cases, to the extent that we have the means to do so.

As will appear, that science and the other sciences deriving from it *all* depend on the unprecedented discovery thanks to which Marx opened up a new 'continent', the continent of history, to scientific knowledge. The general theory of this scientific discovery is known as *historical materialism.*

That is why we shall have to make a long detour through the scientific results we need, produced by historical materialism, in order to reach our goal, a *scientific* definition of philosophy.

In the last analysis, this long detour will explain the structure of our study. Here, in the order in which they occur, are the chapter titles:

Chapter 1: What is Philosophy?
Chapter 2: What is a Mode of Production?
Chapter 3: The Reproduction of the Conditions of Production
Chapter 4: Base and Superstructure

I wish to warn readers from the outset, *solemnly*, as it were, in order to avoid all misunderstanding, all confusion, and all unfounded criticism, that the order of exposition I have adopted has a serious disadvantage, one no other order of exposition can overcome. It is that the present volume proposes to discuss, above all, the mode of functioning of the superstructure (the state, the state apparatuses) as reproduction of the relations of production. It is, however, impossible to talk about the state, law and ideology without bringing class struggle into play. Proper logic would therefore seem to indicate that I should have adopted the opposite order of exposition, and begun by talking about the class struggle before talking about the state, law and ideology. The latter order of exposition, however, would have run into the same difficulty the other way around: for it is impossible to talk about classes and class struggle without first talking about the state, law and ideology. Thus we are caught in a circle, since we would have to *talk about everything at once*. The reason is quite simple: in reality, all the things that we would like to discuss go hand in hand, and all depend, albeit in a very precise way, on each other. They pay no mind at all to their complex functioning and the distinctions we must make to understand them; *a fortiori*, they are oblivious to *the order of exposition* we have to adopt to explain how they work.

Since the essence of what I have to say, to the extent that it involves new theoretical refinements of certain limited points, bears on the superstructure, it is legitimate, because one must choose in any case, to choose the order of exposition that offers as many theoretical and pedagogical advantages as possible. For, as readers will eventually see, we also have

---

4   [EN: Althusser incorporated into the second draft of his manuscript, the basis for the present edition, the chapter that has here become Chapter 7 ('Brief Remarks on the Political and Associative Ideological State Apparatuses of the French Capitalist Social Formation'). What is identified as Chapter 7 in his list has here become Chapter 8, and so on. Chapter 10, here Chapter 11, was ultimately given the different title, 'Further Remarks on Law and Its Reality, the Legal Ideological State Apparatus'; Chapter 11, here Chapter 12, was renamed 'On Ideology' and the title of Chapter 6 was truncated.]

reasons of principle for thinking that the order of exposition we have chosen is the right one.

The *class struggle* will therefore constantly come into play after a certain – very early – point in our analysis. It will do so by way of a whole series of effects that remain unintelligible unless we refer to its reality and presence *outside* the objects we analyze, but inside them as well. However, as we are unable – for good reason – to present a theory of the class struggle beforehand, we shall constantly have to bring its effects into play without first having provided a thorough explanation of their causes.

It is the more important to spell this out in that *the reality of the class struggle infinitely exceeds the effects of the class struggle that we will encounter in the objects analyzed in Volume 1.* We state this principle clearly, in advance, so as to forestall criticisms based only on the inevitable one-sidedness of our order of exposition. Had we chosen the other order of exposition (beginning by talking about the class struggle before going on to talk about the state), just as many criticisms could have been raised, but from the other direction. On this point, therefore, we ask readers, not for their indulgence, but, simply, for their understanding. It is materially impossible to discuss everything at the same time if one wants to expound things with a modicum of order and clarity.

Two final remarks: we shall endeavour, precisely, to be as clear as possible. We must, however, warn our readers that, so as not to traduce our subject, we shall sometimes have to enter into explanations that are complex and call for sustained attention. This is not our fault. The difficulty of our explanations has to do with the objectively complex nature of philosophy, law, its apparatuses, and ideology.

Finally, we ask readers to take the present book for what it is, without asking that it do the impossible (for us). It is a simple essay, the beginnings of an investigation. While it is a product not of improvisation but of reflection, it obviously cannot avoid the risks of inadequacy, approximation and, of course, error that all research involves. All that we ask is a certain indulgence for the one who takes these risks. At the same time, however, we ask for the assistance provided by the most severe sort of criticism on condition, of course, that it be *real criticism*, that is, seriously argued and backed up with evidence, not a simple judgement handed down without reasons to justify it.

One last 'warning', if I may put it that way: nothing of what is advanced here should be taken, on any grounds whatsoever, as 'the Bible truth'. Marx demanded that his readers 'think for themselves'. That rule holds for all readers, whatever the nature of the text one submits to them.

1

What Is Philosophy?

I COMMON-SENSE PHILOSOPHY AND PHILOSOPHY

Everyone thinks she knows, spontaneously, what philosophy is. Yet philosophy is also supposed to be a mysterious activity that is difficult and beyond the reach of ordinary mortals. How is this contradiction to be explained?

Let us look a little more closely at its two terms.

Everyone thinks she knows, spontaneously, what philosophy is, on the basis of a conviction that all people are, more or less, *philosophers*, even when they are not aware of it (like Monsieur Jourdain, who uttered prose without being aware of it).

This is the thesis defended by the great Italian Marxist theoretician Gramsci: '*everyone is a philosopher*'. And Gramsci provides interesting details. He observes that, in everyday language, the expression 'to take things philosophically' designates an attitude that itself involves a certain conception of philosophy, bound up with the idea of *rational necessity*. Someone who, confronted with a painful occurrence, 'takes things philosophically' is someone who takes a step back, gets the better of her immediate reaction, and conducts herself in a rational way: she understands the event affecting her and acknowledges its *necessity*.

Of course, says Gramsci, there can be a streak of passivity in this attitude ('to be a philosopher' is 'to cultivate your own garden' or 'mind your own business' or 'see only what suits you'. In short, 'to be a philosopher' is also, most of the time, to *resign* oneself to necessity and withdraw into this resignation, into one's private life, one's inner life, one's day-to-day affairs, while waiting for 'the dust to settle'). Gramsci does not deny this. But he insists on the fact that such passivity contains, paradoxically, the acknowledgement of a certain order of things, one that is necessary and comprehensible.

At the same time, however, as Plato already notes, we find another idea of what philosophy is in the popular conception of it, an idea embodied in the stock figure of the philosopher who goes around with his head in the clouds or in abstraction and 'falls down wells' (there were no well walls in Greece, as there are today) because he keeps his eyes trained on the heaven of ideas instead of the ground. This caricature, thanks to which the 'people' can make fun of philosophers, is itself ambiguous. On the one hand, it represents an ironic criticism of the philosopher: an affectionate or bitter settling of accounts with philosophy. On the other hand, it contains the acknowledgement of a fact of sorts: philosophers practice a discipline that is beyond the ken of ordinary men and women, of common people, while being, as the same time, a discipline involving serious risks.

Gramsci takes the first term of the contradiction into account, but not the second. But it is not good method to chop things in half and keep only what suits us. We have to take *every* aspect of the popular conception of philosophy into account. When we do, it appears that, in the everyday expression 'to take things philosophically', what first meets the eye is *resignation* to necessity, conceived as something inevitable (one waits 'for things to settle down' or for the onset of death: 'to philosophize is to learn how to die', says Plato). The acknowledgement that it is a '*rational* necessity' thus takes a back seat. Indeed, it may be a necessity and nothing else (we may not know the *reasons* for this necessity, so that it is not *rational*). That is, it may be a fatality ('there is no other way'). That is usually the case. This remark is crucial.

It is crucial, first of all, because it puts the accent on the idea that *philosophy = resignation*. One cannot say that this equation in fact contains, despite itself, as it were, an idea of philosophy that has *critical* value. Indeed, we shall be showing that the vast majority of philosophies are forms of *resignation* or, to be more precise, forms of *submission* to the 'ideas of the ruling class' (Marx) and thus to class rule.

It is crucial, *secondly*, because it does in fact contain a distinction between two altogether different types of *philosophy*. There is, on the one hand, the passive, resigned 'philosophy' of those who 'take things philosophically' while 'cultivating their gardens' and 'waiting for the dust to settle' (we shall call this 'philosophy' *common-sense philosophy*). On the other hand, there is the *active* philosophy of those who submit to the order of the world because they know it by means of Reason, either in order to know it or in order to change it (we shall call this 'philosophy' *Philosophy* tout court, writing its name with a capital letter). Take, for example, a Stoic philosopher: he is a 'philosopher' to the extent that he actively adapts to the order of the world, and this rational order is, for him, rational because he knows it through the exercise of reason. Take, for example, the communist philosopher: she is a 'philosopher' to the extent that she militates in order to hasten the advent of socialism, the historical necessity of which she has understood (by means of scientific reason). We shall say that all the adepts of Stoicism and all communist militants are, in this respect, *philosophers* in the second, strong sense of the word. They 'take things philosophically', if you like; in their case, however, this expression has to do with knowledge of the rational necessity of the course of the world or evolution of history. Of course, there is a big difference between the adept of Stoicism and the communist militant, but, for the moment, it does not interest us. We shall discuss it in due course.

What is essential, for the moment, is to see clearly that the common-sense philosophy to which the everyday expression refers should not be confused with *Philosophy* in the strong sense, the philosophy *'elaborated'* by philosophers (Plato . . . the Stoics and so on, Marx, Lenin), which may or may not disseminate or, rather, be disseminated among the broad mass of the people. When, today, we encounter philosophical elements in the popular conceptions of the masses, we have to take this *dissemination* into account. Unless we do, we may mistake Philosophical elements in the strong sense that have been *'inculcated'* (Lenin, Mao) into the masses as a result of the union of Marxist theory and the workers' movement for *spontaneous* mass consciousness.

A) Moreover, the popular conception of Philosophy, when it ironically shows us the philosopher with his head 'in the clouds,' explicitly recognizes that philosophy can be something altogether different from common sense 'philosophy'. This irony, which is a settling of accounts, indulgent, sardonic, or severe, with *speculative* Philosophy, incapable of concerning itself with down-to-earth problems, also contains its 'grain of truth' (Lenin): namely, that the true philosopher 'circulates' in a 'world different' from that of spontaneous popular consciousness. (Let us call it, provisionally, the world of 'ideas'.) The philosopher 'knows' and says certain things that ordinary people do not know; he has to negotiate the difficult roads of abstraction in order to attain this lofty 'knowledge', which is not *immediately* given to everyone. In this sense, one can no longer say that everyone is spontaneously a philosopher, unless one plays on the sense of the word 'philosopher', the way Gramsci does – unless one confuses common-sense philosophy with Philosophy (tout court).

This brings us back to our question: *What is philosophy*? But, at the same time, we can now see that our first question is pregnant with another: What is *common-sense* philosophy?

To answer this two-part question, we shall be developing a certain number of theses in orderly fashion. We will thus be brought to discover a certain number of realities. Only after we have put these realities in place can we come back to our questions and answer them.

II   PHILOSOPHY HAS NOT ALWAYS EXISTED

Let us begin with a simple observation: while common-sense philosophy has, it seems, always existed, Philosophy has not.

Everyone knows how Lenin begins his famous book *State and Revolution*: he points out that the state has not always existed. He adds that the state is observed to exist only in *societies* in which *social classes* exist.

We shall make a remark of the same sort, but it will be a little more complicated. We shall say that Philosophy has not always existed. Philosophy is observed to exist in societies in which

1) social classes (and therefore the state) exist;
2) science (or one science) exists.

Let us be more precise. By science, we mean, not a list of empirical findings (*connaissances*), which can be quite long (thus the Chaldeans and Egyptians were familiar with a considerable number of technical procedures and mathematical results), but an abstract, ideal (or, rather, idea-dependent [*idéel*]) discipline that proceeds by way of *abstractions* and *demonstrations*: for example, the Greek mathematics founded by Thales (or those designated by this no doubt mythical proper name).

To stick with our observation, the facts do indeed appear to show that we are right. We can confirm it in both past and present. It is a fact that Philosophy as we know it begins for us with *Plato*, in the Greece of the fifth century [before] our era. We can see that Greek society comprised social classes (our first condition) and that the world's first known science, mathematics, began to exist as a *science* (our second condition) shortly before the turn of the fifth century. These two realities – social classes and mathematical (demonstrative) science – are registered in Plato's Philosophy, and combined there. On the pediment of the school in which he taught Philosophy, Plato wrote: 'Let none enter here who is not a geometer'. And he made use of the 'geometric proportion' (which grounded the idea of proportional equality, in other words, inequality) to establish class relations among people that flattered the convictions of the reactionary aristocrat he was. (There are people who are made for work, others who are made to command and, finally, still others who are made to ensure that the dominant class's order reigns over slaves and tradesmen.)

But let us not proceed too quickly. For we can observe another fact as well. Other class societies existed well before fifth-century Greece; yet they did not possess the idea of demonstrative science and, plainly, they did not have the idea of Philosophy. Examples: Greece itself prior to the fifth century, the great Near Eastern kingdoms, Egypt, and so on. It would clearly seem that, in order for Philosophy to exist, the two conditions that we have mentioned must obtain: the necessary condition (the existence of classes) and the sufficient condition (the existence of a science).

It will be objected that there were men who called themselves 'philosophers' before Plato, such as the Seven Sages, the 'Ionian philosophers', and so on. We shall reply to this objection a little later.

Let us return to the conditions that we have defined and pursue our observations. The *unprecedented* discipline of Philosophy, founded by Plato, did not disappear with his death. It survived him as a discipline and there have always been people to practice it. It is as if it were necessary that Philosophy exist – and not just that it exist, but that it perpetuate itself in singular fashion, as if it were *repeating* something essential in its very transformations.

Why did it continue and why was it transformed even as it was perpetuated?

Let us note that it was continued and developed in what we call the 'Western world' (which was relatively isolated from the rest of the world until the advent of capitalism): a world in which classes and the state have continued to exist and in which the sciences have seen great developments, but in which the class struggle has also seen great transformations.

As for Philosophy, what has happened to it? We may observe the following.

III POLITICAL–SCIENTIFIC CONJUNCTIONS AND PHILOSOPHIES

We note that Philosophy, too, has seen major transformations. Aristotle is something other than Plato, Stoicism something other than Aristotle, Descartes something other than St Thomas Aquinas, Kant something other than Descartes, and so on. Did these transformations occur for no reason other than that these great authors were inspired? Or, to put the question another way, why were these authors *great* authors, whereas a throng of other philosophers, who wrote a host of books, have remained, so to speak, in the shadows, without playing any *historical* role?

Here, too, we can note certain things. We observe, perhaps to our surprise, that all great transformations in philosophy intervene at moments in history *either* when noteworthy modifications occur in class relations and the state *or* when major events occur in the history of the sciences:

with the additional stipulation that the noteworthy modifications in the class struggle and the major events in the history of the sciences appear, most of the time, to reinforce each other in their encounter in order to produce prominent effects in Philosophy.

Let us give a few examples. In view of the rudimentary facts we have provided so far, we have to present them in *extremely schematic* form. We shall modify it later, when we have other analytical principles in hand.

As far as most of the great 'authors' of Philosophy are concerned, we can indeed observe, in the conjuncture in which they thought and wrote, a conjunction of *political and scientific* events representing important modifications of the previous conjuncture.

Political events	Scientific events	Authors
Creation of the Macedonian Empire (end of the city-state)	Idea of a biological science[1]	Aristotle
Creation of the slave-holding Roman Empire; Roman Law	Idea of a new physics	The Stoics
Feudalism + the first signs of a revival of Roman Law	Propagation of the Arabs' scientific discoveries	St Thomas Aquinas
Development of legal mercantile relations under the Absolute Monarchy	Foundation of mathematical physics by Galileo	Descartes
Rise of the bourgeoisie; French Revolution	New foundation of physics by Newton	Kant
Contradictions of the French Revolution (threat of the 'Fourth Estate' eliminated by Thermidor and Napoleon: Civil Law Code)	First approaches to a theory of history	Hegel
Emergence, growth and first struggles, failures and victory of the workers' movement	Science of history founded by Marx	Marx-Lenin (dialectical materialism)
Imperialism (rise of the 'petty bourgeoisie')	Axiomatization of mathematics, mathematical Logic	Husserl
Crisis of imperialism	Developments in technology	Heidegger
And so on . . .		

---

1   Once one science (mathematics) exists, we may say that the *idea* of science taken from it can serve to *authorize* theoretical constructions, not yet scientific, that are brought to bear on empirical facts. Hence the 'idea' of a biological 'science' that Aristotle's Philosophy takes as its authorization.

We shall leave it to our readers to 'breathe life into' the elements of this schematic table. We shall restrict ourselves to putting them on the right track with a few simple remarks that are themselves extremely schematic. We shall take just one example, Descartes.

The table should be read as follows: Descartes' Philosophy, which marks a crucial moment in the history of Philosophy, since it inaugurates what we may call 'Modern Philosophy', came into existence with the *conjunction* of important modifications in class relations and the state on the one hand and the history of the sciences on the other.

In class relations: we are referring to the development of bourgeois law, which sanctioned, in its turn, the development of commodity relations in the manufacturing period *under* the absolute monarchy. The absolute monarchy was a new form of state representing a form of transitional state between the feudal and capitalist state.

In the history of the sciences: Galileo's foundation of the science of physics, which represents the great scientific event of the modern period, comparable in importance to only two other great discoveries known to us: the discovery that led to the foundation of mathematics in the fifth century and the discovery, due to Marx, that laid the foundations for a science of history in the mid-nineteenth century.

Let there be no mistake: we are not claiming that Descartes' philosophy can be *deduced* from the conjunction of these two decisive events, political-economic and scientific. We contend only that the *conjuncture* in which Descartes thought was *dominated* by this *conjunction*, which radically distinguishes it from the preceding conjuncture, the one in which, for example, Italian Renaissance Philosophers had to think.

For the moment, we shall content ourselves with bringing Descartes' Philosophy into relation with this conjuncture (and this conjunction). What interests us in this conjuncture is this *conjunction*, which would seem to confirm the validity of the twofold condition that we stated in order to begin to account for what Philosophy might be. We shall leave it at that for the moment.[2]

Reading the other examples in our table this way, we observe that the transformations of Philosophy seem to stand in relation with a *complex* (but unmistakable) *interplay* [*jeu*] between transformations in class relations and their effects, on the one hand, and major events in the history of the sciences on the other. We ask the reader to grant us no more than that the conditions of existence of Philosophy that we have defined *are plausible*.

---

2   We shall go much further in due course, at the end of our study.

So much for the past. What about the present?

We invoke the present in order to make our definition even more plausible. For we are referring not just to the present of societies in which Philosophy exists, but also to that of societies without Philosophy.

For, in our world, there still do exist societies or groupings of people in which Philosophy as we know it has never managed to arise. For instance, the so-called 'primitive' societies, traces of which still subsist. These societies have neither social classes nor science: they know nothing of Philosophy. For instance, great societies in which we cannot yet isolate what has been brought into them from outside in order to consider, so to speak, what they were *before* this importation (of the sciences and Philosophy). We might take the example of nineteenth-century India or China in order to ask ourselves whether these societies which had social classes (even if they were disguised in the form of castes, as in India) *but not science* (as far as we know, but we may be mistaken) had what we call *philosophies* in the strict sense.

People readily speak of Hindu philosophy and Chinese philosophy. In question here, however, may be theoretical disciplines that have only the external appearances of Philosophy, so that it would doubtless be preferable to give them another name. After all, we, too, have a theoretical discipline, theology, which, while plainly theoretical, is not, *in principle*, a Philosophy. Provisionally, we can hypothesize that the question of the nature of so-called Hindu or Chinese philosophy is of the same order as the question of the pre-Platonic Greek 'philosophies'. Later, we shall attempt to answer this question.

Here, to sum up, is what we have 'found' so far, setting out from the simple observation *that Philosophy has not always existed*: we have found (empirically) that the existence and transformations of Philosophy seem to bear a close relation to the *conjunction* of important events in class relations and the state, on the one hand, and the history of the sciences on the other.

Let there be no confusion about what we have said and what we have not. So far, we have merely observed that there is a *relation* between these conditions and Philosophy. *We do not yet know anything about the nature of that relation.* To arrive at a clear understanding of it, we shall have to put forward new theses, making a very long detour in the process. As I have indicated, this detour passes by way of an exposé of the scientific results of historical materialism that we need if we are to produce a scientific definition of Philosophy. To begin with, it leads us to the question: what is a 'society'?

2

What Is a Mode of Production?

With his discovery, Marx opened up the 'continent of history' to scientific knowledge. He laid the groundwork for a theory constituting the foundation of all the sciences that bear on objects belonging to the 'continent of history': not just what is known as 'history', sociology, human geography, economics and demographics, but also psychology, 'social psychology' [*psychosociologie*] and, generally, the disciplines known as 'social sciences' and, still more generally, all the 'human sciences'. The fact that these social and human sciences do not acknowledge that Marx's theory is the foundation for their true existence as sciences, the fact that they persist in upholding ideological notions which make them semi-sciences, pseudo-sciences or mere techniques of social adaptation is due to the dominant influence of bourgeois ideology, which prevents them from recognizing Marx as the founder of their true theory. But let us say no more about that.

What matters for present purposes is the fact that Marx, with his discovery, provided us with scientific concepts capable, for the first time, of making intelligible what 'human societies' and their histories are – that is, of making the structure, persistence, development, stagnation and decline of societies intelligible, along with the transformations whose sites they are. This does not mean that nothing important was ever said about the nature of 'human societies' before Marx – by, for example, 'philosophers' (Spinoza, Hobbes, Montesquieu, Rousseau and others); *historians (feudal or bourgeois) who discovered the reality of the class struggle*; or economists such as Smith and Ricardo. All the efforts of Marx's predecessors, however, their most positive aspects included, were dominated by ideological notions and depended in every instance on an (explicit or implicit) idealist 'philosophy of history', not on a true scientific theory of history.

Human 'societies': let us note straight away that Marx very early (beginning in 1847 with his polemic against Proudhon, *The Poverty of*

Philosophy) rejected the notion of 'society' as non-scientific. This term is in fact fraught with moral, religious and legal overtones; in short, it is an ideological notion that must be replaced by a scientific concept: the concept of 'social formation' (Marx, Lenin). It is not simply a matter of substituting one word for another. The concept of social formation is scientific insofar as it belongs to a *theoretical system* of concepts that has nothing whatsoever to do with the system of ideological notions to which the idealist notion of 'society' must be referred. We cannot now elaborate on this system of concepts, in which the concept of mode of production plays the central role.

Let us simply say, so as to be understood by one and all, that 'social formation' designates every 'concrete society' that has historical existence and is *individualized*, so that it is distinct from other societies contemporaneous with it, and is also distinct from its own past, by virtue of the mode of production dominant in it. Thus we can speak of so-called 'primitive' social formations,[1] the Roman slave-holding social formation, the French social formation based on serfdom (known as 'feudal'), the French capitalist social formation, such-and-such a 'socialist' social formation (in transition towards socialism), and so on.

Marx showed, precisely, that in order to understand how a given social formation functions and what occurs in it (including the revolutionary transformations that shift it from one mode of production to another), we have to bring the central concept of *mode of production* into play.

I FOUR CLASSICAL THESES

I here recall four classical theses in order to show how the central concept of mode of production 'comes into play' in Marxist theory.

1) Every concrete social formation is based on a *dominant* mode of production. The immediate implication is that, in every social formation, there exists more than one mode of production: at least two and often many more.[2] One of the modes of production in this set is described as *dominant*, the others as dominated. The dominated modes are those surviving from the old social formation's past or the one that may be emerging in its present. The plurality of modes of production in every social formation and the current dominance of one mode of production

---

1 See Emmanuel Terray, *Marxism and 'Primitive' Societies: Two Studies*, trans. Mary Klopper, New York, Monthly Review Press, 1972.

2 Analyzing the late nineteenth-century Russian social formation, Lenin distinguished four modes of production!

over those that are disappearing or coming into being make it possible to account for the contradictory complexity of the empirical facts observable in every concrete social formation, but also for the contradictory tendencies that clash within it and find expression as its history (the observable real transformations in the economy, politics and ideology).

2) What constitutes a mode of production? It is *the unity* between what Marx calls the productive forces and the relations of production. Thus every mode of production, dominant or dominated, has, in its unity, its productive forces and relations of production.

How should we conceive of this unity? Marx speaks of the 'correspondence' between the productive forces and relations of production. 'Correspondence', however, is just a descriptive term. The theory of the very special 'nature' of the *unity* between the productive forces and the relations of production of a determinate mode of production has yet to be constructed.

This first theory commands the theory of an altogether different problem, too often confused with the first: the theory of another 'unity' – quite different, because necessarily 'contradictory' – between the dominant and dominated mode or modes of production in a given social formation. For example, when we say that the relations of production no longer 'correspond' to the productive forces and that this contradiction is the driving force behind every social revolution,[3] it is no longer a question or no longer just a question of non-correspondence between the productive forces and relations of production of *one* given mode of production. In the great majority of cases, doubtless, it is also a question of the contradiction, in the social formation under consideration, between the productive forces *of the whole set of modes of production* in that social formation, on the one hand, and, on the other, the relations of production *of the mode of production currently dominant*. This distinction is crucial. If we fail to make it, we will talk wildly and inaccurately about 'correspondence' and 'non-correspondence', confusing two very different types of unity: first, the unity, internal to a mode of production, between its productive forces and relations of production, and, second, the (always contradictory) 'unity' between the dominated modes of production and the dominant mode of production.

3) When we consider a mode of production in the unity productive forces/relations of production that constitutes it, it appears that this

---

3   See the famous Preface to Karl Marx's 1859 *A Contribution to the Critique of Political Economy*, [trans. S.W. Ryazanskaya, in Karl Marx and Friedrich Engels, *Collected Works*, London, Lawrence and Wishart, 1975–2002, vol. 29, pp. 261–5].

unity has a material basis: the productive forces. But these productive forces are nothing at all if they are not rendered operational, and they can only operate *in* and *under the aegis of* their relations of production. This leads to the conclusion that, on the basis of the existing productive forces and *within the limits they set, the relations of production play the determinant role.* The whole of *Capital* and all of Lenin's and Mao's work comprise a commentary on this thesis; Marxists have not always acknowledged this. On this decisive thesis, the reader may consult Appendix 1.

4) This last thesis, which bears on the determinant element *in* the unity between productive forces/relations of production, and thus in the economic 'base' or 'infrastructure', should not be conflated with another classic thesis, which affirms that in another very complex unity, that which unites the superstructure (law, state, ideologies) with the base (the unity of the productive forces and the relations of production), the economic infrastructure is '*determinant in the last instance*'. The thesis that I just presented, Thesis 3, must therefore itself be placed under the present thesis. Thesis 3 can accordingly be stated as follows: in the base, which, in the last instance, determines everything that happens in the superstructure – in the base, that is, in the unity productive forces/relations of production – the relations of production are determinant, on the basis of the existing productive forces and within the material limits they set.

We have to be very careful here.

We need only compare these four theses with each other to see that we are virtually identifying the mode of production with the unity between productive forces/relations of production, which is to say that we are classing the mode of production with the base. Simply in order to evoke an issue that is the subject of still unsettled theoretical debates,[4] we shall say that we are provisionally leaving aside the question as to whether we should ultimately define a mode of production 'in the narrow sense' (*as we are doing here*) – namely, by bringing only its productive forces and relations of production into play – or whether we should, rather, affirm that every mode of production necessarily 'induces' or includes its own superstructure.

For some time, we favoured the latter hypothesis. *Provisionally,* we now prefer to maintain the 'narrow' sense of the concept mode of production (unity of the productive forces and the relations of production peculiar to a given mode of production), while affirming, again provisionally, that the question of the superstructure pertains, rather, to

---

4   A trace of these debates may be found in Poulantzas and Terray.

the nature of the concrete *social formation*, in which at least two modes of production are combined under the dominance of one of them. In the present state of our knowledge, it seems to us preferable to retain the present hypothesis, while reserving the right to modify it, should that prove necessary.

II THE PRODUCTIVE FORCES

In what follows, we shall consider what happens in a *single* mode of production.

A mode of production is, as its name indicates, a way or manner (a mode) of producing. Of producing what? The material goods indispensable to the material existence of the men, women and children living in a given social formation. A way of 'producing' is a way of 'tackling nature', since it is from nature and nature alone that all social formations, which do not live on thin air or the Word of God, extract the material goods necessary for their subsistence (food, clothing, shelter, and so on), that is, for their stagnation or 'development'.

A way of tackling nature in order to *wrest* from it the goods required for subsistence (hunting, gathering, fishing, extraction of minerals, and so on) or *make it produce* them (agriculture, animal husbandry) is not a state of mind, a behavioural style, or a mood. It is a set of *labour processes* that together form a system constituting the production process of a particular mode of production. A labour process[5] is a series of systematically regulated operations performed by the *agents* of that labour process, who 'work on' an *object of labour* (raw material, unprocessed material, domesticated animals, land, and so on), using, to that end, *instruments of labour* (more or less sophisticated tools, and then machines, and so on) in such a way as to 'transform' the object of labour into, on the one hand, *products* capable of satisfying immediate human needs (food, clothing, shelter, and so on) and, on the other hand, *instruments of labour* for the purpose of ensuring that this labour process can continue to be carried out in future.

In every labour process, the agents of that process must be 'qualified', that is, capable of properly using the instruments of labour in accordance with specific technical rules. Hence they must have technical experience of a kind that is rigorously *defined by*, because *required by*, the existing instruments of labour; if they did not have such

---

5 For an analysis of the labour process, see Karl Marx, *Capital*, vol. 1, trans. Samuel Moore and Edward Aveling, in Marx and Engels, *Collected Works*, vol. 35, pp. 187–95.

experience, the instruments of labour would be improperly used or not used at all.

Every generation of individuals always finds the existing instruments of labour to hand; it can improve them or not. In any case, the limits on these improvements (or innovations) depend on the state of existing instruments, those that the generation in question has inherited, not invented itself. The technical level of the agents of a labour process is thus always *determined* by the nature of the instruments of labour and, more generally (see below), by the existing *means of production*. Hence the following important Marxist thesis: in the productive forces, in which people figure as agents of the labour process, it is not these people but, rather, *the means of production which are the determining element*. Marx was always categorical on this point.[6]

Only for the last 200 years has it been possible to observe, as a consequence of the capitalist mode of production, a constant revolution in the means of production, a consequence of the development of technology, linked, in its turn, to the development of the natural sciences. For millennia, however, modifications of the means of production were either virtually non-existent or all but imperceptible. The constant modernization of technology specific to the capitalist mode of production,[7] including the spectacular developments that we have been witnessing for the past thirty years (above all, atomic energy and electronics), do not alter Marx's thesis by a jot.[8]

Throughout the labour process, its agents either work in a non-cooperative mode (isolated fishermen or hunters, small 'independent' producers) or cooperate. The introduction of cooperation and, above all,

---

6   In this connection, one is quite simply stupefied to read, in a recent official work by Soviet Marxist theorists, *Fundamental Principles of Historical Materialism*, the following phrase, which *revises* the classical thesis: [TN: The phrase is missing from Althusser's manuscript.]

7   Marx points out time and again that one of the essential characteristics of the capitalist mode of production, one distinguishing it from previous productive modes, is that it *incessantly 'revolutionizes'* the existing means of production. Thus what is occurring today comes under a classical Marxian thesis.

8   I note the incontestable topicality of this thesis of Marx's, at a time when the *conjunction* between the vogue of the Marxist-'humanist' interpretation, on the one hand, and, on the other, the unbridled technocratic lyricism that the 'impetuous development of the sciences and technology' inspires in certain Marxists, leads them to formulate theses tending to affirm 'man's' primacy over the means of production. These theses are converted into hazy formulas about, say, 'the increasingly determinant role, in production, of intellectuals as elements of the collective worker', or the revisionist thesis that '*science has become a direct productive force*'. We shall return at our leisure to these seemingly 'theoretical' questions.

its different forms also depends, in the final analysis, on the state of the existing means of production. People can fish all alone, angling with hook and line or using a small net. When, however, they possess long-range trawlers and huge nets, the kind of fishing they practice mandates a specific form of cooperation.

The existing dominant relations of production and the politics that correspond to them can either impose or allow forms of cooperation which, *with the same productive forces*, make possible results that the previous relations of production and politics ruled out. For instance, cooperation based on colonial 'forced labour' (on big plantations owned by whites, or for road-building and other construction projects) made it possible to achieve – using the same instruments of production as in the past, or other, almost equally rudimentary instruments – results that had previously been beyond the reach of the colonized 'social formations'. For instance, the very large-scale cooperation practised in China after the Revolution in order to build gigantic earthen dams, especially in the People's Communes (to cite just this one example), made it possible, without in any way altering the existing instruments of production (small baskets carried on shoulder poles, hoes and shovels), to achieve results that were impossible and unimaginable in the older forms of familial cooperation (individual peasants) or cooperation based on a single village.

Let us also simply note the following: every productive process in a mode of production involves *several different* labour processes, which must therefore be carefully combined in such a way that the manpower needed to perform the various tasks (seasonal or not) suffices to accomplish the whole of the labour process called for by that one mode of production. By itself, this requirement necessarily implies a *division of labour*, even if it takes only rudimentary forms.

To take an extremely simple example, we can observe, in the surviving 'primitive' African social formations, divisions of labour between different labour processes: the men hunt and build the huts, in regulated forms of cooperation, while the women, for their part, tend the vegetable garden or raise the small barnyard animals, pound the grain, and so on. We can also observe crossover phenomena: the same men switch from one labour process to the other, depending on the season.

This simple example provides some idea of the extreme complexity that reigns even in a 'primitive' social formation's productive process. As one can readily imagine, the process of production becomes infinitely more complex in our highly industrialized 'modern societies'.

Let us leave it at that and go back to our basic concepts.

Our contention is that the productive forces of a mode of production are constituted by the *unity* of a complex, regulated interplay [*jeu*] of factors that brings on stage:

– *the object of labour*: nature, in various forms (including the 'natural energy' that must always, under all circumstances, be either 'harnessed', even if what is involved is simply wind or a flowing stream, or exploited (gravity); but, above all, raw material, whether passive (minerals) or active (animals, land);[9]

– the *instruments of production*;

– the *agents of production* (or labour-power).

Marx uses the term *means of production* for the set encompassing the object of labour + instruments of labour (or production). Marx uses the term *labour-power* for the set encompassing the various ways in which activity (either physical or of some other kind) is expended by the set of agents of the labour process, that is, individuals who have the technical skills needed to utilize the existing means of production in the required cooperative or non-cooperative forms.

If we recapitulate these terms, we arrive at the famous equation: *productive forces = (unity) means of production + labour-power*.

All this holds for *a single* mode of production.

This equation has the theoretical advantage of highlighting the set *means of production*; that is, it distinguishes this set from the set 'labour-power'. This distinction is essential to understanding what happens in every 'class society' – for example, in a capitalist social formation, in which the *means of production* are held, not by those who dispose of *labour-power*, but by individuals outside the labour process: capitalist exploiters.

Before going further, let me bring a theoretical problem with far-reaching implications to my readers' attention, including those of my readers who may have illuminating suggestions as to how to resolve it.

It will have been understood that it is, to begin with, crucial to distinguish the productive forces specific to *one* particular mode of production from the *whole set of productive forces* in a concrete social formation, in which several modes of production 'coexist' under the dominance of one

---

9 Livestock and the land have a double status: they are objects of labour (livestock must be 'raised' and land must be 'cultivated') but, at the same time, 'machines' of a sort, since they themselves work on an 'object of labour' with which they are provided: pasturage or animal fodder and, in the case of the land, seed. This twofold character of livestock and land is of decisive importance when it comes to understanding the very special nature of agricultural labour – as well as the role played by the concept of the differential 'fertility' of land in the theory of ground rent (see Karl Marx, *Capital*, vol. 3, Part 3, trans. David Fernbach, London, Verso, 1981).

of them. The set of the latter forces of production is the set of the productive forces of the different modes of production coexisting in a social formation under the dominance of one of them. In this case, the plural 'productive forces' seems to be justified by the plurality of the modes of production, although the set of these productive forces obviously cannot be a simple aggregate, a simple sum, but has to possess, even in its contradictions, a kind of unity: the unity conferred on it by the dominance of the mode of production that dominates the others. This is in itself a problem for which we do not yet have a real theory.

The principal difficulty, however, has to do with the plural of the 'productive forces' belonging to *one* given mode of production. We have, in a word, described the productive forces and presented their unity in the form of a list and a sum: object of labour + instruments of production + labour-power.[10] Hegel long ago warned us that a sum is just a sum: that is, to be very rigorous, it is the absence of a concept, if not, as Spinoza put it in another context, 'the sanctuary of ignorance'. To be less rigorous, let us say that a sum is the index of a provisional lacuna that clearly has to be filled.

For we clearly 'sense' that the productive forces put into operation in the various labour processes in the productive process of *a single* mode of production are not just *added up* or added up any which way. Addition is the record of an observation that 'counts things up'. We have to set out from it, of course, but we cannot remain at that level. We suspect that what we are describing in the form of a sum is not a random aggregation, but a specific combination that has, for each mode of production, a *specific unity* which, precisely, founds the material possibility of this combination or *conjunction*; we come to terms with it empirically by breaking it down into the form of elements that we then *add up*. Among the important theoretical questions requiring clarification, then, we must include the question of the type of unity which, for each mode of production, organizes its productive forces in specific forms.[11]

However this last difficulty is resolved, we have, by bringing the concept of productive forces into play, begun to form a clearer picture

---

10　We find this sum in the form of a list in Joseph V. Stalin, *Dialectical and Historical Materialism*, New York, International Publishers, 1970.

11　In *Reading Capital* [trans. Ben Brewster, London, Verso, 1997], Etienne Balibar has undertaken this investigation for the transition from manufacturing to big industry. I would like to point out to those who have read or will read Balibar's discussion that what he has given us, albeit in keeping with the spirit of *Capital*, *is not in Capital*; it is an original, fruitful 'contribution'. This is worth noting, in order to distinguish those who make the risky attempt to *discover something* from those who content themselves with *repeating* things they owe to others so as not to have to 'think for themselves'.

of one of the two elements of the mode of production. In question here, after all, are facts that anyone who keeps his eyes open and is reasonably methodical can, if not discover, then at least recognize. It is not on the subject of the forces of production that we can decently pick a quarrel with Marx. The vast majority of 'experts' (the 'economists') will agree, but will further observe that all that goes without saying. They will even add, 'We have understood what a mode of production is: productive forces set in motion in certain labour processes by agents with special skills.'

From the foregoing, a good many 'experts' will conclude: 1) that Marx invented nothing new, since all this is blindingly obvious (without suspecting that it has only been blindingly obvious since Marx); and, above all, 2) that we have to do, in all this, with nothing more than *technology* pure and simple: material technology (tools, machines), technical training of the workforce, and technical organization of the labour process. The experts will feel reassured, and their 'spontaneous' tendency, which is technicist or technocratic, will be reinforced. Since they find themselves, unfortunately, in certain Marxists' company in this matter, everything will, for them, be for the best in the best of all (bourgeois) worlds.

In fact, we must squarely rebut them. The productive forces do not suffice to account for a mode of production, since they are just *one* of its elements. The other is represented by the relations of production.

Marx effectively shows in *Capital* (as does Lenin throughout his work) that the mobilization of the productive forces (means of production + labour-power) is incomprehensible unless we understand that it takes place under the aegis of definite relations of production, which play the determinant role in the unity productive forces/relations of production.

III THE RELATIONS OF PRODUCTION

What are the relations of production? They are relations of a very special kind between (in classless societies) the agents of production, when all the members of a social formation are agents of production, or between (in class societies) the agents of production on the one hand and, on the other, personages *who are not agents of production*, although they intervene in production.

These personages hold [*détiennent*] the means of production and *appropriate* a share of the products of the labour of the agents of production without providing anything 'in return': they appropriate a share of surplus labour. Thus they may, *so to speak*, be found at both 'ends' of the productive process, since they own [*détiennent la propriété de*] the means of production *before* the process of production and, after it, *appropriate* its product, conceding only a *share* of it to the agents of production so that the latter may live and reproduce. They keep the remainder (in the capitalist regime, surplus-value) for themselves.

Of course, they do not 'consume' the whole of this remainder at celebrations or spend it on other personal whims. They must consecrate a *share* of this remainder (that is, of surplus labour) to renewing the means of production in the requisite proportions, because means of production are gradually depleted (a mine) or wear out (tools, machines).[12] If those who hold the means of production do not take care to renew them, they will end up, one fine day, no longer holding them at all and be unable to avoid falling to the level of individuals of the sort who have nothing to sell but the strength of their two hands, when they do not sell their bodies. (One can find, in Balzac or Zola, stories of rich heirs who 'fritter away' the family fortune and end up as wage-workers in what was once their own factory – or in the gutter.)

Thus we can, at the point we have now reached, define the relations of production in class societies as relations of the one-sided *distribution* of the means of production between those holding them and those without them. We can add that this distribution of the means of production determines the distribution of the goods produced.

Here, however, we have to be very careful.

We may be tempted to think: Granted, there are people who hold the means of production and others without them. It is all a question of '*property*'. So what? What does that change as far as the labour process, for example steel-making, is concerned and, generally speaking, as far as the mobilization of the productive forces is concerned? We have been told that the personages who hold the means of production and who appropriate surplus labour are, '*so to speak*', *at both ends of the process: before and after*. But then the process of production remains what it is: mobilization of the productive forces, full stop. Our 'economists' will once again conclude: 'process of production' = 'the reign of *technology*', relegating 'all that business about the ownership' of this or that to the level of secondary considerations.

Yes, precisely: we said that these individuals are, 'so to speak', at both ends of the process of production. If we take things at the level of pure appearances, our 'economists' (there are even 'Marxists' among them) are

---

12 Machines wear out not only 'materially' but also 'historically': they are made obsolete by new, improved machines, the results of technological progress.

right: who holds or does not hold the means of production is simply a matter of *legal* clauses, a question of '*property*'. '*I'm* the one', says the capitalist, 'who owns the means of production, and the legal consequence (have a look at the Civil Code) is that I also own its products; I'm free to concede a share of them to my workers in the form of wages – something that is, moreover, quite "normal" – in exchange for their "labour".'

But we said '*so to speak*'. That was a way of suggesting that all this is not true. We can now show why.

Capitalist relations of production are relations of capitalist exploitation. To demonstrate this, we shall, from now on, restrict our analysis to what goes on in the capitalist mode of production – to be very precise, in a social formation, such as the contemporary French social formation (I am writing in 1969), dominated by the capitalist mode of production.

The fact that the capitalist mode of production is dominant in this social formation means that there still exist elements of one or more earlier modes of production in France, which is to say, in the case to hand, 'sectors' in which decomposition products of the feudal mode of production, the mode of production based on serfdom, still endure – big landed estates,[13] to begin with (the basis for ground rent), followed by the 'small independent producers', urban or rural craftsmen (referred to as 'small family farmers'), and so on.

However, the capitalist mode of production dominates these archaic forms, not just by virtue of the transformation of 'natural' ground rent into capitalist ground rent, but also by virtue of the capitalist market's nearly total domination of the surviving 'small independent producers'. As for buyers', sellers' or producers' cooperatives (the last-named are extremely rare), they are incontestably part of the capitalist mode of production, constituting a direct 'anticipation' of the socialist mode of production only in the fancy of a handful of opportunists or superannuated utopian thinkers.

The fact that 1969 France is a social formation dominated by the capitalist mode of production means that *production* (of socially useful goods or use-values, marketed in the form of commodities or exchange-values – thus the real, effective production of objects of real social utility) takes place

---

13 Let us recall one effect of this 'survival' (= the 'class' of big landowners) that has nothing to do with the capitalist mode of production. It is well known that Lenin defended the thesis (which is 'imaginary', but interesting from a theoretical standpoint) that, in a 'purely capitalist' social formation (one without residues of the 'feudal' mode of production), the land could or even should be . . . 'nationalized', that is, the property of the state, which would rent it to capitalist farmer-entrepreneurs (and charge a purely capitalist 'rent', that is, a differential rent shorn of absolute rent).

under the aegis of capitalist relations of production. But these capitalist relations of *production* are simultaneously relations of capitalist *exploitation*. And
we shall see in a moment that it is necessary to go further still.

Here, we must beware. The point is not to conflate everything and, as
soon as it has been understood that capitalist production is simultaneously
capitalist exploitation, to whisk production off stage and consider only
exploitation. One of the effects of the capitalist mode of production
(among others) is effectively to *produce* objects of social utility that are
consumed either 'individually', 'collectively'[14] (bread, sugar, apartments,
automobiles, radios, airplanes and also . . . weapons) or 'productively' (as
means of production). Every mode of production in every social formation, whether or not there are social classes in that social formation, has,
among other effects, this basic material effect. In this regard, and depending on the existing – today, international – level of technology,[15] 'Soviet'
or 'Chinese' wheat is well and truly *wheat*, identical to 'capitalist' wheat,
and an automobile, 'Soviet' or 'Chinese', is well and truly an automobile,
identical to a 'capitalist' automobile, simply because social and political
categories (such as 'socialist' or 'capitalist') do not apply to objects of
social utility or even to means of production. To be sure, those wishing
to efface all distinctions between social regimes invoke the international
(because physical) nature of products of social utility (of the overwhelming majority of such products) and technology in order to justify their
theories of 'industrial societies' or other such drivel.

We can even do them the favour of giving them, for free and to all
appearances, an additional argument, by saying that all identical labour
processes or even all labour processes in general, no matter what the
mode of production or 'regime' under which they are carried out, mobilize the invariable elements of a labour process: object of labour,
instrument of labour, labour-power. Here the imaginations of our utopian
thinkers, apologists for neo-capitalism and reformists start churning and
promise us the moon (either the disappearance of classes or communism)
just as soon as automation becomes universal . . . because automation will
put an end, 'to all intents and purposes', to nearly every intervention by
labour-power . . . and, consequently, to the exploitation of labour-power!

Let us be serious. While the capitalist mode of production does indeed

---

14   Be it recalled that *Capital* contains neither a theory of the basic unit of production
nor a theory of the basic unit of consumption. We need to elaborate both theories.

15   Technology has not always been international. It became international with the
constitution of the '*global market*' or 'universal history', which really only dates from
the period in which the capitalist mode of production came into existence.

produce objects of social utility, it produces them only under the aegis of very specific relations of production (we have briefly seen which ones, in a very provisional way) that simultaneously make them relations of *exploitation*. The same thing holds for all class societies, but these relations of exploitation take a specific form in capitalist social formations.

Let us now see in what respect capitalist relations of production are relations of capitalist exploitation. In principle, this finds very concrete expression in the following way.

The *means of production*: the unprocessed material processed in a factory, the factory buildings, the instruments of production (machines) in them, and so on, are the sole property of a capitalist proprietor (or corporation – that makes no difference here). It likewise makes no difference whether the capitalist proprietor directs the process of production himself, as his 'orchestra's' 'conductor' (Marx) or delegates this task to a factory director.

In contrast, *labour-power*, in each of its atomistic subdivisions, belongs to a large number of individuals who possess no means of production, but only their personal 'labour-power', with different degrees of qualification. These individuals sell the use of their labour-power for a set length of time to the owner of the means of production. In exchange for wages, they are hired by the day, the week or (in certain cases) the month. Wage-workers always *advance* the use of their labour-power, as Marx shows, inasmuch as they are paid *at the end* of the day, week or month. Among these wage-workers, there are different categories of 'personnel': common labourers and unskilled workers at the lowest level, then skilled workers, technicians of various levels, supervisors of various kinds, production engineers and various managers. There are also office workers (typists, accountants, and so on).[16]

As everyone knows, real 'production' cannot take place unless the means of production (which do not 'work' all by themselves) are set into relation with – and set to work by – labour-power, that is, *waged* workers. But this act of bringing wage-workers into relation with means of production belonging, not to them, but to the capitalist owner of those means

---

16 I leave aside two questions that are today 'on the agenda', and for good reason: that of the difference between productive and non-productive workers, and that of the 'collective worker'. Ink is being spilled on the latter concept in the same proportions as it is 'fuelling hopes'. Let me point out that the concept of the collective worker, if it is to be brought into play from the apposite theoretical standpoint, has to be paired off with an unprecedented concept that I submit to the reflection of 'collective worker' fans: the concept of the 'collective exploiter'. The latter bears a name familiar from Marx himself: *the holders and the agents or auxiliaries, direct or indirect, of capital*.

of production – the act thanks to which material production can proceed – takes place, precisely, in a capitalist regime, and only within relations of control of the means of production in the one case and, in the other, non-control of the same means of production (those who have no means of production at their disposal have nothing but their individual labour-power). These relations *automatically convert capitalist relations of production into relations of exploitation.*

We have already seen where this exploitation resides (this is Marx's great discovery): in the value that the capitalist concedes to the 'free' workers in exchange for the purchase of the use of their labour-power. The capitalist concedes to his wage-workers (contractually) only their wages, that is, only *part* of the value produced by their labour. By law, all the products remain in the capitalist's hands: their value represents: 1) the value of the commodities that are used up in the process of production carried out by the workers, such as raw material, wear and tear on machines, and so on; and 2) a surplus product that is itself divided up (unequally) into two portions: the wage conceded to the workers and the 'surplus-value' extorted from them, which is pocketed by the capitalist without further ado. And 'everyone is happy', says the capitalist, because he has 'risked' his capital, because he surely must pocket a 'profit' that rewards him for . . . the 'risk' he has run, and because the workers' labour has been paid for at 'its value'.

The trouble with this 'line of reasoning', which Marx took to pieces, is that: 1) no category, legal or of any other kind, can register the 'necessity' of giving the person who is lucky enough to hold capital a profit 'in exchange . . . for the risk' he has run, which, moreover, he generally does not run at all; and 2) the value conceded to the individual worker in the form of a wage by no means represents the 'value of his labour', but only the value required to reproduce his individual labour-power, a value that has nothing to do with the 'value of labour', an expression that, properly speaking, is devoid of all theoretical meaning.[17]

This is why the capitalist relations of production that ensure the real production of use-values (or products of social utility) simultaneously ensure, inexorably, capital's exploitation of labour-power. That is why capitalist relations of production are simultaneously relations of capitalist exploitation.

To this, we must add a determination specific to the capitalist regime. A number of readers will agree that the foregoing analysis is realistic.

---

17 Labour, the 'quantity' of which serves to measure/compare the value of products, cannot, by definition, 'have value' (Marx) (yellow logarithm).

They will, however, add: granted, the capitalist mode of production is indeed a mode of production that produces objects of social utility, but the capitalist avails himself of the *opportunity* that this production provides in order to squeeze surplus-value from workers. In sum, the capitalist is a man shrewd enough to 'cash in' on the real production of objects of social utility required to meet 'men's' needs.

This is not at all true. Marx shows that, contrary to most earlier modes of production, for which this explanation may perhaps hold, capitalism is a mode of production whose overriding objective is to produce, not objects of social utility, but surplus-value and capital itself. That is what is meant by the common expression which has it that the driving force behind the capitalist regime is the 'profit motive'. We should say, more rigorously, that the driving force behind capitalism is the production of surplus-value *by means* of the production of objects of social utility; it is the *uninterrupted* growth, and thus the growth *on an extended scale*,[18] of exploitation *by means* of production.

In the capitalist mode of production, the production of objects of social utility is wholly subordinate to the 'production' of surplus-value, that is to say, the production of capital on an extended scale, or what Marx calls 'the valorization of value'. The capitalist mode of production does indeed produce goods of social utility ('use-values'), but it does not produce them as objects of social utility for the seemingly primordial 'purpose' of satisfying social needs. It produces them as commodities that are produced through purchase of the commodity known as labour-power, and it does so for one purpose and one purpose alone: to 'produce' surplus-value, that is to say, to extort it from workers thanks to the unequal play between two values: the value of the surplus-product and the value of wages.

In a day and age in which both ideologues of neo-capitalism and neo-anarchists are sweeping exploitation under the carpet, the former by way of a defence of the notion that the capitalist economy no longer exists, that we have a 'service economy', the latter by declaring that the essence of exploitation is repression, we need to recall this truth that Marx brought to light. Everything that happens in a capitalist social formation, including the forms of state repression that accompany it (we shall see which forms and why), *is rooted in the material base of capitalist relations of production, which are relations of capitalist exploitation, and in a system of production in which production is itself subordinated to exploitation and thus to the production of capital on an extended scale.*

---

18   The concept of the 'extended scale' plays an altogether crucial role in the theory of the capitalist mode of production, as we shall have occasion to confirm.

Before we come to these notorious forms of state repression, however, we must examine more closely, even if only by adducing a few limited examples, the manner in which this primacy of the relations of capitalist exploitation is expressed and exercised in the forms of capitalist production itself, its technical forms included.

IV THE SOCIAL DIVISION OF LABOUR IS THE REALITY BEHIND THE 'TECHNICAL' DIVISION OF LABOUR: PRODUCTION, EXPLOITATION AND THE CLASS STRUGGLE IN PRODUCTION

The thesis that we shall be defending is a perfectly classical thesis. We find the basis for it everywhere in Marx's *Capital*, Lenin's work, and the work of their intellectual heirs. It runs as follows:

1) The relations of production radically determine *all* the seemingly '*technical*' relations of the division and organization of labour.

2) By virtue of what we have said so far, since the relations of production are relations of capitalist exploitation, the relations of capitalist exploitation radically determine, not in general and indistinctly, but *in specific forms*, all the apparently 'technical' relations that come into play in material production itself.

In other words, the relations of exploitation are not just expressed in terms of the extortion of surplus value, which is consecrated by wages and all the effects of the market economy. Exploitation has its primary effect in wages, but it has other specific effects in the practice of production itself, in the guise of the division of labour.

To bring out the existence of some of these effects, we introduced the concept of the *social division* of labour some time ago[19] (in a sense different from the one in which Marx uses the term), opposing the social to the technical division of labour. Marx employs the expression '*social division of labour*' in *Capital* to designate what we propose to call *the division of social labour*, that is, the division of social production into different branches: agriculture and industry, to begin with, but also different branches of industry. Because the term is convenient and seems to us to be very apt, we propose to retain the terminological innovation that we introduced then. Thus we shall use the term *social*

---

19 In 'Problèmes étudiants', an essay that was published in *La Nouvelle Critique* [no. 152 (January 1964), pp. 80–111; partially translated by Dick Bateman as 'Student Problems', *Sublation* (1967), pp. 14–22, reprinted in *Radical Philosophy*, 170 (November–December 2011), pp. 11–15]. We here rectify the 'technicist' and 'theoreticist' tendency that marked some of the arguments in that essay.

division of labour to designate the effect that the relations of production, *qua* relations of exploitation, have at the heart of the production process itself.

Our 'adversary' is, here too, the same as before: namely, the technocratic-technicist ideology that we may describe as '*economistic*'.

As we have already seen, every mode of production mobilizes a combination of labour processes which require that certain defined operations be carried out by qualified agents in a strictly defined order and in strictly defined forms. For each labour process, this entails a technical division into defined *posts* of various kinds, as well as organization of the labour process and thus management of the organization resulting from the defined division of labour. This holds for every labour process; it holds *a fortiori* when a process of production subsumes, as it always does, a large number of labour processes.

From all this, our stalwart 'economists' promptly draw the very simple conclusion that only *purely technical* phenomena occur in the production process: a purely technical division of labour, a purely technical organization of labour, and a purely technical management of labour. Invoking the requirements of production itself, they will argue that division, organization and management of labour are surely needed to ensure production; that there must therefore be 'manual workers' and 'intellectual workers', and thus workers and diversely qualified technicians on the one hand and, on the other, the whole hierarchy of managers, administrators, engineers, upper-level technicians, supervisors, and so on. These are all 'blindingly self-evident truths'. Did Marx himself not acknowledge the fact? There has to be someone to supervise each department on the shop-floor, and the whole 'orchestra' needs a 'conductor' to organize the division of labour and lead the resulting organization. To which our worthy 'economists' add that all one has to do is to 'humanize' relations in the enterprise between supervisors, engineers and managers on the one hand and workers on the other. This provides workaday proof of the fact that 'economistic' ideology and 'humanist' ideology are two faces of one and the same ideology. We need only read Louis Armand or [François] Bloch-Lainé.

But all Marx's work is a commentary on the fact, and all the workers' practical experience – their grinding, pitiless daily experience of the real relations that dominate and regulate the 'technical' division and organization of labour – is proof of the fact that these 'self-evident truths' about the division, organization and purely technical management of labour are pure and simple illusions or, worse, pure and simple impostures, milked for all they are worth in the capitalist class struggle against the workers' class struggle for the purpose of maintaining workers in the condition of the exploited.[20]

It is indeed in production itself that the implacable class struggle between exploiters and exploited is rooted, for it is present there at every moment.

The primary argument of the capitalist class struggle consists, at this level, in the ideological imposture about the 'purely technical' division, organization and management of labour. Squarely taking our stand, with Marx, against this mystification, we affirm that all the *forms* in which the putatively 'technical' functions of the division of labour are carried out are direct or indirect effects of the dominant relations of production (in our country, capitalist relations of production). Consequently, we maintain that every technical division of labour is in fact a *social division of labour*. As Marxists, we must take the view that all arguments to the effect that the currently existing forms of the division of labour are purely technical, and all such presentations of them should be rejected and denounced as pure and simple arguments of the capitalist class struggle. I will restrict myself to developing three points to prove it.

1) Every process of production entails the existence of several labour processes and thus of a set number of *posts* for qualified labour, including the posts required to organize, coordinate and manage that process of production. In the final analysis, the state of development of the means of production, first and foremost the technological unity object of labour/instruments of labour,[21] commands the way these posts are defined.

In our capitalist class society, these posts are filled on the basis of an implacable, insuperable class division. Posts requiring 'manual labour' of the kind performed by workers as well as certain posts for technicians and low-level supervisors (foremen and, at the limit, the heads of the various departments on the shop-floor) are *held for life* by members of the working class. The other posts, involving somewhat more elevated

---

20   The fact that engineers, even young engineers, who are stuffed with a heavy dose of 'economistic-humanist' ideology in their school years, really 'experience' (for themselves, and even when they have the 'best of intentions') their status and work as *purely technical* makes no difference here. Given that they are educated in their schools in conformity with an ideology which, by a happy coincidence (such is not always the case: hence the 'friction' that can indeed go quite far when 'circumstances' are favourable, as happened in May, for example), also holds sway in the enterprises in which they are employed, how can anyone expect them not to 'experience' their ideology as if it were the 'nature of things'? It takes no ordinary experiences to disabuse them, assuming that they wish to be disabused when it is not in their interest to be.

21   See Balibar's demonstration in *Reading Capital*.

organizational tasks and, higher up, 'planning' and partial management of the labour process, are monopolized by members of other social strata: engineers and technicians, as well as middle-level and upper-level supervisory personnel. Finally, the most important posts are held by the capitalists themselves or their direct representatives.

The division into social classes is thus present in the division, organization and management of the process of production, *by virtue of the distribution of posts on the basis of the class affiliation* of the individuals who hold them (and, correspondingly, the number of years they have spent in school getting an 'education', whether 'truncated' or complete). The fact that a majority of these individuals – engineers, upper-level supervisory personnel, even directors – are increasingly simple wage-earners[22] makes no difference here. *There are class differences among those who work for wages*, for source of revenue does not determine class affiliation.[23] That this division into classes has inexorable effects on the division of labour is strikingly revealed by the circumstance that only a *rare* handful of workers ever succeed in climbing up a few rungs and, thanks to gruelling efforts, acquiring somewhat better qualifications. As for the worker who becomes an engineer or even a manager, he is, in our society, a museum piece exhibited to encourage belief in the 'possibility' of the impossible and the idea that there are no social classes or that someone born a worker can 'rise above his class'. Plain, unvarnished reality cries out against these disgraceful exhibitions.

The immense majority of workers are workers *for life*. The opposite is still more indubitably true: an engineer or upper-level supervisor never 'falls to the level' of a worker, except in the case (an exceedingly rare limit case, and even that is understated) of disastrous economic crises. A pitiless line of class demarcation unmistakably separates two categories of human beings: the 'technical' division of labour is quite simply a mask hiding the fact that some people are permanently 'penned' in the situation of the working class while others can have either high-level posts that are immediately attributed to them, or fairly or (very) broadly open-ended 'careers'.[24]

---

22   'Simple wage-earners': we would have to examine the matter more closely even in this respect. An engineer's income, for example, allows him to 'invest his savings' in the stock market, to cite only that case. From the standpoint of his revenue, such an engineer is no longer 'a mere wage-worker', but takes part in capitalist exploitation by way of the redistribution of speculation on surplus-value.

23   The last lines of *Capital*, unfortunately broken off, prove it.

24   Let me point out an extremely tenacious and, from a theoretical and political standpoint, noxious illusion here: What happens in an enterprise (since we are taking an

2) This line of demarcation exactly coincides with another, the one that 'justifies' the first. Some people (engineers, upper-level supervisors and technicians, factory directors and all their assistants) hold a *monopoly* on certain contents and forms of knowledge, and thus on a form of 'know-how', while others (common labourers, unskilled and skilled workers) are '*penned*' *in other* contents and forms of know-how. The monopoly of the managers, engineers and upper-level supervisors and technicians has its counterpart in *what is in practice a prohibition* for the great majority of workers, exhausted by the production rate. The myth about all imaginable 'evening courses' notwithstanding, this prohibition prevents them from 'breaking out of' the contents and forms of 'knowledge' in which exploitation pens them.

This segregation, internal to all productive processes, throws the 'social' nature of every putatively technical division of labour into sharp relief. It is not always to the advantage of the supposedly 'knowledgeable' engineers and other upper-level technicians, who are ignorant of very many things that the workers learn in their practice or through personal effort. This does not go unnoticed by the workers, who often 'resolve' problems that baffle certain engineers. The workers judge them accordingly – a circumstance which, combined with the experience of being

---

enterprise as our example) is never more than an *effect* of what happens in the capitalist system as a whole, and thus an effect that can in certain cases be literally *undecipherable* at the level of the enterprise alone. Precisely that holds for the social 'distribution' or 'penning in' of people that we are here denouncing. Any 'engineer' will tell you: 'Fine, but so what? I need someone to run a milling machine, so I run an ad. A milling machine operator answers it. I hire him. Is it my fault that he's *just* a milling machine operator?' Literally, taken in its own limits, this is not 'wrong'. But, precisely, 'competencies', that is, qualifications or the lack of them, *owe their existence not to the enterprise* as such, but to a system *external* to the enterprise, the school system that 'educates', more or less, different individuals (employing mechanisms that we shall be studying) in ways that vary with the milieu from which they come. These mechanisms reinforce the practical, economic and ideological prohibitions (or 'cultural' prohibitions, those studied by Bourdieu and Passeron) which *distribute in advance*, on a class basis, the individuals recruited by the enterprise. In this respect, the entrepreneur's [*sic*] reasoning is not 'wrong'. It simply proves that he is not 'in control of' events. But these events that 'are beyond his control' nicely correspond *in advance*, by an amazing coincidence, to a dispositive for 'distributing-penning in' people that is always already ready and waiting in his enterprise, for the purpose, precisely, of exploiting workers. The reason is that the school system that supplies ready-made, at the national level, a predisposition for the 'distribution-penning in' of people that becomes concrete reality in the enterprise is the capitalist school system corresponding to the capitalist class's system of exploitation, *not some other school system*. It cannot be other than what it is, whether certain dreamers like that or not, as long as the foundations of capitalist exploitation remain in place – namely, capitalist relations of production.

'penned' in one's position, contributes to class consciousness and the working-class struggle.

As far as the great mass of its effects goes, however, the official monopoly on certain kinds of knowledge and the practical prohibition that keeps workers from acquiring such 'knowledge' maintain the omnipotence of the social division of the relations of production in the relations of a supposedly purely technical 'division of labour'. They do so by virtue of the *authority* that that monopoly and prohibition exercise over the relations of production. There is never organization, management and division of labour without *hierarchical relations of authority*. But authority is always on the same side: it is always the same people who wield it and the same who are subjected to it, for all intents and purposes *their whole lives long*.

3) The proof is that no organization of the labour process in any factory can ever do without *sanctions* enforcing this class domination, without a form of *repression* in no way beholden to policemen, since it is exercised in the division of labour itself and by its agents. Nothing – unless a factory has an 'ultramodern' staff trained in the pseudo-scientific techniques of 'human-resources' 'social psychology', and perhaps not even then – can eliminate the need for functions of surveillance and repression, which may or may not be performed by the same agents who are responsible for the organization of labour: supervisors, engineers, and so on. Fines, demotions, the attribution or withholding of bonuses, and dismissals are workers' daily lot. An unspoken class struggle plays itself out at this level. In limit cases, it involves hiring procedures accompanied by more or less 'political' checks, if not police-like enquiries, as well as constant 'surveillance' of trade union representatives and activists and even dismissals, illegal dismissals included. In fact, many employers would rather be fined by a labour court – they lump the fines in with 'overheads' – than 'tolerate' the presence of an 'undesirable element' whose activity, they rightly fear, may end up costing them more than a court condemnation. Most labour inspectors, as everyone knows, have no power to stop 'abuses', when they do not collude with those who commit them.

Internal repression is brought to bear on wage-workers *by wage-workers* taking their orders from the management of an enterprise, which is always a class management implementing a policy of exploitation or super-exploitation. This completes the practical demonstration that the purely 'technical' division of labour is just a facade for a very different kind of division, the *social division of labour*, which is an effect of the division between classes. It is no accident that the workers call engineers, very aptly, 'little bosses'. The fact that a certain evolution is under way among some engineers makes no real difference as far as the overall problem is concerned.

That is why the class distinction between 'manual labour and intellectual labour', to which Marx refers from *The German Ideology* on, is indeed a reality, despite the crude, crass nature of the formula.[25] It is produced by all class societies. It is still produced, and increasingly produced, by modern capitalist class society, despite the 'spectacular progress of science and technology' and the growing numbers of 'intellectual workers' in new categories, such as 'researchers', whom we shall discuss when the time comes. That is why Marx was on the mark when he said that socialism should 'abolish the distinction between manual and intellectual labour'.

That is why Lenin's desperate insistence on the need to establish a new, *polytechnic* school education (it unfortunately had small success), which would, moreover, *combine manual labour in real production* with intellectual labour, was – and is – so important.[26] That is why it seems to us that the news reaching us through what we can gather about certain experiments of the Cultural Revolution (mandatory training periods in basic production units for 'intellectuals' of all orders, 'controlled' shake-ups in the distribution of different manual and intellectual jobs among the producers, a real upgrading of jobs involving only implementation to posts of great authority and responsibility) has something to do with the class struggle against the radical determination, in our country, of the 'technical division of labour' by the 'social division of labour'.

There is no further need, in my view, to demonstrate that it is a question of class struggle in all this, and that this class struggle is directly rooted

----

25   This opposition between 'manual labour' and 'intellectual labour' obviously has to be much more thoroughly elaborated at the theoretical level, for it is no more than a *first* formulation pointing to an incontestable reality. When Marx coined this phrase, he plainly had in mind very 'classical' references to a situation in which those who either did nothing at all (beyond enjoying their fortunes or giving orders to the exploited) flattered themselves that they were all 'working' with their intelligence alone, so as to make it clear that the lower classes, since they lacked intelligence, could plainly only work with 'their hands' (Plato). Marx was also thinking of big industry, in which the worker is a pure and simple (automatic) extension of the (automatic) machine. The reality of the matter is more complex: no manual labour is possible without a modicum of intellectual 'labour'. However, as far as the basic *principle* goes, Marx's distinction is perfectly justified, in that it points to *a real class distinction* the *precise* forms and effects of which require further investigation.

26   In *Schools* (forthcoming), we will publish a long text by Krupskaya on this question. The text leaves no room at all for doubt: it evokes Lenin's almost desperate efforts and the failure of his educational policies. [EN: The projected book was not successfully completed as planned. See Etienne Balibar's preface to the present volume.]

in the effects of the relations of production in the process of production itself.

Recapitulating the results of our analysis, we may say the following:

1) Capitalist relations of production are relations of capitalist exploitation. This exploitation is accomplished by way of an extortion of surplus-value consecrated by the limits of the wage relation. Wages are paid in exchange for work performed in productive enterprises.

2) Within this production, the relations of production find expression in effects which, overlapping with and reinforcing the effects of class and class struggle, culminate in the following overriding result: the irreducible dominance exercised by the social division of labour over the 'purely technical' pseudo-division of labour. That social division of labour, an effect of the distribution of individuals in classes, culminates in a double, joint line of demarcation, in the enterprise itself, between a *monopoly on certain jobs* (associated with certain kinds of 'knowledge') reserved for one part of the 'personnel', and the *'penning'* of another part of the 'personnel', the workers, *in subaltern jobs* (plus a prohibition on 'knowing').

3) We can, then, put all of an enterprise's employees in three major categories:

a) The category of those who perform only *functions of production*. It includes all the workers: common labourers, unskilled labourers, skilled labourers and (sometimes) a handful of technicians. These are the proletarians, in the strict sense.

b) The category of those who perform *functions of exploitation* that are always *simultaneously* functions of production (engineers, upper-level technicians, production managers, and so on).

c) The category of those who perform *functions of repression* that may be combined with functions of exploitation (supervisors, from foremen to certain engineers) or may not be (the goons expressly recruited in a number of factories to serve as informers and execute, among other tasks, all the police manoeuvres of the gutter-level anti-union struggle).

All these employees are *waged* and must therefore be counted, on one ground or another, among the 'exploited'. There are, however, major disparities in their wages and working conditions (workers are subjected to exhausting work rhythms, while engineers work under completely different conditions), to say nothing of the basic distinction between functions of pure production on the one hand and the highly varied combination of functions of exploitation, production and repression on the other. When all this is taken into account, it will be agreed that the *forms of class struggle*, unconscious and conscious, that obtain within the process of production alone are *complex in the extreme*.

4) It must in any case be understood that the sole basis and purpose of all the elements (including the three functions) just analyzed is *exploitation* of wage-workers, especially those who are the 'most exploited', always more harshly exploited: pure agents of production or *proletarians*.

It must be understood that the whole system of monopoly and 'penning in' and all the differences in function, including the repressive 'function' (just one of the system's internal elements), converge to the sole end of accomplishing this exploitation or super-exploitation.

It is an anarchist mistake to claim that 'production runs on repression'. To do so is to foreground just one of the component elements of the process of production-exploitation, and a subordinate one at that: repression.

How does production-exploitation 'work'?

First and foremost, it 'works' because proletarians and other wage-workers must, just to *survive*, take jobs in the production that exploits them, *since none of the means of production are in their hands*. That is why they show up 'all by themselves' at the personnel office and, after they have been given work, set out 'all by themselves' to take their jobs on the day-shift or night-shift. That is the absolutely determinant cause, but not the only one.

Production-exploitation also 'works' thanks to *the currently existing dispositive of the means of production*, the assembly line [*chaîne*] that pulls the workers in and inexorably forces them to adapt to its pace. As Marx long ago compellingly pointed out, workers have ceased to be 'working hands' and have become mere automatic extensions of their machines.

Production-exploitation also 'works' thanks to *the bourgeois ideology of 'work'*. The workers are the first to be subjected to its effects, because it is an ideology of the capitalist class struggle. This ideology that 'makes the workers go'[27] comprises the following basic elements, which are so many illusions and impostures, yet 'are successful' as long as the workers' class struggle does not combat them: 1) the bourgeois legal illusion according to which 'labour is paid for at its value'; 2) the corresponding legal-moral ideology which has it that one must 'respect one's labour contract' and, through it, the enterprise's house rules and regulations; 3) the technicist-economistic ideology which has it that 'there must, after all, be different jobs within the division of labour' and such-and-such individuals to fill them. This ideology does a great deal more to make workers 'go' than repression does.

---

27   [TN: *Fait marcher*, a key phrase in *On Reproduction*. It means 'makes go/function/work/fall into line/march', and also 'hoaxes', 'bamboozles'.]

Production-exploitation 'works', *finally*, with the help of certain repressive measures, some spontaneous, others very carefully thought out (by the 'bosses on the front line'): goons plus 'house unions' (consider Simca and Citroën).

It will readily be understood that, under these conditions, the workers' class struggle in production does not unfold all by itself. It is rooted in, and takes shape in, exceedingly harsh day-to-day realities of exploitation, of the *experience* of exploitation; in the experience of the class line between 'manual' and non-manual workers, a line that is not blurred by one or another technician's or engineer's 'liberal' or even 'progressive' behaviour (often just a mask for 'paternalism'); and in the experience of the actual behaviour of supervisors, engineers and agents of repression. This class struggle, however, runs squarely up against the powerful weapons of the capitalist class struggle, which are the more redoubtable in that they do not always resemble weapons: above all, after control of the means of production and extortion of surplus-value, *the illusions/impostures of the bourgeois ideology of work* just discussed. Trade union activists waging the class struggle are well aware of this: they have to fight this ideology step by step, taking up the same combat day after day to root this mystification out of their own consciousness (no easy task) and their comrades'. Struggle against exploitation (wages, production rates, unemployment), struggle against the impostures of the bourgeois ideology of work, struggle against repression: such are the three *always interlinked* forms of the economic class struggle in production.

If this is right, then we can understand:

1) why *the class struggle* is basically conducted in the forms of the division of labour and the working conditions prevailing in enterprises, and why *the political class struggle is rooted in the economic class struggle*;

2) why the economic class struggle is a struggle against incessantly intensified exploitation: not only against the brutal material form of exploitation, capitalism's tendency to reduce wages, and against the class 'techniques' for increasing productivity (speed-up, and so on), *but also* around the question of the technical-social division of labour that prevails in enterprises, and against bourgeois ideology and repression. The working class's class consciousness is built up thanks not only to its experience of its material exploitation (wages, production rates), but also to its experience of the forms in which it is 'penned' in the division of labour. It can be built up only in an ongoing ideological struggle against the bourgeois ideology of work.

It will be understood, then, why the capitalist class and its ideologues have so powerful an interest in presenting the technical-social division of labour, which is, in the final analysis, a class division of labour, as a *purely technical* division. It will be understood why overt struggle against this mystification and imposture of the capitalist class struggle can acquire such importance for the proletariat's revolutionary class struggle. Economism, in whatever form it appears, including that of 'self-evident truths' about 'technology' and 'technicity', is the primary danger threatening the very foundations of working-class consciousness, at the point where capitalist exploitation is carried out: in production.

It will further be understood why those who have an interest in disguising the class relations of the social division of labour as the 'neutral' relations of a supposedly 'technical division' of labour, denounced by Marxist theory in its entirety, also have so deep an interest in treating capitalist relations of production as mere *property* relations, mere legal relations. We are beginning to understand that, between a 'technicist-economistic' interpretation of the division of labour and a legalistic conception of the relations of production, one and the same unity obtains: the unity of the bourgeois ideology of the capitalist class struggle. We shall see in a moment the practical consequences that this can have for the workers' movement itself.

V CONCLUSION: THE RELATIONS OF PRODUCTION MUST NOT BE MISTAKEN FOR PURELY TECHNICAL RELATIONS OR LEGAL RELATIONS

If what we have just said is on the mark, it is clear that the relations of production no longer have anything to do with mere *property* titles. Legal titles and, consequently, legal relations are merely a form that sanctions a real content altogether different from that form: namely, the relations of production and their effects.

We have just seen at how deep a level the relations of production and class relations and, therefore, the class struggle deriving from them, operate in the real relations prevailing in the production process itself.

The description with which we began our exposition for the sake of convenience is clearly untenable. The relations of production do not come into play, in the form of property titles, *before* and *after* the process of production, simply in order to justify and lend legal sanction to control of the means of production and its products, and, thus, extortion of surplus-value. The relations of production are not a legal 'umbrella' under the protection of which a perfectly and purely technical productive process is realized.

Hence a twofold ideological confusion that must be avoided at all costs:

1) The technical confusion: as we have seen, the relations of production are not purely technical relations, but, rather, relations of capitalist exploitation, inscribed as such in the concrete life of production as a whole.

2) The legal confusion: the relations of production are not legal relations. They are something quite different: they affirm class relations in production itself.

If that is right, we begin to glimpse what is covered by the scientific Marxist concept of the mode of production. We have defined it as 'a way of tackling nature'. We have seen that 'tackling' here means mobilizing productive forces under the aegis of relations of production. In class societies, these relations of production are relations of exploitation. The mode of production of a class society (of a social formation divided into classes) is quite the opposite of a mere technical process of production. At the same time as it is the locus of production, it is the locus of class exploitation and of class struggle as well. It is in the productive process of the mode of production itself that the knot of class relations and the class struggle bound up with exploitation is tied. This class struggle pits the proletarian class struggle against the capitalist class struggle: it is an *economic* class struggle, but also, from the outset and simultaneously, an *ideological* class struggle, and thus a class struggle that has, consciously or not, *political import*. Every other form of class struggle is rooted in this basic class struggle, including the *political* class struggle properly speaking, in which all forms of class struggle are tied together in a knot of critical importance.

It is easy to understand the capitalists' interest in depicting the process of production as the opposite of what it is: as a purely technical rather than an exploitative process. It is also easy to understand their interest in depicting the relations of production as something quite different from what they are: as legal relations, not relations included in class relations and the class struggle.

It is also easy to understand that the destiny of every class struggle, the *victorious* revolutionary class struggle included, ultimately depends on an accurate conception of the relations of production. To 'build socialism', it will be necessary to establish new relations of production that abolish, concretely, the exploitative effects of the previous relations of production, together with all their class effects. The construction of socialism can therefore not be settled with purely legal formulas: *ownership* of the means of production plus better technical organization of the labour process. At the limit, these are formulas which, if they are not seriously criticized and corrected, and very soon at that, may end up trapped in the economistic-technicist-legal-humanist-bourgeois ideology of work.

Every misunderstanding of these formulas and their inexorable logic does an objective disservice to the revolutionary cause and the construction of socialism.

3

The Reproduction of the Conditions of Production

We have not yet finished with the mode of production. We must now bring out something that we glimpsed in the course of our analysis when we discussed the necessity of *renewing* the means of production to make production possible. That was a passing hint. We shall now consider the matter in full.

As Marx said, even a child knows that if a social formation did not *reproduce* the conditions of production while producing, it would not last a year.[1] Thus the ultimate condition for production is *the reproduction of the conditions of production*. It can be 'simple' (only just reproducing the conditions of previous production) or 'on an extended scale' (expanding them). We shall leave this crucial distinction aside in Volume 1 and return to it in Volume 2.

What, then, is *the reproduction of the conditions of production*?

The reader should be warned that we are here entering a domain that is both very familiar (since *Capital* Volume 2) and singularly misunderstood. The tenaciously self-evident truths (the empiricist kind of ideological self-evident truths) of the point of view of *production* alone, or even of simple productive practice (which is itself abstract with respect to the process of production), are so much a part of our everyday 'consciousness' that it is extremely difficult, not to say practically impossible, to rise *to the standpoint of reproduction*. Yet, outside this standpoint, everything remains abstract (not just one-sided, but distorted). That holds even at the level of production and, *a fortiori*, at the level of simple practice.

Let us try to examine matters methodically and clearly.

To simplify our discussion, and bearing in mind that every social formation is characterized by a dominant[2] *mode of production*, we may say

1   Karl Marx, Letter of 11 July 1868 to Kugelmann, *Selected Correspondence*, Moscow, 1955, p. 209.

2   We repeat: *dominant*. For in every social formation in a process of historical

that the process of production puts the existing *productive forces* to work under determinate *relations of production*.

It follows that, in order to exist, every social formation must, while it produces, and in order to be able to produce, *reproduce* the conditions of its production. It must therefore *reproduce*

1) the productive forces;
2) the existing relations of production.

I REPRODUCTION OF THE MEANS OF PRODUCTION

Everyone now admits (including both the bourgeois economists who work in national accounting and modern 'macroeconomic theorists'), because Marx compellingly proved it in *Capital* Volume 2, that no production is possible unless it ensures reproduction of the *material* conditions of production in strictly regulated proportions: reproduction of the *means of production*.

The average economist is, in this respect, no different from the average capitalist. He will tell you that, every year, it is necessary to make provisions to *replace* what is used up or wears out in production: raw materials, fixed facilities (buildings), instruments of production (machines), and so on. We say the average economist = the average capitalist, because both express the viewpoint *of the enterprise*; they content themselves with simply commenting on the terms of its financial accounting *practice*.

We know, however, thanks to the genius of Quesnay, the first person to pose this problem that was 'staring everyone in the face', and the genius of Marx, who solved it, that the reproduction of the material conditions of production cannot be thought of at the level of the *enterprise*, because it does not exist in its real conditions at that level. What happens at the level of the enterprise is an *effect* that only gives some *idea* of the necessity of reproduction, but does not at all enable us to think its mechanisms.

A moment's reflection will convince us of this. Mr X, a capitalist who produces woollens in his mill, has to 'reproduce' his raw material, machines, and so on. However, *he* does not produce them for his own production, other capitalists do: Mr Y, a big Australian sheep-breeder;

---

development (or non-development), there is a mode of production that *dominates* the earlier modes still *surviving* in that social formation. That is why we once wrote that, to the present day, there are *at least* two modes of production in every social formation. (Cf. Emmanuel Terray, *Marxism and 'Primitive' Societies*, trans. Mary Klopper, London, 1972, pp. 178–9.)

Mr Z, a big machine-tool manufacturer, and so on. *They, too*, in order to produce these products necessary for the reproduction of Mr X's conditions of production, have to *reproduce* the conditions of their own production, and so on to infinity. And everything has to happen in proportions such that, on the national and even world market, *the demand for means of production (for reproduction) is satisfied by the supply*.

To envisage this mechanism, which entails a sort of 'endless spiral', we have to take Marx's 'global' approach. That is, we have to study the *relations of the circulation* of capital between Department I (production of means of production) and Department II (production of means of consumption), as well as the realization of surplus-value, in *Capital* Volumes 2 and 3.

We shall not go into an analysis of this question. Here, it is enough to have evoked the necessity of reproducing the *material* conditions of production.

II REPRODUCTION OF LABOUR-POWER

Yet something will surely have struck the reader. We have discussed the reproduction of the *means* of production, but not that of the *productive forces*. Thus we have ignored the reproduction of that which distinguishes the productive forces from the means of production: the *reproduction of labour-power*.

Observing what goes on *in* the enterprise, especially the financial accounting practice of anticipating investment and depreciation, gave us a rough idea of the *existence* of the material process of reproduction. Now, however, we are entering a domain in which observing what goes on in the enterprise is, if not totally blind, then very nearly so, and for good reason: the reproduction of labour-power takes place essentially *outside* the enterprise.

How is the reproduction of labour-power ensured?

It is ensured by giving labour-power the material means of reproducing itself: *wages*. Wages appear in every firm's account books, but as 'wage capital',[3] not at all as a condition of the material reproduction of labour-power. Yet that is clearly how wages 'work', since they represent only that *portion* of the value produced by the expenditure of labour-power that is *indispensable for its reproduction*: that is, indispensable for reconstituting the wage-worker's labour-power (what he needs to procure food, clothing, and shelter; in short, what he needs to present himself at the

---

3   Marx has provided the scientific concept for wages: *variable capital*.

factory gate again *the next day*, and every further day God grants him). Let us add: what is indispensable for raising and educating his children as well, in whom the proletarian reproduces himself as labour-power (in n copies, where n = 0, 1, 2, and so on).

Let us recall that the quantity of value (wages) required to reproduce labour-power is not determined by the needs of a '*biological*' minimum wage alone, but by those of a *historical* minimum. (English workers need beer, Marx says, while French proletarians need wine.) Thus it is a historically *variable* minimum.

Let us also recall that this minimum is historical in a twofold sense, in that it is defined not by the historic needs 'recognized' by the capitalist class, but by those *imposed* by the proletarian class struggle (a twofold class struggle: *against* lengthening the working day and *against* wage cuts). We can, however, leave this crucially important point aside, since it does not directly bear on what we are trying to show here.

For it is not enough to guarantee labour-power the *material* conditions of its reproduction if it is to be reproduced as labour-power. We have said that the available labour-power must be 'competent'. That is, it must be such that it can be put to work in the complex system of the productive process, in specific posts and specific forms of cooperation. As a result of the development of the productive forces and the *type of unity* historically constitutive of the *productive forces* at a given moment,[4] labour-power must be (diversely) *skilled*. Diversely: that is, as required by the social-technical division of labour, its different 'jobs' and 'posts'.

How is this reproduction of (diversely) qualified labour-power ensured in a capitalist regime? It is ensured differently than in social formations based on slavery or serfdom: the reproduction of the qualification of labour-power *no longer tends* (it is a question of a tendential law) to be ensured '*on the job*' (instruction during production itself) but, increasingly, *outside* production, by the capitalist school system[5] and other instances and institutions that we shall discuss at greater length in a moment.

But what do people learn at school? Everybody 'knows' the answer: they stay in school for longer or shorter periods but, at all events, they learn reading, writing and arithmetic. That is, they learn a handful of techniques, and quite a few other things besides, including elements (rudimentary or, on the contrary, advanced) of 'scientific culture' or 'literary culture' that are of direct use in different jobs in production (one curriculum for

---

4   See Etienne Balibar, *Reading Capital*, [trans. Ben Brewster, London, Verso, 1997].

5   See *Schools*, forthcoming in autumn 1969. [See Chapter 2, n. 26.]

workers, another for technicians, a third for engineers, still another for senior managers, and so on). Thus they acquire 'know-how'.[6]

What everybody also 'knows', however – that is, what nobody *cares to know* – is that, *alongside* these 'techniques' (reading, writing and arithmetic) and this 'learning' (elements of 'scientific and literary culture') that function as 'know-how', *alongside, but also in the process of acquiring* these techniques and this learning, people also learn, at school, the 'rules' of good behaviour, that is, the proprieties to be observed by every agent in the division of labour, depending on the post he is 'destined' to hold in it. These are rules of professional ethics and professional conscience: that is, to put it plainly, rules of *respect* for the social and technical division of labour, and, in the final analysis, the rules of *the order established by class domination*. People also learn 'to speak proper French' at school, to 'write properly', which in fact means (for the future capitalists and their underlings) to 'order workers around properly', which in fact means (the ideal case) to 'talk properly' to them so as to intimidate or cajole them – in short, to 'con' them. The 'literary' curricula in secondary and higher education serve that end, among others.

To put this in more scientific terms, we shall say that the reproduction of labour-power requires not only that its *qualifications* be reproduced, but that its *submission* to the rules of respect for the established order be reproduced at the same time. This means, for the workers, reproduction of labour-power's *submission to the dominant ideology* and, for the agents of exploitation and repression, reproduction of *its capacity to handle the dominant ideology* properly, so as to ensure the domination of the dominant class 'verbally'.

In other words, the school (but also other state institutions such as the Church or other apparatuses such as the army, which is as free

---

6 'Know-how'. This can mean simple *techniques* (knowing how to read, write, count, read a map, find one's way in a chronology, recognize this or that object or reality, and so on). But it can also mean 'knowledge' [*savoirs*], that is, the rudiments or elements (sometimes even relatively advanced) of scientific learning (let us leave literature aside). We must here introduce a very important distinction. One does not learn 'science' at school, nor even at university, as a rule. One learns scientific results and methods of reasoning and demonstration. Basically, one learns to '*solve problems*' or do '*practical exercises*'. That is not, however, 'science', but, rather, elements of methodology and scientific results that constitute *by products* of living science. Living science exists, let us say, in scientific research alone. (Lengthy commentaries could be made on that simple sentence.) To capture the difference in a phrase, let us say that the essence of living science consists less in solving problems than in *posing* the problems to be solved. Thus what one learns of science in schools and universities is techniques for manipulating and exploiting certain scientific results and methods completely detached from their 'real life'. That is why we can range all of the following under a single rubric: know-how; elementary techniques; and elements, even if they are relatively advanced, of scientific learning.

and mandatory as school, to say nothing of the political parties, whose existence is bound up with the state's) teaches 'know-how', but in forms that ensure *subjection to the dominant ideology*, or else the 'practice' of it; every agent of production, exploitation, or repression, to say nothing of 'professional ideologues' (Marx), has to be 'steeped' in that ideology in one way or another in order conscientiously (and with no need to have his own personal gendarme breathing down his neck) to carry out his or her task: the task of the exploited (the proletarians), the exploiters (the capitalists), the auxiliaries of exploitation (supervisory personnel), or the high priests of the dominant ideology, its 'functionaries', and so on.

Thus we see that the *sine qua non* for the reproduction of labour-power is the reproduction not only of its 'qualification', but also *of its subjection* to the dominant ideology or of *the 'practise' of this ideology*. Let us clearly spell out that one has to say 'not only but also', for it is *in the forms and under the forms of ideological subjection that the reproduction of the qualification of labour-power is ensured*.

With that, however, we discover a new reality: *ideology*. A long analysis is required to broach this question. We shall introduce it with two remarks.

The first remark will round off our analysis of *reproduction*. We have just rapidly examined the forms of the reproduction *of the productive forces*, that is, the means of production and labour-power. But we have not yet broached the question of the *reproduction of the relations of production*. This question is *the number-one question, the crucial question* for the Marxist theory of the mode of production. To neglect it would be a theoretical omission – worse, a *serious* political mistake.

We shall therefore discuss it. To acquire the means we need to discuss it, however, we have to make another long detour. We ask the reader to follow us patiently and attentively.

The second remark is that, to make this detour, we have to ask our old question again: *what is a society?*

4

Base and Superstructure

We have already had occasion to insist on the revolutionary nature of the Marxist conception of the 'social whole' with regard to what distinguishes it from the Hegelian 'totality'.[1] We said (this thesis simply restates well-known propositions of historical materialism) that Marx conceives the structure of every society as constituted by 'levels' or 'instances' articulated by a specific determination: *the infrastructure* or economic base (the 'unity' of the productive forces and the relations of production) and the *superstructure*, which itself comprises two 'levels' or 'instances': the political-legal level (law and the state) and the ideological level (the various ideologies: religious, moral, legal, political, and so on).

I ADVANTAGES OF A TOPOGRAPHICAL REPRESENTATION

This conception is of theoretical and didactic interest: it *makes us see* the difference between Marx and Hegel. It has a crucial theoretical advantage as well: it allows us to inscribe in the theoretical *dispositive* of its essential concepts what we have called the *index of effectivity* of each one. What does this mean?

It will be readily agreed that this representation of the structure of every society as an *edifice* comprising a base (or infrastructure) on which the two 'floors' of the superstructure are erected is a metaphor. To be quite precise, it is a spatial metaphor: the metaphor of a topography [*topique*].[2] Like all

---

1 In *For Marx* and *Reading Capital*, Paris, Maspero, 1965 [Louis Althusser, *For Marx*, trans. Ben Brewster, London, Verso, 2010; Louis Althusser and Etienne Balibar, *Reading Capital*, trans. Ben Brewster (abridged English version), London, Verso, 2009].

2 Topography, from the Greek word *topos*, place. A *topography* represents, in a defined space, the respective *places* occupied by various realities: thus the economic is *at the bottom* (the base) and the superstructure is *on top*. In this way, the topography makes visible what is at the 'foundations' (the base) and what is determined by the base (the superstructure).

metaphors, this one, too, suggests or makes us see something. What? Precisely the fact that the upper floors could not 'stay up' (in the air) all by themselves if they did not rest, precisely, on their *base*, and its foundations.

Thus the object of the metaphor of the edifice is, above all, to represent 'determination *in the last instance*' by the economic base. The effect of this spatial metaphor is accordingly to assign the base an *index of effectivity* known by the famous terms: determination in the last instance of what happens in the 'upper floors' of the superstructure by what happens in the economic base.

Setting out from this index of effectivity 'in the last instance', the 'floors' of the superstructure are obviously endowed with *different* indices of effectivity. What kind of indices?

We can say straight away, with no risk of error, that the upper floors of the superstructure are not determinant in the last instance, but are, rather, *determined* by *the effectivity* of the base; and that if they are determinant in their own way (which we have not yet defined), they are such insofar as they are *determined by the base*.

Their index of effectivity (or determination), as determined by the determination in the last instance of the base, is *thought* in two forms in the Marxist tradition: 1) the superstructure is 'relatively autonomous' with respect to the base; and 2) the superstructure 'reacts back on' the base.

We can therefore say that the big *theoretical* advantage of the Marxist topography, that is, of the spatial metaphor of the edifice (base and superstructure), is that it simultaneously *makes us see* that questions of determination (or of index of effectivity) are crucial; that it makes us see that it is the base which determines the whole edifice in the last instance; and, consequently, that it *requires us to pose* the theoretical problem of the type of 'derivative' effectivity that is specific to the superstructure, or, in other words, that it *requires us to think* what the Marxist tradition designates with the linked terms of the relative autonomy of the superstructure and the action of the superstructure back on the base.

On the other hand, the major disadvantage of this representation of the structure of all societies by the spatial metaphor of the edifice is, obviously, that it is metaphorical; in other words, that it remains *descriptive*.

It now seems to us imperative to represent things differently. Let there be no mistake: we are *in no sense* rejecting the classic metaphor, since it is

---

[EN: The following sentence in the footnote has been crossed out: 'Everyone "knows" and "sees" that the upper floors of a house do not stay up in the air all by themselves, but "rest" on a base and its foundations.']

this metaphor itself which requires that we go beyond it. And we are not going beyond it in order to reject it as obsolete. We would simply like to try to *think* what it gives us in the form of a *description*.

II LIMITS OF A TOPOGRAPHICAL REPRESENTATION

Let us lay our cards on the table. We think that it is by setting out from reproduction that it becomes possible and necessary to envisage the exist-ence and nature of the *superstructure*. Simply adopting the standpoint of reproduction sheds light on several questions whose existence the spatial metaphor of the edifice *indicated*, but to which it could not furnish a conceptual response.

We have to make a new stipulation here.

In the texts we referred to a moment ago,[3] we tended, taking up certain indications made by Marx and his successors, to emphasize the *distinction*, within the superstructure, between what we called, on the one hand, the legal-political superstructure (law and the state) and, on the other, the ideological superstructure (the various ideologies). To emphasize this distinction was itself a way of *making the reader see* that there are differ-ences in indices of effectivity between these two 'levels' of the superstructure as well.

Here, the spatial metaphor of the edifice also helped us to show that the legal-political superstructure is, as a rule, '*more*' effective than the ideological superstructure, although the ideological superstructure, too, is endowed with 'relative autonomy' in its relations with the legal-political superstructure and is capable of 'reacting back' on it.

However, in emphasizing this *distinction* (between the two forms of the superstructure), we remained within the logic of our metaphor and, accordingly, within its limits: those of a *description*. Here, too, it has become imperative to represent things differently. That is, we should represent the relations between, first, the law-state and, second, the ideologies in a way *different* from that dictated by the logic of the descrip-tive metaphor of the edifice.

Let us take our idea to its logical conclusion. We should also represent *differently* from how we have so far what is involved in the singular dyad designated by our expression *legal-political* superstructure. We should account for the *hyphen* that unites law and the state in the expression legal-political, asking exactly what we can and should *think* to justify (or question) this hyphen. Finally, we should also ask why we use (and

---

3 *For Marx* and *Reading Capital*.

whether it is legitimate to use) an expression that puts law *before* the state, and whether it would not, rather, be preferable to put law *after* the state – or whether these questions of before and after, far representing a solution, are merely the index of a problem that should therefore be posed in completely different terms.

All these questions, which we are raising in summary fashion, but, we think, correctly, can be summed up in the form of the following problems:

What is law?

What is the state?

What is ideology?

What are the relations between law, the state and ideology?

In what kinds of 'groupings' (law–state or state–law, and so on) can we represent these relations in order to think them?

Our basic thesis is that it is only possible to pose these problems (and therefore to resolve them) *from the viewpoint of reproduction*.

We will briefly analyze law, the state and ideology *from that viewpoint*. And we will try to bring out what happens from the viewpoint of practice and production on the one hand and, at the same time, of reproduction on the other. Only by taking this *difference* between reproduction and production into consideration can we provide the solution to the problems that we are here posing.

One final remark before we enter into this analysis. Since we are looking for answers to complex questions that bear on the very *order* that they imply, and since we are, for the time being, ignorant of that order, we shall adopt a *provisionally arbitrary* order, which we shall of course have to rectify once we have made these analyses. We propose, then, to proceed in the following arbitrary order: law, state, ideology. We shall see that, as we proceed, we shall have to modify that order for an unexpected reason: we are going to discover a new reality.

5

Law

We shall here examine what is given the name 'law' in the social formations that fall under the capitalist mode of production. It should be made
clear in advance that we shall be making, for the moment, a purely *descriptive* analysis. We shall take up the same question in more theoretical form
once we have acquired the means to do so (Chapter 11).

Law is *a system* of codified *rules* (consider the Civil Code, the Penal
Code, Public Law, Commercial Law, and so on) which are *applied*, that
is to say, both respected and circumvented, in day-to-day practice. To
simplify our discussion, we shall focus on Private Law, contained in the
Civil Code. Private Law is, moreover, the legal base from which the
other sectors of law set out to systematize and harmonize their own
notions and rules.

We can say, very schematically, the following.

Private law states, in systematic form, rules governing commodity
exchange, that is, purchases and sales – based, in the last instance, on
'property rights'. Those rights, in turn, are derived [*s'explicite*] from the
following general legal principles: legal *personality* (civil personality, which
defines individuals as legal persons endowed with defined legal capaci-
ties); the legal *freedom* to 'use and abuse' the goods one owns; and *equality*
before the law (for all individuals endowed with a legal personality – in
our present law, this means all human beings with the exception of a
certain number of 'rejects', excluded from equality before the law).[1]

That said, what shall we say about law?

We should note three characteristics, on which, moreover, Marx and
Engels (following Kant and, to some extent, Hegel) put the accent.

---

1 Because of pathologies – mentally ill individuals who have been involuntarily
detained; as a penal measure; or in accordance with non-statutory rules applying to children,
minors, foreigners, women (to a certain extent), and so on.

I THE SYSTEMATICITY OF LAW

Law necessarily takes the form of a *system* which, by its nature, aspires to internal consistency and compehensiveness. We beg the reader's pardon for introducing these two apparently technical concepts here. They are easy to understand.

Insofar as law is a system of rules that are applied – that is, both respected and circumvented – there has to be *consistency* among all the rules of the system, such that one cannot *invoke* one rule against another; if that were possible, the effect of the first rule would be cancelled by the effect of the second. That is why law tends to eliminate all possibility of internal *contradiction*, and why jurists engage in the extraordinary activity of systematization that has, from time immemorial, elicited the admiration of ordinary mortals. That is what makes jurists jurists, with a maniacal concern for rules and the cases to which they apply.

At the same time, however, law must be *comprehensive* [*saturé*]. In other words, it must represent a system of rules which, *tendentially*, cover every case that could possibly present itself in 'reality', so that one is not brought up short by something that is not juridically 'covered' and could allow non-juridical practices to make their way into the law itself, undermining the integrity of the system. Hence another 'admirable' aspect of the activity of jurists, who have from time immemorial striven to absorb the disparities of 'customary law' and the gaps and deviations of *case law* (application of the existing rules to 'concrete' cases that, often, go beyond them) in the law itself.

This activity of systematization is accordingly to be understood not only as elimination of the contradictions that can arise among the rules of existing law, but also, and above all, as elimination of the eventual *contradictions* that may arise between the rules already defined in the internal system of law and the paralegal limit-practices of case law, the essential role of which is to identify 'cases' that the law has not yet really integrated and systematized. In this regard, case law must obviously be brought into relation with *law's outside*, the existence of which the history of law recognizes in the form of what is known as '*customary*' as opposed to *written* legislation (every system of legal rules gives rise to a written codification). Let us, however, leave this point aside; it interests us only insofar as it indicates, from the standpoint of the security of the law itself, the existence of a more or less threatening *outside of the law*.

II FORMALISM OF LAW

Law is necessarily *formal*, in that it bears not on the *content* of what is exchanged between legal persons in contracts of purchase and sale, but on the *form* of these contracts regulating exchange, a form defined by the (formal) acts of legal persons who are formally free and equal before the law. It is to the extent that law is formal that it can be *systematized* as tendentially non-contradictory and comprehensive. Law's formalism and its correlative systematicity constitute its formal *universality*: the law applies to – and may be invoked by – *every* person legally defined and recognized as a legal person.

The formalism of law is usually regarded as, and criticized for being, 'formalistic': thus it is judged and criticized from a *moral* standpoint. A moral standpoint is a moral standpoint: it produces approval or condemnation. But law is indifferent to whether it is approved or condemned: law exists and functions, and can only exist and function, *formally*.

The obvious effect of law's formalism is to bracket, *in law itself*, the different contents to which the form of law is applied. But it by no means makes these contents disappear by enchantment. Quite the contrary: the formalism of *law* makes sense only to the extent that it is applied to defined contents that are necessarily *absent from law itself*. These contents are the *relations of production and their effects*.[2]

Hence we can begin to see that:

1) Law only exists as a function of the existing relations of production.

2) Law has the form of law, that is, formal systematicity, only on condition *that the relations of production* as a function of which it exists *are completely absent from law itself*.

This singular situation of law, which exists *only as a function of a content from which it abstracts completely* (the relations of production), explains the classical Marxist formula: law 'expresses' the relations of production while making no mention at all, in the system of its rules, of those relations of production. On the contrary, it *makes them disappear*.

The distinction between the relations of production on the one hand and law on the other is fundamental in Marxist theory.

---

2 The law recognizes that all people, as equal legal subjects, have a right to own property. No article of the law code, however, recognizes the fact that certain subjects (the capitalists) own the means of production, while others (the proletarians) have no means of production at all. This element (the relations of production) is accordingly absent from the law which, at the same time, *guarantees* it. See Chapter 11.

Confusing them gives rise not only to very serious theoretical mistakes, but also to the very serious political errors that follow from those theoretical mistakes.[3]

It is in fact imperative that we make this distinction not only in order to analyze what happens in the capitalist mode of production, but also in order to anticipate what will happen in the socialist mode of production.

It is perfectly obvious, to take just this one example, that it is wrong to define the socialist mode of production in terms of collective or socialist *ownership* of the means of production. It is wrong to define the socialist revolution as the 'transition' from one *kind of ownership to another:* from ownership of the means of production by individuals or monopolistic groups (reduced to a 'handful')[4] to ownership of the same means of production by *the* collectivity . . . that is, the state on the one hand and cooperatives on the other.

For to talk about collective *ownership* of the means of production is to talk about, not socialist relations of production, but, let us say, socialist *law*, and to mistake (so-called) socialist law for socialist relations of

---

3 [EN: The manuscript includes the following crossed out passage: 'For example, a formula seeking to define socialism as founded on *"collective ownership"* (as opposed to *individual* – capitalist – ownership) of the means of production remains caught up in legal relations (collective *ownership*) in that it maintains the basic principle of bourgeois law: *legal personality (collective* legal personality – the state – or collectives such as the kolkhozes – instead of *individual* legal personality).]

'This definition can be of some rough use when, starting from bourgeois law, we try to anticipate what will "happen" in the socialist mode of production. However, precisely because it confounds the relations of production with (bourgeois) legal relations, it completely misses its object: *socialist relations of production.*

'It is easy to understand the kind of theoretical and practical aberrations such a formulation can induce among those who are building socialism, since if the capitalist relations of production themselves can under no circumstances be confused with bourgeois law, it is a *fortiori* scandalous to define socialist relations of production not only in terms of law, but, to boot, in terms of *bourgeois law.*

'One should beware of a potential trap for the imagination of readers who may be tempted to say: granted, we must abandon the standpoint of bourgeois law and adopt that of *socialist law.* This comes down to repeating the same mistake in different terms: for if law must necessarily subsist in the period of transition from capitalism to socialism, the law that subsists, even if it is called "socialist" because legal persons are "collective", is still *bourgeois law, for law as such is the law of commodity relations and thus bourgeois.* The socialist mode of production will *abolish* all law. Marx understood this perfectly. He states it in his own terms in a passage of his "Critique of the Gotha Programme" that is often quoted, but rarely understood.'

4 [TN: As in many other passages of 'The Reproduction of the Relations of Production' and 'Note on the ISAs', Althusser is alluding to ideas defended by the French Communist Party (PCF) or leading PCF theorists. The immediate target here is the theory of 'state monopoly capitalism'.]

production. If we stick to this purely legal definition of the socialist mode of production, we risk very serious disillusions. Experience is there to prove it.

We know that Marx always defined the relations of production constitutive of the socialist mode of production not in terms of collective (socialist) *ownership* of the means of production, but in terms of their collective or common *appropriation* by freely 'associated' men and women. Thus he refused to define in terms of law that which cannot be defined in terms of law, even if it is called socialist law. This refusal goes very far in Marx, for in his view all law, since it is in the last instance the law of *commodity* relations, is marked by this indelibly bourgeois defect: thus all law is by essence, in the last instance, inegalitarian and bourgeois. See on this question the admirable, but too brief, comments to be found in the 'Critique of the Gotha Programme'.[5]

What, then, are we to understand by collective, common *appropriation* of the means of production by freely 'associated' 'men and women'? Clearly, while the problem is posed by this programmatic formula, which eschews all reference to law and all legal domination, the solution is not provided. The debates that this problem has occasioned and continues to occasion in the history of the Marxist workers' movement are well known (and far from over). Some do not go beyond state and cooperative ownership of the means of production; socialism then becomes a matter of economic planning. They claim that good socialist law and good planning realize, spontaneously and concretely, the 'appropriation' of the means of production of which Marx spoke. Others wish to move immediately to direct appropriation by the agents of production by establishing 'self-management', which, for them, *is* this appropriation. Slogans such as 'workers' power' or '*economic* democracy'[6] issue or have issued from this tendency. Things are not simple.

They are not simple because we must not confuse the *socialist* relations of production enabling common appropriation of the means of production, and, later, *communist* relations of production, with the relations to be established in *the phase of the transition* to socialism. For if socialism must not be confused with communism, the phase of the transition to socialism (of the construction of socialism) must *a fortiori* not be mistaken for socialism.

---

5 [TN: As a parenthetical phrase in the manuscript shows, Althusser intended to include passages from the 'Critique' and related texts in an appendix.]

6 The slogan 'economic democracy' is social-democratic. From the standpoint of Marxist theory, it is a piece of nonsense. As Lenin reminds us, democracy is a *political* concept that concerns politics – and has nothing to do with the economy.

In the transitional phase in question, the phase of the dictatorship of the proletariat, one does not yet have to do, as Lenin repeated a thousand times, with socialist relations of production, but with transitional relations in which so-called socialist law remains, by its form, inegalitarian and therefore bourgeois law, and in which state ownership and cooperative ownership are merely transitional forms that the dictatorship of the proletariat must utilize as such *in order to* prepare in them, patiently, tenaciously, over a long period, the constitution of the future socialist relations of production. Lenin repeated this incessantly, against all those who, ignoring the need to proceed step by step and, to boot, proposing petty-bourgeois solutions already quite classic in utopian socialism, wanted to establish 'workers' power', 'self-management' and 'economic democracy' or 'the democracy of production'.[7]

If, however, we can agree to leave the problems of the transitional phase of the dictatorship of the proletariat to that phase (the first of them consists in knowing whether or not one has gone beyond the phase of the dictatorship of the proletariat . . .)[8] and not confuse them with the problems of already *constructed* socialism, we can pose the question of the nature of collective, socialist, *appropriation* of the means of production in its own right. We can ask, to begin with, what Marx meant by this programmatic term.

Marx obviously meant something like the withering away of law, a correlative of the withering away of the state. The withering away of law can only mean the withering away of *commodity* exchange, exchanges of goods in the form of commodities (naturally including, first and foremost, the commodity that labour-power becomes in capitalist commodity relations) and their replacement by *non-commodity* exchange. We are thus inevitably led to the question as to how such non-commodity exchange is to be realized. The classic response runs: through socialist planning. But what is socialist planning?

It is plain that this is a burning question today, but it is one that bears the terrible mark *of the very particular form* that Stalin's politics impressed on Soviet planning from the 1930s on. We shall call it *state [étatique] planning* rather than 'bureaucratic' planning (since the bureaucracy effect is a secondary effect of a more general politics).

7　Here [in a planned appendix, see n. 5 above], Lenin, *Oeuvres*, vol. 32, p. 19 [Moscow, 1962].

8　Khrushchev very imprudently declared that the dictatorship of the proletariat had been transcended in the USSR and that the USSR was on the way to constructing *communism* . . .

All those trying, in the USSR, Czechoslovakia, Hungary and other countries, to make planning more 'flexible' by introducing 'liberal' measures are, even today, thrashing about within the limits established by this very particular form. The effect of such measures is to acknowledge and extend commodity relations at the very heart of these countries' economies.

Likewise posed within the limits established by this very particular form are the 'theoretical' problems over which theorists in these countries are agonizing and arguing, and also proposing methods for resolving key questions: for example, the question of how 'prices' should be determined.[9] The labour theory of value, placed at the heart of these 'theoretical' questions, as proper Marxist doctrine requires, is, if I may say so, put to a hard test in these debates!

At the limit, an appeal is made to the double myth of automation and electronics, which are together supposed to make it possible, thanks to a hyper-centralization facilitated by gigantic computers, to 'resolve' all these problems by magic mathematical planning,[10] with a little 'help'

---

9   On these debates and the dead-end to which they lead, see Charles Bettelheim ['Les problèmes des prix dans les pays socialistes d'Europe'], *La Pensée,* [no. 133, June 1967, and no. 134, August 1967].

10   To get to the bottom of the question involved here, beyond all the theoretical-technical discussions of the means of ensuring planning, it seems to me necessary to make the following observation. Basically, people think, or rather hope, that the essential aim of planning is to realize, to constitute, in short, to create socialist relations of production, the celebrated relations of real appropriation. In fact, to the extent that planning tends to be assigned sole responsibility, or the main responsibility, for solving this gigantic problem, its real function is misunderstood, which is less to create socialist relations of production than to organize, in the most 'rational' way possible, the existing *productive forces*, and, essentially, the productive forces alone. Here we once again encounter a politics I discuss in the Appendix: that of the primacy of the productive forces over the relations of production. This politics is false in its very principle and at odds with Lenin's famous slogan: 'Socialism is the Soviets plus electrification'. With this pithy phrase, Lenin states an accurate, fundamental thesis. Neglecting it always has fatal consequences. Lenin affirms, with this phrase, the primacy of the Soviets over electrification, and, thereby, the political primacy of the problem of the relations of production over the productive forces. I say the *political* primacy. For the Soviets are the masses' political organizations, and socialist relations of production will not be established as a side effect of the planning of the productive forces (here symbolized by electrification), but, rather, by *the political intervention of the masses* (here, the Soviets). Planning (the primary objective of which is to organize the productive forces) is *one means* of political intervention and of the political line that must constitute or 'invent' (the masses 'invented' the Soviets in 1905, after all) the new socialist relations of production. Planning, its conception and methods included (I say nothing about its objectives: that is self-evident), is thus not the solution, but *a means subordinate* to a political line based on the primacy of the relations of production that the (political) dictatorship of the proletariat has to put in place. This is a long and exacting business, the business of the class struggle. At

(which just happens to be indispensable) from the 'profitability criterion' in the enterprises . . . I doubt that this technocratic solution, tempered with a dose of economic liberalism (which is uncontrollable in the long run) and the requisite sort of right-thinking 'humanist' ideology (the necessary counter-point), will provide us with the kind of socialist planning capable of materializing *relations of appropriation* of the means of production by 'freely associated men and women'.

We would do well to take a big step back from the form of planning imposed by Stalin's politics, which still commands these 'problems', in order to put things into historical, political and theoretical perspective and re-examine them from a more correct point of view. That, at any rate, is my personal opinion; I offer it as such. But this step back and its effects presuppose political and theoretical conditions which, if the present course of events is any indication, are not likely to prevail any time soon and will not come about without serious transformations that it will be painful to carry out. For very serious questions lurk behind these problems, even in the socialist countries: questions of class and the class struggle, a circumstance that should not surprise Marxists.

However that may be, it is clear that by way of the various experiments in progress – the Yugoslav experiment, from which we may already draw the certain conclusion that it is only a stage in a transition-regression towards capitalism; Soviet planning, marked by Stalin's conception; Chinese planning (the form and spirit of which are considerably different) – in these various experiments, I say, it is well and truly a question of a search for unprecedented *forms* in which these much discussed relations of socialist production may one day exist as relations of *real appropriation*. It is also clear that the search for such forms is not just a theoretical question, even if theory has a very important part to play in it (the theory of Marx and Lenin, of course), but an eminently political question that can be settled only after the conclusion of political struggles (at bottom, economic, political and ideological class struggles) of which we are now experiencing just the beginnings.

Those are some of the reasons for which the Marxist distinction between the relations of production and legal relations is of the first importance.

---

any event, the question has to be posed in the right terms and, against the tendency towards economism-humanism, politics has to be put in command, so that the primacy of the relations of production is ensured in actual fact.

III THE REPRESSIVE NATURE OF LAW

Law is necessarily *repressive*. Kant sees and states this very clearly in his *Metaphysics of Morals* (a work that has very little of the metaphysical about it, its title notwithstanding). In this regard, the Hegelian conception of Law, with its delirious idealism, trails far behind Kant's.

Law is repressive in that it could not exist in the absence of a corresponding system of sanctions. In other words, there can be no civil code without a penal code, which is the realization of the former at the level of the law itself. This is easy to grasp: a legal contract can exist only on condition that it is *applied*; in other words, on condition that the law is respected or circumvented. Hence there must be a law of the application (or non-application) *of law*, that is, of the observance (or non-observance) of the rules of the legal contract.

In a contract, two legal persons *promise* to make certain defined exchanges. At the same time, they *promise* to *submit to sanctions* if they fail to observe the terms of the contract.[11]

By way of the essential legal complement to law comprised by the system of legal rules for the sanction of (non)observance of the terms of a contract, by way of the legal complement of the civil code comprised by the penal code, law recognizes, internally, that it could not 'exist', that is, be practiced by legal persons, without rules of *repressive constraint*.

This is what Kant very clearly sees in his *Metaphysics* 'of law': *law entails constraint*. Naturally, however, he sees it from the standpoint of *morality*, hence as a difference between law (a formal, non-contradictory-comprehensive *repressive* system) and morality (a formal, non-ontradictory-comprehensive system that includes an obligation – Duty – which is *without sanction* and thus *without repression*). No one will be surprised to learn that our viewpoint on law is not Kant's (the viewpoint of its difference from morality), but an altogether different viewpoint (that of its difference from the relations of production).

Things are now simple. Constraint implies sanction; sanction implies repression, and therefore, necessarily, an *apparatus of repression*. This apparatus exists in the *Repressive State Apparatus* in the narrow sense. It is called

---

11 Unless, obviously, they can find (legal) means of circumventing them, either by discovering (thanks to legal experts who are paid for the purpose) a legal rule that 'covers' their operation, or by discovering (the same way) an absence of legal rules, a loophole in the law that puts them beyond the reach of any appeal whatever to law (either law in the proper sense or case law).

courts, fines, prisons, and the various detachments [*corps*] of the police. It is by virtue of this that law is inseparably bound up with the state [*fait corps avec l'Etat*].

At the same time, however, it is clear that the practice of law is not exclusively based on repression *in actu*. Most of the time, repression is, as the expression goes, '*preventive*'. It intervenes in legal-state forms in a very small number of cases, over against the infinite number of contracts that are respected without the intervention *in propria persona* of the repressive apparatus or the initiation of a repressive process. In the vast majority of cases, things go without a hitch: the terms of the contract are *observed*.

We must, however, pay close attention here.

IV LAW, LEGAL IDEOLOGY, AND THE SUPPLEMENT OF MORAL IDEOLOGY

Common sense (that *Almanac Vernot*[12] of public asininities) will burst out laughing, with its coarse laugh: it is 'fear of the gendarme' which makes the parties to a contract respect the promises they make in the articles of a contract! For, as everyone 'knows', fear of the gendarme is the 'beginning of wisdom'.

To which 'decent people'[13] will respond, to all appearances with good reason, that if the gendarme is plainly on the horizon of legal obligations, he is by no means present on the horizon of the *consciousness/conscience* of the contracting parties. Better, he is *absent in person*.

The 'decent people' are right. Indeed, they are always right; but one must understand the reasons for which they are right. In the present case, we need only listen to what they say: 'If we observe the terms of the contract we sign, it is not – God forbid! – out of fear of the gendarme, but "*out of simple decency*".'

There do in fact exist honest people who sign contracts, people who do not at all need the fear of the gendarme to be honest. They are honest for reasons of simple 'professional conscience' or simple 'moral conscience', and they sometimes derive a certain pride from this, when they do not derive (more or less discreetly) commercial advantages from it, for everyone in the national or international market 'knows' that such-and-such a 'Company' is perfectly 'law-abiding' and punctual, or even that

---

12   [TN: A conservative, folksy almanac with a mass readership, launched in 1886.]

13   [TN: The contrast is between *honnêtes gens* ('decent people'; *honnête* can also mean 'honest') and *gendarmes*, which was earlier written *gens d'armes* ('people of arms') and meant 'knights'.]

such-and-such a people is (Germans, Japanese, and so on), whereas other companies or peoples do not know how (properly) 'to behave in business matters', that is, how to 'honour their promises' (Honour!).

We had better take the 'decent people' at their word. For, in spite of all the sarcastic remarks of a latent Poujadism and the petty-bourgeois bitterness that does not imagine that it (the petty bourgeoisie) could ever have gone to ruin if it had not been swindled, the decent people are fundamentally in the right, for good reason. Let us call that right reason by its name.

Since, a moment ago, we gave the repressive apparatus (part of the state apparatus) required by bourgeois law its name, let us give its name to this right reason as well. It is *legal ideology*, and also *moral ideology*, which serves legal ideology as a 'supplement'.

The vast majority of legal persons observe the terms of the contracts they sign, and they do indeed do so without the intervention of, and even without preventive threats from, the specialized repressive state apparatus. They do so because they are 'steeped' in '*the decency*' of '*legal ideology*', which inscribes itself in their behaviour of respect for law and, in the proper sense, enables law to 'function' – enables, that is, legal practice to 'go all by itself', without the help of repression or threats.

But we must pay close attention here, too.

Legal ideology is obviously required by the practice of law, and therefore by law (law that is not practiced is not law at all), but it is not the same thing as law.

Law says (writes in its Codes), for example: every individual (except for the rejects comprising the exceptions we mentioned earlier) is *legally* free (to sign contracts or not, to use and abuse his or her property, and so on). This is a *legal* definition of freedom, that is, a definition of freedom *by law*, by the system of its rules – a perfectly precise definition of freedom that holds only within the limits of law and has nothing to do with moral or philosophical freedom, or even, as we shall see, with the freedom of legal ideology.

Law says, for example: all individuals (except for the rejects, and so on) are legally equal before every contractual act and its consequences (especially its penal consequences). This is a *legal* definition of equality, that is, a definition of equality by law, by the system of its rules – a perfectly precise definition of equality that holds only within the limits of law and has nothing to do with moral, political or metaphysical equality, or even, as we shall see, with the equality of legal ideology.

Law says, for example, that we must respect the obligations we have signed. This is a *legal* definition of obligation, that is, a definition of obligation by law, by the system of its penal rules – a perfectly precise definition of obligation that holds only within the limits of law and has nothing to do with moral obligation or metaphysical obligation, or even, as we shall see, with the obligation of legal ideology.

If we wish to talk about *legal ideology* with a modicum of respect for the facts and with some rigour in our terminology, we must say that, while it does indeed take up the notions of freedom, equality and obligation, it inscribes them, *outside the law* and thus outside the system of the rules of law and their limits, in an ideological *discourse* that is structured by completely different notions.

To sum up the essence of these basic notions of legal ideology, we must pay attention to the following 'little difference'.

Law says: individuals are *legal* persons, legally free, equal and bound to honour their obligations *as legal persons*. In other words, law does not leave the domain of law: it brings everything back to law, 'honestly'. It should not be reproached for this: it honestly plies its 'trade' as law.

Legal ideology, for its part, utters a discourse that is apparently similar, but in fact *altogether different*. It says: men are free and equal *by nature*. Thus, in legal ideology, it is *'nature'*, not law, which 'founds' the freedom and equality of 'men' (not of legal persons). That is a little different . . .

There remains, obviously, obligation. Legal ideology does not say that men are bound to honour their obligations by *'nature'*. It needs a little supplement on this point – very precisely, a little *moral* supplement. This means that legal ideology can stand upright only if it leans on the moral ideology of 'Conscience' and 'Duty' for support.

The reader will have understood what we wanted to show. Law is a formal, systematized, non-contradictory, (tendentially) comprehensive system *that cannot exist all by itself.*

On the one hand, it rests on part of the state repressive apparatus for support. On the other hand, it rests on legal ideology and a little supplement of moral ideology for support.

On the horizon of every legal practice there is, doubtless, a gendarme (part of the state apparatus) who keeps an eye on things and intervenes when he must. Most of the time, however, he does not intervene and is even completely absent from the horizon of legal practice.

What, then, is present, not on the horizon of this space, but in this space itself? *Legal ideology plus the little supplement of moral ideology.* It is quite as if legal and moral ideology played the role of the absent gendarme and were his 'representative' in the space of the legal practice of contracts.

Someone who is absent is someone who is absent. The representative of the one who is absent is not the one who is absent, but his representative. (Our diplomats know well – and thank God! for they would otherwise be crushed under the weight of France – that, unlike De Gaulle, they are not 'France!', but only its 'representatives'. This allows them to have a little life of their own, a family, holidays and prospects, career prospects included.)

Legal-moral ideology thus stands in for the gendarme; but insofar as it stands in for the gendarme, *it is not the gendarme.*

This is not nitpicking or an idle distinction. This distinction is manifest *in fact*, very precisely, in the circumstance that the gendarme is a repressive *force* of *physical* intervention. He is accredited after taking an oath empowering him to *arrest* a delinquent and bring her (handcuffed, if necessary) before the proper legal authority [*à qui de droit*] who will require that she give an account of herself, with detention, jail, a trial and condemnations, at the end of the process. The gendarme is the *violence* of the state cloaked by an inoffensive (or not so inoffensive) uniform; operettas are composed about him precisely so as to 'forget' that he exists only by *violence*. We shall say that, in the guise of the gendarme, legal practice functions 'on the violence' (the regulated violence) of the state apparatus.

However, as a general rule, in the vast majority of cases, there is no need for state violence to intervene. For legal practice to 'function', *legal-moral ideology is sufficient*, and things go '*all by themselves*', since legal persons are steeped in the glaringly obvious 'self-evident truths' that men are free and equal *by nature*, and 'must' respect their promises by virtue of simple legal-moral 'conscience' (baptized 'professional conscience' to mask its *ideological* grounds). We shall therefore say that the practice of law 'functions' in the vast majority of cases 'on legal-moral ideology'.

Of course, the consequence of the way law thus 'functions' (on state 'violence' and, at the same time, on non-violent 'ideology') are incalculable, as far as both the relations of production and the *forms of existence* of the relations of production in the division and organization of labour are concerned. We shall obviously have to come back to this. But for the moment we shall leave this crucial question in suspense in order to focus our attention on the following remark.

Our analysis of the nature and 'functioning' of law has brought us face to face with two realities (although we have made no special effort to seek them out) in whose absence the existence and functioning of law are literally unintelligible. These 'realities' are the state on the one hand and ideology on the other. It is time to discuss them.

6

The State

The Marxist tradition is categorical: from the *Manifesto* and the *Eighteenth Brumaire* on (and in all the later classic texts, above all Marx on the Paris Commune and Lenin in *State and Revolution*), the state is explicitly conceived as a *repressive apparatus*. The state is a repressive 'machine' that enables the dominant classes (in the nineteenth century, the bourgeois class and the 'class' of big landowners) to ensure their domination over the working class in order to subject it to the process of extorting surplus-value (that is, to capitalist exploitation).

The state is thus, above all, what the Marxist classics have called *the state apparatus*. This term covers not only the specialized apparatus (in the narrow sense) whose existence and necessity follows, as we have seen, from the requirements of legal practice – that is, the police, courts and prisons – but also the army, which, apart from its 'national defence' role (the proletariat has paid for this experience with its blood), intervenes directly as the auxiliary repressive force of last resort when the police (and its specialized corps: the riot police, and others) are 'overwhelmed by events'. Presiding over this ensemble are the chief of state, the government, and the administration.

Presented in this form, the Marxist-Leninist 'theory' of the state touches *on the essential point*, and there can be no question at all of not recognizing that this is indeed the essential point. The state apparatus, which defines the state as a repressive force of execution and intervention 'at the service of the dominant classes' in the class struggle waged by the bourgeoisie and its allies against the proletariat, is well and truly the state, and this well and truly defines its basic 'function'.

I FROM A DESCRIPTIVE THEORY OF THE STATE
TO THEORY IN THE FULL SENSE

Nevertheless, here too this presentation of the nature of the state remains *descriptive*, as we have already noted about the metaphor of the edifice (base and superstructure).

Since we shall often have occasion to use this adjective ('descriptive'), a word of explanation is in order to eliminate all ambiguity.

When, in discussing the metaphor of the edifice or the Marxist 'theory' of the state, we say that these are descriptive conceptions or representations of their object, we have no negative ulterior motives. On the contrary, there is every reason to believe that great scientific discoveries cannot avoid going through a first phase of what we shall call *descriptive* '*theory*'. This would be the *first* phase of every theory, at least in the domain that concerns us (that of the science of social formations). Accordingly, one could – and, in our view, one must – regard this phase as a *transitional* phase necessary for the development of the theory. We inscribe the fact that it is transitional in our expression 'descriptive theory', bringing out, by way of the conjunction of the two terms employed, the equivalent of a kind of 'contradiction'. For the term *theory* is partially 'at odds' with the adjective '*descriptive*' attached to it. This means, to be very precise, 1) that the 'descriptive theory' really is, beyond the shadow of a doubt, the irreversible commencement of the theory; but 2) that the 'descriptive' form in which the theory is presented *requires*, precisely as an effect of this 'contradiction', a development of the theory that goes beyond the form of 'description'.

Let us clarify this idea by returning to the subject to hand, the state.

To say that the Marxist 'theory' of the state at our disposal remains largely 'descriptive' means, first and foremost, that this descriptive 'theory' is, beyond the shadow of a doubt, the real *commencement* of a Marxist theory of the state, and that this commencement provides us with the essential point, that is, the *decisive* principle [of] every later development of the theory.

But that is not enough. We shall say that a theory is 'descriptive' when we can perfectly well bring the vast majority of observable facts in the domain on which it bears into correspondence with its definition of its object. Thus the definition of the state as a class state that exists in the repressive state apparatus sheds a very revealing light on all the facts observable in the various orders of repression in whatever domain: from the massacres of June 1848 and the Paris Commune, of Bloody Sunday and May 1905 in Petrograd, of the Resistance, of Charonne,[1] and so on, through the simple (and relatively harmless) interventions of a 'censorship' that banned Gatti's play on Franco or the translation of Diderot's *La Religieuse* into the cinematographer's moving pictures,[2] to all the direct or indirect forms of the slaughter of the popular masses (imperialist wars), their exploitation, and the subtle everyday domination in which is revealed, in the forms of political democracy, for example, what Lenin called, after Marx, the dictatorship of the bourgeoisie. That is the first aspect of the definition of a 'descriptive theory'.

In its second aspect, it is, obviously, a stage in the constitution of a theory which itself demands that we 'go beyond' that stage. For it is clear that, while the definition in question really does provide us with the means of identifying and recognizing the facts of oppression by linking them to the state conceived as Repressive State Apparatus, this 'linkage' gives rise to a very special kind of obviousness, about which we shall soon have occasion to say a word: 'Yes, that's really how it is, that's really *true!*'[3] And although accumulating facts under the definition of the state multiplies examples, it fails to advance the definition of the state – the scientific theory of it – by a jot.

If this definition were to remain at the first stage, in which it functions as a 'descriptive theory', it would risk finding itself in unstable equilibrium, as if it were poised on a narrow mountain ridge, on the point, that is, of falling to one side or the other. This instability and the attendant risk of a fall have been very well analyzed in a recent book.[4] Here we shall note only the book's reminder that, precisely because of the instability of the 'descriptive theory' of the state, certain Marxists, and by no means the least of them, have 'fallen' to the wrong side of the path on the ridge by presenting the state as a *mere instrument* of domination and repression in the service of *objectives*, that is, of the dominant class's *conscious will*. This is a bourgeois, instrumentalist–idealist conception of the state reinforced by a bourgeois idealist (humanist) conception of social classes as 'subjects'. Such a conception has nothing to do with Marxism, because it perverts

---

1   [TN: A Paris underground station in which nine demonstrators against the French colonial war in Algeria were killed by the police in 1962.]

2   [TN: Armand Gatti, *La passion du général Franco*, banned from the stage by the French government in 1968; Jacques Rivette, *Suzanne Simonin – la Religieuse de Denis Diderot*, banned by the French government in 1966. The film was shown and the play was performed in France despite the bans.]

3   See below, 'On Ideology' [Chapter 12].

4   Nikos Poulantzas, *Pouvoir politique et classes sociales* [Paris, Maspero, 1968; *Political Power and Social Classes*, trans. Timothy O'Hagen, London, Verso, 1975], Chapter 11.

what is ultimately the most valuable thing the 'descriptive theory' gives us. Hence the need to 'fall to the right side' of the mountain path . . . or, to drop the metaphor, the need to develop the descriptive theory into a theory in the full sense.

Here, too, we have to be careful.

To develop this descriptive theory into a theory in the full sense, that is, in order to grasp the *mechanisms* of the state in its functioning, rather than merely identifying and ranging the facts of repression under the concept of state apparatus, we think it is imperative to add something to the classic definition of the state as state apparatus.

II THE ESSENTIALS OF THE MARXIST THEORY OF THE STATE

What must be, if not added, then at least made very precise, is, to begin with, the fact that the state (and its existence in its apparatus) is intelligible only as a function of *state power*. The whole *political* class struggle revolves around the state: around the possession, that is, the seizure or conservation of *state power* by a certain class or 'power bloc', in other words, an alliance between classes or class fractions.[5] This first stipulation accordingly requires us to distinguish between, on the one hand, *state power* (conservation of state power or seizure of state power), the objective of the political class struggle, and, on the other hand, the *state apparatus*.

We know that the state apparatus can remain in place even after political events which affect *the possession of state power* without affecting or modifying the state apparatus. This is proved by the nineteenth-century bourgeois 'revolutions' (1830, 1848) or coups d'état in France (2 December 185[1], 13 May 1958), the collapse of regimes (the fall of the Empire in 1870 or of the Third Republic in 1940), the political rise of the petty bourgeoisie (1890–5 in France), and so on. Even after a social revolution, like that of 1917, a large part of the state apparatus remained in place after an alliance of the proletariat and poor peasantry seized state power. Lenin repeated that often enough; it was an anguishing preoccupation of his to the day he died.

The book we have cited offers an illuminating, detailed discussion of this point.[6] It may be added that this distinction between state power and the state apparatus has been an explicit part of the 'Marxist theory' of the state from Marx's *Eighteenth Brumaire* on.

---

5   See Poulantzas, who provides a very good commentary on Marx and Lenin.
6   See Poulantzas, *Political Power and Social Classes*.

To summarize the 'Marxist theory of the state' on this point, let us recall that the classics of Marxism have always maintained that:

1) the state is the (repressive) state apparatus;

2) state power and state apparatus must be distinguished;

3) the objective of the class struggle has to do with the possession of state power and, consequently, the use of the state apparatus by the classes (or alliances of classes or class fractions) holding state power as a function of their class objectives; and

4) the proletariat must seize state power in order to destroy the existing bourgeois state apparatus. In a first phase, the phase of the dictatorship of the proletariat, it must replace it with an utterly different, proletarian state apparatus, before going on, in later phases, to set a radical process in motion, the destruction of the state (the end of state power and all state apparatuses).

From this standpoint, consequently, what we just proposed to add to the 'Marxist theory' of the state is already there, black on white. It seems to me, however, that this theory, even completed in this way, remains partly descriptive, although it now contains complex, differential elements whose play and functioning cannot be grasped without the help of a decisive theoretical enrichment.

III THE IDEOLOGICAL STATE APPARATUSES

What has to be added to the 'Marxist theory' of the state is therefore something else. Here we shall be advancing cautiously on a terrain on which Marx, Lenin, Stalin and Mao have long since preceded us, but without systematizing, in theoretical form, the decisive progress that their experiences[7] and procedures implied. Why? Because these experiences and procedures were restricted in the main *to the terrain of political practice*.

By that, we mean to suggest that the classics of Marxism in fact treated the state, in their political practice, as a *reality* that is *more complex* than the definition of it given in the 'Marxist theory of the state', even when that definition is completed as we have just completed it. Thus they acknowledged this complexity in their practice without expressing it in a corresponding theory.

We would like to try to sketch that corresponding theory.

We know very well the sort of objection we will be opening ourselves up to, since we cannot put forward a single proposition *that is not already*

---

7   [TN: *Expériences*, which also means 'experiments'.]

contained in the records of the political practice of the proletarian class struggle.
Thus it can be objected at every turn that we are not adding anything
new at all; and in a sense, that is perfectly true. We nevertheless believe
that we *are* adding something new – doubtless very little, since we are
merely *giving theoretical form* to something that has already been recognized in the practice of the proletarian class struggle. Yet we know, thanks
to the same Marxist classics, that this 'very little' (casting the practical
experience of the class struggle in theoretical form) is, or can be, *very
important* for the class struggle itself. Without revolutionary theory (of the
state), no revolutionary movement.

We shall lay our cards on the table. We are going to advance and
defend the following thesis.

To produce a theory of the state, it is imperative to take into account
not only the distinction between *state power* (and those who hold it) and
state apparatus, but also another 'reality' that must clearly be ranged alongside the Repressive State Apparatus, but *is not conflated with it*. We shall
take the theoretical risk of calling it the Ideological State Apparatuses.
The precise point on which our theoretical intervention bears is thus
these *Ideological State Apparatuses* in their distinction from the state apparatus in the sense of Repressive State Apparatus.

Be it recalled that the state apparatus comprises, in 'Marxist theory',
the government, administration, army, police, courts and prisons, which
together constitute what we shall henceforth call the *Repressive State
Apparatus*. 'Repressive' should be understood, at the limit (for there exist
many, very varied and even very subtly occulted forms[8] of *non-physical*
repression), in the strong, precise sense of 'using *physical violence*' (direct
or indirect, legal or 'illegal').

What, then, are the *Ideological State Apparatuses* (ISAs)? The following
provisional list will give us a rough idea of them:
  1) the Scholastic Apparatus
  2) the Familial Apparatus
  3) the Religious Apparatus
  4) the Political Apparatus
  5) the Associative Apparatus
  6) the Information and News Apparatus
  7) the Publishing and Distribution Apparatus
  8) the Cultural Apparatus
This list is provisional because, first, it is not exhaustive (see Chapter

---

8   [TN: Crossed out, 'Example: the administration'.]

12) and, second, because it may be that apparatuses 7 and 8 are just one apparatus. The reader will perhaps bear with this last hesitation, for I have not yet made up my mind on this point, which calls for further research.

This list (in which, for example, the family figures) and these terms will not fail to cause surprise. Let us be patient and proceed in orderly fashion in order to arrive at a provisional but clear definition.

First remark: one can observe, empirically, that there exist 'institutions' or 'organizations', as they are called, corresponding to each ISA. For the scholastic ISA: the various schools and their various levels, from the primary to the tertiary, the various institutes, and so on. For the religious ISA: the various churches and their specialized organizations (for example, youth organizations). For the political ISA: the parliament, the political parties, and so on. For the information and news ISA: the press (the various newspapers or newspaper groups), the RTF,[9] and a large number of publications and organizations. For the familial ISA: all the institutions that have to do with the family, including the famous associations of parents of schoolchildren, and so on. For the cultural ISA: all kinds of entertainment, sport included, as well as a series of institutions that may dovetail with what we have called the publishing ISA.

Second remark: for each ISA, the various institutions and organizations comprising it form a *system*. That, at any rate, is the thesis we are putting forward. We shall see what constitutes the unity of the system in each case. If this is right, we cannot discuss *any one component part* of an ISA without relating it to the *system* of which it is a part. For example, we cannot discuss a political party, a component part of the political ISA, without relating it to the complex system of the [political][10] ISA. The same holds for a trade union, which is a component part of the system constituted by the associative ISA, and so on.

Third remark: it can be seen that the institutions existing in each ISA, the system they form, and, consequently, each ISA, although defined as *ideological*, is [*sic*] not reducible to the existence 'of ideas' without a concrete, material *support*. I mean by this not only that the ideology of each ISA is realized in material institutions and material practices; that is clear. I mean something else: that these material practices are *'anchored'* in *non-ideological* realities. Take the family: it is an ISA, but the ideology

---

9   [TN: Radiodiffusion-Télévision française, French state television and radio.]

10   [TN: The word is missing in the manuscript.]

that it realizes is 'anchored' in a reality that is not purely ideological. For the family is the site of the biological reproduction of representatives of the 'human race', of their rearing and training, and so on (let us say that it reproduces *the existence* of labour-power). But the family is clearly also something else. Even in our capitalist societies, in which it is now 'disappearing', it preserves, at least in certain now disintegrating sectors, the role of a *production unit* (for example, in the countryside: 'family farms'). In the mode of production based on serfdom, the family was the dominant production unit. In our mode of production, this is a survival. On the other hand, the family still is a *unit of consumption* in our societies. It is not the only kind of unit of consumption there is, but, of those in existence, it is a kind that still plays an extremely important part and it is not about to disappear (it subsists in the socialist regimes with which we are familiar, albeit in transformed or waning forms). For example, the cultural ISA: the ideology that it realizes is anchored in practices either aesthetic (the theatre, film, literature) or physical (sport) that are not reducible to the ideology for which they serve as a support. The same holds for the political and associative ISAs: the ideology they realize is 'anchored' in a reality irreducible to that ideology – here, the class struggle. The same holds for the ISA we are calling the scholastic apparatus: the ideology it realizes is 'anchored' in practices that make it possible to acquire and use objective 'know-how' irreducible to that ideology. An ISA such as the religious apparatus, in contrast, does in fact seem to 'exist' up in the air, as a function of the pure and simple ideology that it realizes. But this is by no means certain. Later, we shall attempt to say why.

These three remarks will allow us to state a *provisional definition*. It foregrounds the 'reality' (namely, ideology) which unifies, in *systems*, the various institutions or organizations and the various practices present in each ISA. We shall say that:

An Ideological State Apparatus is a system of defined institutions, organizations, and the corresponding practices. Realized in the institutions, organizations, and practices of this system is all or part (generally speaking, a typical combination of certain elements) of the State Ideology. The ideology realized in an ISA ensures its systemic unity on the basis of an 'anchoring' in material functions specific to each ISA; these functions are not reducible to that ideology, but serve it as a 'support'.

When the time comes, we will explain what we mean by *the State Ideology*, the existence of which accounts for the fact that the ISAs are *ideological* apparatuses and *state* apparatuses, and also for the unity that makes each ISA a specific *system* distinct from the other ISAs.

We can now come back to the concept that we are proposing – *Ideological State Apparatus* – in order to examine each of its three terms and justify the fact that we have associated them in our concept.

Readers will doubtless be surprised at seeing these 'realities' (diverse institutions or 'activities') designated as *apparatuses*, a concept that obviously brings the expression state 'apparatus' to mind; and they will be intrigued at seeing us attach the adjective 'Ideological' to the term 'Apparatuses', only to discover, finally, at the tail end of this expression, the state itself: *Ideological State Apparatuses*. It is as if we wanted to bring out that the ideological is, as it were, 'stuck in the middle' of the expression *Appareil . . . d'Etat*,[11] with the small 'difference' that the term state apparatus tout court is *in the singular*, whereas our 'Ideological State Apparatuses' are *in the plural*. All this obviously calls for explanation.

In presenting our explanation, we shall set out from this singular situation in which *Idéologie* is 'stuck' between *Appareil . . .* and *Etat*, precipitating the passage from the singular (state apparatus) to the plural (Ideological State Apparatus*es*).

We shall go straight to essentials. In our capitalist societies, what distinguishes the Ideological State Apparatuses from the Repressive State Apparatus is the following *difference*.

Whereas the Repressive State Apparatus is by definition a repressive apparatus that makes direct or indirect use of *physical violence*, the Ideological State Apparatuses cannot be called repressive in the same sense as the 'state apparatus', because they do not, by definition, use *physical* violence. Neither the Church nor the school nor political parties nor the press nor radio and television nor publishing nor entertainment nor sport *have recourse* to *physical violence* in order to function with their 'clientèle'. At any rate, the use of physical violence is not *manifest* or *dominant* in them.

It is 'of our own free will' that we go to church or school (although school is 'mandatory'),[12] join a political party and obey it, buy a newspaper, switch on the TV, go to a cinema or a stadium, buy and 'consume' records, paintings or 'posters', and literary, historical, political, religious, or scientific works. This is to say that Ideological State Apparatuses are distinguished from the state apparatus in that they function, not 'on violence', but 'on ideology'.

---

11   [TN: In the French term corresponding to 'Ideological State Apparatus', *Appareil Idéologique d'Etat*, 'apparatus' comes first and 'state' comes last, the object of a prepositional phrase which literally means 'of the state'.]

12   Let us therefore say that we (apparently) 'pursue our educations' beyond the 'mandatory' period 'of our own free will'.

We have already uttered this sentence in discussing the way law 'functions' on 'legal-moral ideology'. We know what that means: these apparatuses apparently function '*all by themselves*', without recourse to violence. In fact, they function thanks to means other than violence, namely, on *ideology* or, rather, *ideologization*. With that, we have very clearly marked the distinction that sets the state apparatus apart from the Ideological State Apparatuses.

It remains to explain why we consider it imperative to use the apparently enigmatic term 'state apparatuses' to designate these 'institutions' and 'activities' (churches, schools, the political system, radio and TV, the theatre, the press, publications, and so on). Why State . . . Apparatus? And why this plural (State Apparatus*es*)?

Our affirmation becomes still more enigmatic when we take the trouble to note (and it is in our 'interest' to note this ourselves, for, if we do not, others will not fail to take issue with us) that if some of these 'institutions' are now state institutions (in our country, the school, certain theatres, radio and television), *not all of them are*. The Church, in our country, is officially separate from the state, as are some schools, and so on.

The press, political parties, trade unions and other associations, the vast majority of cultural institutions and activities (entertainment, sport, publications, the arts) are 'free', that is, part of the private 'sector', not the state sector. Better, in certain capitalist countries, a large proportion of the schools (for example, two-thirds of higher education in the USA), and even radio and television (in the USA and Great Britain), belong, or can belong, to the private sector. By what right, then, do we say that these 'institutions' or 'activities' fall into the category of Ideological *State* Apparatuses?

IV PUBLIC AND PRIVATE 'INSTITUTIONS'

We have to clear away the following objection: By what right do we list *private* institutions such as those that belong to the religious apparatus, political apparatus, cultural apparatus, and so on, among Ideological *State* Apparatuses?

This objection is in fact based on a distinction drawn in bourgeois law, the distinction between public and private. This distinction concerns only the status, that is, the definition, of the legal *persons* who hold formal title to this or that institution. Such persons can be *individual* private legal persons (Mr Gallimard)[13] or *collective* private legal

---

13 [TN: Gaston Gallimard (1881–1975), owner of a major French publishing firm.]

persons (the Dominican Order); *collective state* legal persons (our state educational system), and so on.

The legal grounds for personhood are legal grounds: since law is universal and formal, we already know that it abstracts, by its nature, *from the content* of which it is the 'form'. But since it is precisely that content that matters to us here, the objection based on the private / public distinction is trivial.

Our point is that the 'legal' objection that might be raised against us is not germane. Our subject is not 'law', but something quite different – at the limit of the class struggle and class relations – which the law is perfectly incapable of encompassing, even if it sanctions certain of its *formal* aspects, since that is its function.

To put this in a way Marxists will understand (even certain non-Marxists know this, since they sometimes find themselves saying it): Marxists are well aware that the state itself, despite all the articles of constitutional law defining it (it is exempt from the Civil Code and that is no accident!), is always the state *of* the dominant class. It is not that the state is the dominant class's '*property*' in the legal sense, inasmuch as class does not yet figure, as far as I know, among the legal personalities recognized by law, although they are numerous: it is quite simply because the state is *its* state, the bourgeoisie's state, in the sense that the bourgeoisie *holds* state power and exercises it by way of the Repressive State Apparatus and Ideological State Apparatuses.

Let us take another example which, this time, will not admit the least objection. The papers that are legally owned by Mr Prouvost,[14] like the peripheral radio and television channels that are owned by Mr Sylvain Floirat and others and are therefore in the private sector (and come under the Civil Code),[15] have a 'right' to exercise their imaginations a bit; this credits the notion that they are 'free' and independent. But everyone is aware that they *know* perfectly well how to toe the bourgeois state's political line when they have to – that is to say, day in, day out, and with great fanfare on the 'big days' – and to

---

14　[TN: Jean Prouvost (1885–1978), a media magnate who at one point or another owned most or all of the right-wing newspapers *Paris-Soir*, *Paris-Match*, and *Figaro*, the TV guide *Télé 7 Jours*, and Radio-Télé Luxembourg.]

15　[TN: In the mid-1950s, Sylvain Floirat (1899–1993) bought the radio station Europe 1, which had acquired a mass audience by the early 1960s, when the French state became the indirect owner of about a third of it. In 1969, some of its reporters were fired for excessively sympathetic coverage of the May events. Privately owned 'peripheral television' broadcast to France from countries nearby, such as Monaco and Luxemburg.]

disseminate, in variants suited to their respective audiences, the grand themes of the bourgeois state's never-ending ideological litany: the grand themes of *the State Ideology*.

Thus the private / public distinction cannot call our thesis about the Ideological State Apparatuses into question. All the private institutions we have mentioned, whether owned by this or that individual or the state, *function* willy-nilly as component parts of determinate Ideological State Apparatuses, under the State Ideology, in the service of the state's politics, the politics of the dominant class. They do so in the form specific to them: that of apparatuses that function primarily on ideology – not on repression, like the Repressive State Apparatus. That ideology is, as I have said, the State Ideology itself.

I mention, for good measure, one last argument, which completely invalidates the 'legalistic' objection that might be raised against our concept of Ideological State Apparatuses. The 'legalistic' argument applies, at best, to 'institutions'. But as we have said, and repeat here, an institution is not an Ideological State Apparatus. What constitutes an Ideological State Apparatus is a complex system that encompasses and combines *several* institutions and organizations, as well as their practices. Whether they are all public or all private, or whether some are public and others private, is a secondary detail, because what interests us here is the *system* they form. This system, its existence, and its nature owe nothing to law; they are indebted to the altogether different reality that we have called the State Ideology.

V IDEOLOGICAL STATE APPARATUSES AND THE IDEOLOGICAL BY-PRODUCTS OF THEIR PRACTICES

Precisely because we are foregrounding ideology, we have to draw a distinction of great importance.

May we make a personal confession here? For years, we were baffled by a very brief hint of Stalin's that practically came down to saying, 'ideology and the institutions *corresponding to it*'. What in the world did that mean? Was it not an astonishing slip and, what is more, an *idealist* slip, to grant that institutions could, in a list, *follow* their ideology,[16] that ideology could, in some sense, 'produce' institutions, when a right-thinking materialist should, putting the horse before the cart, have talked *first* about the institutions, and *then* (only afterwards: because determined

---

16   One may find this list, in which we found our 'hint', in Joseph Stalin, *Dialectical and Historical Materialism* (1938) [New York, International Publishers, 1970].

in the sense of derived) about the ideology *corresponding to them*? For do we not in fact daily see the institutions we know (the Church, the schools, the political parties, and so on) 'producing', precisely, the ideology that 'corresponds to them' because they need it? Does a Sunday gardener not 'produce' on his little fenced-off plot of land the vegetables and flowers that his wife 'needs'?

I am afraid that, on this point at least, I will have to show a little personal gratitude to Stalin for his hint, which I cite from memory.[17] For, in order to grasp the new concept that we are proposing (Ideological State Apparatuses), it is necessary to grant the paradoxical fact that institutions do not 'produce' the ideologies corresponding to them. Rather, *certain elements of an ideology (the State Ideology) 'are realized in' or 'exist in' the corresponding institutions and their practices.*

Let there be no mistake. We do not deny that the institutions in question 'produce', internally and in their practices, certain forms of ideology that would be inexplicable without references to those practices. Thus we shall say that religious practice 'produces', inside the Church, certain forms of ideology: ecclesiastical ideology, for example. But there are other ideologies in the Church, to stick with that example: these days, it is teeming with them. Consider Isolotto,[18] the 'letter' by the 360 French priests,[19] Father Cardonnel's Lenten sermon,[20] *Frères du Monde*[21] – and, lest we forget, *Esprit*,[22] which long ago had its 'avant-garde' moment. Consider all the extraordinary developments in the religious ideology of certain groups among the *lower* clergy and even a few members of the *high* clergy in some Latin American countries, to say nothing of Father Torres,[23] who died fighting with the guerrillas.

---

17   [EN: Crossed out: 'Because, without it, the author of these lines might never have arrived at the theses he is here expounding.']

18   [TN: A Christian community established in the mid-1950s by worker-priests in the proletarian Florence suburb of Isolotto and maintained in the 1960s over the politically motivated protests of the Church hierarchy.]

19   [TN: A 1967 open letter urging clergymen in the United States to pressure their government into negotiating an end to the Vietnam War.]

20   [TN: Jean Cardonnel (1921–2009), a Dominican who in 1968 delivered a sermon titled 'The New Testament and Revolution' in the Mutualité, a big Paris conference centre, prompting the Church hierarchy to try to prevent him from speaking in public.]

21   [TN: A radical journal published by Franciscans in Lyon from 1959 to 1974.]

22   [TN: On 5 May 1967, Althusser gave a talk on Marxism and the workers' movement to a group associated with this left-leaning Catholic journal in which he had published extracts from his first book in 1959 and, in 1962, the essay on Bertolazzi and Brecht later collected in *For Marx*.]

23   [TN: Camilo Torres Restrepo (1929–1966), a priest and Marxist sociologist who joined the Colombian National Liberation Army (ELN) in 1966.]

Thus we shall say that scholastic practice produces particular forms that may be termed *scholastic ideology* (the ideology of elementary school teachers, realized in the publications and initiatives of the SNI,[24] or of teachers in secondary schools and higher education, and so on), and many other forms that we cannot, for material reasons, discuss here. We shall do so elsewhere.[25]

For example, political parties, too, produce forms of internal ideology. There is no need to draw the reader a picture: since we have already mentioned Stalin, let us simply note that *the ideology* of a certain practice of the USSR's political leadership became *manifest*, at a certain point in the country's history, in what is called the 'personality cult', a purely, 'discreetly', descriptive term (as if a 'personality' could by itself 'produce' the ideology of its 'cult', and so on). We could go on indefinitely, discussing entertainment, sport, news, publishing, and so on; that would be fascinating. The examples already adduced, however, are enough to make our thesis clear. We must now state it, not negatively, but positively.

We shall therefore say that a distinction must be made here. We must distinguish between, on the one hand, the determinate elements of the State Ideology that are realized in, and exist in, a determinate apparatus and its practices, and, on the other, the ideology that is 'produced' in this apparatus by its practices. To mark this distinction terminologically, we shall call the former ideology the 'Primary Ideology', and the latter – a by-product of the practice in which the Primary Ideology is realized – the 'secondary, subordinate ideology'.

Let us note another important point. We shall say that this secondary ideology is 'produced' by the practice of the apparatus that realizes the Primary Ideology. But that is just a convenient way of putting it: for *no practice in the world produces 'its' ideology all by itself*. There is no 'spontaneous' ideology, although it can be useful, in other words, terminologically convenient when making a specific point, to use the expression 'spontaneous' ideology. In the case to hand, these secondary ideologies are produced by a conjunction of complex causes. Among them are, alongside the practice in question, the effect of other, external ideologies, other external practices and, in the final instance, the effects – however veiled – of the *class struggle*, even its remote effects, which are in fact very close. No one will presume to deny it if he pays a little attention to what has been going on for a while now in the ideology of

---

24 [TN: The Syndicat National des Instituteurs, then the main schoolteachers' union.]
25 See *Schools*, Maspero, forthcoming in autumn 1969. [EN: See Chapter 2, n. 26.]

certain religious circles, in and around 'schools' (from May on), and in families (since May).

Thus, if we want to understand what 'institutions' (the Church, the schools, and so on) are, and, on top of that, what the secondary ideological sub-formations 'secreted' by the practices of these institutions are, we have to set out from the ideological formations deriving from the State Ideology and realized in those institutions and their practices. For it is these ideological formations which provide us with the key to both the institutions in question and their practices, and also some of the causes that produce the ideological sub-formations that we see emerging in those practices.

Doubtless none of this is very easy to envisage in the immediate notions offered us by the 'self-evident truths' in which we live, since we live in ideology,[26] even if we also have a few scientific concepts in our heads. But we have to think it.

The initial form of the 'thought' that occurs to us will of course be couched in terms of the famous common-sense schemes that Hegel already dismissed as drivel: the *interaction* schemes. Someone will say, straining to make a big 'concession' in the first part of his statement: True, the primary ideological formations (religious ideological formations, and so on) are realized in institutions. But he will add: 'since there is action and reaction everywhere in the world', institutions produce the secondary ideology that we observe in them by *reacting back on* the primary formations. It is with fustian of this sort that we make our peace with the 'dialectic'! The reader will not be surprised to learn that, inasmuch as action and reaction are 'the night in which all cows are grey', because they effectively mean that 'everything is in everything and the other way around', we shall be sending our grey cows back into their night.

We think, on the contrary, that it is necessary to keep a firm grip on the first part of the statement, 'primary *ideological formations* are realized in institutions', while temporarily leaving aside an element (that is, while abstracting from an element, as Marx does in order to carry out his scientific analyses in *Capital*) that can only confuse everything, since it is secondary, subordinate, and derivative – namely, the *internal* ideological formations that we have identified as *by-products*.

We shall say that a church is, *qua* 'institution', a realization of religious ideology. We shall say that a school (or educational system) is a realization

---

26 If I may be allowed to add a supplementary 'definition' of ideology to the list of famous definitions, I would say, by paraphrase: 'Man is by nature an ideological animal.'

of ideology. (What kind of ideology? Let us leave the question in abeyance.) We shall say that a political party is a realization of a political ideology, and so on. The same goes for all the institutions we have listed. But beware: a church, a school, a party do not *each* constitute *one* Ideological State Apparatus; rather, each forms a component part of different *systems*, which we term Ideological State Apparatuses: the religious system, scholastic system, political system, and so on.

We shall add, at the risk of *repeating* ourselves: the ideological formations that we can correlate with the practices at work in these institutions are not the product of the primary ideologies realized in these institutions, but by-products of that ideology [*sic*], insofar as they are the 'products' of practices at work in those institutions. It is perfectly plain that there also exist direct relations between the primary ideological formations, which are external to the institutions, and the secondary ideological sub-formations internal to them. However, these relations cannot be conceived in terms of action and reaction – for the good reason that these relations *do not always exist*, and, when they do, are realized in accordance with *laws altogether different* from the so-called dialectical laws of interaction. To put it very precisely, they are realized as a result of the intervention of another reality that we have not yet been able to discuss (because it is unfortunately impossible to say everything at once). We can, anticipating, call this reality by its name: *the class struggle and its ideological effects*.

Provisionally, then, we shall content ourselves with our thesis, because we want to proceed in proper order: the Ideological State Apparatuses are the realization, the existence, of the ideological formations dominating them.

VI   THE DOUBLE FUNCTIONING OF THE STATE APPARATUSES AND THEIR 'CONCERTED ACTION'

Since I just introduced the clarification 'functioning *primarily on*', a word of explanation is in order. It will account for the use of the common term 'apparatus' in two different expressions: Repressive State Apparatus, Ideological State Apparatus.

I think I can claim that *all* state apparatuses, repressive and ideological alike, function *simultaneously* on repression and on ideology, but with one very important distinction that precludes *confusing* the repressive apparatus with the Ideological State Apparatuses. The Repressive State Apparatus, for its part, functions *in overwhelmingly preponderant fashion* on repression (at the limit, direct physical repression), while functioning secondarily on ideology.

The army and police, for instance: internally, they train their own recruits both by repression and ideological inculcation; externally, they act by violent repression, but also by 'discussion' and 'persuasion'. The latter *watchwords* appear black on white in the circulars issued by police chiefs and army generals possessed of a modicum of good sense. In May 1968, Mr Grimaud, the Paris police chief, 'conducted discussions' in person with the 'wild ones' during the battles in the Place Maubert. The army and police also operate with the help of their own 'ideological aura' ('Join the Army and learn a trade!') and the prestige of their uniforms ('Join the riot police and you'll stand guard over the beaches!'), and so on.

Similarly, we may say, but the other way around, that the Ideological State Apparatuses, for their part, function *in overwhelmingly preponderant fashion on ideology*, while functioning secondarily on repression, even if it is, at the limit – but only at the limit – quite attenuated and more or less symbolic.

Let us give a few examples of this secondary repressive functioning of apparatuses that function in overwhelmingly preponderant fashion on ideology. The school and the Church, to take only those two examples, 'train' not just their officiants (teachers and priests), but also their wards (schoolchildren, the faithful, and so on) with the appropriate methods of punishment (once exclusively and often still physical, and also, of course, 'moral'): expulsion, selection, and so on. News and information, publishing, and entertainment carry out, with or (much more subtly) without the backing of the law, daily *censorship*, which is unremitting and extremely vigilant, since this censorship lodges itself *in advance* in the heads of authors who take the precaution of censoring themselves, in the name, of course, of their 'professional conscience' and 'decency', or 'the proper behaviour' that one owes the fatherland, the dead, and families – leaving aside Virtue, which has lost a bit of its lustre these days, since 'intellectual freedom' has to be lodged somewhere – for instance, in (two-bit) eroticism.

I do not think I need to multiply illustrations for the reader to understand, from the ones just adduced, that very subtle combinations of repression and ideologization, explicit or tacit, are forged *in and among all the state apparatuses*, whether they are primarily repressive or primarily ideological, and that these very subtle combinations would allow us, if we succeeded in analyzing their mechanisms, to account for the manifest pacts and unambiguous (or even ambiguous) objective forms of complicity that are *forged* among the various state apparatuses, not only on Major Occasions, when the bourgeois state is threatened by open working-class struggle, but every single day of our humdrum lives.

A little police or a lot; a little army on the move here; a little UNR or CDR[27] there; a little Paul VI or Archbishop Marty in their sector: a little *France-Soir* in its; a little or a lot of De Gaulle, Couve, Faure, 'Cardinal' Daniélou on the radio;[28] a little Grand Rabbi on Israel; a little Jean-Jacques Servan-Schreiber on the American challenge; a little Louis Armand on Teilhard de Chardin;[29] a little Siné for the Club Med on the back of the bus; Publicis posters of naked young mothers or tomato juice on all the walls; inspired articles or works by our great ideologues, living or dead, in *Le Figaro* and the bookshops;[30] the obligatory Sermons on Literature, Humanism, and Our Lord in the universities and the churches alike . . . In the domain of ideologization, all this constitutes the multiform arsenal of a power whose centre is and remains the state, that is to say, the (bourgeois) holders of state power, who exercise their class power through the various specialized apparatuses with which the state is endowed.

---

27 [TN: Union pour la Nouvelle République, the Gaullist ruling party, in existence from 1958 to 1976; Comités de Défense de la République, created by an alliance of Gaullists and the far right in May 1968 to show support for De Gaulle, notably in a big demonstration staged in Paris on 30 May.]

28 [TN: *France-Soir* was a conservative, middle-brow daily. Maurice Couve de Murville became Prime Minister after the June 1968 elections; Edgar Faure was his Minister of Education. The French Jesuit Jean Daniélou, a moving spirit behind Vatican II, became a Cardinal on 28 April 1969, as did the Archbishop of Paris since March 1968, François Marty.]

29 [TN: Jean-Jacques Servan-Schreiber, a journalist and politician, published *The American Challenge* in 1968 and, in October 1969, became General Secretary of the left-liberal Radical Party. The Jesuit Teilhard de Chardin (1881–1955) was a palaeontologist whose spiritual philosophy found favour with certain Marxist humanists in the PCF. Louis Armand wrote a Preface for André Monestier's *Teilhard ou Marx?* (Paris, Lettres Modernes, 1965).]

30 [TN: Siné (Maurice Sinet), a French political cartoonist who also designed advertisements for the Club Med, co-founded the satirical review *L'Enragé* in May 1968 and published work in *Action* (see Chapter 12, p. 178) in the same period. Publicis is a big advertising agency. *Le Figaro*, founded in 1826, is France's main highbrow conservative daily.]

VII FRAGILITY AND SOLIDITY OF THE
IDEOLOGICAL STATE APPARATUSES

Let us take the example of contemporary France.

The state, under the class leadership of the representatives of French imperialism ('France is great, France is beautiful, France is generous!'[31]), who hold state power in France and are in command of its apparatuses, executes their class politics by means of those apparatuses, repressive and ideological. The apparatuses 'conscientiously' do their daily duty. They constantly lend one another a hand, in an overtly and tacitly 'concerted' operation, and in the forms required by the ticklishness or brutality of the situation.

That this does not take place without 'contradictions', and that, in particular, the *ideological sub-formations* 'produced' in the apparatuses by their own practice should sometimes 'make the gears grate and grind' is inevitable.[32] It would even appear that the police 'hesitated' at a certain point in May and that people in high places did not have much confidence in how the troops would have acted had it become necessary to call on their services. Everyone knows that, because 'protest' is infectious, some priests and even some teachers are balking, now that their pupils, those little devils, who (my God, but why?) no longer have any respect for 'authority' and are no longer inclined to take the moon for green cheese – to the utter dismay of the Most Respectable Associations of Parents of Schoolchildren,[33] a

---

31   [TN: The phrase is De Gaulle's.]

32   And for good reason, if we recall the *effects of the class struggle* that operate in them to 'produce' these ideological sub-formations.

33   For a laugh, although it is in fact no laughing matter, let us note that while every schoolchild (orphans excepted) has a father and mother, not every father and mother considers themselves (thank God!) the parent of a schoolchild. To come forward as the parent of a schoolchild is a political act, by virtue of which one joins this or that association, with a certain political tendency, obviously. It is doubtless no coincidence that the aforementioned Associations of Parents of Schoolchildren – which are of different shades (for one association can, under cover of 'secularism', be more 'open' [TN: Crossed out, 'less reactionary'] than another) – are, as one says, 'very concerned' about the 'disorder' reigning in the schools. Other associations (the CDR and the Gaullist organization of the modern university) cultivate a still saltier discourse: their word is 'gangrene'. High school and college students will not fail to note the delicacy of the language some of their parents (parents of schoolchildren, precisely) use in talking about their own progeny. Things have come to such a pass that one wonders what has become of the family virtues: I mean, of course, the virtues of the aforementioned parents of schoolchildren. When will an *Association of Children of*

component part of a redoubtable Ideological State Apparatus.

But, somehow or other, when an Ideological State Apparatus such as the school or family is ailing, the others, thank the Lord, manage to hold out for a while, and, with De Gaulle's help, and if the dominant ideology is still functioning properly among broad sectors of the 'population', the bourgeois state manages to hold up, and its various apparatuses do, too. For how long? That is another story: until state power and the state apparatus themselves are taken by storm in what is known as a revolution.

But, precisely, since we have just invoked revolution, we can spell out what we meant by 'grating' in the ISAs. We may say that the 'stuff' of which the ISAs are made is such, and that they 'function' in such a way, that we must consider them to be *relatively fragile* apparatuses, given the shocks of the class struggle which affect them through the ideological sub-formations anchored in certain aspects of their practices. In this they differ from the repressive apparatus, made of completely different 'stuff' that is much harder to put a dent in.

Rather, we should say that the ISAs are *apparently* fragile apparatuses. For we have to say, at the same time, that they *are extraordinarily strong and tough*.

It is enough to read the texts that Lenin wrote in the last years of his life in order to see how profoundly he was haunted by this problem after the victory of the revolution. The repressive apparatus of the feudal-capitalist state (army, police) had basically been destroyed. This did not hold for the administration. Yet that was not Lenin's essential concern. His essential, anguished concern was, above all, with the

---

Parents of Schoolchildren be founded to denounce the 'gangrene' that threatens, on the parents' side of the line, the traditional paternalistic virtues of (among others) familial understanding, generosity and tolerance? I am not joking; what is going on in families these days should be far greater cause for 'concern' for our worthy vice-principals [TN: responsible for school discipline] than what is going on in the schools. The reader would do well to recall this when we speak, as we shall in a moment, of a certain school-family dyad. It is also no wonder that, in comparison with the big brouhaha about 'disorder' in the schools, the discussion of what is going on in families is much more discreet, '*Honneur*' oblige. Family business is settled *in the privacy of the family*. It is, in fact, as if some parents of schoolchildren *were demanding that the state settle the problems that they are having in their own families with their own children by . . . restoring 'order' in the schools!* These are things that really should be kept hush-hush; for, if they were not, would we not have to admit that, in a certain regard, the family does indeed have something to do with an Ideological State Apparatus and that the class struggle even produces some of its effects in families? We think so. Interestingly, the 'facts' themselves are coming forward to lend support to our thesis.

proletarian state's Ideological State Apparatuses: its *political* apparatus (the party, the Soviets: the number one problem being their connections to the masses, their capacity to control the state administrative apparatus and root out its 'bureaucratic' tendency); its trade union apparatus (here, too, the number-one problem was, what should a trade union be? A *non-coercive* apparatus, a *'school of communism'* that could reliably ensure, via a series of 'transmission belts', the right connection to the masses); finally, its *scholastic* apparatus, which was, for Lenin, the problem of problems, for he knew that the scholastic ISA is determinant, since it has the future in its power: the younger generations.

What conclusion should we draw from this tragic concern of Lenin's after the seizure of state power and the destruction of the better part of the bourgeois Repressive State Apparatus? The conclusion that follows.

It is not enough to destroy the repressive apparatus; it is also necessary to destroy and replace the Ideological State Apparatuses. New ones have to be put in place, urgently; otherwise – Lenin was right – the very future of the revolution will be jeopardized. For it is extremely hard to replace the old ISAs (in this case, the Russian bourgeois ISAs), and it takes a long time. A long time is needed, for example, truly to establish a whole new proletarian political, trade union, and school system. One must first know exactly *what* to put in place, what new systems to *invent*,[34] and *how* to put them in place. The right *line* must be found for each of these systems, *down to the details*. Finally, competent personnel loyal to the revolution have to be trained to apply the new, revolutionary politics in each new ISA: in short, to imbue the practice and consciousness of all Soviet citizens with the new State Ideology, proletarian ideology.

If one does not succeed in this and, *a fortiori*, if one does not make a serious, thoroughgoing attempt, with no concessions, to come to grips with this crucial problem, what happens?

The old (bourgeois) ISAs remain in place, wholly or partially, or they are hardly undermined. If the old personnel remains in place, whatever one does and whatever one claims, the old-model ISAs, either intact or half reformed, pursue their old 'work' in new institutional forms. The proletarian ideology of the proletarian state is not realized; that is, the masses are not imbued with proletarian ideology and the gigantic 'school of communism' that the new ISAs should represent does not go into operation. Instead, what remains of the old ISAs in fact continues to

---

34   For, with the exception of the Paris Commune, there were *no precedents* and there was no theory.

imbue the masses with *the old bourgeois or petty-bourgeois ideology*, even *alongside* new elements that clash with that ideology, elements that it is their mission to inculcate.

In this matter, Lenin, who abhorred 'decrees', was perfectly well aware that things could not be settled by 'decree' or from on high. He also knew that there existed no prefabricated, ready-made, a priori plan or line for establishing these new ISAs. He knew that it was a task that had to be worked on every minute; better, that it was a long *experimentation* involving huge risks, to which all available resources of intelligence, imagination and political dedication had to be committed, a long struggle that would brook no weakness or failure, a struggle that could not be waged simply by dint of coercive administrative measures, but that called for detailed knowledge, for education and persuasion, as well as explanation, constant explanation: a struggle that could not be carried out by a handful of militants, however lucid and courageous, but that depended on appeals to *the masses*, to their judgement and their reactions, their initiatives and inventions.

If this struggle is not won (it can certainly not be won in the space of a few months or even a few years), and, *a fortiori*, if it is not truly, seriously *begun*, on the right political mass basis, the future of the 'construction of socialism' may encounter forbidding obstacles and may even be compromised.

If, instead of functioning ever more clearly on proletarian State Ideology, the new proletarian Ideological State Apparatuses continue to function, by some mischance, on the old bourgeois and petty-bourgeois ideology or a questionable 'mix' of the old and new ideologies – if the old ideology is not rooted out – who can prove to us that *the old ideology* will not, even under the official facade of socialist state institutions (*formally and officially socialist*), survive, reproduce itself, and spawn a terribly dangerous effect – insinuating itself for good and all into one or another weak spot in the relations of production or the political relations of the socialist state?

What becomes of the Soviets in that event? What becomes of the trade unions? What becomes of the proletarian school system?

When Lenin made such frequent reference, couched in the terms of a dramatic, solemn warning, to the danger of capitalist 'survivals' in a socialist regime, to the terrible onus of 'tradition' and, in particular, of petty-bourgeois ideology, he plainly had in mind the reproduction of capitalist relations of production *owing to the survival and re-emergence of 'petty production'*.

But he was surely also thinking of these questions, which haunted him, and which he hoped would find a temporary solution in the proper 'functioning' of the Workers' and Peasants' Inspectorate: the questions of *ideology*, whose fate in the new proletarian state's new Ideological State Apparatuses was still far from settled.

Lenin died before he could see to settling these decisive questions. He handed them down to his successor, Stalin. Did Stalin settle them? Where are the Soviets, the trade unions, and the proletarian school system today, after Stalin, in the USSR?

If Stalin neglected these questions, as a number of effects give us reason to believe he did (precisely the effects of the 'personality cult'), have they been seriously and thoroughly re-examined since? To spell out our preoccupation: is it not, to a great extent, the fact that these questions were not settled or were only 'half-settled' which explains the 'principles' now commanding Soviet politics, its difficulties, the problems it is having with the 'reform of planning', and even some of its otherwise incomprehensible impasses and 'initiatives', such as the military intervention in Czechoslovakia?

VIII SUMMARY

To close this long analysis, let us try to summarize our results.

We can now put the essential elements of the state in place.

The number-one question when it comes to the state is the question of the possession of state power. The whole *political* class struggle revolves around this question.

In a class social formation, possession of state power is always possession of state power by a social class or an alliance of social classes, the exploiting class or classes – the proletarian class in the transitional phase of the dictatorship of the proletariat that should lead to socialism, a social formation dominated by a mode of production without classes.

With possession of state power comes power over the state apparatuses, which constitute the very 'nature' of the state.

The state apparatus comprises two types of apparatuses:

1) The Repressive State Apparatus (the government, administration, army, police, and specialized repressive corps: gendarmerie, courts, judiciary, prisons, and so on). This apparatus is a single, centralized corps.

2) The Ideological State Apparatuses (in our social formations, scholastic, religious, familial, political, associative, cultural, the news and information apparatus, and so on). These apparatuses are multiple, relatively independent, and unified as a distinct system by all or part of the State Ideology.

The Repressive State Apparatus 'functions' primarily on repression (physical or not). The Ideological State Apparatuses function primarily on ideology. The overall unity of the system formed by all the state apparatuses is ensured by the unity of the class politics of the class holding state power and by the State Ideology corresponding to the fundamental interests of the class (or classes) in power. The object of the politics of the class in power and of the State Ideology (dominant ideology = ideology of the dominant class) is to guarantee the conditions for the exploitation of the exploited classes by the dominant classes, above all the reproduction of the relations of production in which this exploitation takes place, since these relations of production are the relations of exploitation of the class social formation under consideration.

Thus everything is clearly based on the infrastructure of the relations of production, that is, the relations of class exploitation. The base or infrastructure of the class state is thus well and truly, as Lenin said, *exploitation*. The effect produced by the superstructure is simultaneously to ensure the conditions under which this exploitation is carried out (Repressive State Apparatus) and the reproduction of the relations of production, that is, of exploitation (Ideological State Apparatuses).

There can be no question of examining the functioning of the individual Ideological State Apparatuses in an essay whose sole aim is to establish that they exist and to indicate their function. Indeed, each Ideological State Apparatus, if its mechanisms are to be fully clarified, merits detailed, thoroughgoing analysis. We shall soon provide a first example with an analysis of the capitalist scholastic apparatus.

What matters to us here is, first of all, to understand how ideology brings off the feat of making things and people 'go all by themselves'. However, before we can get to that point, that is, before we can sketch a theory of the functioning of Ideology in general, it is imperative, to avoid all misunderstanding, that we make a few remarks about what we call, using a term that may surprise readers, especially Marxist readers, the political and associative Ideological State Apparatuses.

7

Brief Remarks on the Political and Associative Ideological State Apparatuses of the French Capitalist Social Formation[1]

I

It is indeed imperative that we insert a few remarks here to enable readers to understand our concepts and perceive their theoretical and political utility, which is possible only if all misunderstanding is avoided.

Two misunderstandings complicate, from the outset, the extension of the concept ISA to the 'world' of politics and the 'world of the unions'. Indeed, as the present remarks will show us, they complicate any utilization of the concept of the ISA. Our aim here is to eliminate these two misunderstandings from the very beginning of our discussion.

I shall go straight to the heart of what will inevitably pose an apparent 'problem' for all readers: classifying organizations of the *proletarian* political class struggle (the party) or economic class struggle (the trade union) under the rubric of ISAs of the *bourgeois* state.[2] To make this only apparent 'problem' disappear, we have to spell out two points.

---

1 [TN: The French noun *syndicat* and the corresponding adjective *syndical* are used of both trade unions and a wide variety of organized interest groups, including professional and employers' associations, a key point in the argument of the present and the following chapter. However, as Althusser points out in Chapter 8, the word *syndicat* 'makes everyone think first of trade unions'. Accordingly, *syndical* is here translated as 'associative' or trade union, depending on the context.]

2 [TN: The specific referents of 'the party' and 'the trade union' are the French Communist Party (PCF, created in 1920) and the trade union confederation that explicitly allied itself with the PCF in 1947, the Confédération générale du travail (CGT), founded in 1895.]

1) A proletarian political party and a proletarian trade union have indeed figured among the ISAs of the French social formation since the 1920s, although they were outlawed for a certain period (under Pétain) and have managed to survive only at the price of constant repressive measures (the condemnation and imprisonment of communist leaders at various times between 1921 and 1939; the Rif War; and again in 1929, for example). They are officially registered as organizations, have been recognized, and enjoy the corresponding legal 'rights'. They are 'component parts' of the corresponding French ISAs.

Their ideology, however, insofar as it is the proletarian ideology of class struggle, cannot be considered to be a 'realization' of the bourgeois State Ideology that is realized in the ISAs of which the party and trade union are 'component parts'. It is, in its very principle, radically opposed to the bourgeois State Ideology.

Hence the paradox: How can a 'component part' of the system of an ISA figure in the system of a bourgeois ISA, while being the realization of an ideology of proletarian class struggle?

The answer is simple. It has to do, not with the 'logic' of the system of the corresponding ISAs, but, rather, with the logic of a long *class struggle* that *imposed* legal recognition of the party and the proletarian class-struggle trade union as well as their inscription in the ISAs in question.

It was as organizations of proletarian class struggle that these organizations, by dint of their struggle in the history of the French social formation, imposed this recognition and this inscription: *hence by force*. It is by dint of class struggle that they are able to preserve their proletarian class ideology in the ISAs in question.

Thus the proletarian party and trade union have a place in these ISAs. Legally, they are part of them, and legally, they should enjoy all the rights that accrue to them as a result of their recognition and inscription in them. In actual fact, they are constantly treated as the object of special measures in them. In the parliament, 'Communist votes are not taken into account'; the Communist Party is declared to be the party of a foreign country or a 'separatist' party and is walled off in a political 'class ghetto' in the apparatus itself. The same tactic is applied to the proletarian trade union: except when there is no other choice, it is refused advantages granted to the others, and 'negotiations are conducted' with the others.

There is an antagonistic contradiction here that the bourgeoisie is in principle incapable of assimilating. If it has consented to the compromise, it is because it could not do otherwise. There we have an effect of the development of the class struggle.

Formally speaking, there is no contradiction in saying that one of the 'component parts' of a system, while figuring in the system, does not radically compromise the nature of the system. Proletarian ideology has not 'conquered' the system of the political or the associative ISA. On the contrary, bourgeois State Ideology continues to dominate them. It is clear that this creates, under certain circumstances, 'problems' for the 'functioning' of the bourgeois political and associative ISAs. The bourgeoisie disposes, however, of a whole series of tried and tested techniques for meeting this danger. We shall see which ones.

2) The products of a class struggle external to the ISAs under consideration, the proletarian party and trade union wage their class struggle within the limits of the ISAs and, obviously, their legal forms. Great dangers obviously threaten this delicate practice of the class struggle by proletarian organizations in bourgeois ISAs. They can be collectively summed up as the danger of lapsing into class collaboration: 'parliamentary cretinism' for the party and 'economism' for the trade union, both of which are forms of reformism. We shall come back to this.

However that may be, the class struggle that has imposed the presence of the proletarian party and trade union in the corresponding ISAs infinitely exceeds the very limited struggle that they can conduct in these ISAs. Created by a class struggle external to the ISAs, sustained by it, charged with furthering and sustaining it by all available legal means, the proletarian organizations that figure in the ISAs concerned would betray their mission if they reduced the external class struggle, which merely finds a reflection in very limited forms in the class struggle carried out in the ISAs, *to* this class struggle internal to the ISAs.

The social-democratic workers' parties are perfect examples of 'component parts' of the bourgeois ISAs which allow themselves to be assimilated by both bourgeois State Ideology and the 'rules' of the 'political and associative game' of these ISAs. These parties' ideology is merely a sub-product, for workers' consumption, of bourgeois ideology: petty-bourgeois reformist ideology. Their politics is, at the price of the right to get worked up now and again or work their jaws, a politics of class collaboration.

We can, then, understand Lenin's categorical warnings against the social-democratic parties' or trade unions' reformist ideology and politics of class collaboration; 'component parts' of the ISAs in question, they let themselves be wholly integrated into them and assimilated by them. When their 'leaders' are in 'power', that is, at the head of the government (bringing down a government must not be confused with taking state power), they conduct themselves, in Léon Blum's lovely phrase, as 'loyal managers of the capitalist regime', which they have no desire really to 'overthrow', at least not in deeds, whatever their declarations. I am well aware that, in certain conjunctures, they can let themselves be 'dragged into' doing more than they would really like, but, when that happens, they really cannot be blamed for it . . .

It is no accident that the social-democratic organizations are included with 'full rights' in the bourgeois ISAs. From the bourgeoisie's standpoint, they take their places as full-fledged members of them, and are not confined to any political or trade union 'ghetto'. More: they are the essential 'component part' of the corresponding ISAs, and the bourgeoisie makes very able use of them to counter the very troublesome 'component part' represented by a proletarian party or trade union. The whole history of bourgeois politics for the last eighty years has been based on this tactic of *dividing* the working-class forces, at the level of politics and trade union organization alike. Thanks to this technique, the bourgeoisie effectively 'annuls' the presence of proletarian organizations in its ISAs.

II A FEW HISTORICAL FACTS

To bring out the full significance of the two points I have just very schematically developed, I propose to recall a few empirical facts that will help us grasp how and why proletarian class-struggle organizations figure in bourgeois ISAs.

To begin with, it is enough to consider what happens in social formations other than the French (or Italian) formation in order to understand that this result is unintelligible if the history of the class struggle specific to these countries is not taken into account. Let us first adduce two examples that simple comparison makes instructive.

The bourgeois fascist regimes, whether in Europe or Latin America, to take only those two cases, created working-class organizations that were wholly in their service, fully integrated component parts of the ISAs of the fascist state: in fascist Germany and fascist Italy as well as in Peron's Argentina, there existed 'labour fronts' or 'state trade unions'. Peron even came up with the following admirable phrase: 'The bourgeoisie should *organize* the working class: that is the best way to protect it against Marxism.' The Franco regime's state trade unions exemplify this even today. The fact that, in these unions, things are not going for the best for Franco's politics is assuredly not the fault of the State Ideology or the minister in charge of the state workers' or students' unions . . .

Another example: in a number of capitalist countries, proletarian class-struggle organizations are quite simply *banned*. The balance of power in the class struggle, especially in certain Asian, African and Latin American countries directly or indirectly controlled by US imperialism, has not been able to impose recognition of these organizations.

One final example: in a number of capitalist countries, workers' organizations are very well integrated into the system of the capitalist ISAs – for instance, in the Scandinavian countries, ruled by 'socialists', or in England. The course of the class struggle in England has culminated in the victory of a reformist line: trade unionist in the unions, 'Labourite' in the Labour Party. There is, of course, unrest among the rank-and-file, but, for the moment, the trade union and Labour Party[3] leadership still basically work hand in hand. The result is that the trade unions and the Labour Party are indeed perfectly integrated component parts of the system of the political and associative ISAs of the capitalist-imperialist English state. Is there any need to make the demonstration for the American trade unions or the German trade unions and German Social-Democratic Party? It is sometimes even the case that reformist political and trade union organizations are capitalist economic powers, as in England, the USA and Germany.

How does it happen, then, that the 'situation' is different in France? How does is it happen that the French bourgeoisie has had to resign itself to recognizing, without being able to neutralize, organizations that the bourgeoisie in other countries and other circumstances has either succeeded in 'organizing' by taking over their leadership itself, or in banning, or in purely and simply subordinating to itself and assimilating? The answer lies in the history of the French class struggle.

The history of the French bourgeoisie is dominated by a great event that it 'botched': the French Revolution. From the bourgeois point of view, this was truly a 'dirty' revolution. In a 'clean' revolution, as in England, for example, things would have been the object of a 'gentleman's agreement'[4] between the leading classes, feudal-aristocratic and bourgeois industrial-mercantile. Unfortunately, thanks to the stupidity of a bankrupt rural petty aristocracy which, in the 1780s, had the 'bad taste' to demand its 'feudal rights' at all costs in a day and age in which (consider Turgot) they were being quietly abolished (and for other reasons as well, of course), things took a nasty turn: the people made

---

3 [TN: 'Trade unionist', 'trade unions' and 'Labour Party' are in English in the original.]

4 [TN: In (misspelled) English in the text.]

their entrance onto the scene and did not pull their punches. There were peasant uprisings in the countryside, where castles started going up in flames, and '*journées révolutionnaires*' in the cities, especially Paris, where, very quickly, despite the 'Night of 4 August'[5] and the Girondists' reform-ist politics, the most 'uncontrollable' of the plebeians poured onto the streets of Paris, imposed their revolutionary committees, and brought Robespierre and the Committee of Public Safety to power, among other things. The counter-revolutionary war (the fraternal feudal states rushed to the rescue of the King and Queen who had, together with the émigrés, requested that they intervene) made the class war even harsher and more radical. For a time, the popular masses' Patriotism and the Revolution, reinforced by the measures of public safety that the bourgeoisie has labeled 'the Terror', confronted that bourgeoisie with the threat of something altogether different from 'its' Revolution: sinister prospects in which a certain 'Fourth Estate' of sans-culottes – poverty-stricken plebs – demanded a social, egalitarian Republic from which mercantile and industrial capitalism had everything to fear. On the horizon were the pamphlets and speeches of Marat and other agitators and propagan-dists for equality; there was something in the air that found expression in the 'communism' of a Babeuf and a Buonarotti, in forms that were still primitive, yet unmistakable.

The French bourgeoisie has not forgotten the Terror (the Commune filled it with the same Terror, and it reacted with the same White Terror in both cases). It had to take emergency measures to put the popular masses back *in their place*: not in power, but at work, under its exploitation and domination. The stages in this process were Thermidor, then the Consulate, then Bonaparte and Napoleon.

Bonapartism is a *typically French* solution to the problem represented by the style of the class struggles unleashed in France by this 'unfortunate revo-lution' of 1789. It is the standard bourgeois solution for putting the popular masses back [in their place] when conflicts between the dominant classes have not been able to prevent their direct, armed intervention on the stage of the overt class struggle, or, worse, have made it necessary. It is no acci-dent that the bourgeoisie has entrusted power to a providential 'Bonapartist' figure whenever the division between the dominant classes and the inter-vention of the popular masses has put the bourgeois class's domination in jeopardy: after the 1789 Revolution, to put the people in their place and establish the apparatuses of the bourgeois state, its superstructure, law (the

---

5   [TN: On 4 August 1789, the Constituent Assembly decreed the abolition of feudal privileges in France, which had until then been enshrined in law.]

Civil Code), and Ideological State Apparatuses (its universities no less than its chambers of commerce and so on, as well as . . . the Comédie Française, to say nothing of the Concordat); after the terribly frightening alert constituted by the proletariat's June 1848 intervention on the barricades; in the wake of the twofold crisis that divided the French bourgeoisie (the 1940 defeat and then the Algerian insurrection).[6] Napoleon I, Napoleon III and De Gaulle are the 'price' that the French bourgeoisie had or still has to pay for the history of its own class struggles, during which it has had to resign itself to the outpouring of plebs and then the proletariat into the streets in order to achieve its own objectives. It was not enough that the bourgeoisie diverted the results of popular struggles (in 1789, 1830 and 1848) to its own exclusive advantage. It also 'made the popular masses pay' a very high price in blood (the White Terror, the 1848 massacres) and in the mass arrests, condemnations and deportations of 2 December [1851], for 'contributing' to its own class struggles. Bonapartism and ferocious repression have been 'its' solutions.

It is the French bourgeoisie's misfortune that the plebeians and, very soon, the proletariat were 'steeled' in the struggles of the *journées révolutionnaires*, learning the art of building barricades and fighting the army on them, and that the bourgeoisie was in some sense forced by its own history to educate the popular masses and the proletariat, which saw that it could one day take up arms and fight 'on its own behalf', as a famous phrase has it: 'The emancipation of the working class must be the work of the working class itself.'

These words were inscribed in history by Marx and Engels. *The Manifesto* was published in 1848. In 1864, the International was founded. The lesson was not lost on the French proletariat. There followed what is known as the Paris Commune.

One of the disadvantages (for the bourgeoisie itself) of the 'Bonapartist' solution is its instability. It always comes to a bad end. The reasons vary: the arbitrariness of 'personal power', which ultimately becomes an encumbrance – the providential man really takes himself for France and, in the long run, can maintain his position only by staging military expeditions (Napoleon I, Napoleon III) which, since they meet with the resistance of the peoples occupied as a result, ultimately take a bad turn, culminating in 'adventurist' military operations (Spain, Mexico, and so on). Things took a very bad turn at Sedan, against Prussia.

---

6   [TN: The 13 May 1958 putsch staged in Algiers to prevent the 'abandonment of French Algeria'. It put an end to the French Fourth Republic and brought De Gaulle to power.]

There occurred, after Sedan, an unprecedented event, one that left its stamp on human history – the history of socialism, but also the history of the class struggle as a whole: the Commune. While Mr Thiers's big bourgeoisie was colluding with the Prussian occupiers in Versailles, the Parisian proletariat assumed the leadership of the patriotic resistance, wresting, for the first time in history, the cause of the defence of the nation away from the bourgeoisie. For class reasons, this sudden turnabout led to the first attempt to make a socialist revolution in human history: that reckless, unheard of, desperate, but formidable experiment in which the working-class and popular masses invented what theory had only had a presentiment of, the destruction of the state and its apparatuses . . . that experiment that left its mark on Marx and Lenin, and is still being invoked at the other end of the world, in China. Everyone knows how the French bourgeoisie, relying on the Prussian occupier, put the 'people' back in their place: it put it up against the walls, where tens of thousands of men and women were killed in broad daylight, before the people were sent back to their posts in production, in exploitation.

I shall cut this short in order to say that the lesson of all these class struggles, which were 'exemplary' (Engels), not for the bourgeoisie, but for the proletariat and the French people, was such that the bourgeoisie had to recognize the political and trade union organizations of the proletarian class struggle, once they had succeeded, despite tremendous difficulties and unheard-of sacrifices, in imposing themselves. The bourgeoisie, taken at its word, not only the one it had uttered in the course of the struggles of its eighteenth-century ideologues and writers, but also that of its 'democratic' tradition (Liberty, Equality, Fraternity), tripped up by the fact that the working masses had offered it support that it had not disdained in 1830, nor in February 1848, nor in the ultimate paroxysms of its class struggle against the aristocracy (for instance, its late nineteenth-century struggle against the Church) – in short, taken by the throat by the power of the popular and then proletarian class struggle, the bourgeoisie opted to recognize the political and trade union organizations of proletarian class struggle in its ISAs. It did so in the hope of defeating them there, getting the better of them, perverting them, if need be, or neutralizing them by pitting the social-democratic organizations against them: that is certain. But, reason or ruse, impotence or finesse, the facts are the facts.

That the same does not hold for other countries is, in the final analysis, a question of the balance of power in a historical class struggle. What I have just said about this question in France shows, at any rate, the true nature of the class struggle. It can unfold, in the forms prescribed by the law prevailing in the ISAs under consideration, only as a simple effect, a simple relay of an altogether different class struggle, which infinitely exceeds all the legal forms in which it may *also* manage to find expression.

8

The Political and Associative
Ideological State Apparatuses[1]

I NECESSARY PRELIMINARY REMARK

We here take up a question which is as important as it is hard to present properly, that is to say, without giving rise to the least misunderstanding.

That is why we wish to repeat here, in the same terms, a solemn statement that we included in our 'Preliminary Remark to My Readers'. It is a question, in the political and associative Ideological State Apparatuses, of the class struggle. But beware: it is not a question of the whole class struggle, nor even of the terrain in which the class struggle has its roots. It is a question of a domain in which the class struggle assumes *legal forms*, the conquest of which was itself the result of a history of class struggle that was necessarily external to those legal forms. Once they are conquered, the class struggle is pursued in them within the more or less narrow limits that they impose and, in any case, within rigorously defined limits. At the same time, the class struggle unfolds, massively, *outside these forms*.

That the system of political and trade union forms which the dominant class has either taken control of in its class struggle, or has been forced reluctantly to concede as an effect of the conquests of the proletarian and popular class struggle, or, again, has incorporated into the dominant class's state apparatus as Ideological State Apparatuses, so that it is, above all, the State Ideology that is realized in these apparatuses – all this can be effortlessly understood. But it can just as easily be understood that the class struggle that has imposed these apparatuses, around which and in which part of the class struggle between the bourgeoisie and the proletariat is unfolding today, profoundly marks *certain*

---

1 [TN: See Chapter 7, n. 1.]

of their component parts, conferring, in particular, an *exceptional* position, within these apparatuses' legal forms themselves, on certain institutions of proletarian class struggle. Examples are provided by the proletariat's organization of political class struggle and its organization of trade union class struggle.[2]

An exceptional position is an antagonistic position. For the bourgeoisie did not, after the tumultuous events that we shall discuss in a moment, recognize the existence of reformist and then revolutionary workers' parties with joy and gladness. The same holds *a fortiori* for its recognition of the existence of trade union organizations of the economic class struggle. The bourgeoisie knows that what is at stake, behind these organizations' legal forms of existence, goes infinitely beyond those legal forms themselves. It is given proof of this whenever a crisis that is at all serious brings into the broad light of day the reality that the legal existence of these organizations expresses but also obscures: the fact that the class struggle is not confined, and for good reason, to this or that communist party's oppositional activity in parliament, or this or that trade union confederation's 'negotiations' with the bosses or the government; the fact that an extremely violent class struggle is waged without let-up in every domain of the practice of production and also well beyond production, although it is silent and, observed from the outside, invisible, since it does not find sanction in existing legality. This exceptional position both reflects and betrays a position that is – in principle – antagonistic (except when the organizations in question lapse into class collaboration). We are thus confronted with the following paradox.

Within an Ideological State Apparatus such as the apparatus of the political system, there can exist a proletarian party (as is already the case in a number of countries) whose ideology is, albeit radically antagonistic to the State Ideology, realized in the forms and practices of the Ideological State Apparatus in which that proletarian party figures. The fact remains that this antagonism unfolds in the very forms imposed by the State Ideology (for example, bourgeois democracy, the dictatorship of the bourgeoisie in the forms of a parliamentary or presidential democratic apparatus). This singularly complicates the proletarian party's task. However, as Lenin has shown, this complicated task is not therefore impossible, on the absolute condition that certain imperative conditions are met. The first of them is that the proletarian party should not sink into 'parliamentary cretinism' or 'bourgeois-democratic cretinism' and, *a fortiori*, that it should not allow its ideology of proletarian class struggle to be

---

2   [TN: See Chapter 7, n. 2.]

sapped by the State Ideology, the ideology of the dominant class. It must, rather, know how to make use of the political Ideological State Apparatus, including some of its forms and certain elements of its ideology (for example, certain democratic slogans), in order to *foster*, by way of elections and also from the high tribune of the bourgeois parliament, the development of the class struggle, which basically unfolds outside these legal, bourgeois-democratic forms. The same holds *a fortiori* for workers' trade union activity.

If things are very clear in this regard, we can set out on our analysis of the political and associative Ideological State Apparatuses.

To provide, straight away, a classic point of reference for my thesis, I shall refer to a well-known text of Lenin's, drawn from a speech he delivered on 30 December 1920: 'The Trade Unions, the Present Situation and Trotsky's Mistakes', which one would do well to read in its entirety, and also supplement with a second text, a speech delivered shortly after the first (on 25 January 1921): 'Once Again on the Trade Unions'. Lenin is here talking about trade unions under the dictatorship of the proletariat, and thus about their existence in the framework of the proletarian state, which is a state in the strong sense, under the control of the Bolsheviks and their allies and endowed with the repressive and ideological apparatuses characteristic of any state. Lenin declares:

[T]he trade unions have an extremely important part to play at every step of the dictatorship of the proletariat. But what is their part? I find that it is a most unusual one, as soon as I delve into this question, which is one of the most fundamental theoretically. On the one hand, the trade unions, which take in all industrial workers, are an organisation of the ruling, dominant, governing class, which has now set up a dictatorship and is exercising *coercion through the state.* But it is not *a state organisation; nor is it one designed for coercion,* but for education. It is an organisation designed to draw in and to train; it is, in fact, a school: a school of administration, a school of economic management, a school of communism. It is a very unusual type of school, because there are no teachers or pupils; this is an extremely unusual combination of what has necessarily come down to us from capitalism, and what comes from the ranks of the advanced revolutionary detachments, which you might call the revolutionary vanguard of the proletariat.[3]

---

3   Vladimir Lenin, 'The Trade Unions, the Present Situation and Trotsky's Mistakes', in Lenin, *Collected Works*, Moscow, Progress Publishers, 1965, vol. 32, p. 20 [Althusser's emphasis].

A few pages later, Lenin adds these remarkable statements:

> Comrade Trotsky falls into error himself. He seems to say that in a workers' state it is not the business of the trade unions to stand up for the material and spiritual interests of the working class . . . We now have a state under which it is the business of the massively organised proletariat to protect itself, while we, for our part, must use these workers' organisations *to protect the workers from their state*, and *to get them to protect our state*.[4]

Let us single out Lenin's central statement here. He says, in so many words, that 'the trade unions . . . are an organisation of the ruling, dominant, governing class, which has now set up a dictatorship and is exercising *coercion through the state*'. But, he goes on, the Soviet trade union '*is not a state organisation; nor is it one designed for coercion* . . . it is, in fact, a school'.

When we look between the lines of a text about the trade unions of the proletarian state for an answer to the question about the status trade-union organizations (we shall see which ones) can have under the bourgeois state, it appears that Lenin's formulation almost exactly coincides with our own, inasmuch as it distinguishes the state's coercive action from Soviet trade unions' *non-coercive* action. For Lenin, proletarian unions have an ideological/educational mission: they are to act as a 'school of communism'. Keeping things in proportion, that is, paying due attention to the obvious differences between proletarian and bourgeois Ideological State Apparatuses, and with the aforementioned reservations, we may regard the trade union and associative system as an Ideological State Apparatus, and discuss the political system in terms of the same concept.

II THE POLITICAL IDEOLOGICAL STATE APPARATUS

We shall begin with the political Ideological State Apparatus, for reasons that will appear.

The communist parties and the political Ideological State Apparatus: democracy for the people and socialist revolution

Of course, this does not at all mean that a political party such as the Communist Party, because of its topographical inscription in the system

---

4 Ibid., p. 24.

of the political Ideological State Apparatus, is necessarily *reduced* to the role of fulfilling the bourgeois state's wishes, or to the role of His Majesty's opposition.[5]

The latter role is played to perfection, with all the requisite tact, by the 'loyal managers of the capitalist system' known as the *social-democratic* parties. They did not need to hear Léon Blum's marvellous phrase to understand that they had a 'vocation' on – of course – 'the human scale'.[6] This famous 'human scale' does indeed offer a sizeable advantage: it allows those who scale its rungs, that is, progressively attain the bourgeois honours (or even the honours of the nobility: Mr Attlee was well and truly elevated to the 'dignified rank' of Lord by Her Most Gracious English Majesty!), quite simply to '*rise above*' the 'small-minded' '*class struggle*' standpoint in order to practice, in all serenity, proper *class collaboration* (consider Mr Wilson today).

Lenin struggled hard enough, using vehement language ruthless enough, against the people who, even in the communists' ranks, might be tempted by these mirages – that is, the impossible miracles of purely parliamentary-democratic activity ('parliamentary cretinism') – to dispel all conceivable ambiguity. Since, today, everyone is thinking about the 'transition' to socialism, it must be recalled *that there is no parliamentary road to socialism*. Revolutions are made by the masses, not by parliamentary deputies, even if the communists and their allies should fleetingly, by some miracle, attain a majority in the parliament.

For the bourgeois state will never consent to be *seized* and *destroyed* (for it is a question of seizing the state, not of 'bringing down the government' or simply 'changing' the 'regime') by 450 parliamentary deputies armed with nothing but their bare hands, even if they come marching out of the Palais Bourbon sporting their tricoloured sashes. It will never consent, that is, to be seized and destroyed by a simple parliamentary majority, except in some unprecedented situation conceivable, perhaps, once socialism has triumphed over five-sixths of the globe. In the present state of things, it is literally unimaginable, in the short or even the middle term.

For the bourgeois state is something altogether different from the mere

---

5 Be it recalled that *the class struggle goes infinitely beyond those of its effects* which are inscribed in the forms of the Ideological State Apparatuses. Here we are analyzing those effects alone, to the exclusion of all others.

6 [TN: *The Human Scale* (*L'échelle humaine*) was the title of a book Blum published in 1945. It features a polemical account of the differences between the communists' inhuman socialism and the socialists' 'socialism on a human scale'. *Echelle* also means ladder.]

government. The state disposes of many ideological apparatuses besides its *political* ideological apparatus (in which the *government* has its place), which is, after all, just one apparatus among a multitude of others (the Church, the schools, news and information, and so on). Furthermore, it has the day-to-day *repressive apparatus* at its beck and call: the police, specialized repressive units (riot police, mobile security forces, and so on), as well as its repressive apparatus 'of last resort', the *army*, an organization of hundreds of thousands of people marshalled in the infantry, armoured divisions, air force, and navy – to say nothing of the armies of the 'fraternal' imperialist states, which can cross borders (land or other borders) to help out at the right moment.

Even ignoring these extreme cases, the simple experience of the Popular Front or the post-1945 Three-Party government[7] proves that a simple government of *popular democracy*[8] is at the mercy of simple financial procedures (for example, the capital flight that sounded the knell of the Popular Front) or political procedures (the socialist Ramadier's 1947 dismissal of the communist ministers), unless the popular masses intervene directly and forcefully on the political stage to stymie or foil the manoeuvres of the capitalist class struggle and *force* the parliament to take radical measures which, in that case, change the course of history, lending existing democracy class character and setting it on an *irreversible* course in the form of actions that ultimately culminate in the socialist revolution properly so called.

Lenin said that one had to know how to anticipate, accept and practice *transitional periods* in order to reach the Revolution. He himself 'practiced' this theory at the head of the Bolshevik Party between February and October 1917. This was the period in which Kerensky presided over a bourgeois and petty-bourgeois parliamentary majority that had been 'democratically' elected after the February 1917 events, which had 'overthrown' the Czarist regime without overthrowing the feudal-capitalist Russian state, even if its state apparatuses, beginning with the army, had been severely undermined. This very peculiar period of 'democratic' transition, during which the Bolsheviks, albeit a tiny minority in the

---

7   [TN: For the first eighteen months of the existence of the post-war French Fourth Republic, with the exception of a brief interlude from December 1946 to January 1947, successive French governments were formed by the PCF, the Socialists of the Section Française de l'Internationale ouvrière, and the conservative Mouvement républicain populaire.]

8   In Marxist doctrine, a democracy can only be characterized by its *class nature*: bourgeois democracy, petty-bourgeois democracy (bourgeois democracy's appendage and fig leaf), or popular democracy, democracy for the people.

parliament, were able to win over the masses, mobilize them, and rally them to their leadership *in a few months* thanks to their correct line and correct actions, was truly a period of transition *towards* socialist revolution, not, after big electoral successes and even very big victories of popular mass struggles (as in 1936), a period of transition towards the restoration of democracy *against* the people – that is, reactionary bourgeois democracy – culminating in Pétain's fascism.[9]

If the Communist Party and its allies should, one day in our future, win a majority in legislative elections, and if the bourgeoisie were to allow them to assume the responsibilities of 'government' in the framework of existing bourgeois *legality*, one must be aware:

1) that they would thereby open up the prospect of democracy *for the people* (popular democracy or new democracy);

2) but that, *for as long as the bourgeois state remained in place*, with its repressive apparatus intact, and with its Ideological State Apparatuses, including the bourgeois *political* Ideological State Apparatus, *the actions of the popular masses*, assuming that they are educated, mobilized and committed to a struggle based on a correct line, would determine the nature of the *transitional period* thus initiated;

3) that, depending on the balance of power and the political line that the popular masses were mobilized to follow by the Communist Party, this *transitional* period could lead to *either* a victorious bourgeois reaction (after a few popular successes) *or* the triumph of the socialist revolution;

4) that *without the seizure of state power, without a dismantling of the Repressive State Apparatus* (what Marx and Lenin called 'smashing the machine of the bourgeois state'), without a long struggle to smash the bourgeois Ideological State Apparatuses, revolution is unthinkable, or can only triumph for a time, as was seen in Central Europe in the 1920s.

Thus, for us, no *parliamentary* 'transition' to socialism is even conceivable, for such a transition is impossible. Nor is it conceivable that the 'transition' to socialism can be brought about by combining mass political action whose *sole* objective is '*to isolate the bourgeoisie*' in general and the action of an electoral majority 'that professes socialism' or even wants socialism.

---

9   A correct line does not always triumph in six months. Transitional periods can be long and can unfold in stages. The international balance of power can impede their progress. With no correct mass line, however, it is pointless to invoke the need for a transition, which, in that case, is just idle chatter.

If it is supposed that bourgeois dictatorship can be overcome by 'isolating the bourgeoisie' *without seizing state power*, without *smashing the bourgeois state apparatuses*, the bourgeoisie, even if it is 'isolated', will know, whatever the tendency of the *government* in power, how to use the existing state apparatuses, first and foremost the police and army; and it will find itself a chief of state capable of commanding the still intact state apparatus – if need be, by means of a coup d'état such as that of 13 May[10] or of some other kind.

If the masses do not decisively intervene, not to 'isolate the bourgeoisie', but to *disarm/dismantle the Repressive State Apparatus*, the transitional period initiated by an electoral victory promising democracy for the people will be, rather than a transition *towards* socialism, a 'transition' *towards* bourgeois reaction in, without a doubt, its most violent form: openly dictatorial and tendentially fascist. In that case, the Repressive State Apparatus and Ideological State Apparatuses, the *political* state apparatus included, will be put to 'full use' by a bourgeoisie that will have dropped its mask, with the requisite massacres as well as the mass arrests that have become classic in a 'reaction' of this type, perfected by the bourgeoisie in the century-and-a-half or more in which it has ruled France (Thermidor, 1815, June 1848, the Commune, Daladier, Laval-Pétain). What ultimately comes into being after such events obviously is not *just* the bourgeoisie's creature; but we know that there are massacres and overtly dictatorial regimes, whether they are called fascist or neo-fascist, that can crush the mass movement for years.

Again, Lenin issued enough warnings, in terms categorical enough, to all unconditional partisans of the 'putsch' and even the 'insurrection', to the effect that it was not just foolish, but even criminal not to utilize all forms of struggle – not just all legal forms, but also all parliamentary-democratic, and thus electoral, forms[11] – in such a way that whatever parliamentary-democratic action is undertaken by the communist party in the framework of the bourgeois political Ideological State Apparatus is something other than class collaboration. Lenin insisted, however, that the *absolute condition* for this was that such action be one form of struggle among others, subordinate to the system of mass class struggles led by the communist party.

---

10   [TN: See Chapter 7, n. 6.]

11   Let us not forget that in 1908, at a critical moment in the history of the Russian workers' movement, Lenin was for maintaining the Social-Democratic deputies in the Duma. He was opposed by the leftist-rightist Bolsheviks known as the Otzovists, who were for recalling them. [TN: 'Leftist-rightist' means ostensibly leftist but actually rightist; see Louis Althusser, 'Lenin and Philosophy', in *Lenin and Philosophy*, London, New Left Books, 1971, p. 24.]

If we interpret these well-known theses of Lenin's in the light of our distinction between the Repressive State Apparatus and Ideological State Apparatuses, and if we take into account the fact that a democratic system (in which a parliament elected by universal suffrage in a political contest among different parties designates a government representing the parliamentary majority[12]) is part of the *political* Ideological State Apparatus, we will, I think, better understand the real but narrow limits on the *parliamentary-democratic* activity of the communist party.

When the party is in the opposition, its [parliamentory] activity is always confined to the framework of democratic legality prevailing in the political Ideological State Apparatus at a particular moment in history. That activity does not directly effect, or does not effect at all, the state's other ideological apparatuses. Despite all the bills the party may propose, its activity has virtually no effect on the news and information apparatus (no one can claim that 'democracy' extends to the regime of radio, TV, or the press), the publishing apparatus, the religious apparatus, the scholastic apparatus,[13] and so on. What is more – this is the most serious limit on the party's activity, the absolute limit – it obviously puts not the least dent in the repressive apparatus. And if a 'democratic' government in which the party participates is able to exact obedience from the radio–TV regime and a part of the administration, it is with many reservations, and on condition that it remain within the confines of a 'politics' ensuring, at the very least, the 'defence of the national currency' and other 'national interests'. It is a different story as far as the police and, a fortiori, the army are concerned: they 'obey' when they want to, and know how to blow the whistle when they judge that the situation threatens to reach the critical point for bourgeois class domination. The army then steps in directly, as was seen with the Algiers Putsch that brought De Gaulle to power, although *the existence of the bourgeois state* was not even in jeopardy, only the unity of the dominant class, the unity of a bourgeoisie divided by the Algerian people's struggle for national liberation. What would have happened if the bourgeois class state itself had been threatened by the French popular masses?

The distinction between the Repressive State Apparatus on the one hand and the Ideological State Apparatuses on the other, as well as the

---

12   Although the government is elected by parliament, which is part of the political Ideological State Apparatus, the governemnt is part of the Repressive State Apparatus. That is normal. See p. 136 of this edition.

13   One need only consider all the bills for educational reform proposed by the Communist Party. They have never been translated into reality. That is normal.

thesis that the latter include the *political* Ideological State Apparatus, within which the struggles of parliamentary democracy take place, thus grounds and illustrates Leninist principles concerning the distinction between the communists' activity in a parliament or even a parliamentary government (where the existence of the state is not in question) and the masses' revolutionary activity for the conquest of the bourgeois state by way of, first, the destruction of its Repressive State Apparatus and, subsequently, its Ideological State Apparatuses.

To grasp these 'fine points', it suffices to consider:

1) the (seemingly paradoxical) *validity* of our classification of the political *system* of bourgeois democracy – including, consequently, the political parties that bourgeois democracy encompasses and, therefore, the party of the working class as well[14] – under the concept of the *political Ideological State Apparatus*;

2) *the possibility* that a revolutionary party such as the Communist Party can and should find its place in the 'play' of the system of the Ideological State Apparatus comprised by the political apparatus (a place circumscribed by very narrow objective limits, to be sure) and pursue objectively revolutionary politics there, on the absolute condition that the party's parliamentary politics in the forms of 'bourgeois democracy' be subordinated to its overall politics, which can only consist in mobilizing the proletarian masses and their natural allies[15] for the purpose of seizing bourgeois state power and transforming it into the power of a socialist state.[16]

The possibility, for the party of the working class, to intervene in revolutionary (non-reformist) fashion in the 'play' of the system of the *political* Ideological State Apparatus, rests on the possibility of *circumventing* the law *even while respecting it*.

Very precisely, in the case of the parliamentary struggle in bourgeois democracy, it is a question, for the party of the working class, of

---

14   It succeeded in gaining recognition only after a long class struggle, throughout which it was constantly maligned as 'the party of a foreign country' or the 'Separatists' Party'.

15   These natural allies are, *in order of priority*: 1) the small, poor and proletarian peasantry; 2) segments of the rural and urban petty bourgeoisie – some middle peasants as well as craftsmen, small merchants, employees, intellectual workers, secondary school and college students, and so on.

16   [EN: Crossed out: 'This *possibility* attests a necessary effect of the existence of bourgeois law (here, bourgeois democracy's constitutional law) that we noted in passing when we noted that the essence of law consists in being applied, *that is, respected and circumvented*. This will have come as no surprise to jurists or politicians.']

invoking the constitutional law recognized by the bourgeoisie itself so as to make it produce effects of agitation and propaganda favouring overt struggle against the bourgeoisie's politics. In other words, it is a question of taking bourgeois democracy at its word in order to *help* (only to help, for one must steer clear of all forms of 'parliamentary cretinism') the masses to engage ever more deeply in a course of action that will ultimately overturn bourgeois democracy in favour of the *socialist* democracy in which, during the dictatorship of the proletariat, the dictatorship of the working class and its allies will be exercised over their class enemies.

Stalin happened to utter a 'historic' phrase when he declared that the communist parties should 'pick up the banner of democratic freedoms' that 'the bourgeoisie had dropped'. However, he spoke a little too quickly; for history has shown that even a man like De Gaulle, who is contemptuous of those freedoms, also knows how to 'wave' the flag of democratic freedoms in skilful speeches that, as election results prove, still have a certain effect. De Gaulle can find successors to wave the same flag! Stalin's remark likewise betrays his failure to see that, as Lenin has shown, there is democracy and democracy, and that the question of the nature of democracy is, in the last instance, a *class matter*.

The same holds for Stalin's other 'historic' phrase about 'the banner of national independence' 'abandoned by the bourgeoisie', which 'the party of the working class' was supposed to 'pick up'. Here, too, he spoke a little too soon, for De Gaulle, who is not in the least contemptuous of national independence, has proven that he knows very well – as the electoral results prove here, too – how to 'wave' 'the flag of national independence' to the appropriate kind of anti-American music. Stalin's remark also betrays his failure to see that, as Lenin has shown, there are nations and nations, and that the nature of a nation is, in the last instance, a *class* matter.

Under no circumstances should we forget that the themes of democratic freedoms and national independence are, first and foremost, integral parts of the bourgeois State Ideology, especially in periods when the communist party can rightfully invoke them against bourgeois policies.

Thus the reader will allow me to take for granted, or, at any rate, to treat as well-supported hypotheses, the propositions advanced in the preceding discussion, namely, that there exists a specifically *political* Ideological State Apparatus, and that it is constituted, in the French capitalist social formation, by the *realization* of the bourgeois State Ideology (here liberal-democratic-nationalist ideology) in the system comprising the electoral system, political parties, parliament, and so on.

III THE ASSOCIATIVE IDEOLOGICAL STATE APPARATUS

The same demonstration applies to the *associative* Ideological State Apparatus, which falls under the same theory, but with an important difference that leads us to make a new remark.

As early as 1791, as everyone knows, the 1789 bourgeois revolution strictly outlawed, with the Le Chapelier Act, associations of labourers, the former journeymen who were soon to become the new workers, that is, proletarians. The Civil Code clearly recognized the right to use and abuse all (material) goods. As for the 'good' of association for journeymen and workers, a law was required expressly to *prohibit the free use of it*!

The working class conquered the right to association in a long, fierce, bitter, bloody struggle. Notwithstanding the 'individualistic' Civil Code, that right was enshrined in the Labour Code recently created to that end. Even civil servants employed in the administration or various Ideological State Apparatuses (such as the scholastic state apparatus or the news and state information apparatus) eventually saw their right to association enshrined in the 1946 constitution, a circumstance that will give us some idea of the 'lag' affecting this 'branch' of the law . . .

This should remind us of a parallel phenomenon. Parliamentary democracy, in which suffrage was initially based, under the Constituent Assembly,[17] on tax-based qualifications, went through a jolting series of ups and downs in the course of the nineteenth century before finally gaining general acceptance with the 'misunderstanding' that led to the proclamation of the Third Republic, which would doubtless have become a monarchy again for some time if had it not been for the stupidity of Mac-Mahon and his friends.[18] This proves that the Ideological State Apparatuses are very sensitive in nature and made of very sensitive stuff, since it takes so much time and so many struggles to replace old ones with new ones and establish them in their apparently definitive function; this also proves that they can be highly vulnerable as soon as they are shaken up by the conjuncture. In that respect, *they differ from the Repressive State Apparatus*, which displays superb continuity and constancy, inasmuch as it

---

17 [TN: *La Constituante*, the National Constituent Assembly created shortly after the French Revolution began.]

18 [TN: Edmé Patrice de Mac-Mahon, who led the forces that bloodily suppressed the Paris Commune, was elected president of France in 1873. He proved unable to restore the monarchy shortly after his election, although the National Assembly was then dominated by monarchists.]

has not changed for centuries, which have nevertheless seen many different 'regimes', class regimes all.

We can make the same demonstration, then, for the *associative* Ideological State Apparatus. We must, however, introduce a new stipulation.

When we talk about political parties, we know that they extend from the right to the far left. The existence of parties of the right, centre and 'left', and the fact that they have loyally shown up at all the major historical occasions of the capitalist class struggle to shield the bourgeois state with their bodies plainly shows that there is a connection of some kind between the political parties and the system of parliamentary democracy on the one hand, and, on the other, the dictatorship of the bourgeois state. We need only take one more step to understand Lenin's formula: bourgeois democracy is the 'dictatorship of the bourgeoisie'.

When we talk about unions, however, things are not as self-evident. The word makes everyone think first of trade unions, and of the most combative of them: the CGT and, for a few years now, the CFDT.[19] We tend to forget that workers' unions are not the *only* kind of unions in existence. There are also unions of civil servants employed by either the Repressive State Apparatus (tax inspectors' union, and so on, and even a police union) or the Ideological State Apparatuses (unions of primary school, secondary school, and college teachers, and so on).[20]

Yet there also exist unions of supervisory personnel and syndicates of small and middle-sized businesses. Above all, there exist very powerful 'professional' associations of employers, crowned by the most powerful of them all, the National Confederation of French Employers [CNPF].

To make our thesis about the existence of an associative Ideological State Apparatus very clear, we would do well to *look at things from the other end*, beginning, not with the class-struggle workers' union (the CGT, the only trade union to include this definition in its statutes), but with the CNPF, and proceeding back down the ladder. When we do, we discover

---

19 [TN: The Confédération française démocratique du travail, the second largest French trade union confederation after the CGT, is the successor organization to the French Christian Labour-Union Confederation (CFTC). The CFDT was formed in 1964, when the CFTC majority adopted a class-struggle line and changed its name. The CFDT and CGT collaborated between 1966 and 1970.]

20 On the other hand, there are no unions or political parties in the army, the Great Mute Organization in which only generals have the right to speak, when, let us note, they are authorized to do so by the Minister of the Armed Forces, except on 18 June [1940, when De Gaulle made, in London, a radio declaration repudiating the French government's cessation of hostilities with the Axis powers], 13 May [1958], or during putsches such as the Algiers putsches. and so on.

that there exist an unbelievable number of employers' syndicates or interest groups charged with 'defending the interests' of a profession.[21]

The system made up of these organizations forms an apparatus that realizes an ideology of 'defence of the interests of . . .' a profession! Naturally, this ideology goes hand in hand with an ideology of the inestimable services that the profession in question renders the public and the national interest. It thereby realizes one of the grand themes of the State Ideology, that of the general and national interest in freedom of enterprise and the defence of lofty moral values. 'Defence of the profession' is, for associations of middle employers and big employers, a fig leaf hiding their class objective.

That a workers' union waging an economic class struggle was able, at the price of battles lasting more than a century, to 'win recognition' in such company, and that it can, moreover, wage a genuine class struggle in the margins of the very recent juridical legality[22] of the Labour Code, is the fruit of a kind of heroism: the heroism, precisely, of the working class.

History proves that this trade union has been the constant target of indescribable pressure and repression, shameless blackmail, dismissal of activists, as well as corruption and pay-offs pure and simple (FO,[23] as is now official, was created with CIA money); and it has been a victim of the concomitant splits, not to mention the standing temptation to lapse into the economism of the 1906 Charter of Amiens ('No politics in trade unions!') or into anarcho-syndicalism ('Down with political parties! Politics is the business of trade unions alone!').[24] This, however, merely provides additional empirical evidence for our thesis about the existence of an *associative* Ideological State Apparatus.

21　[TN: Crossed out: 'The most resplendent jewels in the French associative apparatus are, incontestably, the Order of Physicians, the Order of Architects, the Order of Notaries, and so on.' See Chapter 11, n. 5 and 'Note on the ISAs', p. 220 below.]

22　It poses serious 'logical' 'problems' as far as the jurists' requirements of systematicity, formalism and universality are concerned!

23　[TN: CGT-Force Ouvrière, the third biggest French union, was created in 1947 with US assistance following a split in the CGT.]

24　'Apoliticism' is one of the themes of the State Ideology realized in the associative Ideological State Apparatus. It proclaims: '"Apolitical" defence of the interests of the Profession . . . in the interests of the Nation!' The struggle against trade union apoliticism is thus the touchstone of the ideological class struggle of a workers' trade union organization. The history of the CGT illustrates this struggle: it was apolitical when it was founded, was combated by the CGTU, and was then reunified on the basis of a rejection of apoliticism. [TN: Adopting the Charter of Amiens in 1906, the CGT declared its complete independence of both the state and all political parties. On the CGTU, see n. 44 below.]

Better, this allows us to make a remark that may seem rather paradoxical when one considers the Marxist tradition.

It is often said that, according to Marx and Lenin, the workers' movement is capable of organizing, by itself, *without the help of Marxist theory*, organizations of trade union struggle capable, after weathering the trying ordeals of their apprenticeship, of leading fights that go beyond the merely local level or corporatist limits to attain the national level. On the other hand, the argument goes, things are infinitely harder when it comes to making the transition to political organization. And there is a tendency to add that this is *only natural*, since the workers who daily experience the economic exploitation whose victims they are *are not equally familiar with the mechanisms of political class struggle*, and thus of political oppression and the ideological subjection exercised by the capitalist state.

There exists, consequently, a tendency, at least on the part of some proletarian political leaders who are not of proletarian origin, and, *a fortiori*, among people, especially intellectuals, of petty-bourgeois origin, to consider the economic struggle as, in some sort, 'natural', but subordinate, and to believe that the political struggle is much harder to set in motion. It is, however, not certain that the reality of the matter corresponds point for point with this judgement. That is why we chose to begin by discussing the *political* Ideological State Apparatus, before going on to discuss the *associative* Ideological State Apparatus.

The reason is simple. The terribly hasty promulgation of the Le Chapelier Act can put us on the right track. The reason is that the same bourgeoisie which demanded the benefit of the freedom to organize politically, and which thus *imposed* at a very early stage, by means of its own class struggle, in which it did not 'turn up its nose' at support from the 'people' (consider 1789–93; 1830; 1848), *its own political* Ideological State Apparatus in opposition to the feudal aristocracy's – *the same bourgeoisie took great pains, from the word go (1791), to repress by means of law and the worst sort of violence the slightest inclination to organize or to wage economic struggle on the part of those it exploited, the proletarians.*

IV THE CLASS STRUGGLE OF THE POPULAR CLASSES INSIDE THE
POLITICAL IDEOLOGICAL STATE APPARATUS (AND OUTSIDE IT)

It must be understood that the bourgeoisie discovered that it was incapable of preventing the popular masses – for the good reason that it could not do without them – from taking part in the bourgeois *political* class struggles against, first, the feudal class in 1789–93, and then against the landed aristocracy throughout much of the nineteenth century, above all the first half of it.

It was the French bourgeoisie's 'historical bad luck' that it had to do with a nobility and feudal Church that were particularly tenacious, hard-headed, and even 'dumb' (the proto-Poujadist 'revolt' . . . of the petty aristocracy in the years 1770–80 really spoiled everything). The result is well known: the violent revolt of the peasantry ('Peace to the huts, war on the castles!'), with the castles in question going up in smoke all over the place – for the peasants went about their business with a vengeance – the repetition of the *'journées révolutionnaires'* in the cities, the reign of the plebeians in the streets and over Paris, the Committee of Public Safety and the Terror meeting the challenge of the frankly counter-revolutionary war that had been unleashed by the fraternal feudal states at the appeal of the highest-ranking French aristocracy (with the King and Queen heading the list, prior to their execution).

Without the decisive support of the popular masses, including the horrid, ominous 'Fourth Estate'[25] that Mathiez has described,[26] the bourgeoisie of the Third Estate would have been able neither to overturn 'feudal' relations of production and exchange, nor to take power and destroy the feudal state of the absolute monarchy in order to create its state apparatuses, nor, finally, to exercise power in order to establish its own relations of production and its law.

Engels says somewhere that France is an *exemplary* country in that to be sure, class struggles are carried to an extreme there, with utter clarity. It is exemplary for the proletariat, to be sure, *but not at all for the bourgeoisie.* From the bourgeois standpoint, the 1789 revolution was, in comparison with the English Revolution, a *'dirty* revolution' that, politically, exacted infinitely too high a price from the bourgeoisie; the damage it caused had to be 'repaired' as best it could be, under the worst of conditions. Above all, those unspeakable popular masses, peasant masses that were becoming increasingly urban and plebeian, had to be put back *in their place*; they had of course been vitally necessary for the bourgeoisie, but they were definitely a little too confident (and how was one supposed to prevent that?) that *'their day had come'*.

---

25   The most 'plebeian' segment of the common people, led by Marat, Duchêne and countless other vigorous, courageous popular agitators. On the horizon was the communism of a Babeuf or a Buonarotti, which was still in search of its theoretical and political positions, as well as its forms of organization and action.

26   [TN: Albert Mathiez, *La Révolution française, Vol. 3,* Paris, 1922.]

A few good mass shootings, Thermidor, the White Terror and, finally, Bonaparte the Saviour (the De Gaulle of his day), crowned Emperor in exchange for the Civil Code and the French bourgeoisie's pre-imperialist wars throughout Europe, settled matters. But at what a price! A twofold price, at least.

First, the bourgeoisie had had to pay the price represented by Napoleon Bonaparte I. It thus inaugurated an original tradition, the typically *French* tradition of *Bonapartism*, a disagreeable, but rational and indispensable bourgeois solution designed to put the plebeian masses back in their place (in 1798 and again in 1852, a tradition pursued down to 1958, with De Gaulle's 13 May).[27] This was a solution, certainly, but a *costly* one, for it showed one and all that bourgeois political 'liberalism' could take the overt form, to the advantage of the bourgeoisie itself, of a non-democratic or non-parliamentary personal *dictatorship* that, while serenely grounding itself on the Grand Parliamentary-Democratic Principles of 1789, betrays whenever its class domination is threatened, the contempt in which it holds those principles.

Second, the bourgeoisie had to pay the price for setting the popular masses a 'bad example' that might prove contagious and, worse, be repeated. For, in its class struggle against the aristocratic reaction of the Restoration (Louis XVIII, Charles X), the bourgeoisie did not 'turn up its nose' at the workers and common people of Paris who, side-by-side with the petty bourgeoisie, 'did the work' on the *Trois Glorieuses* in July 1830.[28] Once again, then, '*journées révolutionnaires*' on which the people poured into the streets and invented both the barricades and the art of fighting on them.[29] Nor did the bourgeoisie 'turn up its nose' at the proletariat's help in 1848, when 'for the first time the proletariat as such, in its

---

27 Pétain was something else again: same end, but different means. The Bonapartist and fascist solutions should not be confused. De Gaulle has so far adopted not the fascist, but the Bonapartist solution, and, what is more, the 'liberal' Bonapartist solution, for the 'solution' represented by his Bonapartism is distinguished by the fact that it has restored (as it did, moreover, in 1945 as well) the terribly jeopardized *unity* of the bourgeois class itself. The French bourgeois class split very dangerously down the middle between 1940 and 1945, in the face of the Nazi invasion, and in 1958, when confronted with the Algerian insurrection. In both cases, De Gaulle's historic role consisted in 'putting the pieces back together' – that is, restoring the unity of the French bourgeoisie. Furthermore, beginning in 1958, he has presented French imperialism with the non-parliamentary democratic plebiscitary state demanded by the monopolies.

28 [TN: The 'Three Glorious Days' of 27, 28 and 29 July, 1830, when an uprising toppled Charles X, putting an end to the Bourbon monarchy of the French Restoration.]

29 In May 1968, the people remembered that the street can belong to the people. they have not forgotten. They will not forget.

first organizations, marched out to battle, launching an assault on the Orleanist monarchy alongside the petty bourgeoisie, and glimpsed, hopefully, albeit still from a very great distance, something that spoke of 'socialism', even if it had to be discerned through the disavowals of a Louis Blanc and the sham of the 'National Workshops'.

Every time, the bourgeoisie had to resign itself to the idea of *armed* intervention by the popular masses – by the petty bourgeoisie, to be sure, but also by craftsmen, journeymen and, finally, in 1848, the proletarians themselves, in their first class organizations. Every time, it had to resign itself to the paradoxical fact that its own bourgeois class struggle was educating the proletariat and preparing it for violent political class struggle, which it would one day wage *in its own interests*.

Need we say something about the Commune as well? At stake this time was the Empire, which had become an encumbrance for the bourgeoisie in view of its inappropriate authoritarianism and the catastrophic consequences of its annexationist, adventurist foreign policy. This time, too, the help of the popular masses – proletarians who were increasingly well organized and politically conscious, despite their ideological divisions (partisans of Proudhon, of Blanqui, and so on) – proved necessary (although it was making the bourgeoisie increasingly uneasy) to bring down the Empire and proclaim the Republic. To top things off, the defeat also did its part. The defeat? But what then becomes of nationalism, a key component of the bourgeois State Ideology?

This is where the French bourgeoisie found its cross: in the encounter between a military defeat and a popular revolution (think of 1917 Russia!). The *national* resistance that the *people* of Paris put up against the Prussian occupier, the appeal to the popular masses to liberate the nation from foreign armed forces, was no longer the work of the patriotic petty bourgeoisie or, obviously, the big bourgeoisie of Mr Thiers in Versailles, which was colluding with the victorious Prussians. It originated in a fact without precedent: *it was the work of the Parisian proletariat*, which, for the first time in history, assumed the leadership of the patriotic resistance and the revolution. The consequence was the Commune: a transition from the popular national struggle against the occupier *to the first socialist revolution in history*: that reckless, unheard of, excessive, inconceivable, mad, but formidable experiment, a source of practical inventions and theoretical discoveries without precedent, which changed the entire course of the international workers' movement in a phenomenal way.

For, this time, it was not one or another *government* or *form of bourgeois state* that was at issue, but the bourgeois state as such, in its *apparatuses*. It was from the Paris Commune that Marx derived the irrefutable *empirical* confirmation of his theses on the necessity of seizing state power, destroying the state apparatuses, and establishing the dictatorship of the proletariat at the head of a new *state*, a proletarian state, fitted out with new – *proletarian* – state apparatuses.[30]

Everyone knows how the bourgeoisie went about 'rewarding' the common people of Paris for their decisive help in 1830: by confiscating the *Trois Glorieuses* for Louis–Philippe's benefit. It rewarded the proletariat for its decisive help in February 1848 by massacring proletarians in June 1848 and then pursuing the repression with the sentences of 2 December: death sentences, prison terms, mass deportations. Everyone knows how the bourgeoisie responded to the Paris Commune's patriotic resistance and revolutionary audacity: by murdering tens of thousands of men and women who were murdered in broad daylight with everyone's full knowledge. They were stood up against Parisian walls in plain view of the beautiful ladies whom these comforting massacres helped to get over their 'dreadful' fright, unforgettable and unforgotten, unforgotten even *today*.

However one assesses these terrible events, the bourgeoisie, once it had basically secured its political victory over the aristocracy, once it felt strong enough to tolerate its existence, that is, to *control* or even *assimilate* it, found itself unable to prevent the creation of *workers' political parties* (in the 1860s and 1870s in Germany, and later, in the 1880s, in France), because its constitutional law *formally* authorized them. A *workers' political party*, even a socialist party, need not be dangerous, if it plays the democratic game. The proof is that the German Social-Democratic Party's huge electoral successes, and the real, if more modest, successes of the *Parti ouvrier français* and, later, the *Section française de l'Internationale ouvrière*, culminated, as is well known, in the two *Unions Sacrées*, the one that the German Social-Democratic Party concluded with the German imperialist state and the one that the French Socialist Party concluded with the French imperialist state (with Guesde serving as minister without portfolio in the first war cabinet) after Jaurès was assassinated. This shows that what has, since Lenin, been known as *imperialism* always *has the last word* about even the most spectacular electoral successes of the workers' parties, Marxist parties not excepted.

The bourgeoisie is very adept at manoeuvring within its *political* Ideological State Apparatus, not only by utilizing the right electoral techniques

---

30 We should reread Lenin's *State and Revolution*. Whenever it is a question of destroying the bourgeois state apparatuses, the example of the Commune surges up – its example and practical *political inventions*.

to put more deputies in parliament the fewer votes it has in the country, but, above all, *by dividing the working-class forces*. Thus it tolerated the Communist Party in France after the First World War (while imprisoning its leaders every now and then), but *alongside* the Socialist Party, and *constantly* used the Socialist Party *against* the Communist Party. It knows the score and is not as stupid as Mr Guy Mollet once had the audacity to say. (The audacity? Rather, the *complicity*: to create the impression that the French bourgeoisie is stupid is also a way of deceiving the workers as to its real strength once again, and thus of once again serving the bourgeoisie.)

The *division* of the workers' political parties went hand-in-hand with the *division* of the workers' trade union organizations. Such is the bourgeoisie's constant tactic.

This is irrefutable proof that *what the bourgeoisie fears above all things* is (listed in order of increasing importance):

1) political unity between the workers' parties;

2) trade union unity between the workers' unions;

3) and, *above all, above all*, unity between these two forms of unity, that is, *the fusion, behind a unified line and a unified leadership, of the mass trade union activity and mass political activity of the working class and its natural allies.*

These stages (1, 2, 3) may be regarded as *absolute* thresholds and touchstones. Hence we must advance the following *thesis*:

The bourgeois class struggle reaches the level '*state of alert*' with the first event (political unity between the workers' parties). It reaches the level '*state of emergency*' with the second event (trade union unity between the workers' unions). It reaches the level '*martial law*' with the third event (unity of the economic and political class struggles of the masses of workers and their allies). For, at that point, one stage following another, it is the bourgeois state itself that is *directly at issue*.

The bourgeoisie can 'tolerate' a great deal, including an active communist party, active trade unions, a general strike, even if it is relatively politicized, as in May 1968, and the simultaneous ideological revolt of the young people in school (in one segment of the scholastic Ideological State Apparatus). But *under no circumstances* can it tolerate the mortal threat against *the state itself* (state power, the state apparatuses taken as a whole, with the Repressive State Apparatus that forms their core) represented by the *irresistible popular power* that looms up behind the unity of the workers' parties and the unity of the labour unions, that is, *the real fusion of the economic and political struggles of the* popular *masses* in the cities and countryside. May 1968, *albeit miles* from achieving this fusion, warned the bourgeoisie that it had to exercise extreme vigilance in the face of this mortal threat.

The bourgeoisie is not at all stupid. It does everything it can to fend off this mortal threat; and, as a good Cartesian, it 'divides up difficulties', that is, applies a strategic, patient, tenacious, shrewd policy of *dividing*, first, the political workers' movement; second, the trade union movement; and, finally, the relations between them. To do this, it need only rely on the social-democratic parties and the class-collaborationist trade unions *against* the communist parties and the trade unions of economic class struggle. History verifies this empirically, beyond all question. It is up to communists, first of all, and then up to proletarians and their natural allies, to learn the lesson that this history has to teach. It is a vitally important lesson for the cause of the period of transition to socialist revolution and the socialist revolution itself.

V THE ECONOMIC CLASS STRUGGLE IN THE ASSOCIATIVE IDEOLOGICAL STATE APPARATUS

We have now made many observations on familiar topics of the workers' parties' struggle in the framework of the political Ideological State Apparatus. It is time to say a word about the specificity of the struggle of workers' organizations in the framework of the *associative* Ideological State Apparatus.

Since politics is in the foreground, and since the political struggle always represents a higher level of 'consciousness' than trade union struggle does, there is a tendency, as I have pointed out, to regard trade union struggle as both easier and less important – when it is not considered a secondary, if not, indeed, somewhat contemptible business.

It is enough, for example, to read through the 'literature' that has been turned out for years by a handful of 'revolutionary' theorists of the UNEF,[31] but also of certain splinter groups and the PSU,[32] not to mention ideologues such as Serge Mallet[33] and others, or the organs in which they publish (*Le Nouvel Observateur*), in order to learn about a great

---

31 [TN: Union nationale des Etudiants de France, the biggest student union in France.]

32 [TN: The Parti socialiste unifié, a small party founded in 1960, was close to the CFDT. Its candidate in the June 1969 presidential elections, Michel Rocard, joined the Socialist Party five years later and held the post of prime minister from 1988 to 1991 under the Socialist President François Mitterrand.]

33 [TN: Sociologist, former member of the PCF, founding member of the PSU, author of *La nouvelle classe ouvrière* (Paris, 1963) / *The New Working Class* (Nottingham, 1975).]

'Revelation' from them, namely, that 'quantitative' demands must be clearly distinguished from 'qualitative' demands. The former, the 'quantitative' demands, which have to do with the 'defence of the *material interests*' of wage-earners and coincide with or comprise the major objectives of the *economic* class struggle of the workers' trade union organization (the CGT), are considered to be basely materialistic and without 'horizon' or 'global strategic revolutionary' 'perspective' (to use these theorists' jargon). They are therefore treated as somewhat contemptible.

The other demands, *in contrast*, the 'qualitative' demands, are noble and worthy of Universal History, that is, of the interest that these theoreticians bestow on them in order to elaborate their 'global strategy' of World Revolution, in which the proletariat had better hold on to its hat, that is, hold to the position they assign it.

If I mention these errors or asininities, it is because they wreak havoc, not only among 'intellectuals' (students and others),[34] but also in other strata of the petty bourgeoisie (supervisory personnel and engineers, progressive members of both categories included) and even in certain working-class strata. The CFDT's slogans themselves often echo the distinction between 'quantitative' and 'qualitative' demands, *to the advantage of the latter*, of course, since the distinction was invented to that end.

In sum, only politics is noble and worthy of being practiced, since it is revolutionary, whereas material trade union demands are 'basely' materialistic and non-revolutionary – it is all they can do not to dispatch someone to tell the workers they should be ashamed of themselves for demanding money with which to buy fridges, tellies, or even a car, since we know, as the good bourgeois theory of 'consumer society' has it, that these things are, in and of themselves, 'alienating' for the class struggle, because they 'corrupt the souls' of their owners. The counter-argument leaps to the eye: as everyone knows, the handful of 'theorists' (CFDT, PSU, or 'intellectuals', a *few* students included) who graciously share with us the revelation that has been bestowed on them, all go without fridges, tellies and cars themselves, not to mention vacations on the Balearic Islands, the Riviera, or in Greece, so that they will not be 'alienated' or 'corrupted' and can continue to be the 'pure' thinkers, if not *leaders*, of the proletarian revolution they are,

---

34 [TN: The published French text (*étudiants d'âge ou autres*) is garbled. The only partially crossed-out manuscript version reads: 'students of normal age or those who hang on as students for the sake of the "cause"' (that is, in order to be able to continue to play a political role in the UNEF).]

inasmuch as they have *themselves* decreed that they are its 'thinkers' and 'leaders' . . .[35]

If, however, we abandon the 'global' perspective adopted by these 'theorists', and simply pay a little attention to the trade union struggle, its *history* displays a *crucially* important feature. We have stated the reasons that ultimately compelled the bourgeoisie to concede that the workers' political parties, even the Communist Party, have a legal right (which is, to be sure, at the mercy of the first ban to come along) to exist (at least for the time being). The same reasons have produced a completely different result in the domain of the workers' trade union struggle, which comes under the *associative* Ideological State Apparatus.

The workers' *economic* class-struggle organizations have not benefited, unlike the workers' political class-struggle organizations, from the events of the long, spectacular class struggle between bourgeoisie and feudal aristocracy in the eighteenth and nineteenth centuries. Thus they have not benefited from the instructive bourgeois precedents and examples of the political class struggle, or the occasional articles of liberal, egalitarian, bourgeois constitutional law, the grand principles of which were laid down from 1789 on. For the bourgeoisie not only had no need for assistance from the workers' *economic* class struggle; on the contrary, it had everything to fear from it, since this economic class struggle, which targeted capitalist exploitation, in fact targeted, *directly*, the *material basis* for the existence of capitalism and thus for bourgeois society and the bourgeoisie's political domination. The bourgeoisie could therefore risk *no political compromise whatsoever* with the workers' *economic* class struggle, because it lives exclusively on the exploitation of workers. That is perfectly *logical*. However, the immediate conjuncture *requires that we dot the 'i's* here, since people are currently peddling old mistakes which, albeit long since refuted, are still dangerous.

Let us here recall a fundamental classic thesis: the material basis (the infrastructure, as Marx says, or 'the base') for the existence of every capitalist social formation is *economic exploitation* – economic exploitation, *not repression*. Marx, Engels and Lenin, particularly in their relentless struggle against anarchism, which claimed the opposite (and still does in the

---

35   By what miracle do *some* intellectuals and 'students' possessed of all the advantages of consumer society manage to escape the 'alienation' that the same objects of consumer society cause among workers? Answer: they escape it because they, for their part, are 'conscious' of their alienation. It is not, however, consciousness that determines being, but being that determines consciousness (Marx). This truth admits of *one and only one* exception: that of the intellectuals who feel the need to believe that, *in their case*, and in their case alone, *consciousness determines being*.

persons of its petty-bourgeois 'theorists' of the 'avant-garde', that is, of the historical rear-guard), always carefully *distinguished* exploitation from repression, in other words, the economic base on the one hand, in which the economic relations of production of capitalist exploitation hold sway, and, on the other, the political *superstructure*, in which, in the last resort, the *repressive power of the capitalist state* holds sway.

It is here that the metaphor of the edifice (base or infrastructure and superstructure or upper floor resting on the base) renders absolutely decisive theoretical and political service to working-class activists. It can even render important, salutary service to a number of those who, rather than letting themselves be '*intimidated*' by the authoritarian methods of ideological 'leadership' utilized by a handful of intellectuals, the self-appointed theorists and leaders of the 'revolutionary movement', agree to reconsider the question, seriously, scientifically, calmly and honestly.

For the distinction between base and superstructure, as well as the thesis that the superstructure, and thus *all* forms of repression (*all* of which depend on the state apparatuses), are determined in the last instance by the base (that is, by *the material exploitation* of the proletariat and other workers working in relations of production that are relations of *capitalist* exploitation and nothing else) – this distinction puts things definitively back in place.

This is an *elementary* truth of Marxism. Those who today call it into question are nothing other, *in this respect*,[36] than pure and simple *revisionists*.

For what is determinant in the last instance, and thus primary, is *exploitation*, not repression. What is determinant in the last instance are the relations of capitalist production (which are simultaneously relations of capitalist exploitation). What is determined, and thus secondary, is repression: namely, the *state*, which is repression's ultimate centre, *from which all forms of repression emanate*: both the repression that is exercised by the Repressive State Apparatus – physical repression both *direct* (the police, army, courts, and so on) and *indirect* (the administration) – *and all forms of ideological subjection* due to the Ideological State Apparatuses.

---

36 I say, emphatically, *in this respect*, and in this respect alone. For the masses of young people, for example, bear no responsibility for the erroneous declarations of a tiny handful of 'leaders'. What is more, the ideological revolt of young workers and young people in the schools is, at bottom and as far as the great mass goes, profoundly progressive. It should be judged on the basis of the objective tendency informing it in the national and global class struggle – not on the basis of a simple mistaken formula put forward by someone who is temporarily a personality. This holds *a fortiori* for proletarians and other wage-workers in the CFDT.

And if, as we have tried to show, if not, indeed, to prove, the super-structure's effective function is to ensure the *reproduction* of the conditions of production through the system of the various forms of repression and ideologization, all of which are ascribable to the capitalist state, it follows that reproduction is merely the condition for the continuing existence of *production*. This means that *it is in production, and in production alone, not in reproduction,* that *exploitation* is carried out, the material condition of exist-ence for the capitalist mode of production.

If the state is, as Engels puts it, a 'concentrate' of society, it is such only in consequence of its role in *reproduction,* and because we can, *on that grounds,* discover in it the significance of the *political* class struggles of which it is the object and objective. But these political class struggles are not materially grounded in the existence of the state.

They are grounded in the existence of *irreconcilable* antagonistic classes, whose *existence* as antagonistic classes is grounded in, and determined by, the material conditions of class *economic exploitation.* On the one side stands the class of exploiters – exploiters because they have the means of production in their hands; on the other stands the class of the exploited, exploited because they have no means of production and are forced to sell their labour-power as if it were an ordinary 'commodity' – even in our supposed 'consumer society'.

Therein resides the essential, albeit paradoxical, difference distinguish-ing the working class's *economic* class struggle from the (more or less officially recognized or tolerated) forms of its political class struggle.

The paradox is that, in order to destroy the class relations of *capitalist exploitation,* the working class *must* seize bourgeois state power, destroy the state apparatus, and so on, because the state is the key to the *reproduc-tion* of capitalist relations of production. To overthrow the infrastructure of exploitation, therefore, the proletariat and its allies must take state power and destroy the state machine. This proposition is perfectly correct from the standpoint of the proletarian *class war,* which must direct the political attack *against the state,* because the state is that which guarantees the conditions of reproduction of the system of exploitation; or, in short, that which maintains the capitalist system *upright,* by perpetuating it.

However, as every soldier knows very well, a country's last military defence (this or that strategic battlefield) is not the country itself; nor does the battle for this ultimate bastion sum up the whole of the war that preceded it. The same applies to the class war between the proletariat and the bourgeoisie. What *decides* it is whether state power remains in the hands of the bourgeoisie or is seized by the proletariat. That, however, is the culminating point of a very long battle, an incessant, daily, extraordinarily difficult battle, a sort of interminable trench warfare that can never be abandoned and is usually masked by the spectacular political battles in the foreground. This silent, obscure, interminable, bloody trench warfare is the *economic* class struggle.

In this war, the bourgeoisie gives, *in principle*, no quarter. From 1791 on, it has been waging preventive battle, outlawing, with the Le Chapelier Act, all 'associations' of journeymen and craftsmen and, later, workers. One must read the stupefying history, as recounted by honest historians,[37] of the workers' economic class struggle associations. Banned, they had initially to be organized behind the screen provided by various unlikely associations (relief associations, associations of mutual aid, 'correspondence' societies, or even associations for the fight against alcoholism), generally in legal grey zones, when they were not purely and simply illegal – with, on the one hand, all the obscure heroism, incessant sacrifice, tenacity, imagination and subterfuge, and, on the other, the pitiless condemnations or, quite simply, mass killings (Fourmies,[38] to cite just one bloody example) that this entailed – since these practices were, at the time, expressly prohibited by repressive bourgeois law.

Simply to take the measure of this difference, let us simply note that it was infinitely harder for workers' unions to secure recognition of their legal, concrete existence and 'rights' in the associative Ideological State Apparatus than it was for workers' political parties to gain recognition in their Ideological State Apparatus. The workers' unions had to assert their *de facto* existence in the face of the most cynical sorts of bourgeois legality and repression, in heroic, protracted battles, before they were formally recognized in 1884, and actually recognized . . . only under the Popular Front, in 1936! It was only in 1946, after the Resistance, that French civil servants' right to organize unions was recognized! It was at Grenelle,[39] in May 1968 (!), that shop committees were granted a legal right to exist . . . in companies employing more than 200 workers!

Is there any point in adding that, since the law is the law, and since applying it consists in respecting it *while circumventing it*, the bourgeoisie

---

37   See Jean Bruhat, ['Le mouvement ouvrier français au début du XIXe siècle et les survivances de l'Ancien Régime'], *La Pensée*, [no. 142, December 1968].

38   [TN: The site of a massacre of May Day demonstrators perpetrated in 1891 by French army units in a centre of the textile industry in the Pas de Calais.]

39   [TN: The Grenelle accords crowned negotiations involving the French government, employers' organizations and trade unions. The concessions made to the labour movement, although rejected by much of the rank-and-file as insufficient, were subsequently institutionalized.]

did not and still does not hesitate to make use *of all the procedures in its power* against union activists, by subjecting them to sanctions or, quite simply, firing them? Or that labour inspectors either collude with employers or are quite simply helpless in the face of the procedures employers use? Or that some employers write off, as overhead expenses, the fines they are condemned to pay by the labour courts for 'unfair dismissal' of 'people with bad attitudes' who are just a little too politicized? Is there any need to add, on top of everything else, that the bourgeoisie is a past master at exploiting the *divisions* between trade union organizations, which it carefully cultivates (divisions between the CGT, CFDT, CFTC, CGC,[40] and FO, to say nothing of 'company unions' such as those at Simca or Citroën)?

Thus it is no wonder, to take 1969 France as our example, that it is *often easier* to be a member of the Communist Party in France – that is to say, for certain activists, to carry a party card in their pockets, hold occasional meetings *outside* the firm, distribute leaflets or the party cell newspaper by mail or in some other discreet way – than to be a genuine trade union activist. For trade union activity can only be carried on *in* the firm, in the broad light of day, collectively, it is true, but also individually, under the constant, terribly vigilant surveillance of engineers, supervisors and foremen who *in the overwhelming majority of cases are the direct agents*, in forms that are sometimes brutal, but sometimes infinitely subtle, of the *bosses' exploitation* and *repression*.

The thesis that I am advancing by way of these empirical remarks is simple and classic in the workers' movement. It has been defined in very clear terms by Lenin and the Red International of Labour Unions.[41] It runs as follows.

The economic class struggle, which cannot *by itself* determine the outcome of the decisive battle for the socialist revolution, that is, the battle for state power, is not a *secondary or subordinate* struggle. It is the material basis for the political struggle itself. Without bitter, uninterrupted, day-to-day economic struggle, the political class struggle is impossible or vain. There can be no concrete political class struggle capable of carrying the day that is not *deeply rooted* in the economic class struggle, and *in it alone*, because the economic class struggle is, to hazard

---

40 [TN: The CGC (Confédération générale des cadres) was founded in 1944 to defend the interests of supervisory personnel.]

41 [TN: The RILU or Profintern, in existence from 1921 to 1937, was affiliated with the Third International. The manuscript includes a note here: 'See the documents in the appendix'. See Chapter 5, nn. 5 and 7.]

a somewhat metaphorical expression, the base, *determinant in the last instance*, of the political struggle itself, which is for its part – for such is its function – the *only one* that can *lead* the popular masses' decisive battle. Primacy of the political class struggle, then; but this primacy will remain a hollow phrase if the basis for political struggle, the economic class struggle, is not waged daily, indefatigably, profoundly, and on the basis of a correct line.

Obviously, this thesis pulverizes those of petty-bourgeois 'theorists" about the primacy of 'qualitative' over 'quantitative' struggles, and also Marxist pseudo-theses about the 'trade unionist'[42] 'limits' on the workers' class struggle when it is left to itself. The latter theses are ascribed to Lenin when he is read a little too hastily.

For Lenin *by no means says* that the working class, when left to itself, can wage only an *economic* class struggle. The trade unionism of which Lenin speaks is a *political* struggle, but one waged on the basis of an incorrect political line, a *reformist* line, which confines itself to calling on the bourgeois state and bourgeois government to make reforms, without ever calling the existence of the bourgeois class state into question. Trade unionism is the utilization and perversion of the struggle of workers' trade union organizations for the benefit of a reformist political line, that is, a *class-collaborationist* political line. In this case, too, there exists a close relationship between trade unions and party: what would Labour in England be without the trade unions? We can even grant that there exists a certain implantation of Labour in the big British trade unions; we must, however, immediately add that the major trade union leaders, the Bevins, Bevans, Wilsons, and so on, *once they are in power* (that is, at the head of Her Gracious Imperialist Majesty's government), are never slow to cut themselves off from their 'roots' in the trade union struggle, and then to 'contain' that struggle, before overtly combating it. This is always what happens when one is a 'government socialist', that is, a flunky of the bourgeois *state*.

It is, therefore, completely wrong to interpret Lenin's statement that 'trade unionism' is the *furthest limit* that the workers' movement can attain *on its own power* as if it referred to the spontaneous *economic* class struggle of the workers' movement. It refers to something completely different: the absolute limit of the spontaneous *political* struggle of the workers' movement, which trade unionism pushes into the reformist trap of class collaboration. At the limit, trade unionism

---

42 [TN: 'Trade unionist' is in English in the original, as is 'trade unionism' in the following paragraph.]

can set out to conquer the 'government' – but *never the capitalist state*. The result is that it becomes the 'loyal manager of the capitalist regime'.

VI THE POLITICAL CLASS STRUGGLE MUST BE DEEPLY ROOTED IN THE ECONOMIC CLASS STRUGGLE

We must, then, establish the facts again. And, because the trade union struggle is today under attack from certain 'avant-garde theoreticians' and is also, in effect, treated as *secondary* by certain communists, who, be it added, cultivate for that reason an equally *false* notion of their role in the political struggle, we must also emphatically *rehabilitate the trade union struggle*, which takes on the character of a *direct economic class struggle* when big *workers'* union federations (such as the miners, metal workers, rail workers, construction workers, and so on) are involved. (In civil servants' unions, for example, the relationship to economic class struggle *is not direct*.) We must establish the facts again, and understand why no *communist* political class struggle is possible unless it is deeply implanted in the masses' *economic* class struggle, and unless the communists take up a correct position and carry out correct actions in the *economic* class struggle, that is, in the struggle for 'bread-and-butter demands'.

We have brought out the principle that ultimately justifies this thesis: because the whole capitalist regime rests *in the last instance* on direct economic exploitation of the working class and other wage-earners who are not workers, both urban and rural, the anti-capitalist struggle inevitably takes the path of a direct struggle against direct *exploitation*. It also takes the path, secondarily, of a struggle against indirect forms of exploitation.[43]

Because this struggle *can* be led as a mass struggle, it is led by *mass organizations*, which are by nature distinct (by virtue of their statutes, operating rules – the broadest possible trade union democracy – and practices) from the communist parties. It is plainly a question of the *masses*, for exploitation affects *all* workers and labourers *without exception*; it is their daily lot, they experience it directly every day. Thus it is by way of the struggle for material demands that *the masses* can be rallied to objective actions against the capitalist system. The masses: not just the vanguard of the proletariat, not just the proletariat, but also the non-proletarian wage-workers in town and country, poor peasants, small peasants in the process of becoming proletarians, and all those, including many civil servants

---

43 For 'non-proletarian wage-workers', for example: white-collar workers, civil servants in various state apparatuses, and so on.

working in the Ideological State Apparatuses (teachers, for instance) or even certain Repressive State Apparatuses (for example, some categories of civil servants in the administration), *who are objectively victims of capitalist exploitation*.

It is the masses who make history. But if the masses can lead history to the victory of the socialist revolution *only* in the political class struggle and under the *leadership* of the political organization of the vanguard of the proletariat, it is clear and correct that the masses, when they go into motion, will not accept the party's political leadership *unless* they have long since been unified and mobilized in the struggle against *the economic exploitation* of the capitalist regime by a long, hard, heroic, tenacious, unspectacular, *trade union* struggle for *bread-and-butter demands* on the basis of a correct line.

This is an unmistakable sign. If a communist party disappears, as a party, from the enterprises, that is proof that its line and practice were not correct with respect to its own political function and its function vis-à-vis the trade unions. If, in the enterprises, the party cell 'hides' behind the trade union; *a fortiori*, if it purely and simply *disappears*, leaving it to the trade union (which can on no grounds assume this function) to 'stand in for the party'; if the party contents itself with '*supporting* workers' struggles' (read, trade union struggles), instead of *leading* them, which is its role; in short, if, at the national level, the party finds itself, in its non-electoral practice, *objectively lagging behind* the activity and initiatives of the organization of economic class struggle – this is, in all cases, a sign that 'something is wrong somewhere'.

For the party must be *ahead of the masses* by, not ten miles or a thousand miles, as the famous 'revolutionary' 'avant-garde theorists' about whom I have already said a word would have it (speaking on behalf of their 'organization', which exists only in their imaginations), but, as Lenin's formula has it, by *one step, and one step only*. What holds at the national level holds *a fortiori* at the level of *each enterprise*. This presupposes correct definition of the communists' political line vis-à-vis the shop committee, as well as correct practice of it. To forge ties with the masses in the enterprise, the communists have to concern themselves, *down to the details*, with concrete trade union demands and questions, without, however, substituting themselves for the trade union; they have to carry out the work that is theirs, the work of *political* explanation, propaganda, agitation and organization. This presupposes, as its absolute condition, that the party exists *in* the enterprise, that it makes its presence felt there *in actual fact* and *as such* (with its own initiatives, its cell newspaper, and so on). It presupposes that everyone in the enterprise knows and appreciates it, that it has a correct line there and occupies the position it should vis-à-vis the masses organized in the trade union: *one step ahead of the masses, and thus one step ahead of the trade union organizations.*

For, to go back to what we have said about the union between the mass economic struggle and mass political struggle, in short, to discuss this *fusion* again, which is a deadly terror because it is, objectively, a *mortal threat* to the very existence of the capitalist system, this politically revolutionary *fusion* will never come about in forms capable of ensuring its victory if one does not begin to forge it, far in advance, *at the very heart of the enterprises.* But the material basis for this fusion is the implantation of the political class struggle in the economic class struggle, which is, I repeat, *determinant in the last instance.* In more concrete terms, it is *the implantation of the activity of the communists who are members of the shop cell in the activity carried out by the members of the shop committee to win concrete material demands.*

This is the basic principle of the communists' political practice with respect to the trade unions. The old militants who were formed in France by the CGTU and the Leninism of Maurice Thorez have not forgotten it; they know it. They have to teach it to the many young militants who have flocked or will flock to the CGT[44] and then the party. This is not, be it added, their *personal* affair. It is *the number-one task of political education,* which the whole party should take in hand, assuming responsibility for it and carrying it through to the end. I am well aware, we are all well aware, that this is no easy task. That is especially true in the present conjuncture, in which bourgeois and petty-bourgeois ideology, which always has an influence on the working class, because it is and remains the dominant ideology, never ceases to suggest two deviations to the workers' movement: the *economistic* deviation on the one hand and the hyper–political, '*revolutioneering*' deviation on the other (whether anarcho-syndicalist or anarchist).[45] It is especially true in the present conjuncture, in which imperialism's death agony also assigns a high priority to the task of forming activists *for the anti-imperialist struggle* in France itself,[46] and in

---

44   [TN: The CGTU (CGT unitaire) resulted from a 1921 split led by revolutionaries in the CGT, which had rallied to the Union sacrée in 1914. The strong anarchist and libertarian currents in the CGTU grew gradually weaker as it settled into the PCF orbit in the first half of the 1920s. The CGT and the CGTU were reunited in 1936. Maurice Thorez was the PCF's General Secretary from 1930 to his death in 1964.]

45   [TN: 'Anarcho-Maoist' has been crossed out and replaced by 'anarchist'.]

46   Not only with correct slogans – 'Victory for the Vietnamese people! Victory for the Palestinian Resistance!', and so on – but also in practical struggles. Think of the dockers' refusal to load war materiel for the Indochina Expeditionary Corps and of the

particularly delicate conditions at that (the split in the international communist movement and the resulting enfeeblement of proletarian internationalism).[47] In any case, this educational task remains the number-one task of political education, and must be carried out.

Implant the political class struggle as deeply as possibly in the economic class struggle, in the trade union struggle for the masses' material demands: such is *the golden rule of the revolutionary struggle*.

The workers' movement, in its fusion with Marxist theory, learned this golden rule in the course of struggles which cost the international working class unimaginable sacrifices. The workers' movement owes its great historical victories (the 1917 Russian Revolution, the 1949 Chinese Revolution) to its respect for this golden rule. Its great historical defeats (for example, that of the German social-democracy before and after 1914, the defeats of the Central European revolutions in the 1920s, and so on) occurred because it forgot it or disdained it.[48]

It is clear that, even if this golden rule is neglected, the popular masses can still, in such-and-such a critical conjuncture, 'mobilize', or even launch a very powerful movement, capable, if the situation happens to be 'revolutionary', of taking state power by assault. However, if, by accident or for any other reason, the party has not forged *profound ties* with those masses through a very long practice of implanting the political class struggle in the economic class struggle, the movement of the popular masses can either fail to lead to the seizure of state power or, even if it should have the good fortune to take state power, risks *not being able to keep it*.

For one has to go that far to give concrete content to the Marxist-Leninist thesis that it is the masses who make history. Since the history that interests us is the history of the Revolution, the masses must be mobilized and led towards truly revolutionary objectives. Only the party of the vanguard of the proletariat can do that. But the party can assume this leadership role (which presupposes that it explains things to the

---

many different actions undertaken by the working class in this period; think of Henri Martin, and so on. [TN: Martin, a communist sailor, was imprisoned for treason in 1950 for agitating inside the armed forces against the French colonial war in Indochina. He was freed in 1953 after a broad PCF-led campaign.]

47   At the point we have reached in this regard, it is clear that we should objectively take stock of the current 'blockage' produced on both sides by the split, and of its effects, and that we should take action in the field of these effects itself, without *underestimating* the split (that would be a serious political error that would directly serve imperialism), in order to conduct a *real* struggle *against* imperialism, and thus *for* the international revolution.

48   Obviously, *other* causes were also to blame for these failures. I shall ignore them here.

masses, and mobilize and organize them) only if it *has forged deep ties with them*, if it is at one with them. *Nothing but the deep, irreversible implantation of the political class struggle in the economic class struggle*, and thus in 'bread-and-butter trade union demands', can guarantee that it will be able to establish such ties.

This classical thesis restores the trade union struggle as such, which is determinant in the last instance, to its true place. It does so at a time when some consider that struggle to be secondary, if not contemptible, while others would like to transform it into a pure and simple political struggle. I appeal to the activists of good will to whom I am alluding here (there are many among those whom people call 'far leftists'[49] without making the necessary distinctions, especially among lycée and college students as well as young intellectual workers) to think about the *content* of this classical thesis, about the fact that this classical thesis is the tried and tested *result* of a century of class struggle by the workers' movement across the globe, and about the fact that this result has cost hundreds of thousands of anonymous worker militants an *unheard of* price, paid in dedication, sacrifice and blood. Simply, they remained at their posts in a combat infinitely harsher, riskier and more dangerous than the one facing the younger generations of today, thanks to the sometimes tragic sacrifices of their elders, whether they perished or survived.

VII THERE IS ONE REPRESSIVE STATE APPARATUS, BUT THERE ARE *SEVERAL* IDEOLOGICAL STATE APPARATUSES

Let us briefly return to our thesis about the distinction between the Repressive State Apparatus and the Ideological State Apparatuses.

For there is another difference (apart from the one between repression and ideologization) between the Repressive State Apparatus and the Ideological State Apparatuses. It is that while there is *one* Repressive State Apparatus, there are *several* Ideological State Apparatuses. This difference is important.

The state apparatus that we are identifying as repressive presents itself as an *organic whole*; more precisely, as a *centralized* corps that is *consciously and directly led* from a *single centre*. It must be borne in mind that this repressive apparatus, a 'specialized component' of which we singled out in discussing the physical (and other) sanctions imposed by the law, has a

---

49 [TN: *Gauchistes*, which had heavily negative connotations in PCF circles, designated a broad range of radical leftists at the time Althusser wrote, including Trotskyists, Luxemburgists, anarchists, Guevarists, and Maoists, some of whom he himself had inspired.]

centralized organic dispositive that is particularly conspicuous in France, whose chief of state has announced that he is not interested in 'inaugurating chrysanthemums'. At the head of the Repressive State Apparatus, then, is *the real chief of state*. Under his direct orders is *the government*[50] (as well as the farce of the current parliament: the appearances of a 'parliamentary' regime must be maintained, since 'democrats' have attached importance to it since 1789). Under his or their orders are the administration, the army, the police, the judiciary (the story goes that it is independent), the courts, the prisons, and so on.

When it comes to repression, of course, there is a division of labour among these different 'corps', which are merely *members*,[51] and repression is exercised in different or even very different forms by them. A civil servant in the central administration does not, even if he is a tax inspector, use the same 'methods' as a policeman; a customs officer does not use the same methods as an army officer, and so on.

But the fact remains that all of these members belong *to one and the same corps* of repressive agents under the orders of those who hold state power, the political representatives of the dominant class, who implement its *class politics*. (In France today, this dominant class is the imperialist French bourgeoisie.) We may therefore say that the Repressive State Apparatus comprises an organic whole, because it is organized/unified under a single leadership: that of the political representatives of the class in power.

It is a different story with the *Ideological* State Apparatuses. They exist in the plural and have a relatively independent material existence.

The Church is, despite the schools it still has, its chaplains in the public schools, and its ideological representatives in the state school system, an Ideological State Apparatus that can no longer, in 1969, be conflated with the school. That is the result of a ferocious class struggle which opposed, throughout the nineteenth century, the landed aristocracy allied with the Church on the one hand, and, on the other, the capitalist bourgeoisie that emerged from the French Revolution in alliance with the petty bourgeoisie. It was a very dearly purchased result that, today, is established fact.

Similarly, although the Church has its publishing houses and 'shows'

---

50 The government *really* belongs to the Repressive State Apparatus, even if it *formally* belongs, in *parliamentary democracy*, to the political Ideological State Apparatus, since it is 'elected' by the parliament. But its 'formal' inclusion in the political Ideological State Apparatus can fool only those who, lapsing into 'parliamentary cretinism', believe that an 'elected' government stands *above* state power and the state apparatuses.

51 [TN: The French word *corps* means, among other things, (human) body.]

(masses, processions, pilgrimages, and so on), as well as ideological representatives in the other apparatuses, it cannot be identified with the Ideological State Apparatuses comprising publishing, the cultural apparatus (spectacles of all kinds), or the news and information apparatus.

The same may be said of all the Ideological State Apparatuses, the political apparatus included. Despite the inevitable overlaps between them, they are objectively distinct, relatively autonomous, and do not form an organized, centralized corps with a single, conscious leadership. For example, there is no longer a Ministry of Religion in France, and De Gaulle, in spite of 'His Highness', does not command Archbishop Marty's Ideological State Apparatus, his complicity with Marty notwithstanding, the way he commands Edgar Faure's Ideological State Apparatus or the news and information Ideological State Apparatus, the most effective part of which, the RTF, has been presided over by Mr d'Ormesson, 'in complete independence and objectivity'.[52]

If these Ideological State Apparatuses are distinct, relatively autonomous, more or less malleable, and under more or less direct state control (even when they are state institutions, like the schools or radio, they are not all equally malleable, at least not in certain periods; they even 'grate' on certain occasions, terribly), what makes them Ideological *State Apparatuses*? Above all, *the ideology that is realized in them*. This ideology, being the dominant ideology, *is that of the dominant class, the class that holds state power* and directly and imperiously commands the Repressive State Apparatus.

At this point, we need to return to Marx's and Lenin's theses on the state and the ideology of the dominant class. We can now better evaluate their import and scope.

To put things in a nutshell:

1) Marx's and Lenin's theory holds that the state is the 'concentrate' and the 'machine' of the dominant class's domination. If we take Marx and Lenin at their word, this means that *the superstructure is centred, concentred, on the state, as a class superstructure*. This thesis thus allows us to rectify the useful, but overly cut-and-dry, distinctions of the 'topography' on

---

52 [TN: The French equivalent of 'highness' is *hauteur*, which also means haughtiness and tallness; De Gaulle was both haughty and tall. François Marty became archbishop of Paris in March 1968 and was made a cardinal on 28 April 1969. De Gaulle appointed Edgar Faure Minister of Education after the May events. Wladimir d'Ormesson was named head of French state radio and television (RTF) after it was reorganized as the Office de la Radiodiffusion et de la Télévision Française (ORTF) in 1964, for the ostensible purpose of giving it greater autonomy.]

which we insisted only recently, especially those between the legal–political and ideological superstructures. That distinction remains correct, but on condition that we stipulate, from now on, that the difference between these superstructures exists and *exists only under the domination of an absolutely determinant unity: that of the state*, of *state power* and *the state apparatuses*, repressive and ideological.

2) Marx's and Lenin's theory holds, consequently, that the dominant ideology, that of the dominant class, is also, despite its internal variations and the differences between the apparatuses in which it exists, arrayed around, and concentrated in the form of, the ideology of the dominant class, the class holding state power. Hence it is concentrated in the form of an *ideological unity* which, despite the contradictions internal to this unity, can and should be called *the ideology of the class state* in question. Thus what makes for the unity of the various Ideological State Apparatuses is the fact that they realize, each in its own domain and each in its proper modality, an ideology that, notwithstanding its differences or even its internal contradictions, is the *State Ideology*.

Definition: the state is therefore, under the power of the state, 1) the Repressive State Apparatus, and 2) the Ideological State Apparatuses. The unity of the State Apparatus and the Ideological State Apparatuses is ensured by the class politics of those who hold state power, acting directly in the class struggle by means of the Repressive State Apparatus and indirectly by means of the realization of the State Ideology in the Ideological State Apparatuses.

What is the State Ideology? We will discuss it at greater length in Volume 2. Suffice it to say, for the moment, that the State Ideology brings together a certain number of major themes, borrowed from various ideological 'regions' (religious, legal, moral, political, and so on), in a system that *sums up* the essential 'values' which the domination of the class holding state power needs in order to make the exploited and the agents of exploitation and repression, as well as the agents of ideologization, 'go'; that which it needs, therefore, in order to ensure the reproduction of the relations of production. As far as the bourgeois state is concerned, the essential themes brought together in the State Ideology seem to me to be the following:

1) Nationalism: the theme of France, of France's World Role, of the Mission and Grandeur of France. France becomes, as need dictates, 'the Eldest Daughter of the Church';

2) Liberalism: the theme of free enterprise above all, and the theme of Freedom in general, of the Defence of Freedom in the world, of the Free World, and so on;

3) Economism: the theme of interest, not only the national interest (see above), but also the theme of the defence of the interests that . . . one and all have in the 'general progress of the sciences and technologies' and the national economy. Appendix: 'The Ideology of Work';[53]

4) Humanism, the obligatory counterpoint to the theme of Economic Interest; it forges the synthesis between Nationalism and France's Mission, Man's Freedom, and so on.

Every Ideological State Apparatus 'accommodates', in its fashion, some or all of these themes, their component parts and their resonances.

---

53   [EN: This projected appendix is not to be found in the manuscript.]

The Reproduction of the Relations of Production

Only here and only now can we at last answer our central question, which has been left in suspense for many pages: *how is the reproduction of the relations of production ensured?* In topographical terms (base, superstructure), we can say that *it is ensured by the superstructure*, by the legal-political superstructure and the ideological superstructure. However, since we have argued that it is imperative to go beyond this still descriptive terminology, we shall say: *it is ensured by the exercise of state power in the state apparatuses*, the Repressive State Apparatus on the one hand and the Ideological State Apparatuses on the other.

Let us also take what was said earlier into account. It can be assembled under the following three points:

1) All the state apparatuses function on both repression and ideology. The difference is that the Repressive State Apparatus functions in overwhelmingly preponderant fashion on repression, whereas the Ideological State Apparatuses function in overwhelmingly preponderant fashion on ideology – with all the requisite nuances in each case.

2) Whereas the Repressive State Apparatus constitutes an organized whole whose various components are centralized under a commanding unity – that of the class struggle politics applied by the political representatives of the dominant classes holding state power – the Ideological State Apparatuses are multiple, distinct, relatively autonomous, and prone to providing an objective field to contradictions which express, in forms that are as a rule limited, but in some cases extreme, the effects of the clashes between the capitalist class struggle and the proletarian class struggle, as well as their subordinate forms (for instance, the struggle between the bourgeoisie and the landed aristocracy in the first two-thirds of the nineteenth century, or the struggle between the big and the petty bourgeoisie, and so on).

3) Whereas the unity of the Repressive State Apparatus is ensured by the fact that it is organized in centralized, unified fashion under the

leadership of representatives of the classes in power who carry out those classes' class-struggle politics, the unity of the various Ideological State Apparatuses is ensured by the dominant ideology, that of the dominant class. To account for its effects, we have to call it the *State Ideology*.

I   A CERTAIN 'DIVISION OF LABOUR' IN THE REPRODUCTION OF THE RELATIONS OF PRODUCTION

If we agree to take these characteristics into account, we can represent the reproduction of the relations of production in the following way, along the lines of a kind of 'division of labour'.

The role of the Repressive State Apparatus, insofar as it is a repressive apparatus, consists essentially in guaranteeing *by force* (physical or not) the political conditions for the reproduction of the relations of production. The state apparatus not only has a very large part *in its own reproduction*;[1] it also, *and above all*, guarantees the general political conditions for the operation of the Ideological State Apparatuses by means of repression (from the most brutal physical force to simple administrative orders and prohibitions, open or tacit censorship, and so on).

For the Ideological State Apparatuses, by definition, ensure the reproduction, as such, of the relations of production, behind the 'shield' of the Repressive State Apparatus. It is here that the *State Ideology* comes massively into play, the ideology of the dominant class holding state power. It is by way of the dominant ideology, the State Ideology, that the (sometimes grating) 'harmony' between the Repressive State Apparatus and the Ideological State Apparatuses is ensured, as well as that among the different Ideological State Apparatuses.

We are thus led to envisage the following hypothesis, as a consequence, precisely, of the diversity of the Ideological State Apparatuses in their *single*, because *shared*, role of reproducing the relations of production.

We have listed a relatively large number of Ideological State Apparatuses in *contemporary capitalist* social formations: the religious apparatus, scholastic apparatus, familial apparatus, political apparatus, associative apparatus, news and information apparatus, publishing apparatus, 'cultural' apparatus (including sport), and so on. In contrast, in the

---

1   Just as there once existed hereditary monarchical dynasties, there exist, in the capitalist state, dynasties of politicians and dynasties of military men (consider the naval officers who are traditionally recruited, like the diplomatic corps, from the strata of the old aristocracy).

social formations dominated by the mode of production based on 'serf-dom' (commonly called feudal), we observe that, while there existed a single Repressive State Apparatus which, not only in the absolute monarchy, but, indeed, in the earliest known states of antiquity, was formally *very* similar to the one we know today, the number of Ideological State Apparatuses was smaller, and they were individualized differently.

For instance, we observe that the Church (the religious Ideological State Apparatus) combined a number of functions which have today devolved upon several *distinct* Ideological State Apparatuses that are new with respect to the past we are evoking here. Alongside the Church, there existed a *familial* Ideological State Apparatus, which played an incomparably bigger role than it does in capitalist social formations. The Church and family were not, despite appearances, the only Ideological State Apparatuses. There also existed a *political* Ideological State Apparatus (the Estates General, the *Parlement*, various political factions and Leagues, the ancestors of modern political parties, and the whole political system of the free communes and then the *villes*). There also existed a powerful '*proto-associative*' Ideological State Apparatus, if we may hazard that necessarily anachronistic expression: the powerful merchants' and bankers' guilds as well as journeymen's and other associations. Even publishing as well as news and information undeniably underwent development, as did entertainment; initially integral parts of the Church, they became more and more independent of it.

II THERE IS ONE DOMINANT IDEOLOGICAL STATE APPARATUS – TODAY, THE SCHOOL SYSTEM

In the pre-capitalist historical period that we are examining in very broad outline, there patently existed a dominant Ideological State Apparatus, *the Church*, which concentrated within itself not just religious, but also educational functions, and a very large part of the functions of information, 'culture' and publishing as well.[2] The *absolutely dominant* position of the *religious* Ideological State Apparatus explains why all ideological struggle from the sixteenth to the eighteenth century, beginning with the first shocks of the Reformation, was concentrated in anti-clerical, anti-religious struggle.

---

2 Over and above its other functions, if one may put it that way, for the Church was directly involved in feudal exploitation and possessed immense 'ecclesiastical fiefs'; thus it was an *economic* power.

The main objective and result of the French Revolution was not just to transfer state power from the feudal aristocracy to the mercantile capitalist bourgeoisie, destroy part of the old Repressive State Apparatus, and put a new one in its place (for example, the national popular army), but also to attack the number-one Ideological State Apparatus, *the Church*. Hence the civil constitution of the clergy, the confiscation of church property, and the creation of new Ideological State Apparatuses to replace the religious Ideological State Apparatus *in its dominant role*.

Naturally, things did not happen all by themselves. Witness the Concordat, the Restoration, and, throughout the nineteenth century, the long class struggle that the industrial bourgeoisie waged against the aristocracy to establish bourgeois hegemony over functions earlier fulfilled by the Church. We can say that the bourgeoisie relied on the new *political*, parliamentary-*democratic* Ideological State Apparatus, established in the first years of the Revolution and restored, after long, violent struggles, for a few months in 1848 and for decades after the fall of the Second Empire, in order to conduct its struggle against the Church and wrest its ideological functions from it – in a word, in order to ensure not only its political hegemony, but also its ideological hegemony, *essential for reproducing capitalist relations of production*.

That is why we believe we are justified in advancing the following thesis, with all the risks it involves. We think that the Ideological State Apparatus that has been elevated to the *dominant* position in mature capitalist formations, at the end of a violent political and ideological class struggle against the old Ideological State Apparatus, is the *scholastic* ideological apparatus.

This thesis may seem paradoxical, since it plainly *seems* to everyone – according, that is, to the ideological representation that the bourgeoisie was at pains to forge for both itself and the classes it exploited – that the Ideological State Apparatus dominant in capitalist social formations is not the school, but the *political* Ideological State Apparatus, that is, the parliamentary democratic regime, accompanied by universal suffrage and struggles between parties.

Yet history, even recent history, shows that the bourgeoisie has been and is still easily capable of accommodating highly variegated forms of its political Ideological State Apparatus, other than parliamentry democracy: the First and Second Empires, the constitutional monarchy based on the Charter (Louis XVIII and Charles X), parliamentary monarchy (Louis-Philippe), or presidential democracy (De Gaulle), to consider only France. Matters are even clearer in England. There, the Revolution was especially 'successful' from the bourgeois standpoint. For, in contrast to what happened in France, where the bourgeoisie – thanks, be it noted, to the petty aristocracy's stupidity – had to consent to be brought to power by peasant and plebeian '*journées révolutionnaires*', for which it had to pay dearly, the English bourgeoisie was able to strike, more or less adroitly, a 'compromise' with the aristocracy, 'sharing' possession of state power and the state apparatus with it for a very long time. (Peace to all men of good will in the *dominant classes*!) In Germany, things were even more striking. Here, the imperialist bourgeoisie made its sounding entrance onto the stage of history behind a *political* Ideological State Apparatus in which the Imperial Junkers (symbol: Bismarck), their army, and their police provided it with a shield and leading personnel, before it put itself in the hands of the very 'national', very 'socialist', but . . . not particularly 'democratic' political apparatus known as Nazism.

Thus we believe we have solid reasons for thinking that, behind the 'theatre' of the political struggles which the bourgeoisie has offered the popular masses as a spectacle, or imposed on them as an ordeal, what it has established as its number-one, that is, its *dominant*, Ideological State Apparatus is *the scholastic apparatus*, which has in fact replaced the previously dominant Ideological State Apparatus, the Church, in its functions. We may even say that the school-family dyad has replaced the Church-family dyad.

Why is the scholastic apparatus the dominant Ideological State Apparatus in capitalist social formations, and how does it function? We shall explain that in a forthcoming book.[3] For the moment, suffice it to say that:

1) *All* Ideological State Apparatuses without exception contribute to the same end: the reproduction of the relations of production, that is, of capitalist relations of *exploitation*.

2) *Each* of them contributes to this single end in its own way. The political apparatus does so by subjecting individuals to the political State Ideology: indirect (parliamentary) or direct (plebiscitary or fascist) 'democratic' ideology. The news and information apparatus does so by stuffing every 'citizen' with his daily doses of nationalism, chauvinism, liberalism, moralism, and so on, by means of the press, radio and television. The same goes for the cultural apparatus (the role of sport in

---

3 *Schools*, forthcoming in Autumn 1969 (Maspero). [EN: This project was not realized. See Etienne Balibar's preface to the present volume.] Let us, however, here and now point out the very big difference between the capitalist school system and the feudal Church: the former, unlike the feudal Church, is not an 'economic power' and takes no part in capitalist exploitation. To be sure, we cannot say as much, even with all the required nuances, about certain domains of scientific research.

fostering chauvinism is of the first importance), and so on. The religious apparatus does so by reminding us, in sermons, the grand ceremonies of birth, marriage and death, and so on, that man is only ashes unless he loves his neighbour enough to turn the other cheek to the neighbour who smites him on the first. The scholastic apparatus does so . . . we shall soon see in detail how. The familial apparatus . . . but let us leave it at that.

3) This concert is dominated by a single score, in which we hear a few 'false notes' (among others, those of the proletarians and their organizations, which are terribly discordant, and those of petty-bourgeois dissidents or revolutionaries as well): the score of the *State Ideology*, the ideology of the current dominant class, which knows very well how to integrate into its music the great themes of the humanism of the Great Ancestors, who wrought the miracle of Greece before Christianity, and, thereafter, the Grandeur of Rome, the Eternal City, as well as the themes of interest, particular and general, as is only proper. Nationalism, moralism and economism. Pétain said, more cynically: Work, Family, Fatherland.

4) In this concert, nevertheless, one Ideological State Apparatus well and truly plays the dominant role, although no one, or almost no one, lends an ear to its music: it is so hard to hear! This is the *school*.

From nursery school on, the school takes children from all social classes and, from nursery school on and *for years* thereafter, the years when children are most 'vulnerable', *stuck fast* as they are between the scholastic and familial Ideological State Apparatuses, pumps them full, with old methods and new, of certain kinds of 'know-how' (French, arithmetic, natural history, science, literature) *packaged* in the dominant ideology, or, simply, of *the dominant ideology in the pure state* (ethics, civics, philosophy). Somewhere around the age of fourteen, an enormous mass of children are dumped 'into production', to become workers or small peasants. Another segment of the school-age population sticks with it and somehow manages to go a bit further, only to fall by the wayside and find jobs as lower-level supervisory personnel or junior managers, white-collar workers, minor or middle-level civil servants, and petty bourgeois of all kinds. A last group makes it to the summit, either to sink into intellectual underemployment or semi-unemployment or to fill the posts of agents of exploitation or agents of repression, professional ideologues (priests of all kinds, most of whom are convinced 'secularists'), and also agents of scientific practice.

Every mass that falls by the way is by and large, a few errors and miscarriages aside, practically provided with the ideology that suits the role it is to play in class society: the role of the exploited (with a highly 'developed' 'professional', 'moral', 'civic', 'national' and apolitical 'consciousness/conscience'); the role of agent of exploitation (knowing how to order workers around and talk to them), agent of repression (knowing how to issue orders and exact obedience 'without discussion', or how to put the demagogy of political leaders' rhetoric to work), or professional ideologue (knowing how to treat consciousness/conscience with the appropriate respect, that is, the appropriate contempt, threats and demagogy, couched in the accents of Morality, Virtue, 'Transcendence', the Nation, France's World Role, and so on).

Of course, many of these contrasting virtues (modesty, resignation and submissiveness on the one hand, and cynicism, contempt, confidence, self-importance and arrogance, even smooth talk and suavity on the other) are also acquired in families, in the Church, in the army, from good books, from films, and even in the stadiums. No other Ideological State Apparatus, however, has a *captive* audience *of all the children of the capitalist social formation* at its beck and call (and – this is the least it can do – at no cost to them) *for as many years* as the schools do, eight hours a day, six days out of seven.

The relations of production of a capitalist social formation, that is, the relations of exploited to exploiters and exploiters to exploited, are primarily reproduced in this process of acquiring what comes down, in the end, to a handful of limited types of know-how, accompanied by massive inculcation of the ideology of the dominant class. I here anticipate demonstrations that we shall soon be providing when I say that the mechanisms that produce this result, vital for the capitalist regime, are of course covered up and concealed by *a universally reigning ideology of the school*, since it is one of the essential forms of the dominant bourgeois ideology: an ideology which depicts the school as a neutral environment free of ideology (because it is . . . not religious) where teachers respectful of the 'conscience' and 'freedom' of the children entrusted to them (in complete confidence) by their 'parents' (who are free in their turn, that is, are the *owners* of their children) set them on the path to adult freedom, morality and responsibility by their own example, and provide them access to learning, literature, and the well-known 'emancipatory' virtues of literary or scientific humanism.

I beg the pardon of those teachers who, in impossible or appalling conditions, are striving to turn the scientific and political weapons that they manage to find in the history and knowledge that they 'teach' back against the ideology and the system and practices in which they are trapped. They are heroes of a kind. But they are very rare. How many others (*the immense majority!*) do not even begin to suspect the 'work' that the system (which overwhelms and crushes them) forces them to do, or, worse, put their whole heart and all their ingenuity into performing it with extreme conscientiousness (the celebrated new methods!): in, say, the 'pilot' classes of nursery school and elementary school, secondary school and trade school.

So little do they suspect it that they are helping, by their very devotion, to sustain and cultivate this ideological representation of the school, which makes the school today as 'natural' and useful-indispensable or even beneficial for our contemporaries as the Church was 'natural', indispensable and generous for our ancestors of a few centuries ago. The fact is that *the Church has today been replaced by the school*: it has succeeded it and occupies its *dominant* sector, even if there are certain limitations on that sector (because the school system is carefully flanked by the Church, which is not mandatory, and by the army, which is mandatory and . . . free, like school). It is true that the school can count on help from the family, despite the 'snags' that are troubling the family's previous functioning (ever since the *Manifesto* announced its disintegration) as an Ideological State Apparatus. That functioning was once sure; it no longer is. Since May, bourgeois families of the highest rank themselves know something about that – something irreversible that is shaking them up, and, often, even has them 'trembling'.

10

The Reproduction of the Relations of Production and Revolution

There follow just a few words on a vast subject. I beg the reader's pardon for their presumptuousness and, at the same time, their extremely schematic character.[1]

I SUMMARY

So far we have seen, in very broad outline, what a mode of production is. And we have understood that we had to rise to the standpoint of *reproduction* in order to understand the existence and functioning of the *superstructure* (law-state-ideology), which is erected on the infrastructure or 'base' of a mode of production.

We have discovered, contrary to ideas that we once developed and repeated after a *certain* number of classic texts, that it is not enough to represent the *relationship* between the base on the one hand and the legal-political superstructure and ideological superstructure on the other by means of the spatial metaphor of the *topography* of an *edifice*, despite the very great services, indispensable in some cases, that this topographical representation in 'levels' or 'instances' can render. We have come to the conclusion that we have to rise to the standpoint of the reproduction of the conditions of production in order to see what the 'function' and 'functioning' of the superstructure are. For while mere observation of the mechanisms of the economic base (we are here discussing the capitalist mode of production alone) enables us to account for the reproduction of the conditions of the productive forces,

---

1 Be it recalled that I continue to speak from the standpoint of reproduction in general, leaving out of account the fact that, in a capitalist regime, reproduction is always reproduction *on an extended scale*. The latter point, which is crucial, will be discussed in Volume 2.

labour–power included, it by no means enables us to account for the *reproduction of the relations of production.*

We know that what characterizes a mode of production in the last instance is '*the relations of production and exchange specific to it*' (Marx). Since the relations of exchange are a function of the relations of production, a mode of production is ultimately characterized by the relations of production.

Hence we can advance the following very simple proposition: a mode of production *subsists only insofar* as the reproduction of the conditions of production is ensured. Among these conditions of production, the *reproduction of the relations of production* plays the determinant role.[2]

The superstructure ensures the conditions of this reproduction (by means of the Repressive State Apparatus) and this reproduction itself (by means of its Ideological State Apparatuses). It follows, as we saw, that the entire superstructure is grouped around, and centred on, *the state*, considered in its two aspects as a class force of repression and a class force of ideologization. It further follows that ideology, which we earlier tended to treat as an 'instance' clearly distinct from the legal–political, must itself be brought into relation with the state and conceived of, in the unity masking its complex diversity, as the *State Ideology*.

If this is right, the problem of the *duration* of a social formation dominated by a given mode of production (in the case before us, the capitalist mode of production) depends on the 'duration' of the superstructure that ensures the conditions of that reproduction as well as that reproduction itself – that is to say, the duration of the class state, considered as the unity of its repressive apparatus and ideological apparatuses.

II WHAT IS A REVOLUTION?

Given these conditions, it is no wonder that every *revolution* in the relations of production is either a consequence and confirmation of the disintegration of the state (which can be brought down by an 'accident' such as the Barbarian invasions – but I am here advancing a hypothesis

---

2   Given the limited scope of the present discussion, I here leave the reproduction of the productive forces aside. One cannot discount the possibility that certain social formations have disappeared in history as a result of 'accidents' – which have to be studied very closely, of course, since there is no such thing as an 'accident' properly speaking – that made reproduction impossible, even simple reproduction of the productive forces, or of this or that element determinant of the productive forces, at the time. This hypothesis might enable us to account for the disappearance of what the ideologues of history call 'civilizations'. We are indebted to Valéry for the insight that they were mortal . . . since they died.

that is at once very partial and, what is more, very precarious, if not doubtful) or is the effect of the *overthrow* of the existing state pursuant to a conquest of state power, that is, the confiscation of its apparatuses and their replacement. That is why political struggle inevitably revolves around the state: this is an altogether classic Marxist thesis, implying, where a capitalist social formation is concerned, a capitalist class struggle to maintain state power and reinforce the state apparatuses (among other ways, by reforming them), and a proletarian class struggle to take state power, destroy the state's bourgeois apparatuses, and replace them with proletarian apparatuses under the dictatorship of the proletariat.

In the strong sense, consequently, a social revolution consists in dispossessing the dominant class of state power – that is, of control over the state apparatuses that ensure the reproduction of the prevailing relations of production – and establishing new relations of production, the reproduction of which is ensured by the destruction of the old state apparatuses and the (long and difficult) construction of new ones. Examples of revolutions in the strong sense (social revolutions) are the 1789 bourgeois revolutions in France, the 1917 Russian socialist revolution, the 1949 Chinese socialist revolution, and so on.

But there are also revolutions *in the weak sense*. They do not affect the relations of production, that is, state power and the whole set of state apparatuses, but only the *political* Ideological State Apparatus. Examples of these 'revolutions' in the weak sense are the 1830 and 1848 revolutions in France. They consisted in 'revolutionizing' the political ideological state apparatus: very precisely, in replacing the constitutional monarchy of Charles X, based on the Charter, with the parliamentary monarchy of Louis-Philippe in 1830, and, in 1848, in replacing Louis-Philippe's parliamentary monarchy with a parliamentary republic. Thus they involved only modifications to the political Ideological State Apparatus, accompanied, of course, by modifications to other Ideological State Apparatuses, such as the schools. These 'revolutions' were obviously only the effect of the two stages in which the bourgeoisie's and petty bourgeoisie's class struggle rid itself of the landed aristocracy's political representatives at the head of the state. In sum, they represented a family class struggle between dominant classes.

In contrast, although the coup d'état of 2 December [1851] was also a 'revolution' of this kind, formally speaking, it has not been deemed worthy of the honourable title of 'revolution' because it was not the result of popular mass action, but the work of a few individuals conspiring to bring off a *coup de main*. Only Pétain, taking his cue from Mussolini, Hitler and Franco, had the shameless cynicism to confer the name national 'revolution' on the political promotion that France's military defeat at the hands of the Nazi armies netted him towards the end of his career. He thereby demonstrated the servility of an imitator, which should not be mistaken for a sense for ideas. In contrast, De Gaulle, who was both cultivated and prudent, had the political 'tact' not to call his 13 May 1958 coup d'état a 'revolution'. Yet, formally speaking, it was one, because, like Pétain's, it changed something of importance in the political Ideological State Apparatus, reducing the parliament to an echo chamber and universal suffrage to a plebiscitary role.

These are, however, intra-bourgeois affairs, since the 'personalization of power'[3] was never anything more than a simple variant of the impregnable (to date) state of the capitalist class: it answered to the needs of 1960s French imperialism. Let us therefore return to revolutions in the strong sense, those which transform the existing relations of production while destroying the state and its apparatuses.

It is easy to see that, if a mode of production lasts only as long as the system of state apparatuses that guarantees the conditions of reproduction (reproduction = duration) of its base, that is, its relations of production, one has to attack the system of the state apparatuses and seize state power to disrupt the conditions of the *reproduction* (= duration = existence) of a mode of production and establish new relations of production. They are established under the protection of a new state and new state apparatuses which ensure the reproduction (= duration = existence) of the new relations of production, in other words, the new mode of production. When it is a question of the socialist revolution, this new state passes into the hands of representatives of the proletariat and its allies, who hold state power, that is to say, control the state's apparatuses. This is the state of the dictatorship of the proletariat.

This schema is simple, clear, and convincing. But it is formalistic. For we know that the revolutionary conquest of the bourgeois state, its destruction, and its replacement by the state of the dictatorship of the proletariat are not the effect of a simple logical argument, or of simple exhaustion of the old system of the capitalist relations of production, but are, rather, the effect of a *mass class struggle*, which can only be a *long-term class war*, to employ Mao Zedong's accurate formula, an excellent summary of Marx's and Lenin's theses. A moment ago, we evoked the

---

3 [TN: De Gaulle was often charged, notably by communist critics, with having established a regime centred on his undemocratic or even proto-fascist exercise of 'personal power'].

absolute conditions which guarantee that this class struggle of the popular masses will culminate in victory, a lasting victory. Now I would like to add a few words on *one particular* condition of this class struggle.

III THE TWO OBJECTS OF THE REVOLUTIONARY CLASS STRUGGLE

This condition becomes intelligible only if we once again recall the distinction between the Repressive State Apparatus and the Ideological State Apparatuses; the difference in the way they function (the repressive apparatus functions primarily on violence, while the ideological apparatuses function primarily on ideology); and the distinction thanks to which there exists only *one* Repressive State Apparatus, but *several* Ideological State Apparatuses.

We may put forward a thesis in the light of these different distinctions. It can be presented in two points:

1) The hard core of the state is its *repressive apparatus*. It is endowed with a force and a power of resistance that are by definition meant to be 'fail proof'.

The core of this hard core is made up of paramilitary repressive corps (police, riot police, and so on) and the army (as well as the armies of the fraternal imperialist states that readily cross frontiers when they are 'called' to the rescue). This is the ultimate core, the 'last bastion', in that it comprises the dominant class's argument of last resort, the *ultima ratio* of pure violence.

It is also a 'core' in the sense that it comprises the *densest* element and is subject in its turn to iron *discipline* (discipline is 'what makes the armed forces strong')[4] and the most severe sort of internal *repression* (deserters and mutineers are *shot*). It is when this core itself is disabled, when it breaks down and disintegrates (as it did in Russia in 1917, under the impact of the terrible wartime suffering and the Russian defeats) that the state totters on the brink of the precipice, with no last resort available to it (apart from the fraternal states' armies: consider the intervention of the French, Czech and English armies, among others, in Russia in 1917–18).[5]

This innermost core can be sapped by another, purely internal weakness. When it is not a *professional* army (note that De Gaulle was in favour

---

4 [TN: This catchphrase comes from the French Armed Forces' *General Code of Discipline*, in force from 1933 to 1966.]

5 The armies of fraternal states, however, are not always reliable. Consider the 'Black Sea Mutineers' of the French fleet that intervened in 1918: André Marty, Charles Tillon and hundreds of others.

of a *professional* army, in opposition to the tradition of 1789, defended later by Jaurès), it is made up of *conscripts*, that is, 'privates' of popular extraction who, like the 'Brave Soldiers of the 17th Regiment' facing the winegrowers in southern France before the First World War, may 'refuse to fire',[6] or 'refuse to march',[7] like the 'boys' in the army in Algeria, who 'nicked' their officers during the [1961] Generals' Putsch. All in all, however, the police, the riot police and the army are designed to weather the storm, and it is terribly difficult, if not impossible, to make a dent in them, except in the case of a lost war or a revolution.

2) The Ideological State Apparatuses, in contrast, are infinitely more vulnerable.

Since they realize the existence of the *State Ideology*, but piecemeal and in disorganized fashion (for each of them is relatively autonomous), and since they function on ideology, it is *in them* and their forms that much[8] of the protracted war represented by the class struggle takes place, the class struggle which can eventually succeed in overthrowing the dominant classes, that is to say, in wresting state power from their hands.

Everyone knows that the class struggle in the Repressive State Apparatus – the police, the army, and even the administration – is in 'ordinary' periods, if not a virtually lost cause, then, at least, a sharply limited undertaking. In the Ideological State Apparatuses, on the other hand, class struggle is possible, serious, and can go a very long way, for militants, and later the masses, acquire their political experience *in the Ideological State Apparatuses* before fighting the class struggle out 'to the finish'. It is no accident that Marx said that people become conscious of their interests and fight out their class struggle *in ideology*. We have, so far, only formulated this intuition of genius by the founder of scientific socialism in somewhat more exact terms.

I would, precisely, like to make a few remarks on the class struggle in the Ideological State Apparatuses. However, lest they confuse the reader, we need to recall a few fundamental facts first.

---

6   [TN: 'The Brave Soldiers of the 17th Regiment' is part of the refrain of 'Glory to the 17th Regiment', a song celebrating mutineers who refused to fire on striking winegrowers in south-western France in 1907.

7   [TN: The French equivalent of 'march', *marcher*, is the same word that is used in the phrase 'ideology makes subjects go [*marcher*] all by themselves'. See Chapter 2, n. 27.

8   In Volume 2, we shall see that the *class struggle goes far beyond the Ideological State Apparatuses*. We must keep this classic thesis carefully in mind in order clearly to understand the *limits* of the class struggle in the Ideological State Apparatuses, our subject here.

IV RELATIONS OF CAPITALIST PRODUCTION ARE
RELATIONS OF CAPITALIST EXPLOITATION

We have already discussed the class struggle of workers' organizations in the political and associative Ideological State Apparatuses, upholding the classic thesis that the political class struggle should be deeply rooted in the *economic* class struggle, the struggle 'for bread-and-butter demands'. We talked about *enterprises* in this connection, capitalist enterprises in the case to hand.

Well then! Let us set out from what is going on in French firms in 1969 in order to make it clear how Marxist theory accounts for things in all their complexity, so that we can try to provide a *scientific* explanation of the matter.

The fact that 1969 France is a *capitalist* social formation means that *the capitalist mode of production* operates in it in dominant fashion, and therefore that *production* (which takes place *in* enterprises) is dominated and regulated by *capitalist relations of production*. These relations of *production* are, at the same time, relations of capitalist *exploitation*.

This is reflected *concretely*, empirically, in the fact that the buildings belonging to an enterprise (for instance, the factory), the material processed in the enterprise (which can consist of semi-finished goods), the machine tools, and so on, in short, the enterprise's *means of production*, belong to their capitalist *owner*, who can direct the enterprise's production himself or entrust that task to a salaried director.

This is reflected, at the same time (for it is quite simply the same thing, but regarded, now, from the proletarians' standpoint), in the fact that the enterprise 'hires' workers (and other staff who are not workers: typists, accountants, engineers, supervisory personnel, and so on) on a daily, weekly or, more rarely, monthly basis as *wage-workers*. Wage-workers are individuals who, since they do not possess means of production, cannot produce anything with 'their own means' (their own two hands) and, consequently, can only sell *the use of their two hands* to the owner of an enterprise which, precisely, houses means of production.

Once this basic situation, brought about by capitalist relations of *production*, has been well understood, we need to understand why these relations of production are simultaneously relations *of exploitation*.

They are relations of *production* because, if the 'free' workers were not 'put in relation' with the means of production, there would be no production at all. Unfortunately for us, or for them, the means of production do not work all by themselves; they (like God) need people, and not just any people: they need qualified people[9] (common labourers, professionals, workers with various levels of skills, supervisors, technicians, engineers, and so on, including the 'conductor of the orchestra', that is, of the organization of production, who can be the capitalist in person or his number-one 'manager').

But these relations of production are *simultaneously* relations *of exploitation* – of the exploitation *specific* to the capitalist mode of production. It takes the form of the extortion of surplus labour in the form of *surplus-value*.

Marx indicates that the relations of production are simultaneously capitalist relations of exploitation by saying that the process of the capitalist production of goods is simultaneously a process of 'production' of surplus-value.

Such is the material 'basis', that is, not only the material condition for the existence of the capitalist mode of production, but *its material existence tout court*. It is in the process of production itself that the process *of exploitation* takes place. There is no capitalism without this material basis *for exploitation*, this material basis for relations of production that are identical to relations of exploitation. One has to say this over and over again in a day and age in which certain dreamers are once again spouting the old anarchist refrain that reduces the capitalist mode of production to repression, or, still worse, to 'authority'!

I said the *material existence* tout court of the capitalist mode of production. However, when, in this analytical approach, we examine matters more closely, it appears that to say existence is to say duration, and therefore subsistence in time, and therefore reproduction of the conditions of production and, above all, reproduction of the relations of production. We know all this already, just as we know that the state apparatuses, both repressive and ideological, intervene at the level of the reproduction of the relations of production.

V CLASS STRUGGLE IN THE IDEOLOGICAL STATE APPARATUSES

We now come to the subject before us: *the nature of the forms of class struggle in the Ideological State Apparatuses*. We shall take seriously Marx's formula which has it that it is in ideology that people become conscious of the class struggle and fight it out.

Let us begin by noting that Marx says ideology, whereas we say Ideological State *Apparatuses*. This terminological difference will be

---

9   Non-qualification is a defined type of qualification.

problematic only for those who have a bourgeois–idealist conception of the nature of ideology (like the conception typical of the Enlightenment).

For, despite appearances, that is, despite ideological prejudices about ideology and ideas, ideology does not exist *in ideas*. Ideology can exist in the form of written discourses (books) or oral discourses (sermons, courses, speeches, and so on) that are supposed to be vehicles for 'ideas'. But, precisely, one's 'idea' of 'ideas' governs what occurs in these discourses. To anticipate demonstrations we will be making later, let us say that '*ideas*' by no means have, as the ideology of ideas tends to suggest, an *ideal, idea-dependent* [*idéal, idéelle*], or *spiritual* existence; they have a *material existence*. It would take too long to provide a general demonstration of that here. We can, however, verify it in the case of the Ideological State Apparatuses, if we are granted the following proposition, which is itself very general.

Ideology does not exist in the 'world of ideas' conceived as a 'spiritual world'. Ideology exists in institutions and the practices specific to them. We are even tempted to say, more precisely: ideology exists *in apparatuses* and *the practices specific to them*. This is the sense in which we said that Ideological State Apparatuses *realize*, in the material dispositives of each of these apparatuses and the practices specific to them, an ideology *external* to them, which we called the *primary* ideology and now designate by its name: the *State Ideology*, the unity of the ideological themes essential to the dominant class or classes.

Of course, these apparatuses and their practices take as their objects and objectives the *individuals* who occupy the posts of the social–technical division of labour in production and reproduction. Ideology therefore exists, by way of ideological apparatuses and their practices, precisely *in the practices of these individuals*. I say their *practices*: this includes both what are called their 'ideas' or 'opinions', including their 'spontaneous' 'ideas' about the practice (productive, scientific, ideological, political, and so on) that the division of labour assigns them, but also their 'customs' or 'habits', that is, their concrete comportment, whether 'conscious' or 'unconscious'.[10]

---

10   Certain eighteenth-century philosophers who had made considerable progress in the 'theory' of what we call ideology understood that there is a certain practical relationship between, in their terms, 'opinions' and 'customs'; they even glimpsed the fact that 'customs' are more important than 'opinions' because they resist opinions. They even saw that 'laws' are often powerless to affect 'customs' when they are not 'in harmony with them'. One had to be a right-wing dissident (Montesquieu) or a left-wing dissident (Rousseau) to perceive these realities.

It is because the dominant class's ideology thus attains individuals themselves in their most inward 'consciousness' [*conscience*] and their most private or public 'conduct' that Ideological State Apparatuses can ensure the *reproduction of the relations of production* down to the most 'secret' levels of individual consciousness/conscience (professional, moral, paternal, maternal, religious, political, philosophical, and so on and so forth). We shall see, in the next chapter, by virtue of what general mechanism it does so.

Of course, since Ideological State Apparatuses are the realization of the *dominant* ideology (the dominant class's ideology, on which the unity of the state confers the unity of the State Ideology), all talk of dominant ideology automatically implies that there also exists something that likewise involves ideology, but is *dominated*, and thus involves the *dominated* classes. Hence we suspect that ideology and, therefore, the Ideological State Apparatuses in which it exists, bring *social classes* 'on stage' ['*mettent en scène*' *des classes sociales*]: the dominant class and the dominated class (and also what we shall provisionally call the 'middle classes'). These are, in the capitalist mode of production, the class of capitalists (and its allies) and the class of proletarians (and its allies).

Hence, we conclude that the *class struggle unfolds in the forms of the Ideological State Apparatuses*, although it goes far beyond those forms.

VI CLASS STRUGGLE AROUND AND IN THE DOMINANT IDEOLOGICAL STATE APPARATUS

Everyone knows that the class struggle unfolds in the *political* Ideological State Apparatus (struggle between political parties, and so on). Everyone? No. For only a minority of the population realizes that what everyone calls 'politics' is in fact the form that *the class struggle* takes in the political system, which we call, in our terminology, the political Ideological State Apparatus.

On the other hand, only the best-trained militants are aware that the class struggle simultaneously unfolds in the associative Ideological State Apparatus, in the form of the *economic* class struggle. (The same remark applies here, too: how many people know that the 'struggle for bread-and-butter demands' is the economic form of the class struggle? How many people know that employers' associations such as the National Confederation of French Employers, for their part, wage their *capitalist* class struggle in its economic form?)

I am afraid that I will surprise some readers when I tell them that the class struggle also unfolds in all the other Ideological State Apparatuses;

for instance, the schools, the Church, news and information, publishing, entertainment, and . . . the family itself. Of course, it does so in forms specific to each of these ideological apparatuses.

Moreover, because we have found reason to affirm that, in capitalist social formations, the scholastic Ideological State Apparatus, hence the school system, or, more precisely, the *dyad school-family*, is *dominant*, I do not think there is any need for a long demonstration to make our contemporaries see that the class struggle unfolds there *as well*. The May 1968 events and all the ensuing events took it upon themselves to provide empirical verification of our thesis. Or, rather, these events, in addition to the *radical novelty* that they introduced into this class struggle, whose existence the vast majority of people had never so much as suspected, *showed* that the class struggle had *always existed*, naturally in specific forms, in Ideological State Apparatuses such as the schools, family, Church, and so on. The sole difference is that the balance of power in this class struggle was spectacularly reversed in May, and that this revealed or, at least, sowed the suspicion that the class struggle waged in the school-family dyad and even the Church had been, overwhelmingly, the class struggle of the bourgeois class's 'representatives': the elementary school teacher, flanked by school inspector, father, priest, and so on.

To convince oneself of this, it is enough to read the newspapers. The muscular 'raids' that groups from the Association of Parents of Schoolchildren have staged on the schools in 'support of' outraged reactionary teachers and principals with their backs to the wall well and truly show that all these worthies are seeking *vengeance* for the secondary school students' – their own children's – 'scandalous' revolt. This thirst for vengeance and this revolt clearly show what is what: before secondary-school and college students' ideological revolt, the class struggle of the bourgeoisie's representatives or agents *in the scholastic and familial apparatuses enjoyed an overwhelming advantage* – so overwhelming that no one so much as suspected that it was a question, in the silence and the 'peaceful' order of the *lycées* and universities,[11] of a form – specific, to be sure, but a form – of the class struggle.

I hasten to reassure parents, secondary-school teachers and, soon, elementary school teachers, especially if they are militant advocates of the separation of Church and state. They are not the only ones to have experienced the class struggle, out in the open at last, in their respective apparatuses. The same phenomena are occurring in the Church, not only in the form of 'scandalous' 'incidents' between congregation and clergy,

---

11   And, I shall take the risk of adding, in families.

or some members of the lower clergy and the high clergy, or even some prelates (above all in Latin America) and the Vatican, even after Vatican II, but also (oh horrors!) *in the seminaries themselves*, over which the political leaders of the Church (who have long experience in public relations . . .) have cast the veil of ecclesiastical discretion, as befits everything bearing on the sacraments and what is holy. People are raising 'holy hell' in the seminaries, and the effects are *irreversible* here, too.

However that may be, we may say that when the balance of power in the class struggle is reversed *in the number-one Ideological State Apparatus* (or, at least, in one part of it, the least dangerous for the bourgeoisie – for elementary schools, the essential component of the scholastic apparatus because these schools furnish the workers, have not yet been infected by the revolt), the apparatus charged, above all others, with reproducing the relations of production – above all others because it is the *dominant* apparatus – the least one can say is that this is *a sign of the times*.

What is it a sign of? It is a sign, as Lenin used to put it, that the revolution is *on the agenda*. This does not mean – the nuance is crucial – that the *situation is revolutionary* (we are still a long way from that).

VII WHY DOES THE 'IDEOLOGICAL' CLASS STRUGGLE 'PRECEDE' THE OTHERS?

Let us now take some distance from events that are still too recent to allow us truly to assess them. Let us take our distance from them in order to make the following observation.

It is no accident that all the major social revolutions which we know at all well and in sufficient detail – the 1789 French Revolution, the 1917 Russian Revolution, and the 1949 Chinese Revolution – were preceded by *a long class struggle* that unfolded not only *around* the Ideological State Apparatuses in place, but also *in* these ideological apparatuses. This class struggle was at once ideological, economic and political, to employ distinctions that are classic in the masters of Marxism. It is enough to consider the eighteenth century in France, the nineteenth century in Russia, or the half-century that preceded the 1949 Chinese Revolution.

Before the 1789 and 1917 revolutions, we observe extremely violent struggles in the dominant Ideological State Apparatuses: especially around the Church and even in the Church, then in and around the political apparatus, and, later, in publishing and news and information. All these struggles mesh, criss-cross, sustain one another, and confusedly target a *final goal* unknown to most of the combatants: the destruction of the apparatuses that ensure the reproduction of the prevailing relations of production for the purpose of establishing new state apparatuses and, under their protection, new relations of production whose reproduction will be ensured by the new [ideological] state apparatuses.

The economic struggle always remains in the shadows: that is its destiny, for it is the most important class struggle. The political struggle eventually rages out in the open, regrouping all the forces in order to lead them in the final battle, the battle for state power: that is its destiny, for that is its function. The ideological (the so-called ideological) struggle, that is, the class struggle in the news and information apparatus and the publishing apparatus (the struggle for freedom of thought, expression, the press, and the dissemination of progressive and revolutionary ideas) generally *takes place in advance* of the open forms of political struggle; *indeed, it takes place very far in advance of them.*

Suffice it to consider the history of the centuries that preceded the French Revolution, bearing in mind that the bourgeois class struggle, which was merely progressive before becoming pre-revolutionary, took its meaning, at the time (as always) only as a function of the struggle of the dominant class in the same domains. Consider the incredible violence of this 'ideological' class struggle waged by the feudal class and its state apparatuses, first and foremost the Church; its path is littered not just with bans and recantations, but also with torture and burnings at the stake. Galileo and Giordano Bruno, to cite just those two names, while leaving aside the untold multitudes massacred during the Wars of Religion (intense class struggles waged in the religious Ideological State Apparatus, pitting heretics against the orthodox); the throngs of the 'possessed', of 'witches', of 'madmen' condemned to torture or the Great Confinement of which Michel Foucault was the first person in France to have the courage to give us an idea.[12] Consider the universal outcast that Spinoza was before his death, and for three centuries thereafter (cast out of his Church and out of philosophy, a demon to burn or bury alive: since they could not burn him, they buried him).

We have to bear in mind this terrible past of the pre-revolutionary bourgeoisie's ideological class struggle if we are to put the undoubtedly

---

12   *Histoire de la Folie*, [Paris], Plon, [1961]. We have so far ignored what can, we think, justifiably be called, in our capitalist social formations, the 'medical' Ideological State Apparatus. It deserves a study in its own right. Foucault's remarkable book, spurned by our medical authorities (unfortunately for them, they cannot burn it), provides us with the genealogy of important elements of this apparatus. For the history of 'madness', which is the history of a repression, is, even tempered by Pinel's humanism and Delay's pharmacology, an ongoing history. It goes very far beyond what many doctors find it convenient to call 'madness'.

glorious but infinitely less heroic eighteenth-century Enlightenment back in its proper place. This was a period in which, with the help of books that were signed by their authors or were anonymous, were printed in France or abroad, and were disseminated under the counter or with the complicity of an 'enlightened' minister, one could wage an open struggle in books and gazettes, as well as in theatres and operas, against the Church and despotism, even if that despotism was 'enlightened' in its turn. (The despotism of the absolute monarchy had many adversaries on the right – à la Montesquieu – and very few on the left – à la Meslier or Rousseau. It also had a number of partisans, some sincere, others tactical: Diderot.)

Let us, however, leave these historical examples at that and return to our thesis. It allows us, perhaps, if not to understand, then at least to 'situate', albeit in an altogether provisional form (I am more keenly aware of this than anybody), *phenomena* that are the '*antecedents*' of any social revolution.

We may say that these phenomena include all forms of the class struggle conducted in the Ideological State Apparatuses, in line with the modalities specific to each of these apparatuses. We may say that, of all these Ideological State Apparatuses, it is the Ideological State Apparatus dominant in the reproduction of the relations of production which is (or under normal circumstances should be) the number-one object of the class struggle. That explains why the long class struggle of several centuries' duration was centred on the Church and the positions it defended, a struggle marked by mass slaughters and unimaginable measures of violence, terror, repression, extortion and intimidation – the protracted war that paved the way for the final 1789–93 assault, a *political* assault, on the feudal state and its apparatuses.

In attacking the apparatuses specialized in reproducing the relations of production, the bourgeoisie sapped, from within, the most vulnerable part (not only because it was diversified, but also because it was in direct, daily contact with the popular masses) of the state apparatuses. Once the Ideological State Apparatuses had been undermined, it remained only to take the last bastion of the state by force: state power, dug in behind the last battalions of the royal guard.

It seems to me that one could undertake an analysis of the same sort for both the 1917 Revolution, after making due allowance for the differences, and the 1949 Chinese Revolution, with considerable differences (there was no church in China, at least not in the Western sense of the word).

If our interpretation is on the mark, we have to rise *to the standpoint of reproduction* not only in order to grasp the function and functioning of the superstructure, but also so as to have the concepts that will allow us to understand the concrete history of revolutions a little better (so that we can at last found the science of their history, which is at present still much more like chronicle than science): the history of revolutions that have already been made and of others that must still be made. This will also enable us to understand a little better the conditions that must be realized if we are to establish, under the dictatorship of the proletariat, the Ideological State Apparatuses required *concretely to prepare the transition* to socialism – that is, the gradual disappearance of the state and all its apparatuses – instead of floundering around in 'contradictions' that are more or less successfully camouflaged under 'policed' designations, of which contemporary history offers us all too many examples.

VIII   A WORD OF CAUTION: PRIMACY OF THE BASE

One last remark before we conclude this chapter, a remark that is also a warning. We have in no sense just put forward a short treatise on the practice of revolution that might be cast in the form of the following rules:

1) begin by unleashing the class struggle in the Ideological State Apparatuses, while seeing to it that the 'spearhead' of the struggle is directed against the dominant Ideological State Apparatus (today the school);

2) combine all forms of the class struggle in all Ideological State Apparatuses in order to undermine them to the point of making their function of reproducing the relations of production impossible, and then,

3) with all the popular forces marshalled under the leadership of the revolutionary political party, the party of the revolutionary class, launch an assault on state power by destroying its ultimate apparatus, its repressive apparatus (police, riot police and so on, and the army).

That would be absurd, and infantile to boot, because voluntaristic, adventuristic and idealist. Events cannot be commanded that way. And even if, by chance, they could be, this is the place to recall that everything we have just described in discussing the class struggle in the Ideological State Apparatuses concerns *the superstructure alone*, which is determined and secondary, not determinant in the last instance. The *base is determinant in the last instance.* What happens or what can happen in the superstructure thus depends in the last instance on what happens (or does not) *in the base, between the productive forces and the relations of production.* That is where the class struggle has its roots. Thus we can see that it infinitely exceeds the forms of the Ideological State Apparatuses in which it comes into view.

It is a fact that, as the phrase goes, the superstructure 'reacts back on' the base. This fact, however, is merely stated. We have tried to shed a little light on this 'reciprocal action', which is, fundamentally, not a reciprocal action at all, since the specific relation in which the superstructure stands to the base is that of *reproducing* the conditions of its functioning. It is doubtless in the light of this concept and of the effects of the class struggle that we should re-examine the cases flagged with the descriptive term 'reacts back on' or 'reciprocal action'.

This, however, does not at all provide us with the key to what happens *in the base itself*; very precisely, to *what happens* in the base (in the unity forces of production/relations of production) that is capable of fostering and then unleashing the class struggle, which, in the superstructure, begins by attacking the Ideological State Apparatuses, before proceeding to launch an assault on the Repressive State Apparatus, in order to culminate in the seizure of state power by the revolutionary class.

There are, fortunately, a number of indications in *Capital* and *The Development of Capitalism in Russia* about what happens in the base that is of decisive importance for unleashing the revolutionary class struggle in the superstructure, and for its victory. It must, however, be admitted that we are far from having worked out the theory of this process. It will be agreed that it is not with concepts as descriptive and tautological as the concepts of correspondence and non-correspondence between productive forces and relations of production that we can seriously hope to resolve the crux.

On this precise point, then, the question is in suspense. We will, one day, have to propose a solution to it.

11

Further Remarks on Law and Its Reality, the Legal Ideological State Apparatus

This chapter will contain just a few words. They are, however, indispensable if we are to assign 'law' (about which we have already spoken in the form of a 'descriptive theory' in Chapter 5) its proper place.

I REVIEW OF THE CHARACTERISTICS OF LAW

It seems that, in the tradition of Marxist theoretical research and scholarship – especially in the USSR from 1917 until the 'disappearance' of specialists, some of whom were quite remarkable, to judge by the questions it was their merit to pose – there was a great deal of discussion about whether law belongs to the superstructure or should, rather, 'be ranged alongside the relations of production'. This is an altogether pertinent question.

If the explanations just offered are well founded, we can propose a schematic but clear, precise answer to it, at least in principle – for this crucial question warrants lengthy theoretical analyses, which, if we were to go into detail, could only be conducted on the basis of empirical (concrete-historical) investigations and analyses.

In several passages of *Capital*, Marx shows that the nascent constitution of *new* relations of production, when they are gradually forming at the heart of the dominant relations of production, hence under them and, consequently, in opposition to them,[1] is the object of a protracted process that, for a long time, remains a *de facto* process, without being juridically recognized as lawful. There can be *partial* legal recognition of constituted practices, even at the heart of the dominant relations of production, which create a localized, narrowly circumscribed place for the new relations of production or exchange – on the absolute

---

1 Marx here refers to the emergence of embryonic forms of capitalist relations of production under feudalism.

condition that those new relations are limited and subordinated to the dominant relations of production. That is what happened under 'feudalism', when bourgeois law spread to certain limited sectors of the social formations in question (for instance, mercantile law, followed by the 'law of the royal manufactories' and, still later, of private manufacture). The promulgation of laws belonging to a new, partial system of law antagonistic to feudal law simply registered a *fait accompli*: that of the real, undeniable and irreversible consolidation of *new* relations of exchange and production in social formations dominated by very different relations of production.

Let us note, for historians – who have in fact often recognized this phenomenon – that the *renaissance of Roman Law* that began in the twelfth and thirteenth centuries (Marx points out the theoretical interest of this fact in the closing lines of the Introduction – unpublished in his lifetime – to *A Contribution to the Critique of Political Economy*, issued in 1859) had its roots in 'problems' that were at once economic (the development of commodity exchange) and political (the references of the Legists, that is, the ideologues of absolute monarchy, to Roman Political Law). This conjunction is a sign there is no mistaking, and one that surely tells us something about the relations between law and the state.

Without claiming to draw the slightest *direct* general conclusion from these historical facts underpinning a theoretical hypothesis of Marx's, we will content ourselves with making the following remarks.

We have seen the singular status of the bourgeois law at work in capitalist relations of production. It is clearly meant to regulate and sanction precise *economic* practices *above all* (in the guise of its different specialized codes, it regulates other practices as well): practices of exchange, that is, the purchase and sale of commodities, which presuppose – and depend on – property law and the corresponding legal categories (legal personhood, legal freedom, legal equality, legal obligation).

We have seen that bourgeois law tended and still tends, by virtue of an imperious necessity, towards formalism and universality, in spite of all the obstacles (increasingly frequent and insurmountable) that the process of formalization and universalization encounters.[2]

---

2 These obstacles have become greater since the late nineteenth century. They have to do with 1) monopolistic concentration and 2) the effects of the class struggle: the capitalist class struggle (massive violations of constitutional law) and the workers' class struggle (which has *imposed* various articles of a code that is a 'monstrosity' from the standpoint of the Civil Code: labour law).

We have seen that formalism and universality were only possible on condition that law is abstract, that is, actually abstracts from all content, and that this abstraction from all content is the *concrete* condition for the effectivity of the law with respect to its content, the very content from which it necessarily abstracts.

Finally, we have seen that the law is necessarily *repressive* and that it inscribes the sanction of law in law itself, in the form of a penal code. This showed us that law could function concretely [*réellement*] only on condition that there exists a concrete Repressive State Apparatus that *realizes* the sanctions formally inscribed in penal law and handed down as sentences by the judges of the courts to which the infractions are referred. At the same time, however, we clearly saw that, in the immense majority of cases, law is 'respected' by dint of the simple combined interplay of legal ideology plus a supplement of moral ideology – hence in the absence of any direct intervention by the detachment of the Repressive State Apparatus specialized in the practical (physical, violent) realization of the sanctions inscribed in the penal code and pronounced, 'in proper legal form', by the 'competent' courts.

From these observations, we may deduce a few propositions with which we can initiate the transition from a 'descriptive theory' of law to the threshold of a proper theory of law in capitalist social formations.

II CONCRETE REASONS FOR THE CHARACTERISTICS OF 'LAW'

1) Law *formally* regulates the interplay of the capitalist relations of production, since it defines proprietors, their property (assets), their right to 'use' and 'abuse' their property with complete freedom, and the reciprocal right to acquire property. As such, the concrete *object* of law is the capitalist relations of production[3] insofar as it expressly abstracts from them.

A word of caution: an abstraction is always, exactly like a negation, *determinate*. Bourgeois law does not abstract from just anything, but, rather, from the concrete determinate object whose play, or, in other words, functioning, it is 'charged' with regulating: *the capitalist relations of production*.

We must of course not succumb on this point to the ideological illusion that allows magistrates or jurists to act, with a clear 'moral' or 'professional' 'conscience', as servants of the capitalist state. This is the illusion that since all subjects are declared equal and free before the

---

3   Whenever we say 'relations of production', it should be understood that we mean 'the relations of production and the relations deriving from them', such as exchange relations, relations of consumption, political relations, and so on.

law, and since the law is the law of freedom and equality, magistrates and jurists are the servants of freedom and equality, not of the capitalist state.[4]

2) Bourgeois law is *universal*, for the simple reason that in the capitalist regime the interplay of the relations of production is the interplay of an effectively universal commercial [*marchand*] law, since, in the capitalist regime, all (adult, and so on) individuals are subjects of law and *everything is a commodity* [*marchandise*]. Everything: that is, not only the products of social necessity that are bought and sold, but also *the use of labour-power* (a fact without precedent in human history that founds law's pretension to universality on *the very* reality *from which* it abstracts). In Rome, slaves were commodities, but they were things, not subjects of law.

It is because capitalist relations of production force individuals who have been stripped of all means of production, who are, that is, 'free' of all means of production, 'freely' to sell the use of their labour-power as wage-workers, that proletarians are endowed, before bourgeois law, with the same legal attributes as capitalists. They are free, equal, free to alienate (to sell) their 'property' (in this case the use of their labour-power, since they 'own' nothing else), and also free to buy (to buy what they need to live in order to reproduce their existence as 'owners' of their labour-power).

The abstraction, formalism and universality of the law are therefore merely the official, legal *recognition* of the formal conditions regulating the interplay, that is, the functioning, of capitalist relations of production (and, by extension, of the sectors deriving from it: constitutional law, administrative law, military law – since it would seem that the law of privilege no longer exists . . . in this connection, one would do well to take a glance, if not at the Church, which has basically been subjected to the principles of bourgeois law, then at secular orders such as the Order of Physicians, the Order of Architects, and so on).[5]

3) But we have also seen that the law is necessarily bound up, first, with a specialized repressive apparatus that belongs to the Repressive

---

4   This does not mean, however, that one cannot invoke such-and-such an article of existing law as a *guarantee* against such-and-such an abuse, or that honest jurists cannot put their 'science' at the service of rightful claims [*au service du bon droit*], although they have always to act within the limits of the law.

5   [TN: 'Law of Privilege' is here intended in the sense of (feudal) *Privata Lex*. The Orders mentioned here have a kind of hybrid 'legal personality' in French law, which accords them the status of private entities charged with a public mission – the status of quasi-feudal corporations, in the view of some critics. See also Chapter 8, n. 21.]

State Apparatus, and, second, with bourgeois legal-moral ideology. On these grounds, law, which stands in a relation of determinate abstraction with the concrete reality known as the capitalist relations of production, stands at the same time in a relation of determinate abstraction (another, quite different modality of abstraction, to be honest) with another concrete reality known as the state apparatus, in two respects, repressive and ideological.

This reveals, we think, both another function of the state apparatus, and at the same time, perhaps, something that can help us define the status of the law.

It is clear that we can no longer consider 'law' (= the legal codes) in isolation, but must consider it as a component part of a system that includes law, the specialized repressive apparatus, and legal-moral ideology.

A specialized detachment of the Repressive State Apparatus (let us say, to simplify, the gendarmerie plus the police plus the courts plus the prisons, and so on) accordingly appears to us in a function that we need to determine more precisely, after everything we have said about the role of the state apparatuses in the *reproduction* of the relations of production. For this detachment plainly intervenes directly, not just in the *reproduction* of the relations of production, but *in the very functioning of those relations of production*, since it punishes and represses legal infractions of them.

Better, since the direct intervention of the specialized detachment of the Repressive State Apparatus is, albeit frequent and always visible, *exceptional* in the day-to-day functioning of capitalist relations of production, and since law regulates the 'regular' functioning of capitalist relations of production 'on legal-moral ideology' in the vast majority of cases, it can be seen that this legal-moral ideology intervenes not only in the reproduction of the relations of production, but directly and on a daily basis, indeed every second, *in the functioning of the relations of production*.

From this we can perhaps draw two conclusions without great risk.

III THE LEGAL IDEOLOGICAL STATE APPARATUS

1) We can see that, in a certain precise relationship, the reproduction of capitalist relations of production is ensured, *within* the functioning of capitalist relations of production *themselves*, and *simultaneously* with that functioning, both by the relatively exceptional intervention of the repressive state detachment specialized in legal sanctions, and by the constant,

ubiquitous intervention of the legal-moral ideology that 'represents' it in the 'consciousness/conscience' of the agents of production and exchange, that is, in their material comportment.

2) This emboldens us to make the following proposition. If we consider all that was just said; if we bear in mind the fact that the law 'functions' primarily on legal-moral ideology, reinforced by intermittent repressive interventions; if, finally, we recall that we have upheld the thesis that every state apparatus simultaneously combines functioning on repression with functioning on ideology, we have solid reasons for thinking that 'law' (or, rather, the *real system* that this term designates, while also masking it, since it abstracts from it: namely, the law codes plus legal-moral ideology plus the police plus the courts and their magistrates plus the prisons, and so on) ought to be thought of under the concept *Ideological State Apparatus*.

However, we must add this proviso: the law is the Ideological State Apparatus whose *specific* dominant function is, not to ensure the reproduction of capitalist relations of production, which it also helps ensure (in, however, subordinate fashion), but *directly to ensure the functioning of capitalist relations of production*.

If our thesis is on the mark, it brings out a reality of the very first importance: the *decisive* role played in capitalist social formations by *legal-moral* ideology, and its realization, the legal Ideological State Apparatus, which is the *specific apparatus articulating the superstructure upon and within the base*.

Just as we earlier said that, in capitalist social formations, the scholastic Ideological State Apparatus played the dominant role in the reproduction of the relations of production, so we may now advance the thesis that, in the domain of what we shall provisionally call the *practical ideologies*, legal-moral ideology plays the *dominant* role. We say legal-moral ideology, but we know that, in this dyad, when it is a question of the operation of law, *legal* ideology constitutes what is essential, since moral ideology figures only as a complement, indispensable, to be sure, yet still just a complement.

We need to bear these last propositions in mind, including the sort of connection that is beginning to emerge between these two instances of dominance, each in its 'sphere' and role: that of the scholastic Ideological State Apparatus and that of legal-moral ideology. We will need these indications when we go back to our starting point, still in abeyance: the question of the nature of philosophy.

Now that we believe we have succeeded in defining 'law' as an Ideological State Apparatus that fulfils an absolutely specific function in capitalist social formations – now that we have thus answered our question as to the status of 'law' by showing that it belongs, not to the relations of production whose functioning it regulates, but to the state apparatus – we can and must say a few words about ideology in general.

12

On Ideology

What is *ideology*? To begin with: why this term?

I MARX AND THE TERM 'IDEOLOGY'

As is well known, the term 'ideology' was coined by Destutt de Tracy, Cabanis, and their circle. Following a classic tradition in the philosophy of the Enlightenment, in which the notion of genesis holds a central place, they meant by it the theory (-logy) of the genesis of ideas (ideo-). Hence 'ideology'. When Napoleon uttered his famous phrase: 'the Ideologues are no use', he had them and only them in mind – not, obviously, himself, the number-one ideologue (ideologue in the Marxist sense) of the bourgeois social formation that had been 'saved' from the Terror, who knew (or did not know: no matter, because he practiced it) that one cannot do without ideology and ideologues. This held first and foremost for him.

Fifty years after the expressions 'ideology' and 'ideologues' were first used publicly, Marx took them up again, but gave them a completely different meaning. He took these expressions up very early, in his early works, and *had* to give them a completely different meaning. The reason was simple: from his articles in the *Rheinische Zeitung* on, he was waging an ideological struggle, conducting himself like a radical left ideologue, and then a utopian communist ideologue, in combating other ideologues, his adversaries.

Thus it was the practice of the ideological, and later political, struggle that compelled Marx to acknowledge *very early on*, beginning in his early works, the existence and reality of ideology, as well as the necessity of its role in ideological and, ultimately, political struggle: class struggle. It is well known that Marx was not *the first* to acknowledge the existence or even invent the concept of class struggle, since, on his own witness, it figures in the works of the bourgeois historians of the Restoration.[1]

---

1   Mignet, Augustin Thierry, Guizot and Thiers themselves. During the Restoration,

It was most certainly for this reason, at once autobiographical and historical (a situation of opposition to the Rhineland bourgeoisie that propelled its young ideologues from radicalism to utopian communism), that Marx, once he started to become aware of his own class position, paid so much attention to the concept *of ideology*, in *The Holy Family*, the

---

these ideologues/historians depicted the history of the class struggle of the French Revolution: the struggle of the 'Third Estate' against the two other Estates (the Nobility, the Church) of the 'Ancien Régime'. Let us add that the notion of class struggle was present well before these historians and even well before the French Revolution. To restrict ourselves to the period of the French bourgeoisie's pre-revolutionary ideological class struggle: class struggle was explicitly thought, from the sixteenth century on, by the ideologues of the feudality and bourgeoisie alike, in the form of a so-called struggle between *races*, in connection with the central ideological polemic over the 'origins' of absolute monarchy: a struggle between the race of the Germans and the race of the Romans. The *Germanists* defended 'classic' forms of feudality against the 'Despotism' of the absolute monarchy, which was allied with the bourgeois commoners [*roturiers*]. They cultivated the myth of a 'democracy' of the classic feudality, in which the King had been a simple lord elected by his peers in a democratic assembly, against the pernicious influence of the Roman conquerors, who imposed the model of a Prince ruling by despotic divine right. They then wrote the 'history' of the 'Middle Ages' in line with this schema. Montesquieu was the most illustrious representative of this thesis (see the last chapters of *Spirit of Laws*). For their part, the *Romanists* (such as the Abbé Dubois) defended the opposite thesis: against feudal anarchy, the absolute monarchy, supported by the Legists who invoked and commented on Roman Law, and relying on the devotion of bourgeois 'commoners' to the cause of the nation, had succeeded in bringing order, justice and reason to social relations. The Roman conquest of Gaul, a reactionary catastrophe for the Germanists, became, for the Romanists, an emancipatory enterprise. Let us note the singular destinies of these theses, which, albeit products of the exalted historical imagination, had, like all ideological theses, concrete objectives: when the balance of power began to tip for good, that is, in the latter half of the eighteenth century, it proved possible for certain ideologues, struggling, from the left this time, against the absolute monarchy's despotism, to wrest the Germanists' 'democratic' demands from their original advocates. Mably, for example, a left Germanist, used the very same arguments employed by Montesquieu, a right Germanist . . . Here we may discern a true recognition of class struggle as the motor of history, in the ideological disguise of race struggle (Germans versus Romans or the other way round); the explicit object of this ideological polemic (the absolute monarchy); the real object of this ideological struggle (the rise of the bourgeoisie and its struggle against the feudal aristocracy, on the basis of an alliance between bourgeoisie and absolute monarchy – but within the limits of the dominant feudal relations of production). We may also point out that this ideological struggle around the absolute monarchy, Roman Law, the struggle of the races, etc., is contemporaneous with the earliest existing *theories of ideology*: first among them, that of Hobbes, well known, and that of Spinoza, completely unknown, and then all the theories of ideology with which eighteenth-century Enlightenment philosophy teems, as one knows or, rather, does not care to know. We may also point out (we will come back to this when we discuss philosophy again) that the emergence of 'modern', that is, bourgeois philosophy, inaugurated by Descartes, is unthinkable without the prelude of the 'Revival of Roman Law' in its mercantile and political forms.

1844 Manuscripts and, above all, *The German Ideology*. In this regard, there is a very big theoretical difference between *The Holy Family* and the *1844 Manuscripts* on the one hand and *The German Ideology* on the other. Although *The German Ideology* contains a positivist-mechanistic conception of ideology, which is to say a not-yet-Marxist conception of ideology, we find a handful of phenomenal formulas in this text; they are material evidence of the tremendous power with which Marx's political experience irrupted in the midst of a general conception that was still false. We find these two simple formulas, for instance: 'the ruling ideology is the ideology of the ruling class',[2] and the definition of ideology as 'cognition' and 'miscognition'.[3]

Unfortunately, believing, first, that he had 'settled accounts with his former philosophical consciousness' in *The German Ideology*, the text of which he had abandoned to the 'gnawing criticism of the mice';[4] and believing, second, during the positivist transition represented by *The German Ideology*, that all philosophy should be purely and simply 'abolished', because philosophy was nothing but ideology, Marx set out on a study of 'positive matters', that is, after the failure of the 1848 revolutions, a study of political economy. Aware that he had so far acquired only hearsay knowledge of the subject, he undertook a serious examination of it, deciding in 1850 'to begin everything at the beginning'. On the basis of this examination, as is well known, he produced, seventeen years later, the first volume of *Capital* (1867).

Unfortunately, if *Capital* contains a number of elements for a theory of ideologies, especially the ideology of the vulgar economists, it does not contain that theory itself, which depends to a large extent (we shall see to what extent when the time comes) on a *theory of ideology in general* that is still lacking in Marxist theory as such.

I would like to take the considerable risk of proposing a preliminary, very schematic sketch of such a theory. The theses I am about to put

---

2 [TN: The word of Marx's that Althusser here translates as 'ideology' is *Gedanken*, usually translated as 'thoughts' or 'ideas'.]

3 If I may be allowed a personal confession, several years after I had laboriously produced a definition of the function of ideology as recognition/miscognition [*reconnaissance, méconnaissance*], a formula which takes up terms that Lacan, as a good Freudian, applies to the unconscious, I 'discovered' that the formula figures verbatim in *The German Ideology*. [TN: Marx's words are *Erkennung* and *Verkennung*.]

4 This is the proof, be it noted in passing, that Marx was of the opinion that *The German Ideology* – which the vast majority of Marxists take for good coin, citing it copiously to prove their 'theories' – stood in need of a good *critique*, but that this critique was one within the capacity of . . . mice. Alas, how many Marxist men have done what mice could do?

forward are of course not improvisations, but they can be sustained and tested, that is, confirmed or invalidated, only by very long studies and analyses, to which the formulation of these theses will, perhaps, lead. I therefore ask the reader to be extremely vigilant and, at the same time, extremely indulgent towards the propositions that I am about to hazard.[5]

II IDEOLOGY HAS NO HISTORY

Let me first say a word about the reason of principle that seems to me at least to authorize, if not to found, the project of a theory of *ideology in general*, as opposed to a theory of particular ideolog*ies*, considered either with respect to their regional contents (religious, moral, legal, or political ideology, and so on) or class orientation (bourgeois, petty-bourgeois, proletarian ideology, and so on).

In the second volume of the present work, I shall attempt to sketch a theory of ideolog*ies* in the two respects just indicated. It will then appear that a theory of ideolog*ies* depends, in the last resort, on the history of social formations, hence of modes of production combined in social formations and the class struggles that develop in them. In that sense, there can plainly be no question of a theory of ideolog*ies in general*, since ideolog*ies* (defined in the two ways indicated above, with respect to region and class) *do* have a history, whose determination in the last instance obviously lies *outside* them, although it concerns them.

On the other hand, if I can put forward the project of a theory of *ideology in general*, and if this theory is indeed one of the elements on which theories of ideolog*ies* depend, this entails an apparently paradoxical proposition. Laying my cards on the table, I shall state it in the following terms: *ideology has no history*.

That phrase may be found verbatim in a passage of *The German Ideology*. Marx utters it with respect to metaphysics, which, he says, *no more has a history* than does morality (or, by implication, any other form of ideology).[6]

In *The German Ideology*, this phrase figures in a frankly positivist context. Ideology is sheer illusion, sheer dream, in other words, nothingness. All its reality lies outside it. Ideology is thus conceived of as an

---

5 [TN: Written above the word 'hazard' in the manuscript are the words 'expose-confess'.]

6 [TN: Karl Marx and Friedrich Engels, *The German Ideology*, trans. anon., New York, Prometheus Books, 1998, p. 42: 'Morality, religion, metaphysics, and all the rest of ideology and all the forms of consciousness corresponding to these thus no longer retain the semblance of independence. They have no history . . .'.]

imaginary construct whose status exactly resembles the theoretical status of the dream in authors before Freud. For these authors, dreams were purely imaginary – that is, nugatory – results of the 'day's residues', presented in an arbitrary and sometimes even 'inverted' arrangement and order: in short, 'in disorder'. Dreams were the empty, nugatory imaginary, 'patched together' arbitrarily, eyes closed, from residues of the only full, positive reality, that of open-eyed day. That is exactly philosophy's and also ideology's status in *The German Ideology* (since philosophy is ideology par excellence here).

Ideology is an imaginary assemblage, a pure dream, empty and vain, constituted by the 'diurnal residues' of the only full, positive reality, that of the concrete history of concrete, material individuals materially producing their existence. Ideology in *The German Ideology* has no history on these grounds, since its history *lies outside it*, where the only existing history, that of concrete individuals . . . and so forth. In *The German Ideology*, the thesis that ideology has no history is therefore a purely *negative* thesis, since it means both that:

1) ideology is nothing, being pure dream (fabricated by none can say what power – unless it is the alienation of the division of labour, but that, too, is a *negative* determination); and

2) ideology has no history, which does not at all mean that it has no history (quite the opposite, since it is but a pale reflection, empty and inverted, of real history), but, rather, that it has no history *of its own*.

My thesis, although it repeats, formally speaking, *The German Ideology*'s terms (ideology has no history), differs radically from *The German Ideology*'s positivist-historicist thesis. For, first, I think I can affirm that ideologies *have a history of their own* (although it is determined in the last instance by the class struggle in the apparatuses that reproduce the relations of production). Second, I think I can simultaneously affirm that *ideology* in general *has no history*, not in a negative sense (its history lies outside it), but in an absolutely positive sense.

A positive sense, if it is true that a peculiar feature of ideology is that it is endowed with a structure and functioning such as to make it a non-historical – that is, an omni-historical – reality, in the sense that this structure and functioning are, *in one and the same form, immutable*, present throughout what is called *history*, in the sense in which the *Manifesto* defines history as the history of class struggle, that is, *the history of class societies*.

So that readers are not unsettled by this proposition, which will doubtless bring them up short, I would say, returning to my example of the dream one more time, this time in its *Freudian* conception, that our proposition that *ideology has no history* can and must (in a way that has absolutely nothing arbitrary about it, but, quite the opposite, is theoretically necessary, since there is an organic link between the two propositions) be directly correlated with Freud's proposition that *the unconscious is eternal*, in other words, has no history.

If eternal means, not transcendent to all (temporal) history, but omnipresent and therefore immutable in form throughout all of history, I will go so far as to adopt Freud's formulation word for word and write: *ideology is eternal*, just like the unconscious. I will add, anticipating the results of research that must be carried out and now can be, that this parallel is theoretically justified by the *fact* that the eternity of *the unconscious* is based, in the last instance, on the eternity of *ideology* in general.[7] That is why I believe I am, let us say, authorized, at least presumptively, to propose *a theory of ideology in general*, in the sense in which Freud presented a theory of the unconscious in general.

To simplify our terminology, let us agree, taking into account what has been said about ideolog*ies*, to use the word *ideology*, without further qualification, to designate ideology in general, which, I just said, has no history, or (it comes to the same thing) is eternal, that is, omnipresent in its immutable form throughout history (meaning the history of the social formations comprising social classes). I am happy to restrict myself, as can be seen, to 'class societies' and their history. Elsewhere, however, I shall show that the thesis I am defending can and must be extended to what are known as 'classless societies'.

III   REPRESSION AND IDEOLOGY

That said, let me make one more remark before entering into my analysis.

The advantage of this theory of ideology (and that is also a reason I am elaborating it at this point in our discussion) is that it concretely shows how ideology 'functions' at its most concrete level, the level of individual 'subjects': that is, people as they exist in their concrete individuality, in their work, daily lives, acts, commitments, hesitations, doubts, and sense of what is most immediately self-evident. It is here that all those who demand, vociferously: 'Give us something concrete! Something concrete!' will, if I say so myself, be 'well-served'.

We touched on this concrete level when we showed the role played

---

7   One day we shall have to find another, positive term to name the reality that Freud designates negatively as *the unconscious*. In that positive term, all connection, even negative, with 'consciousness' should disappear.

by legal-moral ideology. We did not, however, discuss it, but only pointed it out. And we did not know at the time that the 'legal system' was an Ideological State Apparatus. Since then, we have brought the concept of Ideological State Apparatus into play and demonstrated that there are several such apparatuses, while also showing the function they have and the fact that they realize different regions and forms of ideology, unified under the State Ideology. We have also clearly shown the general function of these Ideological State Apparatuses as well as the effects of the class struggle of which they are both the object and the theatre.

We have not, however, shown how the State Ideology, and the various ideological forms realized in these apparatuses and their practices, whether class forms or regional forms, reach concrete individuals themselves at the level of their ideas and acts: Pierre, Paul, Jean, Jacques, a metallurgist, a white-collar worker, an engineer, a working-class militant, a capitalist, a bourgeois statesman, a policeman, a bishop, a judge, a civil servant, and so on, in their concrete, day-to-day existence. We have not shown the general mechanism by means of which ideology makes concrete individuals 'act by themselves' in the technical-social division of labour, that is, in the various posts held by agents of production, exploitation, repression and ideologization (and also of scientific practice). In a word, we have not shown by what mechanism ideology makes individuals 'act all by themselves', without there being any need to post a policeman behind each and every one of them.

This is no gratuitous paradox I am formulating here, for there exist, in the anti-socialist class struggle, 'anticipatory' works[8] depicting 'totalitarian' socialist society as a society in which every individual will be doubled by his personal 'monitor' (whether a cop or the Big Boss, who is at the same time a Grand Inquisitor), who is present in every bedroom, no matter how secluded, and, using the refined means of avant-garde science fiction – such as microphones in the walls, electronic eyes, or closed-circuit television – observes-monitors-prohibits-commands each individual's every act and gesture.

When we leave this 'political science fiction' behind, the anti-socialist role of which is obvious but crude, in order to turn to the very contemporary forms that are also very widespread in the very narrow circles that are trying to take over the leadership of the 'Movement' that May has spawned among high-school-students-college-students-intellectuals

---

8   The anti-socialist theme of the 'Grand Inquisitor' goes back to Dostoyevsky. Since then: Koestler, *The Twenty-Fifth Hour*, and so on.

(they think they are leading it; however, since it is a mass movement, it eludes their grasp), we find exactly the same incredible myth. When the weekly *Action* recently wrote, as part of a huge drawing on its cover: 'Get rid of the cop in your head!', it took up the same mythology unawares, without suspecting that it is, even in its anarchist guise, profoundly reactionary.

For the 'totalitarian' myth of the ubiquitous Grand Inquisitor, like the anarchist myth of the ubiquitous cop 'in your head', is based on the same anti-Marxist conception of the way 'society' works.

We have already had a word to say about this conception. We have shown that it stands the real order of things on its head, putting the superstructure in place of the base, and, very precisely, whisks exploitation 'under the carpet' in order to focus on repression alone. In another, more elaborate form of the same mistake, it declares that, in the 'stage of state monopoly capitalism', which it presents as imperialism's final stage, exploitation has been reduced to its 'essence': repression – or, if one wants to put the dots on the 'i's, that exploitation has practically become repression.

We can now, going a step further, point out that assimilating exploitation to repression simultaneously entails a second theoretical and political reduction: it reduces the action of ideology to the action of repression pure and simple.

This explains why *Action* could come out with the slogan: 'Get rid of the cop in your head!' That is a proposition that can be thought and uttered only if one whisks ideology 'under the carpet' or confounds it, purely and simply, with repression. From that standpoint, *Action*'s slogan is a little theoretical gem. For, instead of saying: 'Fight false ideas, destroy the false ideas you have in your heads – the false ideas with which the ideology of the dominant class pulls the wool over your eyes,[9] and replace them with accurate ideas that will enable you to join the revolutionary class's struggle to end exploitation and the repression that sustains it!', *Action* declares: 'Get rid of the cop in your head!' This slogan, which deserves a place in the Museum of the History of Masterpieces of Theoretical and Political Error, quite simply replaces ideas, as is obvious enough, with the cop. That is, it replaces the role of subjection played by bourgeois ideology with the repressive role played by the police.

In this anarchist conception, then, we can see that 1) exploitation is replaced by repression or is thought of as a form of repression; and 2)

---

9 [TN: *Fait marcher.* See Chapter 2, n. 27.]

ideology is replaced by repression or is thought of as a form of repression. Repression thus becomes the centre of centres, the essence of the society based on capitalist class exploitation. Repression simultaneously stands in for exploitation, ideology and, ultimately, the state as well, inasmuch as the state apparatuses, which comprise, as we have seen, both a repressive apparatus and ideological apparatuses, are reduced to the abstract notion of 'repression'.

The general 'synthesis' (for there is an admirable hidden logic at work in the whole post-May 'development' of this 'conception', including even its historical 'development') – the general synthesis of this conception, that is, the resolution of the contradiction provided by the statement that one has a 'cop' in one's head, in which, as everyone knows, after all, one can have only 'ideas', is furnished by the same 'theorists'. It comes in the form of a 'discovery' made by the leaders of the 'German student movement'. They have 'discovered' that 'knowledge' is, by nature, directly repressive.

Hence the necessity of 'revolting' against the 'authority of knowledge'; hence the 'anti-authoritarian' revolt against the repression exercised by knowledge; hence the retrospective interpretation of the May Events and their sequel as having been naturally and necessarily centred on the university and schools, where repression, the essence of capitalist society, is exercised directly, in the original, nascent state, in the form of the (bourgeois) authority of 'knowledge'. That is why your daughter is mute; in other words, that is why May took place in the university and among intellectuals, first and foremost. And that is why the revolutionary movement, which the proletarians are invited to join, can (if not must) be led by the aforementioned intellectuals.[10] Publications of all sorts are currently providing the empirical demonstration of these 'theses' and, above all, of the extraordinary labours of the 'old mole'[11] of the 'logic' of the anarchist conception, which produces such pristine theoretical effects.

This, then, is another reason why – after recognizing that exploitation is not reducible to repression; that the state apparatuses are not reducible to the repressive apparatus alone; and that individuals do not have their

---

10 Provisionally, we are told . . . but this provisional situation is sure to last, because, inasmuch as the basic conception on which this whole interpretation rests is wrong, and inasmuch as the mass of the workers will not 'fall for it' [*ne marcheront pas*], since they know that the basis of bourgeois society is not repression but exploitation, the above-mentioned provisional 'leaders' will, if they do not wish to abandon their error, have to persist in it – to persist, that is, in their leadership.

11 [TN: 'Old Mole' (Vieille Taupe) was the name of a Paris bookshop popular with anarchists and *gauchistes* in the late 1960s and early 1970s.]

own personal 'cop' behind them or 'in their heads' – we have to show how the ideology realized in the Ideological State Apparatuses works. It produces the following class result, which is astonishing but quite 'natural': namely, that the individuals in question 'go', and that it is ideology which makes them 'go'.

Plato already knew this. He foresaw that cops ('Guardians') would be needed to monitor and repress slaves and 'craftsmen'. He knew, however, that there is no putting a 'cop' in the head of each slave or craftsman, and that it is not even possible to put, behind each and every individual, his own personal cop (otherwise, a second cop would be needed to monitor the first, and so on . . . and there would ultimately be nothing but cops in society, with no one to produce; and then what would the cops themselves live on?). Plato knew that the 'people' had to be taught, from childhood, the 'Beautiful Lies' that would 'make it go' all by itself, and that those Beautiful Lies had to be taught to the 'people' in such a way that the people would believe in them, so that it would 'go'.

Plato was, to be sure, no 'revolutionary', even though he was an intellectual; he was a reactionary and no mistake. He had enough political experience, however, not to tell himself stories to the effect that, in a class society, mere repression could by itself guarantee the reproduction of the relations of production. He already knew (although he did not have the concept for this) that it is the Beautiful Lies, that is, ideology, which ensure the reproduction of the relations of production better than anything else. Our modern 'revolutionary' anarchist leaders do not know this. This proves that they would do well to read Plato, without letting themselves be intimidated by the 'authority of the knowledge' they will find in him; for they can find in Plato, let us say, elementary 'lessons', albeit purely ideological,[12] about the way a class society works. This proves that 'knowledge' altogether different from repressive-authoritarian knowledge is possible – precisely the scientific knowledge that, since Marx and Lenin, has become emancipatory, because *revolutionary*, scientific knowledge.

That is why – I hope that things have become clear and that I can rest my case – it is absolutely necessary to show, theoretically and politically, the mechanisms by means of which ideology makes people,

---

12 Ideological, not scientific: a distinction our 'theorists' deem outmoded. They prefer to talk about 'knowledge' as such, as if there were not true and false knowledge, ideology and science. The proletarians who are thirsting for true knowledge know that it is not repressive; they know that, when this true knowledge is that of Marxist-Leninist science, it is revolutionary and emancipatory.

that is, concrete individuals, 'march' [*fait marcher*]: whether they 'march' in the service of class exploitation, or 'march' in the Long March that will culminate, sooner than one might think, in the revolution in the Western countries, and thus even in France. For revolutionary organizations, too, 'go' on ideology; however, when it is a question of Marxist-Leninist revolutionary organizations, they go on the proletarian ideology (above all political, but also moral) that has been transformed by the persevering educational activity[13] of the Marxist-Leninist science of the capitalist mode of production, and thus of capitalist social formations, and thus of the revolutionary class struggle and socialist revolution.

IV IDEOLOGY IS AN IMAGINARY 'REPRESENTATION'
OF INDIVIDUALS' IMAGINARY RELATION TO
THEIR REAL CONDITIONS OF EXISTENCE

To broach my central thesis on the structure and functioning of ideology, I shall first present two theses, one negative, the other positive. The first concerns the object 'represented' in the imaginary form of ideology. The second concerns the materiality of ideology.

THESIS I: Ideology represents individuals' imaginary relation to their real conditions of existence.

We often call religious, moral, legal, political, and other ideologies so many 'world outlooks'. Of course, unless we experience one of these ideologies as the truth (unless, say, we profess or 'believe' in God, Duty, Justice, the Revolution, and so forth), we admit that these 'world outlooks' are largely imaginary and do not 'correspond to reality'. We take a critical standpoint on the ideology we are discussing, examining it as an ethnologist examines the myths of his 'little' 'primitive society'. However, while admitting that these ideologies do not correspond to reality and, accordingly, constitute an *illusion*, we also admit that they do make *allusion* to reality and that we need only 'interpret' them to discover the reality of this world beneath the surface of their imaginary representation of it (ideology = illusion/allusion).

There are different types of interpretation. The best known are the

---

13 This educational activity, which transforms spontaneous proletarian ideology into proletarian ideology with ever more distinctly scientific Marxist-Leninist contents, has historically been carried out in complex forms. It includes education in the current sense of the word, through books, brochures, schools and, in general, propaganda, but, above all, through education at the heart of the practice of the class struggle itself: through experience/ experiment, criticism of it, rectification of it, and so on.

mechanistic type common in the eighteenth century (God is an imaginary representation of the real King) and the 'hermeneutic' interpretation introduced by the first Church Fathers and revived by Feuerbach and the theological-philosophical school which descends from him, such as the theologian Barth and the philosopher Ricoeur. (For Feuerbach, for example, God is the essence of real Man.) The essential point is that, provided we interpret the imaginary transposition (and inversion) of ideology, we arrive at the conclusion that, in ideology, 'people represent (in imaginary form) their real conditions of existence'.

This interpretation leaves one 'small' problem in abeyance: why do people 'need' this imaginary transposition of their real conditions of existence in order to 'represent' their real conditions of existence?

The first interpretation (the eighteenth century's) has a simple solution to hand: priests or despots are to blame. They 'forged' Beautiful Lies so that people would, in the belief that they were obeying God, in fact obey the priests or despots, generally allied in their imposture, with the priests working in the despots' service or, depending on the aforementioned theorists' political positions, the other way around. There is therefore a cause for the imaginary transposition of real conditions of existence: that cause is a small handful of cynics who base their domination and exploitation of the 'people' on a skewed representation of the world, which they have imagined in order to enslave minds by dominating imaginations. Thank God, the imagination is a faculty common to one and all!

The second interpretation (Feuerbach's, which Marx repeats word for word in his early works) is more 'profound', that is, just as false. It, too, seeks and finds a cause for the transposition and imaginary distortion of people's real conditions of existence – in short, for the alienation in the imaginary of the representation of people's conditions of existence. This cause is no longer priests or despots or their active imaginations and the passive imaginations of their victims. It is the material alienation reigning in people's very conditions of existence. This is how Marx defends, in *The Jewish Question* and elsewhere, the 100 per cent Feuerbachian idea (enhanced with economic pseudo-considerations in the *1844 Manuscripts*) that people devise an alienated (that is, imaginary) representation of their conditions of existence because those conditions of existence are themselves alienating (in the *1844 Manuscripts*: because those conditions are dominated [by] the essence of alienated society: '*alienated labour*').

All these interpretations thus take literally the thesis which they presuppose and on which they are based: that what is reflected in the imaginary representation of the world found in an ideology is people's conditions of existence, hence their real world.

Here, however, I return to a thesis that I advanced a few years ago, and reaffirm that 'people' do not 'represent' their real conditions of existence in ideology (religious ideology or some other kind), but, above all, their *relation* to those real conditions of existence. That relation is at the centre of every ideological, hence imaginary, representation of the real world. It is that relation which contains the 'cause' that must account for the imaginary distortion of the ideological representation of the real world. Or, rather, to suspend the language of causality, we have to advance the thesis that the imaginary nature of this relation sustains all the imaginary distortion that we can observe in all ideology (unless we live in its truth).

To put this in Marxist terms, if it is true that the representation of the real conditions of existence of individuals holding posts of agents of production, exploitation, repression, ideologization and scientific practice arises, in the last instance, from the relations of production and relations deriving from them, we may say the following: every ideology represents, in its necessarily imaginary distortion, not the existing relations of production (and the other relations deriving from them), but, above all, individuals' (imaginary) relation to the relations of production and the relations deriving from them. What is represented in ideology is therefore not the system of real relations governing individuals' existence, but those individuals' imaginary relation to the real relations in which they live.

If this is so, the question of the 'cause' of the imaginary distortion of real relations in ideology disappears. It must be replaced by another: Why is the representation that individuals make of their (individual) relation to the social relations governing their conditions of existence and their individual and collective lives necessarily imaginary? And what kind of imaginary is involved? Posed in this way, the question rules out the solution that turns on a 'clique'[14] of individuals (priests or despots) identified as the authors of the great ideological mystification, as well as the solution that turns on the alienated character of the real world. We shall see why later in our discussion. For now, we shall go no further.

---

14 I purposely employ this very modern term. For, even in communist circles, it is unfortunately routine to explain this or that political deviation (left or right), [sectarianism]/ opportunism, as the result of the activity of a 'clique'. [TN: The designation for left deviationism has been supplied by the editor. There is a blank space here in the manuscript.]

V IDEOLOGY HAS A MATERIAL EXISTENCE

THESIS II: Ideology has a material existence.

We touched on this thesis when we said that 'ideas', or representations and the like, which seem to make up ideology, have, not an ideal, idea-dependent [*idéale, idéelle*] or spiritual existence, but a material one. We even suggested that the ideal, idea-dependent, spiritual existence of 'ideas' is a notion that belongs exclusively to an ideology of the 'idea' and of ideology, and, let us add, to the ideology of what seems to have 'founded' this conception since the appearance of the sciences: namely, what the practitioners of the sciences represent as 'ideas', whether true or false, in their spontaneous ideology. Of course, presented in the form of a claim, this thesis is unproven. We ask only that the reader entertain a favourable prejudice towards it – say, in the name of materialism. We shall prove it elsewhere than in the present Volume 1.

We need this hypothesis that 'ideas' or other representations have, not a spiritual, but a material existence in order to progress in our analysis of the nature of ideology. Or, rather, we simply find it useful the better to bring out what every even slightly serious analysis of any ideology at all will immediately and empirically show any even minimally critical observer.

In our discussion of Ideological State Apparatuses and their practices, we said that each apparatus was the realization of an ideology (the unity of these different regional ideologies – religious, moral, legal, political, aesthetic, and so on – being ensured by their subsumption under the State Ideology). We now return to this thesis: an ideology always exists in an apparatus and in the practice or practices of that apparatus. This existence is material.

Of course, the material existence of ideology in an apparatus and its practices does not have the same modality as the material existence of a paving stone or rifle. However, at the risk of being called a neo-Aristotelian (let us note in passing that Marx held Aristotle in very high esteem), we shall say that 'matter is expressed in several senses' or, rather, that it exists in different modalities, all rooted, in the last instance, in 'physical' matter.

That said, let us take the shortest way and see what goes on in the 'individuals' who live in ideology, that is, in a determinate representation of the world (religious, moral, and so on) whose imaginary distortion depends on their imaginary relation to their conditions of existence, in other words, in the last instance, to the relations of production (ideology = an imaginary relation to real relations). We shall say that this imaginary relation is itself endowed with material existence. No one can accuse us of dodging the difficulty or of being 'inconsistent'.

We observe the following. An individual believes in God, Duty, Justice, or the like. This belief has its source (for everyone, that is, for everyone who lives in an ideological representation of ideology that reduces it to ideas endowed by definition with spiritual existence) in that individual's *ideas*, and thus in her as a subject possessed of a consciousness containing the ideas of her belief. On this condition – that is, given the perfectly ideological 'conceptual' dispositive thus established (a subject endowed with consciousness in which she freely forms or freely recognizes ideas in which she believes) – the (material) comportment of the subject follows naturally from her ideas.

The individual in question behaves in such-and-such a way, adopts such-and-such a practical line of conduct and, what is more, participates in certain regulated practices, those of the ideological apparatus on which 'depend' the ideas that she has, as subject, freely and in all good conscience chosen. If she believes in God, she goes to church to attend mass, kneels, prays, confesses, does penance (penance was once material in the ordinary sense) and, naturally, repents, and so on and so forth. If she believes in Duty, she will act in the corresponding ways (inscribed in ritual practices), 'observing proper rules of behaviour'. If she believes in Justice, she will unquestioningly submit to the rules of law and, when they are violated, may well protest in the profound indignation of her heart, or even sign petitions, take part in a demonstration, and so on. If she believes in Maréchal Pétain's 'National Revolution', she will do the same. If she believes in the socialist revolution, she will do the same – that is, obviously, something altogether different. I have deliberately chosen the last examples, which are almost provocations, so as not to 'duck the difficulty'.

From first to last in this schema, we observe that the ideological representation of ideology is itself forced to recognize that every subject endowed with consciousness/a conscience and believing in the ideas that it inspires in her or freely accepts should '*act in accordance with her ideas*' and therefore inscribe her own ideas as free subject in the acts of her material practice. If she fails to, '*that is not good*'.

Indeed, if she does not do what she ought to do according to what she believes, then she does something else, and that implies – still according to the same idealist scheme – that she has in her head ideas other than those she proclaims, and acts on *them*, as someone who is either 'inconsistent' ('no one is deliberately evil') or cynical or perverse.

At all events, the ideology of ideology thus recognizes, despite its imaginary distortion, that a human subject's 'ideas' exist in her acts or ought to; and, if they do not, it ascribes to her other ideas corresponding to the acts (even perverse) that she does perform. This ideology of ideology talks about acts; we shall talk about acts inserted into practices. And we shall point out that these practices are regulated by rituals in which they are inscribed, within the material existence of an ideological apparatus, even if it is just a small part of that apparatus: a small mass in a small church, a funeral, a minor match at a sport club, a school day or a day of classes at university, a meeting or rally of a political party, or of the Rationalist Union, or whatever one likes.

We are, moreover, indebted to Pascal's defensive 'dialectic' for the marvellous formula which will enable us to invert the order of the notional schema of the ideology of ideology. Pascal says, more or less, 'Kneel down, move your lips in prayer, *and you will believe.*'[15] He thus scandalously inverts the order of things, bringing, like Christ, not peace, but strife, and, what is more, in a way that is hardly Christian (for woe to him who brings scandal into the world!) – scandal itself. A fortunate scandal which makes him speak, with Jansenist defiance, a language designating reality as it is, with nothing imaginary about it.

We may perhaps be allowed to leave Pascal to the arguments of his ideological struggle with the religious Ideological State Apparatus of his day, in which he waged a little class struggle in his Jansenist party, constantly on the brink of being banned, that is, of excommunication. And we shall try to use, with the reader's permission, a more directly Marxist terminology, if possible, for we are advancing in domains still poorly explored by Marxist theorists.

We shall therefore say, considering only a single subject (such and such an individual), that the existence of the ideas in which he believes is material in that his ideas are his material acts inserted into material practices regulated by material rituals which are themselves defined by the material ideological apparatus from which (hardly by accident!) his ideas derive. Naturally, the four inscriptions of the adjective 'material' in our proposition have to be endowed with different modalities: the materiality of a walk to church to attend mass, of kneeling, of making the sign of the cross or beating one's breast, of a sentence, a prayer, an act of contrition, an act of penance, a gaze, a handshake, an outer verbal discourse or 'inner' verbal discourse (consciousness) is not one and the same materiality. I do not think that anyone will seek a quarrel with us here if we leave the theory of the difference between the modalities of materiality in abeyance.

---

15   [TN: Blaise Pascal, *Pensées*, 250 (Brunschvig edition).]

The fact remains that, in this inverted presentation of things, we are not dealing with an inversion at all (that magic formula of Hegelian or Feuerbachian Marxists!), because we can see that certain notions have purely and simply disappeared from our new presentation, that others, in contrast, survive, and that new terms appear.

Disappeared: the term *ideas*.

Survive: the terms *subject, consciousness, belief, acts*.

Appear: the terms *practices, rituals, ideological apparatus*.

It is therefore not an inversion [*renversement*] (except in the sense in which we say that a government or a glass has been overturned [*renversé*], but a rather strange reshuffle (of a non-ministerial type), since we obtain the following result.

Ideas have disappeared as such (insofar as they are endowed with an ideal or spiritual existence), precisely insofar as it has appeared that their existence is material – is inscribed in the acts of practices regulated by rituals defined in the last instance by an ideological apparatus. It accordingly appears that the subject acts insofar as he is acted by the following system (set out in the order of its real determination): ideology existing in a material ideological apparatus, prescribing material practices regulated by a material ritual, which practices exist in the material acts of a subject acting in all good conscience in accordance with his belief. It may be objected that the subject in question could act differently; but let us recall that we said that the ritual practices in which a 'primary' ideology is realized can 'produce' (in the form of by-products)[16] a 'secondary' ideology – thank God, since, otherwise, neither revolt nor the acquisition of revolutionary consciousness nor revolution would be possible.

But our presentation reveals that we have retained the following notions: subject, consciousness, belief, acts. From this sequence, we shall immediately extract the decisive central term on which everything depends: the notion of the *subject*.

And we shall immediately state two conjoint theses:

1) There is no practice whatsoever except by and under an ideology.

2) There is no ideology except by the subject and for subjects.

We can now come to our central thesis.

---

16 Under what conditions? Essentially, they depend on the class struggle, as we shall see in Volume 2. [TN: In fact, the project to produce a second volume was never realized.]

VI IDEOLOGY INTERPELLATES INDIVIDUALS AS SUBJECTS[17]

This thesis simply comes down to making our last proposition explicit: there is no ideology except by the subject and for subjects. In other words, there is no ideology except for concrete subjects (such as you and me), and this destination for ideology is only made possible by the subject: in other words, by the category of the subject and its functioning.

We mean by this that, even if it appears under this name (the subject) only with the advent of bourgeois ideology, legal ideology in particular,[18] the category of the subject (which may function under other names: for example, the soul in Plato, God, and so on) is the category constitutive of all ideology, whatever its (regional or class) determination and whatever its historical date – since ideology has no history.

We say that the category of the subject is constitutive of all ideology, but we also immediately add that the category of the subject is constitutive of every ideology only insofar as every ideology has the function (which defines it) of 'constituting' concrete subjects (such as you and me). The functioning of all ideology exists in the play of this twofold constitution, since ideology is nothing but its functioning in the material forms of existence of that functioning.

Clearly to grasp what follows, we must bear firmly in mind that both he who is writing these lines and the reader who is reading them are themselves subjects, and therefore ideological subjects (the proposition is itself tautological). That is, we have to be aware that both author and reader of these lines live 'spontaneously' or 'naturally' in ideology, in the sense in which we have said that 'man is by nature an ideological animal'.[19]

The fact that an author, insofar as he writes the lines of a discourse which claims to be scientific, is completely absent as a 'subject' from 'his' scientific discourse (for all scientific discourse is by definition a discourse without a subject; there is no 'Subject of Science' except in an ideology of science) is a different matter. We shall leave it aside for the moment.

As St Paul admirably puts it, it is in the '*Logos*', in other words, in

---

17 [TN: The verb *interpeller* and the corresponding noun are common words in French. In addition to the senses Althusser mentions – hailing to get someone's attention and, not infrequently, as a prelude to harassment such as disciplinary measures in school or police identity checks – *interpeller* is often used in conversation to mean 'to shake up', 'to really get to': 'Her report on our army's reliance on torture really got to me (*m'a interpellé*)'.]

18 Which borrows the legal category of the 'subject of law' and transforms it into an ideological notion: man is by nature a subject.

19 [TN: See Chapter 6, n. 26.]

ideology, that we 'live and move and have our being'.[20] It follows that the category of the subject is a primary 'self-evident fact' for you and me (self-evident facts are always primary): it is clear that you are a (free, moral, responsible, and so on) subject, and that I am, too. Like all self-evident facts, including those that make a word 'name a thing' or 'have a meaning' (including, therefore, the self-evident facts of the 'transparency' of language), the 'self-evident fact' that you and I are subjects – and that that is not a problem – is an ideological effect, the elementary ideological effect.[21] For it is characteristic of ideology to impose self-evident facts as self-evident facts (without in the least seeming to, since they are 'self-evident') which we cannot *not* recognize and before which we have the inevitable and eminently natural reaction of exclaiming (aloud or in 'the silence of consciousness'):[22] 'That's obvious! That's right! That's true!'

At work in this reaction is the function of ideological *recognition*, one of the two basic functions of ideology (the other is the function of *miscognition*).

To take a highly 'concrete' example, we all have friends who, when they knock on our door and we ask 'who's there?' through the closed door, answer (since 'it's self-evident') 'it's me!' And we do indeed recognize that 'it's him' or 'it's her'. The purpose is achieved: we open the door, and 'it's always really true that it really was she who was there'. To take another example, when, in the street, we recognize someone we already know [*quand nous (re)connaissons quelqu'un de notre connaissance*], we show him that we have recognized him (and have recognized that he has recognized us) by saying 'Hello, my friend!' and shaking his hand (a material ritual practice of ideological recognition in everyday life, at least in France; elsewhere, there are other rituals).

With this preliminary remark and these concrete illustrations, I wish to point out only that you and I are *always already* subjects and, as such, constantly practice the rituals of ideological recognition, which guarantee for us that we are indeed concrete, individual, unmistakable and, naturally, irreplaceable subjects. The writing I am currently doing and the reading you are currently engaged in[23] are likewise, in this respect, rituals

---

20 [TN: Acts 17:28, King James Bible.]

21 'Linguists' and those who call poor suffering linguistics to the rescue to different ends run up against problems due to the fact that they ignore the play of ideological effects in all discourses – even scientific discourses.

22 [TN: Jean-Paul Sartre, *Critical Essays*, trans. Chris Turner, London, Seagull, 2010, p. 364.]

23 Note that this recurrent *currently* is further proof of the fact that ideology is 'eternal',

of ideological recognition, including the 'self-evidence' with which the 'truth' of my reflections may impose itself on you (and may make you say 'that's true!').

To recognize that we are subjects, however, and that we function in the practical rituals of the most elementary daily life (hand-shakes, the fact of calling you by your name, the fact of knowing that you 'have' a name of your own thanks to which you are recognized as a unique subject, even if I do not know what your name is) – this recognition gives us only the 'consciousness' of our incessant (eternal) practice of ideological recognition: its consciousness, that is, *its recognition*. It by no means gives us the (scientific) *knowledge* of the mechanism of this recognition, or the recognition of this recognition. Yet it is that knowledge that we have to attain if we want, while speaking in ideology and from within ideology, to outline a discourse which tries to break with ideology, and to risk inaugurating a scientific discourse (a discourse without a subject) on ideology.

Thus, as a way of representing why the category of the subject is constitutive of ideology, which exists only by constituting concrete subjects (you and me), I shall employ a special mode of exposition: 'concrete' enough to be recognized, yet abstract enough to be thinkable and thought, giving rise to a knowledge.

As a first formulation, I would suggest: *all ideology hails or interpellates concrete individuals as concrete subjects*, through the functioning of the category of the subject.

This proposition implies that we should distinguish, for the moment, between concrete individuals on the one hand and concrete subjects on the other, although, at this level, there is no concrete subject that does not have a concrete individual as its support.

We shall go on to suggest that ideology 'acts' or 'functions' in such a way as to 'recruit' subjects among individuals (it recruits them all) or 'transform' individuals into subjects (it transforms them all) through the very precise operation that we call *interpellation* or *hailing*. It can be imagined along the lines of the most commonplace, everyday hailing, by (or not by) the police: 'Hey, you there!'[24]

---

since these two 'currentlys' are separated by an undefined interval: I am writing these lines on 6 April 1969, you may be reading them any time.

24　Hailing as an everyday practice governed by a precise ritual takes spectacular form in the police practice of hailing: 'Hey, you there!' (It functions in very similar forms in interpellating or summoning at school.) Police hailing, however, unlike other kinds of hailing, is repressive: 'Your papers!' 'Papers' means above all *identity* papers, frontal photo of one's face, first and middle names, last name, date of birth, home address, profession, citizenship, etc. Identity, concentrated in first and last names, and so on, makes it possible to identify the subject (presumed

If, to offer readers the most concrete sort of concreteness, we suppose that the theoretical scene we are imagining happens in the street, the hailed individual turns around. With this simple 180-degree physical conversion, he becomes a *subject*. Why? Because he has recognized that the hail 'really' was addressed to him and that 'it really was he who was hailed' (not someone else). Experience shows that the practical telecommunications of hailing are such that hailing hardly ever misses its mark: verbal call or whistle, the one hailed always recognizes that *he* really was the one hailed. This is a strange phenomenon, after all, one that cannot be explained by 'guilt feelings' alone, despite the large numbers of people with 'something on their consciences'. Or is it that everyone always has something on his conscience and that everyone confusedly feels, at least, that he always has accounts to render or obligations to respect – if only the obligation to respond to every hailing? Strange.

Naturally, for the convenience and clarity of exposition of our little theoretical theatre, we have had to present things in the form of a sequence with a before and an after, that is, in the form of a temporal succession. There are individuals walking along. Somewhere (usually behind them) the hail rings out, 'Hey, you there!' An individual (nine times out of ten, it is the one who is meant) turns around, believing-suspecting-knowing that he's the one – recognizing, in other words, that he 'really is the person' the interpellation is aimed at. In reality, however, things happen *without succession. The existence of ideology and the hailing or interpellation of individuals as subjects are one and the same thing.*

We may add that what thus seems to happen *outside* ideology (to be very precise, in the street) really happens *in* ideology. What really happens in ideology thus seems to happen outside it. That is why those who are in ideology, you and I, believe that they are by definition outside ideology: one of the effects of ideology is the practical *denegation* of the ideological character of ideology by ideology. Ideology never says 'I am ideological'. One has to be outside ideology, in other words, in scientific knowledge, to be able to say 'I am in ideology' (a quite exceptional case) or (the general case) 'I was in ideology'. As is very well known, the

---

in police hailing to be more or less suspect; initially presumed, that is, to be a 'bad sort'), thus to identify him without confusing him with another subject, and either 'let him go' ('It's all right') or 'take him in' ('Follow me!'), with consequences familiar to all who have been 'taken in' at a popular demonstration: a shift to casual forms of address or a casual beating, a night at the police station, and the whole terribly material ritual that ensues when a policeman recognizes a 'bad sort' [*mauvais sujet*]: 'He's the one who punched me!' with the corresponding formal accusation for 'attempted violence against a law enforcement official' or other such descriptions. To be sure, there are also thieves and criminals, and policemen who 'do not care for certain practices'.

accusation of being in ideology applies only to others, never to oneself (unless one is truly a Spinozist or Marxist, which, as far as this point goes, is to take exactly the same position). This amounts to saying that ideology *has no outside* (for itself), but, at the same time, *that it is nothing but outside* (for science and reality).

Spinoza explained this perfectly well 200 years before Marx, who practiced it without explaining it in detail. But let us leave this point there, although it is fraught with consequences which are not just theoretical, but also directly political, since, for example, the whole theory *of criticism and self-criticism*, the golden rule of the Marxist-Leninist practice of the class struggle, depends on it. Just one word: how are we to ensure that criticism is followed by self-criticism leading to a *rectification*, in line with Mao's Leninist formula? This is possible only on the basis of Marxist-Leninist science applied to the practice of the class struggle.

Thus ideology hails or interpellates individuals as subjects. Since ideology is eternal, we must now suppress the temporal form in which we have represented the functioning of ideology and say: ideology has always-already interpellated individuals as subjects, which amounts to making it clear that individuals are always-already interpellated by ideology as subjects. This ineluctably leads us to one last proposition: *individuals are always-already subjects*. Hence individuals are 'abstract' with respect to the subjects they always-already are. This proposition may seem to be paradoxical or to be intellectual acrobatics. One moment, please.

That an individual is always-already a subject, even before she is born, is nevertheless the plain fact of the matter, accessible to everyone and not a paradox at all. Freud shows that individuals are always 'abstract' with respect to the subjects they *always-already* are, simply by noting the ideological ritual that surrounds the expectation of a 'birth', that 'happy event'. Everyone knows how much, and how (a good deal could be said about that 'how'), an unborn child is expected. This comes down to saying, very prosaically, if we agree to leave aside 'sentiments', in other words, the forms of familial ideology[25] (paternal/maternal/conjugal/fraternal) in which the unborn child is expected, that it is certain in advance that it will bear its father's name and so have an identity and be irreplaceable.[26] Before its birth, then, a child is always-already a subject,

---

25   We have already said that, in a certain *regard* [*rapport*], the family is an Ideological State Apparatus.

26   Think of the dramas that ensue when one child is substituted for another in a maternity ward, or the dramas of 'recognition' of paternity, or the dramas of children put

marked out [*assigné*] as a subject in and by the particular familial ideological configuration in which it is 'expected' once it has been conceived
('deliberately' or 'by accident'). There is no need to add that this familial
ideological configuration is, in its singularity, terribly structured, and that
it is in this implacable, more or less 'pathological' (if any meaning can be
assigned to that word) structure that the quondam subject-to-be has to
'find' 'its' place, that is, 'become' the sexual subject (boy or girl) it already
is in advance. It needs no genius to suggest that this ideological constraint
and marking out, and all the rituals of family child-rearing-and-training
and family education, bear some relation to what Freud studied in the
forms of the pre-genital and genital 'stages' of sexuality, and thus to the
'take' [*prise*] of what he identified, by its effects, as *the unconscious*. But let
us also leave this point there.

This business of the infant that is always-already a subject in advance,
and, accordingly, not a veteran but a future fighter, is no joke, since we
can see that it is one entryway into the Freudian domain. It interests us,
however, on other grounds. What do we mean when we say that ideology in general has always-already interpellated as subjects individuals who
are always-already subjects? Apart from the limit case of the 'prenatal
child', this means, concretely, the following.

When religious ideology begins to function directly by interpellating the little child Louis as a subject, little Louis is already-subject
– not yet religious-subject, but familial-subject. When legal ideology
(later, let us suppose) begins to interpellate little Louis by talking to
him about, not Mama and Papa now, or God and the Little Lord
Jesus, but Justice, he was already a subject, familial, religious, scholastic, and so on. I shall skip the moral stage, aesthetic stage, and others.
Finally, when, later, thanks to auto-heterobiographical circumstances
of the type Popular Front, Spanish Civil War, Hitler, 1940 Defeat,
captivity, encounter with a communist, and so on, political ideology
(in its differential forms) begins to interpellate the now adult Louis as
a subject, he has already long been, always-already been, a familial,
religious, moral, scholastic and legal subject . . . and is now, lo and
behold, a political subject! This political subject begins, once back
from captivity, to make the transition from traditional Catholic activism to advanced – semi-heretical – Catholic activism, then begins
reading Marx, then joins the Communist Party, and so on. So life
goes. Ideologies never stop interpellating subjects as subjects, never

---

in the custody of their mothers, wrested from their fathers, and so on, and of all the horrors
they spawn.

stop 'recruiting' individuals who are always-already subjects. The play of ideologies is superposed, criss-crossed, contradicts itself on the same subject: the same individual always-already (several times) subject. Let him figure things out, if he can . . .

What will now occupy our attention is the way the 'actors' in this *mise-en-scène* of interpellation, as well as their respective roles, are reflected in the very structure of all ideology.

VII   AN EXAMPLE: CHRISTIAN RELIGIOUS IDEOLOGY

Since the formal structure of all ideology is always the same, we shall content ourselves with analyzing a single example familiar to everyone, that of religious ideology, with the proviso that it is extremely easy to produce the same demonstration for moral, legal, political, aesthetic and philosophical ideologies. We shall, moreover, expressly return to this demonstration once we are in a position to speak of philosophy again.

Let us therefore consider religious ideology, using an example everyone can grasp: Christian religious ideology. We shall use a rhetorical figure and 'make this ideology speak'; in other words, we shall condense in a fictional discourse what it 'says', not only in its two Testaments, its theologians, and its sermons, but also in its practices and rituals, its ceremonies and sacraments. Christian religious ideology says this, more or less:

It says: I address myself to you, a human individual called Peter (every individual is *called* by his name, in the passive sense, it is never the individual who gives *himself* his own name), in order to tell you that God exists and that you are answerable to Him. It adds: it is God who is addressing you through my voice (since Scripture has collected the Word of God, tradition has transmitted it, and papal infallibility has fixed it for ever on 'ticklish' points, such as Mary's virginity or . . . papal infallibility itself). It says: This is who you are; you are Peter! This is your origin: you were created by God from all eternity, although you were born in 1928 Anno Domini! This is your place in the world! This is what you must do! In exchange, if you observe the 'law of love', you will be saved, you, Peter, and will become part of the Glorious Body of Christ! And so on . . .

Now this is a very well-known, commonplace discourse, but, at the same time, a very surprising one. Surprising, because if we consider that religious ideology is indeed addressed to individuals[27] in order to

---

27   Although we know that the individual is always already a subject (if only of familial ideology), we shall continue to use this term, convenient because of the contrasting effect it produces.

'transform them into subjects', interpellating the individual, Peter, in order to make him a subject free to obey or disobey the call, that is, God's commands; if it calls these individuals by their names, thus recognizing that they are always-already interpellated as subjects with a personal identity so much so that Pascal's Christ says (my word, this Pascal!): 'It is for you that I have shed this drop of my blood!'; if it interpellates them in such a way that the subject answers, 'Yes, it really is me!'; if it obtains from them the recognition that they really do hold the place it marks out for them in the world, a fixed abode − 'It really is me, I am here, a worker, boss, or soldier!' − in this vale of tears; if it obtains from them the recognition of a destination (eternal life or eternal damnation) according to the respect or contempt they show for 'God's Commandments', Law become Love; − if everything really does happen this way (in the familiar practices and rituals of baptism, confirmation, communion, confession, extreme unction, and so on), we should note that this whole 'procedure', which stages [*met en scène*] Christian religious subjects, is dominated by a strange phenomenon: there can only be such a multitude of possible religious subjects on the *absolute* condition that there is a Unique, Absolute, *Other Subject*, namely, God.

Let us agree to designate this new, singular Subject by writing subject with a capital S in what follows, to distinguish the Subject from subjects such as you and me.

It then emerges that the interpellation of individuals as subjects presupposes the 'existence' of a unique and central other Subject, in whose name religious ideology interpellates all individuals as subjects. All this is clearly written[28] in what is called, precisely, Scripture. 'And it came to pass at that time that the Lord God (Yahweh) spoke to Moses in the cloud. And the Lord called out to [*appela*] Moses, "Moses!" "It (really) is me!", said Moses; "I am your servant Moses. Speak, and I shall listen and obey!" And the Lord spoke unto Moses and said to him, "*I am That I am*".'

God thus defines Himself as the Subject *par excellence*, He who is through Himself and for Himself ('I am That I am'), and He who interpellates His subject, the individual subjected to Him by His very interpellation, that is, the individual named Moses. And Moses, interpellated-called by [*appelé*] his name, having recognized that it 'really' was he who was called by God, recognizes − yes indeed! − recognizes that he is a subject, a subject of God's, a subject subjected to God, a subject by the

---

28 I am quoting in a combined way, not literally, but 'in spirit and truth'.

Subject and subjected to the Subject. The proof is that he obeys Him and makes his people obey God's commands. And we are on the way, Ladies and Gentlemen, to the Promised Land! For God interpellates and commands, but, at the same time, promises a reward if one recognizes His existence as Big Subject and recognizes His commands, and if one obeys Him in all things. If one disobeys, He becomes the Terrible God: Beware His Holy Wrath![29]

God is thus the Subject, and Moses and the countless subjects of God's people are the Subject's interlocutors, those He has hailed: His *mirrors*, His *reflections*. Was man not created in God's *image* so that God might, with the accomplishment of his grand strategic plan of Creation-Fall-Redemption, contemplate Himself, that is, recognize Himself in him as in His Own Glory?

As all theological reflection proves, although He 'could' perfectly well have done without men, God needs them: the Subject needs the subjects, just as men need God, by all that's holy, just as the subjects need the Subject. Better: God needs men, the Big Subject needs subjects, even in the frightful inversion of His image in them (when the subjects wallow in debauchery, that is, in sin).

Better: God duplicates Himself and sends His Son into the world as a simple subject 'forsaken' by Him (the long complaint of the Garden of Olives which ends on the Cross), subject but Subject, man but God, to accomplish that which prepares the final Redemption, the Resurrection of Christ. God himself thus needs to 'make Himself' man, the Subject needs to become a subject, as if to show the subjects empirically, in a way the eye can see and the hand feel (see St Thomas), that, if they are subjects, subjected to the Subject, it is *solely so that* they may finally re-enter, on Judgement Day, the Bosom of the Lord, like Christ – that is, re-enter the Subject.[30]

Let us decipher this admirable necessity for the duplication of the Subject into subjects and of the Subject itself into a Subject-subject, and translate it into theoretical language.

We observe that the structure of all ideology, interpellating individuals as subjects in the name of a Unique and Absolute Subject, is *speculary*, in other words, a mirror-structure, and *doubly* speculary; and that this speculary duplication is constitutive of ideology and ensures its

---

29   [TN: 'Thou art terrible, and who shall resist thee? from that time thy wrath', Psalms 75:8, Douay-Rheims Bible.]

30   The dogma of the Trinity is precisely the theory of the duplication of the Subject (the Father) into a subject (the Son) and their speculary relation (the Holy Ghost).

functioning. This means that all ideology is *centred*, that the Absolute Subject occupies the unique place of the Centre and interpellates around it the infinity of individuals as subjects in a double speculary relation such that it subjects the subjects to the Subject, while giving them in the Subject in which each subject can contemplate its own (present and future) image the *guarantee* that this really is about them and really is about Him, and that since everything takes place in the family (the Holy Family: the Family is in essence Holy), 'God will *recognize* His own in it', that is, those who have recognized God and have recognized themselves in Him, and they will be saved and sit on the right hand of God (the place of the dead in our countries, where the driver sits on the left), incorporated in the Mystical Body of Christ.

Thus the duplicate mirror-structure of ideology simultaneously ensures:

1) the *interpellation* of individuals as subjects;

2) the mutual *recognition* between subjects and Subject and among the subjects themselves, as well as the recognition of the subject by himself;[31] and

3) the absolute *guarantee* that everything really is so: God really is God, Peter really is Peter, and, if the subjection of the subjects to the Subject is well respected, everything will go well for the subjects: they will 'receive their reward'.

Result: caught in this triple system of subjection, universal recognition, and absolute guarantee, the subjects, unsurprisingly, 'go'. They 'go all by themselves', without a cop behind them, and, as need dictates, when it is truly impossible to deal otherwise with the 'bad sorts', thanks to the intermittent, carefully deliberated assistance, the intervention of the detachments specialized in repression, namely, the magistrates of the Inquisition or, when it is a question of ideologies other than religious ideology, of other specialized magistrates and police officials.[32] The subjects 'go': they recognize that 'it's really true', that 'this is the way it is', not some other way, that they have to obey God, the priest, De Gaulle, the boss, the engineer, and love their neighbour, and so on. The subjects go, since they have recognized that 'all is well' (the way it is), and they say, for good measure: *So be it!*

---

31 As a 'theorist' of Universal Recognition, Hegel is an admirable, albeit partial, 'theorist' of ideology. The same holds for Feuerbach as a 'theorist' of the speculary relation. There is no theorist of the guarantee. We shall come back to this.

32 [Louis Hubert Gonzalves] Lyautey has stated the golden rule of repression: 'show your strength so as not to have to use it'. The formulation can be improved: 'do not show your strength so as to use it without having to use it . . .', and so on.

That is the proof that this *is not really the way it is*, but that that is the way *it has to be*, so that things are what they should be, and – let us come out with it – *so that the reproduction of the relations of production is ensured*, every day, every second, in the 'consciousness', that is, the material behaviour of the individuals holding the posts that the social and technical division of labour assigns them in production, exploitation, repression, ideologization and scientific practice.

We know that, in capitalist social formations, religious ideology (which exists in the religious Ideological State Apparatus) no longer plays the same role that it did in social formations based on 'serfdom'. Other ideological apparatuses play a more important role in them. Their convergent effect always has the same 'objective': the daily, uninterrupted reproduction of the relations of production in the 'consciousness', that is, the material comportment of the agents of the various functions of capitalist social production. But what we have said about the functioning and structure of religious ideology holds for all other ideologies as well. In morality, the speculary relation is that of the Subject (Duty) and the subjects (moral consciousnesses/consciences); in legal ideology, the speculary relation is that of the Subject (Justice) and the subjects (men who are free and equal); in political ideology, the speculary relation is that of the Subject (variable: the Fatherland, the National or General Interest, Progress, the Revolution) and the subjects (the members of the organization, the voters, the militants, and so on).

Revolutionary Marxist-Leninist political ideology is of course distinguished by the fact, *without historical precedent*, that it is an ideology which has been heavily 'reworked', and thus transformed, by a *science*, the Marxist science of history, social formations, the class struggle and revolution. This 'distorts' the speculary structure of ideology without doing away with it altogether ('no saviour from on high . . . no prince or peer', says the Internationale, and, consequently, no subjected subjects! . . .). In this way, the Internationale seeks to '*de-centre*' political ideology itself. To what extent is that possible, or, rather, since it is relatively possible, within what limits has it proven possible so far? That is another question.[33]

---

33 Consider the ideology of the 'personality cult', established on, among other things, survivals of the Czarist ideology (with religious overtones) of the 'Little Father of the Peoples'. The ideology that is currently being elaborated in the Western Communist Parties tends to maintain that these parties have not, for their part, practiced the ideology of the 'personality cult', not at all (PCI) or only in the case of one unfortunate expression, 'the Party of Maurice Thorez' (PCF). The ideology of the 'critique of the personality cult' is still an ideology and therefore has, notwithstanding its attempts at 'de-centring' or . . . denegation, a centre somewhere. Where? Since the 'events' in Czechoslovakia, this

Whatever the truth of the matter, and within the limits set by the resistance to attempts to de-centre, that is, to de-specularize Marxist-Leninist mass political ideology, we will find the same structure in all ideologies, and the same principles of functioning. It would be easy to show this.

Since we have, in passing, already let the phrase slip, let us turn back to the question that is surely on the tip of everyone's tongue. What is really, concretely in question in this mechanism of the speculary recognition of the Subject and the subjects, and in the guarantee given to the subjects by the Subject on condition that they accept their subjection to the 'commands' of the Subject? The reality in question in this mechanism, the reality that is miscognized in the very forms of *recognition*, which is thus necessarily *miscognition*, is, in the final analysis, the reproduction of the relations of production and the other relations deriving from them.

VIII HOW IDEOLOGY CONCRETELY 'FUNCTIONS'

It remains to show, using a few concrete examples, how this whole extraordinary (and simple) machinery functions in its actual, concrete complexity.

Why 'simple'? Because the principle of the ideology effect is simple: recognition, subjection, guarantee – the whole centred on *subjection*. Ideology makes individuals who are always-already subjects (that is, you and me) 'go'.

Why 'complex'? Because each subject (you and I) is subjected to several ideologies that are relatively independent, albeit unified under the unity of the State Ideology. For there exist, as we have seen, several Ideological State Apparatuses. Hence each subject (you and I) lives in and under several ideologies at once. Their subjection-effects are 'combined' in each subject's own acts, which are inscribed in practices, regulated by rituals, and so on.

'centre' is rather hard to identify: it is too military, something political ideology does not like. If, on the other hand, readers are prepared to examine Togliatti's term of the 'polycentrism' of the international workers' movement in the light of our analyses, or the phrase 'there is no longer any leading socialist country', or even the absence, since the dissolution of the Third International, of any International at all, or, finally, the current split in the international communist movement, they will discover in them varied examples of 'decentralization' at work, examples that are, to be honest, oddly heterogeneous and not always 'reworked' or 'monitored' by Marxist-Leninist science. Yet the day will come when the reunification of the international communist movement is ensured in forms ensuring as much 'de-centring' as possible. *Pazienza*.

This 'combination' does not go all by itself. Hence what is called a 'conflict of duties' in the marvellous terminology of our official philosophy. How are familial, moral, religious, political, or other duties to be reconciled when 'certain' circumstances present themselves? One has to make a choice and, even when one does not choose (consciously, after the 'crisis of conscience' that is one of the sacred rituals to be observed in such cases), the choice makes itself. Thus, in 1940, after France's strange defeat in the 'phoney war', De Gaulle made a choice and Pétain did, too. Frenchmen who had neither an aristocratic surname like De Gaulle's nor his means of transport also made a 'choice' – to remain in France and fight there as best they could, in the shadows, with makeshift weapons that they had wrested from the Germans, before proceeding to form armed resistance groups.

There exist other 'conflicts of duties' and other choices that, albeit less spectacular, are quite as dramatic. To take just one simple example, the Catholic Church (not God the Father) has for several years now been forcing Christian couples to bear the very heavy cross of a conflict between familial ideology and religious ideology. The object of the conflict is the 'pill'. I leave it to the reader's imagination and experience to reconstruct other 'cases of conscience', that is to say, other instances of objective grating and grinding between different ideological apparatuses: for example, cases of conscience involving jurists, magistrates, or other civil servants who find themselves torn between the orders they receive (or the objective functions they assume in the state apparatus) and their ideology, whether moral (Justice) or political (Progress and the Revolution). No one is invulnerable to such 'cases of conscience', not even certain police officials.

Let us leave this point there – it would be easy to expatiate on it – and return to our general thesis in order to show in what sense and why one can say that every social formation 'functions on ideology', in the sense in which one says that a gasoline engine 'runs on gasoline'.

We noted in passing, in connection with 'law', that law's basic function was less to ensure the reproduction of the relations of production than to regulate and control the *very functioning of production* (and of the apparatuses ensuring the reproduction of the relations of production). We can now grasp something else, for we have taken note of the fact that, because law can run only on legal-moral ideology, it helps ensure, while also regulating the functioning of the relations of production, the uninterrupted *reproduction of the relations of production* in the 'consciousness' of each subject (each agent of production, of exploitation, and so on) by means of its legal ideology.

We can now say the following. It is characteristic of the Ideological State Apparatuses that they form part of the superstructure and, as such, ensure the reproduction of the relations of production behind the protective shield of the Repressive State Apparatus and the possibility of resorting to it. However, since they ensure the reproduction of the relations of production in the 'consciousness' of subjects who are agents of production, agents of exploitation, and so on, we have to add that this reproduction of the relations of production by the Ideological State Apparatuses and their ideological effects on subjects (the agents of production and so on) is ensured *in* the functioning of the relations of production themselves.

In other words, the externality of the superstructure with respect to the base – a thesis that is justified in principle, a thesis without which nothing in the structure or functioning of a mode of production or social formation would be intelligible – is an externality exercised, in large measure, in the form of *interiority*. I mean by that, very precisely, that ideologies such as religious ideology, moral ideology, legal ideology, and even political ideology (aesthetic ideology, too: think of the craftsmen, artists, and all the others who need to consider themselves 'creators' in their work) ensure the reproduction of the relations of production (in their capacity as Ideological State Apparatuses forming part of the superstructure) at the heart of the functioning of the relations of production, which they help to 'make go all by themselves'.

In contrast, the Repressive State Apparatus does not intervene in the same way in the very functioning of the relations of production. Except when there is a general strike in local transport and military vehicles ensure 'public transport' as best they can, at least in the greater Paris region, neither the army nor the police nor even the administration as a whole intervenes directly in the functioning of the relations of production, in production, or in the Ideological State Apparatuses. There exist well-known limit cases, in which the police, the riot police, and even the army are used to 'quash' the working class, but that happens when it is on strike and thus when production has ceased. Production, however, has its own agents of internal repression (factory directors and all their underlings, from supervisory personnel to foremen, as well as most 'engineers' and even upper-level technicians, whatever they may think and whatever others think), whose existence becomes comprehensible once we have understood that there is no purely technical division of labour, but a *social-technical* division – once we have understood, in other words, that what is determinant in the unity between productive forces/relations of production (which forms the base that determines, in the last instance, what happens in the superstructure) is not the productive forces, but, within limits set by the existing productive forces, the relations of production.[34]

However, this social-technical division of labour in production (and *a fortiori* in other spheres, including the division of labour in the state apparatuses) itself runs on ideology, legal-moral ideology above all, but also, secondarily, religious, political, aesthetic and philosophical ideology. This shows us – clearly, if I may say so – the extreme simplicity and, at the same time, extreme complexity of the way production and the other spheres of activity of a social formation function. This also shows us that it is imperative to rectify our old 'topographical' representation of the relations between superstructure and base once again.

IX BASE AND SUPERSTRUCTURE

The base is dominated by the relations of production. The relations of production function (on the basis, of course, of material labour processes that produce objects of social utility as commodities) simultaneously as relations of production (thus making possible the interplay of the labour processes) and relations of exploitation. This functioning of the relations of production is ensured

1) by agents of exploitation and of the repression internal to the productive process itself, not external to it: the functions of surveillance-control-repression in the process of production are performed by, not policemen or soldiers, but agents of the productive process themselves (factory directors and all those under their orders, from supervisory personnel down to foremen, as well as most 'engineers' and upper-level technicians). This personnel can deploy all the 'tact' imaginable in exercising its functions, and all the 'avant-garde' techniques of public relations or human relations,[35] of, that is, psychology and social psychology, accompanied by all the scruples and 'ethical' considerations one likes, including their own crises of conscience and raised consciousness [*crises et prises de conscience*] which, in certain cases, can make it lean towards the proletarian camp, if not go over to it. This personnel nonetheless belongs, objectively, to the repressive personnel internal to the functioning of the relations of production;

2) by the interplay of the effects of the various ideologies, first and foremost legal-moral ideology. The result to which this leads is that, in

---

34 This thesis will be demonstrated elsewhere. [TN: See Appendix 1.]
35 [TN: In English in the original.]

the vast majority of cases, 'everyone does his duty' at his post, including proletarians at theirs, out of a conscientious sense of 'professional pride' in work well done, including proletarians when they do their (bourgeois) 'political duty' as proletarians, accepting the bourgeois legal-moral ideology that has it that their wages represent 'the value of their labour' and the bourgeois technological ideology that has it that 'after all, there have to be directors, engineers, foremen, and so on to make things work', and the whole song and dance.

In production, the functioning of the relations of production is ensured by a combination of repression and ideology in which ideology plays the dominant role.

The whole superstructure is arrayed around the state. It includes the state apparatuses, which are at the service of the representatives of the class (or classes) in power: the repressive apparatus and the Ideological State Apparatuses. The basic role of the superstructure, hence of all the state apparatuses, is to ensure the perpetuation of the exploitation of proletarians and other wage-workers, that is, to ensure the perpetuation, hence the reproduction, of the relations of production, which are simultaneously relations of exploitation.

The Repressive State Apparatus fulfils several functions. One part of it (the detachment whose special task is to apply the sanctions decreed by the juridical state apparatus) is responsible for preventing infractions, apprehending offenders, and applying material sanctions after judgements that a legal offence has been committed. The general function of this part of the repressive apparatus plus the units specialized in violent class struggle (the riot police and so on) plus the army is to provide a material political guarantee of the conditions that the Ideological State Apparatuses require in order to function.

Thus it is the Ideological State Apparatuses which assume the basic function of reproducing the relations of production – and the relations deriving from them (including those obtaining among their own 'personnel', since it, too, must be reproduced). But we have just seen that this function, although it goes well beyond the one purely internal to the normal operation of the interplay of the relations of production, is also exercised there. We have seen that 'law' is an Ideological State Apparatus specialized, above all, in guaranteeing the functioning of the relations of production. Now it is apparent that we have to broaden this proposition and say that *the other Ideological State Apparatuses ensure the reproduction of the relations of production only on condition that they simultaneously ensure, as one aspect of their own intervention, the interplay of the relations of production themselves.*

From this it follows that the knotting together of superstructure and base, which is not general and vague but extremely precise, is accomplished above all by the Ideological State Apparatuses, which figure in the superstructure only to the extent that most of their 'activity' is accomplished in the interplay of the relations of production themselves in order to ensure the reproduction of the relations of production.

This new stipulation does not call anything of what the topography shows us into question: namely, the determination in the last instance of the superstructure by the base. Quite the contrary: this crucial principle is not merely preserved but even reinforced by our analyses. On the other hand, we gain something by moving from a theory that was still too descriptive to a more 'theoretical' theory. The latter brings out the precise complexity of the intrication of superstructure and base by means of the interplay of the Ideological State Apparatuses, as well as the fact that they ensure the reproduction of the relations of production largely by ensuring the interplay of the relations of production themselves.

X A CONCRETE EXAMPLE

Need we add – so as not to remain at the level of concepts which, albeit precise, remain abstract – that all this can be empirically confirmed in the daily lives of individual subjects, whatever their posts in the social-technical 'division of labour' (production), the social division of labour tout court (exploitation, repression, ideologization), or the scientific division of labour?

Concretely, this means, to give just a few examples that any reader can multiply at will, that:

1) Proletarians would not work if they were not forced to by 'necessity', but, as well, if they were not subjected to work by legal ideology ('of course I have to work in exchange for my wage'); by a moral-economic ideology of work (consider René Clair's veridical mockery: 'work is obligatory because work is freedom'); or, in the case of 'backward' proletarians, by a religious ideology of work (we must suffer to merit salvation; Christ was a worker; the 'community' of labour prefigures the 'community' of spirit), and so on.

2) Capitalists would cease to be capitalists if their 'needs' and, above all, competition (in the final analysis, the competition between capitals confronting each other on the basis of the average rate of profit) did not force them to carry on, but, as well, if they were not sustained by their notion of themselves, shaped by a solid legal and moral ideology of property, profit and the benefits that they themselves bestow on their workers thanks to their capital ('I invest my money, do I not? I risk it,

do I not? Surely I must have something *in return*: profit. What's more, there has to be a boss to tell workers what to do. And what would they live on if it weren't for me?').

3) A civil servant working for the Ministry of Finance, a primary schoolteacher, a secondary school or college teacher, a researcher, a psychologist, a priest, an army officer, a state minister, the head of state himself, a good family man, a mother, a student, and so on and so forth . . . (the reader may provide an illustration for each category.)

To take an example of a different kind and observe the way the effects of different ideologies combine, reinforce one another, coexist, or contradict one another, let us observe what goes on in a few practical rituals of a worker. (Be it recalled that ideology ultimately exists in these rituals as well as in the acts that they determine in the practices in which they figure.)

Let us consider only the rituals of hiring or, still more simply, the ritual of leaving a factory at the end of the day. (What follows is a faithful transcription of a conversation with a comrade who is a lathe operator in a Citroën factory.)

The proletarian, when his workday is over (the moment he has been waiting for since morning), drops everything, without further ado, when the whistle blows, and heads for the lavatories and lockers. He washes up, changes his clothes, combs his hair, and becomes another man: the one who is going to join the wife and children at home. Once he gets home, he is in a completely different world that has nothing to do with the hell of the factory and its production rhythms. At the same time, however, he finds himself caught up in another ritual, the ritual of the practices and acts (free and voluntary, of course) of *familial* ideology: his relations with his wife, the kids, neighbours, parents, friends – and on Sundays, still other rituals, those of his fantasies or favourite pastimes (likewise free and voluntary): the weekend in the forest of Fontainebleau or (in a few cases) his little garden in the suburbs, and sport, the telly, radio, God knows what; and then holidays, with still other rituals (fishing, camping, Tourism and Work, People and Culture,[36] God knows what).

Caught up in these other 'systems', my comrade added, how could he be expected not to become someone other than the man he is at the

---

36 [TN: 'Tourisme et travail' and 'Peuple et culture' were created in the 1940s by communists and others active in the Resistance, the latter to provide workers and peasants access to knowledge and culture in their free time, the former to provide workers affordable holidays while promoting their 'fraternity' and access to culture. In the 1960s, 'Peuple et culture' concentrated on renting workers cheap holiday cottages in touristy areas.]

factory – for example, someone altogether different from the union militant or CGT member[37] he is? This other 'system' is, for example (this is very often the case), the ritual of the petty-bourgeois ideology of the family. Might that mean that this proletarian, 'conscious and organized' when he attends union meetings with his fellow workers, is caught up in another, petty-bourgeois ideological system once he gets back home? Why not? Such things happen. And that would explain a great deal. All the fuss with the kids, who have problems at school, naturally; and even some very odd political goings-on, of the sort that can culminate in certain 'unexpected' electoral results. For everyone knows how it is when you vote. You happen to hear De Gaulle on the TV or radio (the old fox sounded the nationalist theme and the reconciliation of the whole French people, the Greatness of France and all the accompanying tralala). You go to vote with the family on Sunday and stuff an anonymous ballot in the ballot-box when you come out of the voting booth. No one sees, no one knows how you vote. It takes only a moment of conformist vertigo to succumb to petty-bourgeois electoral political ideology, nationalist, above all – and so you vote for De Gaulle. Yet the union had declared that you should not vote for De Gaulle. The day after, it is a safe bet that there will be an article by Jacques Fauvet[38] (this, too, is a ritual) in *Le Monde* about the law of the 'pendulum' that governs electoral results.

Obviously. The next day, however, the proletarian goes back to his factory and sees his buddies again. Thank God, they didn't all react the way he did. But it's hard to be a union militant and even harder to be a revolutionary militant all your life. Above all when 'nothing is happening'.

When nothing is happening, the Ideological State Apparatuses have worked to perfection. When they no longer manage to function, to reproduce the relations of production in the 'consciousness' of all subjects, 'events' happen, as the phrase goes, more or less serious events, as in May, the commencement of a first dress rehearsal. With, at the end, some day or the other, after a long march, the revolution.

By way of a provisional conclusion

I shall end here, at the close of volume 1, the analysis I have undertaken.

I shall pursue it in a second volume that will appear later.

---

37 [TN: See Chapter 7, n. 2.]

38 [TN: In 1969, Jacques Fauvet was elected editor of the leading French newspaper *Le Monde*, which, under his lead, became more favourable to the Left represented by the PCF and the Socialist Party.]

In the second volume, I shall examine the following questions in the order indicated:

1) social classes
2) the class struggle
3) ideologies
4) 'sciences'
5) philosophy
6) the proletarian class standpoint in philosophy
7) revolutionary philosophical intervention in scientific practice and in the practice of the proletarian class struggle.

In this way, we will come back to the 'subject' from which we set out – philosophy – and will be able to answer our initial question: What is Marxist–Leninist philosophy? By the time we do, however, our initial question will have been 'slightly' modified.

APPENDIX 1

On the Primacy of the Relations of Production over the Productive Forces

Things must be *as clear as possible* when it comes to the absolutely fundamental thesis of the primacy of the relations of production, which may be the key[1] to one part of the history of the international socialist and then the communist movement.

Why 'as clear as possible' rather than 'perfectly clear'? Why this limitation and a reservation of this kind?

1) Because things are not clear and are not easy to clarify, even in the minds of a number of Marxist and communist militants, as a result of the history they have experienced.

2) Because, besides the confusions sown by this history, they are exposed to the influence of bourgeois ideology, which is basically 'economistic' and constantly insinuates (or imposes) the 'self-evident' but false idea that everything depends in the last instance on the productive forces and, especially, 'the impetuous development of the sciences and technology' – on the 'prodigious mutation' [*sic*] that we are supposedly witnessing.

3) Because there unfortunately exist texts by Marx that are extremely ambiguous, to say the least – one in particular, the famous 'Preface' to the 1859 *Critique*; and because this text was both the Second International's and also Stalin's Bible.

4) Because it is theoretically very hard to formulate the question in fully elaborated form, and because this will take effort and time.

That said, here is the thesis in question, to which I give the following precise form: '*Within the specific unity of the productive forces and relations of production constituting a mode of production, the relations of production play the determining role, on the basis of, and within the objective limits set by, the existing productive forces.*'

The polemic starts immediately. I shall start it myself.

---

1 [TN: Crossed out: 'qui est la clé' (which is the key).]

One will immediately oppose texts of Marx's to this Thesis. To begin with, the well-known lines from *The Poverty of Philosophy* (1847), in which Marx says: with the water-mill, you have feudalism; with the steam engine, you have capitalism.[2] The productive forces, then, in line with their 'level of development', endow themselves with, as it were, *their* relations of production – that is, with the corresponding relations of production, those adequate to these productive forces. Every revolution in the productive forces, since it leads to non-correspondence with the old relations of production, precipitates a revolution in the relations of production that puts the new relations of production in new (and adequate) correspondence with the new productive forces.

This is plainly stated in the famous 'Preface' (published in 1859, by Marx himself, who thus vouched for its accuracy) to *A Contribution to the Critique of Political Economy*. Here is the core passage in this preface in my translation,[3] based on the German text in the 1953 Dietz edition (*Zur Kritik*, pp. 13–14):

In the social production of their existence, men enter into relations that are determinate, necessary, and independent of their will: relations of production, which correspond to a determinate degree of development of their material productive forces. The ensemble of these relations of production represents the economic structure of society, the real base on which there arises a legal and political superstructure and to which there correspond determinate forms of social consciousness. The mode of production of material life conditions, in general, the process of social, political and intellectual life. It is not men's consciousness that determines their being; on the contrary, their social being determines their consciousness. *The material productive forces of society, at a certain degree of their development, enter into contradiction with*

---

2 [TN: The standard, more accurate, English translation reads: 'The hand-mill gives you society with the feudal lord; the steam-mill, society with the industrial capitalist.' Karl Marx, *The Poverty of Philosophy: Answer to the* Philosophy of Poverty *by M. Proudhon*, trans. Frida Knight, in Karl Marx and Friedrich Engels, *Collected Works*, London, Lawrence and Wishart, 1975–2002, vol. 6, p. 166.]

3 [TN: The present English translation is based on Althusser's French translation. Althusser translates the same passage somewhat differently ten years later in 'Marx dans ses limites', *Écrits philosophiques et politiques*, vol. 1, eds François Matheron and Olivier Corpet, Paris, Stock/Imec, 1994, pp. 421–3 (*Philosophy of the Encounter*, trans. G. M. Goshgarian, London, Verso, 2006, pp. 55–6). For another English translation, see Preface to *A Contribution to the Critique of Political Economy*, trans. S.W. Ryazanskaya, in Karl Marx and Friedrich Engels, *Collected Works*, vol. 29, pp. 261–3.]

the existing relations of production, or – this is merely a legal term designating them – with the property relations *within which they had hitherto
operated. From forms of development of the productive forces, these relations are
transformed into fetters on the productive forces.* There then begins a period
of social revolution. With the changes in the economic base, the whole
immense superstructure is overturned, more or less slowly or
rapidly . . . *A social formation never disappears before all the productive forces
that it is spacious enough to hold have been developed, and new, superior relations of production never take the place of the old ones before their material
conditions have matured-blossomed at the heart of the old society. That is why
humanity only ever sets itself tasks that it can accomplish, for, upon closer
examination, one constantly finds that the task itself arises only when the material conditions for accomplishing it are already present or, at least, caught up in
the process of becoming.* In broad outline, the Asiatic, ancient, feudal and
modern-bourgeois modes of production may be designated as progressive epochs of the economic social formation. Bourgeois relations of
production are the last antagonistic form of the social process of
production – antagonistic not in the sense of individual antagonism,
but of an antagonism that issues from the social conditions of individuals' lives. However, the productive forces that develop in the heart of
bourgeois society simultaneously create the material conditions for
resolving this antagonism. *This social formation therefore closes the prehis-
tory of human society.*

A detail: the words in italics in the text were italicized not by Marx but
by me. We shall see why in a moment.

A remark: there can be no question here of putting so short and, necessarily, sharply condensed text on trial. Be it noted, however, that there is no
explicit mention of the state or social classes in this text, or even any implicit
mention of the *class struggle*, although, as the *Manifesto* had declared, it plays
the role of 'motor' in all of human history and, in particular, 'social revolutions', which are here evoked only in connection with the contradiction
between productive forces and relations of production. This odd silence is
perhaps not due solely to the constraints imposed by the brevity of the exposé.

A second remark: this text is practically the only one of Marx's that
contains an exposé of the basic principles of historical materialism. That
is why it has become classic. Stalin reproduced it nearly verbatim in his
essay 'Dialectical Materialism and Historical Materialism'.[4] On the other

---

4 Joseph Stalin, *Dialectical and Historical Materialism*, New York, International
Publishers, 1970.

hand, to my (limited) knowledge, Lenin never put it at the centre of his thinking or action; nor did he ever suggest it was the Bible, even the heavily abridged Bible, of historical materialism. He cites only the text's incontestable passages.

One final remark: we know, from Marx's correspondence with Engels, that he happened to have 'reread', admiringly, Hegel's *Science of Logic* in 1858. The obvious Hegelian influence in *Grundrisse*, which dates from the 1857–59 period, seems to me to be conspicuous in this Preface. Let us recall that *Capital*, which has a very different ring to it, dates from *eight years later*.

Here is my demonstration:

All the terms that I have italicized belong to Hegelian philosophy, as anyone who has read any Hegel at all (especially *The Philosophy of History*, above all the Introduction) can confirm and must admit. More precisely, Marx has not just borrowed Hegelian terminology, but has taken up the Hegelian *conception* itself, with one difference that is important but basically changes nothing. The set of these Hegelian terms forms a system that functions in Marx's text in accordance with the Hegelian conception itself.

This *conception* is that of alienation, which finds expression in the dialectic of correspondence and non-correspondence (or 'contradiction', 'antagonism') between *Form* and *Content*. The dialectic of non-contradiction (correspondence) and contradiction ('non-correspondence') between Form and Content as well as the dialectic of degrees of development of the productive forces (in Hegel, the *moments* of the development of the Idea) are 100 per cent Hegelian.

What belongs to Marx in this text are the concepts of productive forces, relations of production, base and superstructure, and social formation. These concepts stand in for the following Hegelian notions: content of the moment of the Idea, internalization–objectivation, forms of development of this content, 'peoples'. The new Marxist concepts are simply substituted for the Hegelian notions. The ensemble *functions on the Hegelian dialectic* of non-contradictory, then contradictory alienation between *Content* and *Form*, and thus on the theoretical basis of the Hegelian conception itself.

This Hegelian conception has it that each 'historical people' represents a moment (a degree) of the development of the Idea; that the content of this degree was formed at the heart of the previous developed moment of the previous 'people', like the kernel of an almond; and that, at a given moment, the new content (the almond) enters into contradiction with the previous form (the shell) and bursts it, in order to endow itself with its own forms of development (its new shell).[5] Hegel thinks this process in the form of the content's externalization-alienation in forms specific to it: at the heart of these forms, a new kernel is once again constituted – it is embryonic at first, then becomes more and more substantial: a new almond (a new, 'superior' 'degree' of the 'development' of the Idea). This new kernel will enter into contradiction with the existing Form (shell), and the process continues until the end of History, when the ultimate contradiction is resolved (for Hegel, in the unity of the French Revolution and the German religiosity consecrated by his own philosophy).

Going back to Marx's text, we find, word for word, the same schema, with the development of the material productive forces in progressive, 'superior' degrees standing in for the development of 'degrees' or moments of development of the Idea. We also find the thesis that each degree (of development) of the productive forces has to develop all its resources in the space that the existing relations of production allow it before the intervention of the contradiction that proves fatal for those relations of production, no longer 'spacious enough' to hold the new content as its form, and so on. We also find the finality[6] by virtue of which the future that will replace the past is developing in a social formation at every moment; this grounds the famous thesis that 'humanity' (a strange 'Marxist' concept) 'only ever sets itself tasks that it can accomplish', because the means needed to accomplish it [*sic*] are, every time, already completely ready – providentially, as it were – and to hand. We also find the finality[6] that was the delight of the Second International's evolutionism (later adopted by Stalin): the regulated, 'progressive' succession of modes of production, tending towards the end of class society. Is it, then, any wonder that there is no mention at all of *class struggle*, since everything is apparently regulated by the play of the 'correspondence' and subsequent contradiction between content (the productive forces) and form (the relations of production)?

To repeat: there can be no question of putting Marx [on trial][7] for writing this handful of very equivocal lines, or even for publishing them (whereas he did not publish other, still more dubious manuscripts, such as the *1844 Manuscripts* or even *The German Ideology*). For all of *Capital* protests against this Hegelianism, in its deepest spirit and, barring a few unfortunate but rare formulas, its letter as well. In *Capital*, indeed, 1) the

---

5   The image is Hegel's.
6   [TN: Crossed out: '*téléologie*', replaced with *finalité*.]
7   [TN: The phrase 'on trial', absent from the manuscript, has been supplied by the editor.]

unity of the productive forces and relations of production is no longer conceived of at all as the relationship of a Content to its Form; and 2) the accent is put on the relations of production, the primacy of which is unquestionably affirmed.

We must, however, take note of a historical fact of crucial importance for the history of the workers' movement. Here I consider just one element. It is only a symptom, after all, but I believe it is serious enough to warrant reflection.

The fact is that, in the history of the Marxist workers' movement, this famous, unfortunate 1859 Preface has constituted the Law and the Prophets for some people and been totally neglected by others. One could, in other words, write a history of the Marxist workers' movement by considering the answer given to the following question: Within the unity productive forces/relations of production, to which element should we assign *primacy*, theoretically and politically?

Some have answered (in their texts and acts): primacy must be assigned to the productive forces. Their names are, first, those of most of the Second International's leaders, beginning with Bernstein and Kautsky; and also Stalin.

Others have answered (in their texts and acts): primacy must be assigned to the relations of production. Their names are Lenin and Mao. It is no accident that Lenin and Mao led their communist parties to the victory of the Revolution.

I simply ask the following question. How, if Lenin and Mao had ever taken the central thesis of the Preface literally – '*A social formation never disappears before all the productive forces that it is spacious enough to hold have been developed, and new relations of production never take the place of the old ones before their material conditions have matured-blossomed in the old society*' – how could Lenin and Mao ever have taken the lead of the party and masses and secured the victory of the socialist revolution?

This was the very thesis that Kautsky used against Lenin when he accused him of 'making the revolution too early' in a backward country whose productive forces were a thousand miles from being sufficiently developed to 'warrant' receiving (at the hands of the unspeakable voluntarist-putschist named Lenin) relations of production that were obviously 'premature' . . . Kautsky might even have added (and perhaps did: he ought to be read) that capitalist Russia's productive forces, once freed of the burden represented by Nicholas II, were far from having developed *all* their resources in the new capitalist relations of production that had already undergone considerable development before Czarism fell . . .

What should we say of China, whose productive forces were less developed at the time of its 1949 revolution than Russia's in 1917? Had Kautsky been alive, he might well have excoriated Mao's 'voluntarism' and 'putschism' still more severely . . . But let us here say no more about these questions, which are still burning questions – and not just on account of what we can perceive from afar of what was at issue in China during the Great Leap Forward and, later, Mao's eviction from power and subsequent return to it in the Proletarian Cultural Revolution. It seems to me that, here too, this question of the primacy of the productive forces or relations of production must again have played a certain role.

Let us discuss what is closer and more familiar to us: not the 'personality cult', but Stalin's politics as it took shape around 1930 and was pursued with unremitting tenacity thereafter. I do not think it is any accident that Stalin took up the theses of the 1859 Preface word for word in 1938.

Incontestably, we can characterize Stalin's politics (inasmuch as, from the 1930–32 'turn' onwards, Stalin was, in the last resort, the only one to take political decisions) by saying that it was *the consistent politics of the primacy of the productive forces over the relations of production*. It would be interesting to examine, in this regard, Stalin's policies [*politique*] in connection with planning and the peasantry; the role he assigned the party; and even certain stupefying formulas such as the one which, defining 'man' as 'the most valuable *capital*', obviously treated man with regard to labour-power alone, in other words, as nothing more nor less than a component of the productive forces (consider the related theme of Stakhanovism).

Of course, one can justify this politics by citing the absolutely urgent necessity of endowing Soviet Russia, threatened by imperialist encirclement and aggression, with productive forces and a heavy industry that would enable it to confront the predictable, because virtually inevitable, ordeal of war. Of course, it can also be said that primitive socialist accumulation could only be carried out, in this urgent situation, at the cost of the peasantry, and by virtually 'all available means', and so on. Of course, it can be added that the bulk of the working class, which had made the 1917 Revolution, had been massacred in the overt civil war and the disguised civil war that reigned for years in the countryside, where untold worker militants were quite simply killed; and that Stalin's party could no longer be Lenin's party after these massacres and years of famine. Granted.

Yet I cannot help asking the question that haunts me – for it haunts us all. Might it not be that Stalin fell short of Lenin's politics, as his 1938 text attests, veering towards the tradition of the Second International's politics, the politics of the primacy of the productive forces over the relations of production? All the objective difficulties notwithstanding, would a different politics not have been possible, possible *for a very long time*, down to the moment when the logic of the politics that *was* decided on had gained the upper hand over everything else and precipitated everything we know: the victory over Nazism, but also systematic massacres whose method and magnitude are stupefying – to say nothing else?

Since I am on the subject (I am very well aware of how little I am advancing, in the face of events that still dwarf our understanding of them, and aware as well of the risk I am taking), let me go back to the USSR of the period following the Twentieth Congress and all the thorny problems being debated in connection with the issue of planning, 'liberalization' of the plan, and so on: might it not be that *the contemporary USSR*, now that an end has been put to the police abuses bound up with Stalin's politics, *is pursuing the same politics of the primacy of the productive forces*? All the Soviet texts one can read, all the conversations one can have with Soviet citizens,[8] the improbable thesis put forward by Khrushchev (and not repudiated since) to the effect that the USSR has moved beyond the dictatorship of the proletariat and is entering the period of the construction of . . . communism, as well as the other thesis to the effect that *economic* competition with the United States will determine the fate of socialism in the rest of the world (the well-known talk of 'Goulash Communism': when 'they' see what we *produce*, 'they' will be won over to socialism!) – all this is food for thought. We cannot hold back the question on our lips: *Where is the Soviet Union going? Does it know?*

I return to my proposition about the primacy of the relations of production over the productive forces. We have to perform a gigantic task of theoretical elaboration in order to pronounce on this question: that of knowing what productive forces and relations of production are, not only for a given mode of production, but for a social formation, in which several modes of production exist under the domination of one of them; that of knowing what becomes of this unity in a capitalist social formation *in the imperialist stage*, which adds supplementary determinations that are not secondary but essential to the question of this 'unity'. How is it possible not to see, for instance, that if the 1917 Russian Revolution and the Chinese Revolution broke out at the end of world wars, at the 'weakest links', these weakest links were links in a chain known as *imperialism*? How is it possible not to see that if these revolutions, which triumphed in technologically backward countries, could and can overcome the backwardness of their productive forces in a relatively short

---

8 [TN: Crossed out: 'all the conversations I have managed to have with a few Soviet citizens'.]

span, the reason is the state of the productive forces at the international level, especially the very advanced state of *technology*? That is why, all things considered, and so as not to give the impression that I am indulging a theoretical penchant for voluntarism and adventurism, I have written, and here repeat, that the primacy of the relations of production over the productive forces should not be indiscriminately invoked, but invoked *on the basis of, and within the limits set by, the objectively existing forces of production*, taking into account the fact, the limits of which are also precise – depend, that is, on precise conditions – that the modern productive forces, namely, technology at the highest level, are now basically available to every country that, once it has successfully carried out its revolution, can overcome the backwardness of its productive forces in conditions unimaginable in the past. The USSR proved this between 1917 and 1941. China is proving it as well, if only by the sign represented by its atomic bomb.

Many other considerations on the difference between revolutions we know should be discussed at a theoretical level. The French bourgeoisie had developed not just its productive forces, but also, to a great extent, its relations of production, *before* the 1789 Revolution. The Russian capitalist bourgeoisie had done so as well before the February Revolution. The same holds for the Chinese bourgeoisie. In the case of the Russian and Chinese Revolutions, the bourgeois revolution was made possible only by the participation of huge masses of common people, who promptly moved beyond the bourgeois revolution to the proletarian revolution. That can no longer occur in our country: the bourgeois revolution has already taken place. In the heart of Western capitalist social formations – contrary to what happened in the case of feudal social formations, 'at the heart of which' very powerful elements of the relations of production of the capitalist mode of production had indeed 'grown up' – elements of the socialist mode of production that can be taken at all seriously do not develop anywhere, and for good reason. They do not exist there any more than they existed in Russia or China. The revolution will therefore necessarily take a different form in our country, *without the least support or consent from the bourgeoisie*, but with the support of its victims and its victims alone, grouped around the proletariat.

Note on the ISAs

The charge most often levelled at my 1969–70 essay on the ISAs is *'functionalism'*. Readers thought they saw in my theoretical sketch an attempt to subscribe, on behalf of Marxism, to an interpretation that defined organs by their functions alone, their immediate functions, thus *immobilizing* society within ideological institutions charged with functions of subjection: ultimately, a non-dialectical interpretation the deep logic of which excluded all possibility of class struggle.

I do not think readers have paid enough attention to the notes at the end of my essay, which emphasize the 'abstract' nature of my analysis and explicitly locate the class struggle at the heart of my concerns.

For we can say that the specificity of the theory of ideology deducible from Marx consists in affirming the *primacy of the class struggle* over the functions and functioning of the state apparatus and Ideological State Apparatuses. This primacy is obviously incompatible with functionalism of any kind.

For it is clear that we cannot regard the system by which the dominant class provides society with ideological 'leadership', that is to say, the consensus effects of the dominant ideology ('which is the ideology of the dominant class' – Marx), as a pure and simple *fact*, a *system of defined organs* that *automatically* duplicate the same class's violent domination or are put in place by the clear political consciousness of this class to ends defined by their functions. For the dominant ideology is never a *fait accompli of class struggle* that is itself exempt from class struggle.

For the dominant ideology, which exists in the complex system of Ideological State Apparatuses, is for its part the result of a very long, very harsh class struggle through which the bourgeoisie (to take that example) can achieve its goals only on the twofold condition that it struggle *simultaneously* against the old dominant ideology, which lives on in the old apparatuses, and the ideology of the new exploited class, which seeks its own forms of organization and struggle. This ideology, by means of which the bourgeoisie succeeds in establishing its hegemony over the old landed aristocracy and also the working class, is constituted not just by an *external* struggle against these two classes, but also and at the same time by an *internal* struggle to overcome the contradictions of bourgeois class fractions and realize the unity of the bourgeoisie as the dominant class.

We have to conceive of the *reproduction* of the dominant ideology in this sense. Viewed formally, the dominant class has to reproduce its material, political and ideological conditions of existence (to exist is to be reproduced). But the reproduction of the dominant ideology is not simple repetition, simple reproduction. It is not even an automatic, which is to say mechanical, reproduction on an extended scale of *given* institutions, defined once and for all by their function. Rather, it is the combat for the unification and renewal *of prior ideological elements*, which are disparate and contradictory, within a unity conquered in and through the class struggle in opposition to prior forms and new antagonistic tendencies. The combat for the reproduction of the dominant ideology is a combat that is never over; it has to be taken up again and again, and always under the law of the class struggle.

There are several reasons for the fact that the combat for the unification of the dominant ideology is 'never over' and must always 'be taken up again'. It is not just because of the *persistence* of the old dominant class's ideological forms and Ideological State Apparatuses, which put up fierce resistance (what Lenin calls 'habit'). It is not just because of the vital necessity of forging the *unity* of the dominant class, a product of the contradictory fusion[1] of various class fractions (mercantile capital, industrial capital, finance capital, and so on) and the necessity of making that class realize its *'general interests' as a class*, over and above the contradictions of the 'particular interests' of individual capitalists. It is not just because of the class struggle that has to be waged against the nascent forms of the *ideology of the dominated class*. It is not just because of the historical transformation of the mode of production, which dictates that the dominant ideology be *'adapted'* to the class struggle (today, the legal ideology of the classic bourgeoisie is yielding to technocratic ideology). It is also because of the *materiality and diversity of the practices* whose 'spontaneous' ideology must be unified. This huge, contradictory task is never completely accomplished, and there is reason to doubt that the model of the 'ethical state', whose utopian ideal Gramsci borrowed from Croce, will ever

---

1 [TN: Crossed out: 'encounter' (*rencontre*)].

exist. Just as the class struggle never ceases, so the dominant class's combat to unify existing ideological elements and forms never ceases. This amounts to saying that the dominant ideology *can never completely resolve its own contradictions*, which are a reflection of the class struggle – although its function is to resolve them.

That is why we can derive from this thesis *of the primacy of the class struggle over the dominant ideology* and *the Ideological State Apparatuses* another thesis, its direct consequence: the Ideological State Apparatuses are necessarily both the site and the stake of a class struggle that extends the general class struggle dominating a social formation into the apparatuses of the dominant ideology. If the function of the ISAs is to inculcate the dominant ideology, the reason is that there is *resistance*; if there is resistance, the reason is that there is struggle. In the final analysis, this struggle is a direct or indirect echo of the class struggle, sometimes a close echo, more often a distant one. The May 1968 events brought this fact into the broad light of day, revealing a struggle that had until then been mute and suppressed. However, in revealing, in the form of a revolt, an *immediate* class struggle in the Ideological State Apparatuses (especially the scholastic apparatus, followed by the medical apparatus, architectural apparatus, and so on), they have somewhat obscured the basic phenomenon commanding these *immediate* events: the fact that the historical *constitution* and contradictory *reproduction* of the dominant ideology are inherently characterized by class struggle. May 1968 was 'experienced' in the absence of any historical or political perspective in the strong sense of those terms. That is why I considered it necessary to recall that, in order to understand the facts of the class struggle in the Ideological State Apparatuses and put the revolt in proper perspective, we had to adopt '*the standpoint of reproduction*', which is the standpoint of the class struggle as an *overall process* [*procès d'ensemble*], not a sum of confrontations that are punctual or limited to this or that 'sphere' (the economy, politics, ideology); and as a *historical process*, not *isolated* episodes of repression or revolt.

When I recall these perspectives, I find it truly difficult to understand how anyone can impute to me a 'functionalist' or 'systems-theory' interpretation of the superstructure and ideology, one that ignores class struggle in favour of a mechanistic conception of instances.

II

Other objections to my essay have to do with the nature of political parties, that of the *revolutionary political party* above all. In a word, readers have tended to ascribe to me the view that *each* political party taken by itself is an Ideological State Apparatus. This could have the effect of radically locking every political party into the 'system' of the Ideological State Apparatuses, subjecting it to the law of that 'system', and excluding the possibility of a revolutionary party from the 'system'. If all parties are ISAs and serve the dominant ideology, a revolutionary party, reduced to this 'function', becomes unthinkable.

But I have never written that a political party is an Ideological State Apparatus. I have even said (only briefly, I admit) *something quite different*: that political parties are merely the *'component parts'* of a specific Ideological State Apparatus, the *political* Ideological State Apparatus, which 'realizes' the dominant class's political ideology in, let us say, its 'constitutional regime' (the 'fundamental laws' under the monarchy of the Ancien Régime, the *Parlement*, and so on; the parliamentary-representative regime under the bourgeoisie in its 'liberal' phases).

I am afraid that readers have not clearly understood what I was proposing to think under the term *political* Ideological State Apparatus. To get a better grasp on it, one must carefully distinguish the *political* Ideological State Apparatus from the (repressive) *state apparatus*.

What constitutes the (repressive) *state apparatus*, whose unity, even when it is contradictory, is still infinitely greater than that of the ensemble of Ideological State Apparatuses? The state apparatus comprises the chief of state; the government and the administration, an instrument of the executive; the armed forces; the police; the judiciary; and the courts and their dispositives (prisons and so on).

Within this ensemble, we have to distinguish what I will call the *political state apparatus*, comprising the chief of state, the government that he or she directly leads (in the system current in France and many other countries), and the administration (which *carries out* government policy). The chief of state represents the unity and will of the dominant class – the authority capable of seeing to it that the dominant class's general interests prevail over its members' or fractions' particular interests. [French President] Giscard d'Estaing very conscientiously 'laid his cards on the table' in announcing that if the Left were to carry the 1978 [legislative] elections, he would remain in office 'to defend Frenchpeople's freedoms' (read: the bourgeois class's freedoms). The government (which is currently under the direct orders of the chief of state) executes the politics of the dominant class, while the administration, under the government's direct orders, applies it in detail. This distinction, which brings out the existence of the *political state apparatus*, indicates that the administration is part of that apparatus, notwithstanding the ideology (which it lives on, like the bourgeois state) that has it that it 'serves the general interest' and plays the role of a 'public service'. It is not a question of individual intentions, or of exceptions: the administration's function is, overall, inseparable from the application of the bourgeois government's politics, which is a class politics. The upper levels of the state administration, charged with applying that politics in detail, play a directly political role, while the administration as a whole increasingly plays the role of 'gridding' [*quadrillage*]. It cannot apply the bourgeois government's politics unless it is also charged with supervising the way individuals and groups execute them and denouncing those who fail to respect them to the repressive forces, or handing them over to them.

Understood this way, the *political state apparatus* (chief of state, government, administration) is part of the (repressive) state apparatus. It may legitimately be singled out within the state apparatus.

We now come to the tricky part: the *political state apparatus* (chief of state, government, administration) must be distinguished from the *political Ideological State Apparatus*. The former is part of the (repressive) state apparatus, whereas the latter is one of the Ideological State Apparatuses.

What is to be understood by the term *political* Ideological State Apparatus? The 'political system' or 'constitution' of a given social formation. Thus the French bourgeoisie, like all contemporary bourgeoisies in capitalist countries, has generally deemed the political system of *parliamentary representation*, which has realized bourgeois ideology in a *political* Ideological State Apparatus, to be the one best suited to it. However, it has, in class struggle situations dangerous for it, endowed itself with other regimes as well (Bonapartism I and II; the constitutional monarchy of the Restoration; Pétain's fascism).

The parliamentary political ISA may be defined as an (electoral) mode of representation of the 'will of the people' by elected delegates (more or less universal suffrage) to whom the government, chosen by the chief of state or the parliament itself, is supposed to be 'answerable' or 'responsible' for its politics. It is, however, well known that the government in fact has at its disposal an impressive set of means for dodging and circumventing this 'responsibility' (therein lies the advantage of this apparatus for the bourgeoisie). To begin at the beginning, it can, every imaginable form of pressure aside, falsify the results of 'universal suffrage'. It can, further, use the parliamentary rules in force to the same end (census suffage, disinfranchisement of women and young people, indirect election, the 'separation' of powers, a bicameral system with different constituencies for each chamber, bans on revolutionary parties, and so on). Such are the real *facts*. But what justifies calling the 'political system' an '*Ideological State Apparatus*' is the *fiction*, corresponding to a 'certain' reality, that the component parts of this system, as well as the principle of its functioning, are based on *the ideology of the 'freedom' and 'equality'* of the individual voters and the 'free choice' of the people's representatives by the individuals who 'make up' the people. This choice supposedly depends on the *idea* each individual has of the politics the state should put into practice. It is on the basis of this fiction (for the state's politics is ultimately determined by the dominant class's interests in the class struggle) that *'political parties'* are founded, supposedly in order to formulate and represent the major divergent (or convergent) options for a basic national politics. Each individual can then 'freely' express an opinion by voting for the political party of his or her choice (assuming it has not been condemned to operate illegally).

Be it noted that there *can* be a degree of reality to political parties. Basically, *if the class struggle is sufficiently developed*, they can roughly represent the interests of antagonistic classes or class fractions in the class struggle, or, again, those of social strata seeking to promote their special interests within class conflicts. By way of this reality, the fundamental class antagonism *can* ultimately emerge into the light, notwithstanding all the obstacles and impostures of the 'system'. I say 'can', because we know that there are bourgeois countries (the USA, Great Britain, Federal Germany, and so on) in which the political development of class struggles *does not succeed in attaining the threshold of electoral representation*: in such cases, parliamentary antagonisms are only very remote, or even completely distorted, indices of real class antagonisms. The bourgeoisie in such countries is perfectly invulnerable, shielded by a parliamentary system that goes round in circles or simply idles. On the other hand, cases can occur in which the working class's economic and political class struggle becomes so powerful that the bourgeoisie fears the 'verdict of universal suffrage' (France, Italy), although it also has considerable means to hand with which to overturn that verdict or reduce it to naught. It is enough to recall the Chamber in the Popular Front period in France: it took the bourgeoisie just two years to break its majority and then hand it over to Pétain with the Chamber's *own approval*.

I believe that, if we confront the 'principles' of the parliamentary regime with facts and results, no one can doubt their *ideological* nature.

Bourgeois ideology in its entirety, from legal ideology through philosophical ideology to moral ideology, all of which have been disseminated for centuries, maintains the following 'self-evident truth' of 'human rights': every individual is free to choose his ideas and his camp (his party) in politics. Above all, it maintains the idea underlying this 'self-evident truth', which is ultimately simply an imposture: *the idea that a society is made up of individuals* (Marx: 'society is not made up of individuals', but of classes confronting each other in the class struggle); that the *general will* emerges from the ballot box in an election by majority vote; and that this general will, represented by the parties' delegates in parliament, forges *the politics of the nation*. In reality, it only ever forges the politics of a class, the dominant class.

It is all too obvious that this political ideology is part of the dominant ideology and in full harmony with it: we find the same ideology everywhere in bourgeois ideology (which, let us note, has for the last ten years been undergoing a process of transformation). This will hardly surprise anyone who knows that the 'matrix' of this dominant ideology is *legal ideology*, which is indispensable to the functioning of bourgeois law. The fact that an ideology *can be found everywhere* indicates that we have to do with the *dominant* ideology. And it is *from this permanent reciprocal reference from one 'self-evident truth' to the next*, from the 'self-evident truth' of legal ideology to the 'self-evident truth' of moral ideology, from there to the 'self-evident truth' of philosophical ideology, and from there to the 'self-evident truth' of political ideology that *every* ideological 'self-evident truth' draws its *immediate confirmation*, imposing itself on every individual by way of the various practices of the ISAs. This ideology of the rights of man, freedom, equality, the freedom to choose one's ideas and one's representative, and equality at the polls, has in the end produced – not by dint of the power of 'ideas', but as a result of class struggle – the ideological *apparatus* in which the political ideology of the rights of man has materialized and become – except for Marxist criticism – a 'self-evident truth' that is accepted without visible coercion by the electorate or, in any case, the overwhelming majority of the electorate. We plainly have to do with an apparatus here, since it presupposes an entire rule-bound material dispositive, from the electoral rolls through the paper ballot and the voting booth to election campaigns and the parliaments that result from them, and so on. But we also plainly have to do with an *ideological* apparatus, since it functions without violence, 'all by itself', 'on the ideology' of its agents, who accept its rules and practise them by observing them, convinced as they are that they must 'fulfil their duty to vote' and that that is 'normal'. Subjection and consensus are one and the same thing. This 'self-evident truth', imposed by bourgeois ideology, is accepted as a 'self-evident truth' by the voters; they consider themselves voters and take their places in the system. They 'play the game by the rules'.

If this analysis is accurate, no one can affirm, on any grounds whatsoever – as some have 'hastily' done, in order to lock me into a theory that supposedly rules out all possibility of revolutionary action – that all parties, including the parties of the working class, *are, as parties, so many Ideological State Apparatuses*, integrated into the bourgeois system and therefore incapable of waging their class struggle.

If what I have just said is right, it is, on the contrary, clear that the existence of political parties, far from negating the class struggle, is based on it. And if the bourgeoisie constantly strives to exercise its ideological and political hegemony over the parties of the working class, that, too, is a form of class struggle; the bourgeoisie succeeds to the extent that the working-class parties fall into the trap, either because their leaders are intimidated (the 1914–18 *Union Sacrée*) or simply 'bought off', or because the basis of the working-class parties is diverted from its revolutionary task by material advantages (the worker aristocracy), or, again, because it yields to the influence of bourgeois ideology (revisionism).

III

These effects of the class struggle appear even more clearly when we consider the revolutionary workers' parties – for example, communist parties. Since they are organizations of the workers' class struggle, the interests of the bourgeois class and its political system are utterly *foreign* to them, *in principle* (for they, too, can lapse into reformism and revisionism). Their ideology (on the basis of which they recruit) is inimical to bourgeois ideology. Their organizational form (democratic centralism) distinguishes them from bourgeois parties and even social-democratic and socialist parties. Their objective is not to confine their activity to parliamentary competition, but to extend the class struggle to all workers, from the economic sphere to politics and ideology, in *forms of action* that are specific to them and obviously have nothing to do with stuffing a ballot in a ballot box once every five years. Conducting the proletarian class struggle *in all areas and far beyond the confines of parliament* – that is a communist party's task. *Its ultimate vocation* is not to 'participate' in *government*, but to overturn and destroy bourgeois state power.

We must insist on this point, since most Western European Communist Parties today declare themselves to be 'parties of government'. *Even if a communist party does happen to participate in a government* (and it can be correct to do so in certain circumstances), *it cannot, on any grounds, be defined as a 'party of government'* – whether one is dealing with a government under the domination of the bourgeois class or a government under the domination of the proletarian class ('dictatorship of the proletariat').

This point is crucial; for a communist party has no business entering the government of a bourgeois state (even if this government is a 'left' government of popular unity bent on carrying out democratic reforms) in order to '*administer*' *the affairs* of a bourgeois state. It joins the government, in this case, in order to *widen the scope* of the class struggle and prepare the fall of the bourgeois state. But it also has no business entering a government of the dictatorship of the proletariat on the assumption that its ultimate vocation is to '*administer*' *the affairs of this state, when it should be preparing its decline and demise*. For if it devotes all its forces to such 'administration' – that is, if the party is virtually intertwined with the state, as is the case in the countries of Eastern Europe – it will not be able to help destroy that state. A communist party can consequently not conduct itself on any grounds whatsoever as an ordinary 'party of government', that is, as *a state party*, since that comes down either to serving the bourgeois state or to perpetuating the state of the dictatorship of the proletariat – when its mission is, on the contrary, to help destroy it.

It will be seen that even if a revolutionary party demands its place in the *political* Ideological State Apparatus in order to carry the echoes of the class struggle into parliament, and even if it 'participates' in government, when conditions are favourable, in order to accelerate the development of the class struggle, it is defined neither by its place in an elected parliament nor by the ideology realized in the bourgeois *political* ideological apparatus. The truth of the matter is that a communist party has an altogether different 'political practice' than bourgeois parties.

A bourgeois party enjoys the resources and support of the established bourgeoisie, its economic domination, its exploitation, its state apparatus, its Ideological State Apparatuses, and so on. It does not need, in order to exist, *to make a priority* of uniting the masses that it wants to rally to its ideas: it is, first and foremost, the bourgeois social order itself which sees to this task of persuasion, propaganda and recruitment, ensuring the bourgeois parties their *mass base*. The bourgeoisie's political and ideological grip is such – has been so firmly established, and for so long – that, in 'normal' times, the choices are virtually automatic – allowance made for the variations affecting the parties of the different fractions of the bourgeoisie. Most of the time, the bourgeois parties need only do a good job of organizing their electoral campaigns, during which they mobilize effectively and rapidly, in order to reap the benefits of this domination, transformed into electoral convictions.

That, moreover, is why a bourgeois party does not need a scientific doctrine, or even any doctrine at all, in order to exist: it needs only have a handful of ideas borrowed from the stock-in-trade of the dominant ideology in order to rally supporters convinced in advance, out of fear or self-interest.

In contrast, a workers' party has nothing to offer its members: neither sinecures nor the material advantages with which the bourgeois parties buy off their clientele when it hesitates. It presents itself for what it is: an organization of workers' class struggle, whose sole strengths are the class instinct of the exploited, a scientific doctrine, and the free will of members who have made a commitment to it on the basis of the party statutes. It organizes its members with a view to waging the class struggle in all its forms: economic (in conjunction with trade union organizations), political, and ideological. It defines its line and practices, not solely on the basis of the *revolt* of exploited workers, but on the basis of the *balance of power* between the classes, which it analyzes 'concretely' thanks to the principles of its scientific doctrine, enriched by all its experience of the class struggle. Hence it gives the widest possible consideration to the forms and power of the dominant class's class struggle on not just the national, but also a world scale. It is on the basis of this 'line' that it may deem it useful and 'correct' to enter a left government at a given moment, for the purpose of conducting its class struggle in that government with its own objectives. At all events, it always subordinates the movement's immediate interests to the working class's long-term future interests. It subordinates its tactics to the strategy of communism, that is, the strategy of a classless society. Such are, at any rate, the 'principles'.

Under these conditions, communists are right to talk about their party as a 'party of a new kind', completely different from bourgeois parties, and about themselves as 'militants of a new kind', completely different from bourgeois politicians. Their political practice – illegal or legal, parliamentary or 'extra-parliamentary' – has nothing to do with bourgeois political practice.

It will doubtless be objected that the communist party constitutes itself the way all other parties also do: on the basis of an *ideology*, which the party itself calls, moreover, *proletarian ideology*. That is true. In the communist party as well, ideology plays the role of 'cement' (Gramsci) for a particular social group, *unifying* it in its thinking and practices. In the communist party as well, this ideology 'interpellates individuals as subjects' – to be very precise, as *militant*-subjects: one needs only a little concrete experience of a communist party in order to have seen this mechanism and this dynamic at work. *In principle*, it no more seals an individual's fate than any other ideology does, given the 'play' and the contradictions among the various ideologies. But what is known as proletarian ideology is not the purely 'spontaneous' ideology of the proletariat, in which proletarian 'elements' (Lenin) are combined with bourgeois elements and, more often than not, subordinated to them. For in order to exist as a class conscious of its unity and active in its fighting organization, the proletariat needs not just experience (that of the class struggles it has been waging for more than a century) but also *objective knowledges*, the principles of which Marxist theory provides it. It is on the twofold basis of these experiences, illuminated by Marxist theory, that proletarian ideology is constituted: the mass ideology capable of unifying the avant-garde of the working class in its class-struggle organizations. *It is therefore a very special kind of ideology*. It is an ideology, because, at the level of the masses, it functions the way any ideology does (by interpellating individuals as subjects). It is, however, steeped in historical experiences illuminated by scientific principles of analysis. It presents itself as one of the forms of the fusion of the workers' movement with Marxist theory, a fusion that is not free of tensions or contradictions; for between proletarian ideology as it exists at any given moment, and the party in which it is realized, there can exist a form of unity that is *obscure* to Marxist theory itself, although Marxist theory is an integral component of that unity. Marxist theory is then treated as if it were simply an authoritative text, that is, a password or a dogma; at the limit, it can quite simply *disappear*, albeit proclaimed as the theory of the party, and give way to a pragmatic, sectarian ideology that serves only partisan and state interests. No long speeches are needed here to recognize the situation currently reigning in the parties marked by the Stalin period, and to conclude that 'proletarian ideology' is itself the stake of a class struggle that saps the proletariat's own principles of unity and action when the dominant bourgeois ideology and bourgeois political practice penetrate the organizations of proletarian class struggle.

An ideology, to be sure. Proletarian ideology, however, is not just any ideology. For every class recognizes itself in a particular, by no means arbitrarily chosen ideology, the one that is *rooted in its strategic practice* and capable of unifying and orienting its class struggle. Everyone knows that the feudal class, for example, recognized itself, for reasons that need to be analyzed, in Christian *religious ideology*, and that the bourgeois class, similarly, recognized itself in *legal ideology*, at least in the period of its classic domination, before the very recent developments of imperialism. The working class, for its part, recognizes itself – even if it is receptive to elements of religious, moral and legal ideology – above all in an *ideology of a political kind*: not in bourgeois political ideology (class domination), but in proletarian political ideology, that of the class struggle for the abolition of classes and the construction of communism. It is precisely this ideology, a spontaneous ideology in its earliest forms (utopian socialism) and, later, after the fusion of the workers' movement with Marxist theory, an informed ideology, which constitutes the 'kernel' of proletarian ideology.

It is obvious that such an ideology did not result from a *teaching* that 'intellectuals' (Marx and Engels) dispensed to the workers' movement, which adopted it because it recognized itself in it. Were that the case, we would have to explain how bourgeois intellectuals managed to work this miracle: a theory tailored to the proletariat's measure. Nor was that ideology, as Kautsky claimed, 'imported into the workers' movement from without'; for Marx and Engels would not have been able to conceive of their theory if they had not erected it on class theoretical positions, a direct consequence of the fact that they belonged organically to the workers' movement of their day. In reality, although Marxist theory was of course conceived by intellectuals with vast knowledge, they conceived it *within and from within the workers' movement*. Machiavelli says that 'to understand Princes, one has to be people'. An intellectual who is not born people has to *become people* to understand Princes, and he can only do so if he shares the people's struggles. That is what Marx did: he *became* an 'organic intellectual of the proletariat' (Gramsci) as a militant in its earliest organizations, and it was from the proletariat's political and theoretical positions that he was able to 'understand' capital. The false question of the *injection* of Marxist theory from without thus becomes the question of the *dissemination inside the workers' movement of a theory conceived inside the workers' movement*. Of course, this 'dissemination' was the result of a very long class struggle, with many rude shocks – and it continues today despite dramatic divisions, determined by imperialism's class struggle.

To sum up the essentials of this analysis of the nature of the revolutionary party, we can return to the thesis that the class struggle has primacy over the state apparatus and Ideological State Apparatuses. *Formally*, a party such as the communist party may seem to be a party like others, if it enjoys the right to send representatives to the parliament by playing the electoral game. *Formally*, it may seem to 'play the game by the rules' of the *political* Ideological State Apparatus when it intervenes in parliament or even 'participates' in a popular unity government. *Formally*, it may even seem to ratify those rules and, with them, the whole ideological system realized in them: the bourgeois *political* ideological system. The history of the workers' movement offers enough examples of revolutionary parties which, 'playing the game', are 'taken in' by it, and abandon the class struggle in favour of class collaboration under the influence of the dominant bourgeois ideology. The 'formal' can thus become 'real' under the impact of the class struggle.

This standing risk reminds us of the condition that the workers' movement had to accept in order to come into existence: *the domination of the bourgeois class struggle over the workers' class struggle.* We have a mistaken notion of class struggle if we suppose that it *results from the working class's revolt* against social injustice, inequality, or even capitalist exploitation; in a word, if we reduce class struggle to the working class's struggle against *given* conditions of exploitation and the bourgeois class's response to that struggle. This would be to forget that the conditions of exploitation have primacy; that the process of creating the conditions for exploiting workers is the fundamental form of bourgeois class struggle; that, consequently, exploitation is already class struggle; and thus that *the bourgeois class struggle has primacy.* The whole history of primitive accumulation can be considered the *production of the working class by the bourgeois class,* in a process of class struggle that creates the conditions for capitalist exploitation.

If this thesis is on the mark, we can clearly see in what sense the bourgeois class struggle dominates the workers' class struggle from the very outset; why the workers' class struggle was so long in taking form and finding its forms of existence; why the class struggle is fundamentally *unequal*; why it is not waged through the same practices by the bourgeoisie and the proletariat; and why the bourgeoisie imposes, in the Ideological State Apparatuses, *forms* meant to *forestall* the revolutionary activity of the working class or to subject it to itself [*s'asujettir*].

The working class's great strategic demand for *autonomy* reflects this condition. Subjected [*soumis*] to the domination of the bourgeois state and the effect of intimidation and 'self-evidence' of the dominant ideology, the working class can win its autonomy only on condition that it free itself from the dominant ideology, that it demarcate itself from it, in order to endow itself with forms of organiazation and action that realize its own ideology, proletarian ideology. Characteristic of this break, this radical distance taken, is the fact that it can be achieved only by a protracted struggle which must take the *forms* of bourgeois domination into account and combat the bourgeoisie *within its own forms* of *domination*, but without ever being 'taken in' by the game represented by these forms, which are not simple, neutral 'forms', but *apparatuses* that realize the *existence* of the dominant ideology.

As I said in my 1970 Note:[2]

For if it is true that the ISAs represent the *form* in which the ideology of the dominant class must *necessarily* be realized [if it is to be politically active], and the form in which the ideology of the ruled class must *necessarily* be measured and confronted, ideologies are not 'born' in the ISAs, but from the social classes at grips in the class struggle: from their conditions of existence, their practices, their experience of the struggle, and so on.

The conditions of existence, the (productive and political) practices and forms of the proletarian class struggle have nothing to do with the conditions of existence, the (economic and political) practices and forms of the capitalist and imperialist class struggle. This gives rise to antagonistic ideologies, which, like the (bourgeois and proletarian) class struggles themselves, are *unequal*. This means that proletarian ideology is not the direct opposite, inversion, or reversal of bourgeois ideology – but *an altogether different ideology* that is the bearer of different, 'critical and revolutionary' 'values'. It is because proletarian ideology is, all the vicissitudes of its history notwithstanding, already the bearer of such values, which are already realized in the organizations and practices of workers' struggle, that that ideology prefigures what the Ideological State Apparatuses of the transition to socialism will be and, for that very reason, also prefigures the abolition of the state and Ideological State Apparatuses under communism.

---

2   [TN: The reference is to the closing lines of the 'Postscript' to Althusser's 1970 *Pensée* piece (see p. 272 below). The phrase in square brackets is an addendum.]

APPENDIX 2

Ideology and Ideological State Apparatuses

(Notes towards an Investigation)

Translated from the French by Ben Brewster

I ON THE REPRODUCTION OF THE CONDITIONS OF PRODUCTION[1]

I must now expose more fully something which was briefly glimpsed in my analysis when I spoke of the necessity to renew the means of production if production is to be possible. That was a passing hint. Now I shall consider it for itself.

As Marx said, every child knows that a social formation which did not reproduce the conditions of production at the same time as it produced would not last a year.[2] The ultimate condition of production is therefore the reproduction of the conditions of production. This may be 'simple' (reproducing exactly the previous conditions of production) or 'on an extended scale' (expanding them). Let us ignore this last distinction for the moment.

What, then, is *the reproduction of the conditions of production*?

Here we are entering a domain which is both very familiar (since *Capital* Volume 2) and uniquely ignored. The tenacious obviousnesses (ideological obviousnesses of an empiricist type) of the point of view of production alone, or even of that of mere productive practice (itself abstract in relation to the process of production) are so integrated into our everyday 'consciousness' that it is extremely hard, not to say almost impossible, to raise oneself to the *point of view of reproduction*. Nevertheless,

---

1   This text is made up of two extracts from an ongoing study. The subtitle 'Notes towards an Investigation' is the author's own. The ideas expounded should not be regarded as more than the introduction to a discussion.

2   Marx to Kugelmann, 11 July 1868, *Selected Correspondence*, Moscow, 1955, p. 209.

everything outside this point of view remains abstract (worse than one-sided: distorted) – even at the level of production, and, *a fortiori*, at that of mere practice.

Let us try and examine the matter methodically.

To simplify my exposition, and assuming that every social formation arises from a dominant mode of production, I can say that the process of production sets to work the existing productive forces in and under definite relations of production.

It follows that, in order to exist, every social formation must reproduce the conditions of its production at the same time as it produces, and in order to be able to produce. It must therefore reproduce:

1) the productive forces,
2) the existing relations of production.

Reproduction of the means of Production

Everyone (including the bourgeois economists whose work is national accounting, or the modern 'macro-economic' 'theoreticians') now recognizes, because Marx compellingly proved it in *Capital* Volume 2, that no production is possible which does not allow for the reproduction of the material conditions of production: the reproduction of the means of production.

The average economist, who is no different in this than the average capitalist, knows that each year it is essential to foresee what is needed to replace what has been used up or worn out in production: raw material, fixed installations (buildings), instruments of production (machines), etc. I say the average economist = the average capitalist, for they both express the point of view of the firm, regarding it as sufficient simply to give a commentary on the terms of the firm's financial accounting practice.

But thanks to the genius of Quesnay who first posed this 'glaring' problem, and to the genius of Marx who resolved it, we know that the reproduction of the material conditions of production cannot be thought at the level of the firm, because it does not exist at that level in its real conditions. What happens at the level of the firm is an effect, which only gives an idea of the necessity of reproduction, but absolutely fails to allow its conditions and mechanisms to be thought.

A moment's reflection is enough to be convinced of this: Mr X, a capitalist who produces woollen yarn in his spinning-mill, has to 'reproduce' his raw material, his machines, etc. But *he* does not produce them for his own production – other capitalists do: an Australian sheep farmer, Mr Y, a heavy engineer producing machine-tools, Mr Z, etc., etc. And Mr Y and Mr Z, in order to produce those products which are the condition of the reproduction of Mr X's conditions of production, also have to reproduce the conditions of their own production, and so on to infinity – the whole in proportions such that, on the national and even the world market, the demand for means of production (for reproduction) can be satisfied by the supply.

In order to think this mechanism, which leads to a kind of 'endless chain', it is necessary to follow Marx's 'global' procedure, and to study in particular the relations of the circulation of capital between Department I (production of means of production) and Department II (production of means of consumption), and the realization of surplus-value, in *Capital* Volumes 2 and 3.

We shall not go into the analysis of this question. It is enough to have mentioned the existence of the necessity of the reproduction of the material conditions of production.

Reproduction of Labour-power

However, the reader will not have failed to note one thing. We have discussed the reproduction of the means of production – but not the reproduction of the productive forces. We have therefore ignored the reproduction of what distinguishes the productive forces from the means of production, i.e. the reproduction of labour-power.

From the observation of what takes place in the firm, in particular from the examination of the financial accounting practice which predicts amortization and investment, we have been able to obtain an approximate idea of the existence of the material process of reproduction, but we are now entering a domain in which the observation of what happens in the firm is, if not totally blind, at least almost entirely so, and for good reason: the reproduction of labour-power takes place essentially outside the firm.

How is the reproduction of labour-power ensured?

It is ensured by giving labour-power the material means with which to reproduce itself: by wages. Wages feature in the accounting of each enterprise, but as 'wage capital',[3] not at all as a condition of the material reproduction of labour-power.

However, that is in fact how it 'works', since wages represent only that part of the value produced by the expenditure of labour-power which is indispensable for its reproduction: sc. indispensable to the reconstitution of the labour-power of the wage-earner (the wherewithal to pay for housing, food and clothing, in short to enable the wage earner to present

---

3   Marx gave it its scientific concept: *variable capital*.

himself again at the factory gate the next day – and every further day God grants him); and we should add: indispensable for raising and educating the children in whom the proletarian reproduces himself (in *n* models where *n* = 0, 1, 2, etc. . . . .) as labour-power.

Remember that this quantity of value (wages) necessary for the reproduction of labour-power is determined not by the needs of a 'biological' guaranteed minimum wage [*salaire minimum interprofessionnel garanti*] alone, but by the needs of a historical minimum (Marx noted that English workers need beer while French proletarians need wine) – i.e. a historically variable minimum.

I should also like to point out that this minimum is doubly historical in that it is not defined by the historical needs of the working class 'recognized' by the capitalist class, but by the historical needs imposed by the proletarian class struggle (a double class struggle: against the lengthening of the working day and against the reduction of wages).

However, it is not enough to ensure for labour-power the material conditions of its reproduction if it is to be reproduced as labour-power. I have said that the available labour-power must be 'competent', i.e. suitable to be set to work in the complex system of the process of production. The development of the productive forces and the type of unity historically constitutive of the productive forces at a given moment produce the result that the labour-power has to be (diversely) skilled and therefore reproduced as such. Diversely: according to the requirements of the socio-technical division of labour, its different 'jobs' and 'posts'.

How is this reproduction of the (diversified) skills of labour-power provided for in a capitalist regime? Here, unlike social formations characterized by slavery or serfdom, this reproduction of the skills of labour-power tends (this is a tendential law) decreasingly to be provided for 'on the spot' (apprenticeship within production itself), but is achieved more and more outside production: by the capitalist education system, and by other instances and institutions.

What do children learn at school? They go varying distances in their studies, but at any rate they learn to read, to write and to add – i.e. a number of techniques, and a number of other things as well, including elements (which may be rudimentary or on the contrary thoroughgoing) of 'scientific' or 'literary culture', which are directly useful in the different jobs in production (one instruction for manual workers, another for technicians, a third for engineers, a final one for higher management, etc.). Thus they learn 'know-how'.

But besides these techniques and knowledges, and in learning them, children at school also learn the 'rules' of good behaviour, i.e. the attitude that should be observed by every agent in the division of labour, according to the job he is 'destined' for: rules of morality, civic and professional conscience, which actually means rules of respect for the socio-technical division of labour and ultimately the rules of the order established by class domination. They also learn to 'speak proper French', to 'handle' the workers correctly, i.e. actually (for the future capitalists and their servants) to 'order them about' properly, i.e. (ideally) to 'speak to them' in the right way, etc.

To put this more scientifically, I shall say that the reproduction of labour-power requires not only a reproduction of its skills, but also, at the same time, a reproduction of its submission to the rules of the established order, i.e. a reproduction of submission to the ruling ideology for the workers, and a reproduction of the ability to manipulate the ruling ideology correctly for the agents of exploitation and repression, so that they, too, will provide for the domination of the ruling class 'in words'.

In other words, the school (but also other state institutions like the Church, or other apparatuses like the army) teaches 'know-how', but in forms which ensure *subjection to the ruling ideology* or the mastery of its 'practice'. All the agents of production, exploitation and repression, not to speak of the 'professionals of ideology' (Marx), must in one way or another be 'steeped' in this ideology in order to perform their tasks 'conscientiously' – the tasks of the exploited (the proletarians), of the exploiters (the capitalists), of the exploiters' auxiliaries (the managers), or of the high priests of the ruling ideology (its 'functionaries'), etc.

The reproduction of labour-power thus reveals as its *sine qua non* not only the reproduction of its 'skills' but also the reproduction of its subjection to the ruling ideology or of the 'practice' of that ideology, with the proviso that it is not enough to say 'not only but also', for it is clear that *it is in the forms and under the forms of ideological subjection that provision is made for the reproduction of the skills of labour-power.*

But this is to recognize the effective presence of a new reality: *ideology.*

Here I shall make two comments.

The first is to round off my analysis of reproduction.

I have just given a rapid survey of the forms of the reproduction of the productive forces, i.e. of the means of production on the one hand, and of labour-power on the other.

But I have not yet approached the question of the *reproduction of the relations of production.* This is a *crucial question* for the Marxist theory of the mode of production. To let it pass would be a theoretical omission – worse, a serious political error.

I shall therefore discuss it. But in order to obtain the means to discuss it, I shall have to make another long detour.

The second comment is that in order to make this detour, I am obliged to re-raise my old question: what is a society?

II BASE AND SUPERSTRUCTURE

On a number of occasions[4] I have insisted on the revolutionary character of the Marxist conception of the 'social whole' insofar as it is distinct from the Hegelian 'totality'. I said (and this thesis only repeats famous propositions of historical materialism) that Marx conceived the structure of every society as constituted by 'levels' or 'instances' articulated by a specific determination: the *infrastructure*, or economic base (the 'unity' of the productive forces and the relations of production) and the *superstructure*, which itself contains two 'levels' or 'instances': the politico-legal (law and the state) and ideology (the different ideologies, religious, ethical, legal, political, etc.).

Besides its theoretico-didactic interest (it reveals the difference between Marx and Hegel), this representation has the following crucial theoretical advantage: it makes it possible to inscribe in the theoretical apparatus of its essential concepts what I have called their *respective indices of effectivity*. What does this mean?

It is easy to see that this representation of the structure of every society as an edifice containing a base (infrastructure) on which are erected the two 'floors' of the superstructure, is a metaphor, to be quite precise, a spatial metaphor: the metaphor of a topography [*topique*].[5] Like every metaphor, this metaphor suggests something, makes something visible. What? Precisely this: that the upper floors could not 'stay up' (in the air) alone, if they did not rest precisely on their base.

Thus the object of the metaphor of the edifice is to represent above all the 'determination in the last instance' by the economic base. The effect of this spatial metaphor is to endow the base with an index of effectivity known by the famous terms: the determination in the last instance of what happens in the upper 'floors' (of the superstructure) by what happens in the economic base.

---

4   In *For Marx* and *Reading Capital*, 1965 (English editions 1969 and 1970 respectively).

5   *Topography* from the Greek *topos*: place. A topography represents in a definite space the respective *sites* occupied by several realities: thus the economic is *at the bottom* (the base), the superstructure *above it*.

Given this index of effectivity 'in the last instance', the 'floors' of the superstructure are clearly endowed with different indices of effectivity. What kind of indices?

It is possible to say that the floors of the superstructure are not determinant in the last instance, but that they are determined by the effectivity of the base; that if they are determinant in their own (as yet undefined) ways, this is true only insofar as they are determined by the base.

Their index of effectivity (or determination), as determined by the determination in the last instance of the base, is thought by the Marxist tradition in two ways: 1) there is a 'relative autonomy' of the superstructure with respect to the base; 2) there is a 'reciprocal action' of the superstructure on the base.

We can therefore say that the great theoretical advantage of the Marxist topography, i.e. of the spatial metaphor of the edifice (base and superstructure), is simultaneously that it reveals that questions of determination (or of index of effectivity) are crucial; that it reveals that it is the base which in the last instance determines the whole edifice; and that, as a consequence, it obliges us to pose the theoretical problem of the types of 'derivatory' effectivity peculiar to the superstructure, i.e. it obliges us to think what the Marxist tradition calls conjointly the relative autonomy of the superstructure and the reciprocal action of the superstructure on the base. The greatest disadvantage of this representation of the structure of every society by the spatial metaphor of an edifice is obviously the fact that it is metaphorical: i.e. it remains *descriptive*.

It now seems to me that it is possible and desirable to represent things differently. NB: I do not mean by this that I want to reject the classical metaphor, for that metaphor itself requires that we go beyond it. And I am not going beyond it in order to reject it as outworn. I simply want to attempt to think what it gives us in the form of a description.

I believe that it is possible and necessary to think what characterizes the essential of the existence and nature of the superstructure *on the basis of reproduction*. Once one takes the point of view of reproduction, many of the questions whose existence was indicated by the spatial metaphor of the edifice, but to which it could not give a conceptual answer, are immediately illuminated.

My basic thesis is that it is not possible to pose these questions (and therefore to answer them) *except from the point of view of reproduction*.

I shall give a short analysis of law, the state and ideology *from this point of view*. And I shall reveal what happens both from the point of view of practice and production on the one hand, and from that of reproduction on the other.

III THE STATE

The Marxist tradition is strict, here: in the *Communist Manifesto* and the *Eighteenth Brumaire* (and in all the later classical texts, above all in Marx's writings on the Paris Commune and Lenin's on *State and Revolution*), the state is explicitly conceived as a repressive apparatus. The state is a 'machine' of repression, which enables the ruling classes (in the nineteenth century the bourgeois class and the 'class' of big landowners) to ensure their domination over the working class, thus enabling the former to subject the latter to the process of surplus-value extortion (i.e. to capitalist exploitation).

The state is thus first of all what the Marxist classics have called *the state apparatus*. This term means: not only the specialized apparatus (in the narrow sense) whose existence and necessity I have recognized in relation to the requirements of legal practice, i.e. the police, the courts, the prisons; but also the army, which (the proletariat has paid for this experience with its blood) intervenes directly as a supplementary repressive force in the last instance, when the police and its specialized auxiliary corps are 'outrun by events'; and above this ensemble, the head of state, the government and the administration.

Presented in this form, the Marxist-Leninist 'theory' of the state has its finger on the essential point, and not for one moment can there be any question of rejecting the fact that this really is the essential point. The state apparatus, which defines the state as a force of repressive execution and intervention 'in the interests of the ruling classes' in the class struggle conducted by the bourgeoisie and its allies against the proletariat, is quite certainly the state, and quite certainly defines its basic 'function'.

From descriptive theory to theory as such

Nevertheless, here too, as I pointed out with respect to the metaphor of the edifice (base and superstructure), this presentation of the nature of the state is still partly descriptive.

As I shall often have occasion to use this adjective (descriptive), a word of explanation is necessary in order to remove any ambiguity.

Whenever, in speaking of the metaphor of the edifice or of the Marxist 'theory' of the state, I have said that these are descriptive conceptions or representations of their objects, I had no ulterior critical motives. On the contrary, I have every grounds to think that great scientific discoveries cannot help but pass through the phase of what I shall call *descriptive 'theory'*. This is the first phase of every theory, at least in the domain which concerns us (that of the science of social formations). As such, one might – and in my opinion one must – envisage this phase as a transitional one, necessary to the development of the theory. That it is transitional is inscribed in my expression: 'descriptive theory', which reveals in its conjunction of terms the equivalent of a kind of 'contradiction'. In fact, the term theory 'clashes' to some extent with the adjective 'descriptive' which I have attached to it. This means quite precisely:

1) that the 'descriptive theory' really is, without a shadow of a doubt, the irreversible beginning of the theory; but

2) that the 'descriptive' form in which the theory is presented requires, precisely as an effect of this 'contradiction', a development of the theory which goes beyond the form of 'description'.

Let me make this idea clearer by returning to our present object: the state.

When I say that the Marxist 'theory' of the state available to us is still partly 'descriptive', that means first and foremost that this descriptive 'theory' is without the shadow of a doubt precisely the beginning of the Marxist theory of the state, and that this beginning gives us the essential point, i.e. the decisive principle of every later development of the theory.

Indeed, I shall call the descriptive theory of the state correct, since it is perfectly possible to make the vast majority of the facts in the domain with which it is concerned correspond to the definition it gives of its object. Thus, the definition of the state as a class state, existing in the repressive state apparatus, casts a brilliant light on all the facts observable in the various orders of repression whatever their domains: from the massacres of June 1848 and of the Paris Commune, of Bloody Sunday, May 1905 in Petrograd, of the Resistance, of Charonne, etc., to the mere (and relatively anodyne) interventions of a 'censorship' which has banned Diderot's *La Religieuse* or a play by Gatti on Franco; it casts light on all the direct or indirect forms of exploitation and extermination of the masses of the people (imperialist wars); it casts light on that subtle every-day domination beneath which can be glimpsed, in the forms of political democracy for example, what Lenin, following Marx, called the dictatorship of the bourgeoisie.

And yet the descriptive theory of the state represents a phase in the constitution of the theory which itself demands the 'supersession' of this phase. For it is clear that if the definition in question really does give us the means to identify and recognize the facts of oppression by relating them to the state, conceived as the repressive state apparatus, this 'inter-relationship' gives rise to a very special kind of obviousness, about which I shall have something to say in a moment: 'Yes, that's how it is, that's really true!"[6] And the accumulation of facts within the definition of the state may multiply examples, but it does not really advance the definition of the state, i.e. the scientific theory of the state. Every descriptive theory thus runs the risk of 'blocking' the development of the theory, and yet that development is essential.

That is why I think that, in order to develop this descriptive theory into theory as such, i.e. in order to understand further the mechanisms of the state in its functioning, I think that it is indispensable to *add* something to the classical definition of the state as a state apparatus.

The essentials of the Marxist theory of the state

Let me first clarify one important point: the state (and its existence in its apparatus) has no meaning except as a function of *state power*. The whole of the political class struggle revolves around the state. By which I mean around the possession, i.e. the seizure and conservation, of state power by a certain class or by an alliance between classes or class fractions. This first clarification obliges me to distinguish between state power (conservation of state power or seizure of state power), the objective of the political class struggle on the one hand, and the state apparatus on the other.

We know that the state apparatus may survive, as is proved by bourgeois 'revolutions' in nineteenth-century France (1830, 1848), by coups d'état (2 December, May 1958), by collapses of the state (the fall of the Empire in 1870, of the Third Republic in 1940), or by the political rise of the petty bourgeoisie (1890–95 in France), etc., without the state apparatus being affected or modified: it may survive political events which affect the possession of state power.

Even after a social revolution like that of 1917, a large part of the state apparatus survived after the seizure of state power by the alliance of the proletariat and the small peasantry: Lenin repeated the fact again and again.

It is possible to describe the distinction between state power and state apparatus as part of the 'Marxist theory' of the state, explicitly present since Marx's *Eighteenth Brumaire* and *Class Struggles in France*.

To summarize the 'Marxist theory of the state' on this point, it can be said that the Marxist classics have always claimed that 1) the state is the (repressive) state apparatus, 2) state power and state apparatus must be distinguished, 3) the objective of the class struggle concerns state power, and in consequence the use of the state apparatus by the classes (or alliance of classes or of fractions of classes) holding state power as a function

---

6 See p. 253 below, 'On ideology'.

of their class objectives, and 4) the proletariat must seize state power in order to destroy the existing bourgeois state apparatus and, in a first phase, replace it with a quite different, proletarian, state apparatus, then in later phases set in motion a radical process, that of the destruction of the state (the end of state power, the end of every state apparatus).

In this perspective, therefore, what I would propose to add to the 'Marxist theory' of the state is already there in so many words. But it seems to me that even with this supplement, this theory is still in part descriptive, although it does now contain complex and differential elements whose functioning and action cannot be understood without recourse to further supplementary theoretical development.

The Ideological State Apparatuses

Thus, what has to be added to the 'Marxist theory' of the state is something else.

Here we must advance cautiously in a terrain which, in fact, the Marxist classics entered long before us, but without having systematized in theoretical form the decisive advances implied by their experiences and procedures. Their experiences and procedures were indeed restricted in the main to the terrain of political practice.

In fact, i.e. in their political practice, the Marxist classics treated the state as a more complex reality than the definition of it given in the 'Marxist theory of the state', even when it has been supplemented as I have just suggested. They recognized this complexity in their practice, but they did not express it in a corresponding theory.[7]

I should like to attempt a very schematic outline of this corresponding theory. To that end, I propose the following thesis.

In order to advance the theory of the state it is indispensable to take into account not only the distinction between *state power* and *state apparatus*, but also another reality which is clearly on the side of the (repressive) state apparatus, but must not be confused with it. I shall call this reality by its concept: *the Ideological State Apparatuses*.

What are the Ideological State Apparatuses (ISAs)?

---

7   To my knowledge, Gramsci is the only one who went any distance in the road I am taking. He had the 'remarkable' idea that the state could not be reduced to the (Repressive) State Apparatus, but included, as he put it, a certain number of institutions from '*civil society*': the Church, the schools, the trade unions, etc. Unfortunately, Gramsci did not systematize his institutions, which remained in the state of acute but fragmentary notes (cf. Antonio Gramsci, *Selections from the Prison Notebooks*, International Publishers, 1971, pp. 12, 259, 260–3; see also the letter to Tatiana Schucht, 7 September 1931, in *Lettere del carcere*, Einaudi, 1968, p. 479).

They must not be confused with the (repressive) state apparatus. Remember that in Marxist theory, the state apparatus contains: the government, the administration, the army, the police, the courts, the prisons, etc., which constitute what I shall in future call the Repressive State Apparatus. Repressive suggests that the state apparatus in question 'functions by violence' – at least ultimately (since repression, e.g. administrative repression, may take non-physical forms).

I shall call Ideological State Apparatuses a certain number of realities which present themselves to the immediate observer in the form of distinct and specialized institutions. I propose an empirical list of these which will obviously have to be examined in detail, tested, corrected and reorganized. With all the reservations implied by this requirement, we can for the moment regard the following institutions as Ideological State Apparatuses (the order in which I have listed them has no particular significance):
  – the religious ISA (the system of the different churches),
  – the educational ISA (the system of the different public and private 'schools'),
  – the family ISA,[8]
  – the legal ISA,[9]
  – the political ISA (the political system, including the different parties),
  – the trade union ISA,
  – the communications ISA (press, radio and television, etc.),
  – the cultural ISA (literature, the arts, sport, etc.).

I have said that the ISAs must not be confused with the (Repressive) State Apparatus. What constitutes the difference?

As a first moment, it is clear that while there is one (Repressive) State Apparatus, there is a *plurality* of Ideological State Apparatuses. Even presupposing that it exists, the unity that constitutes this plurality of ISAs as a body is not immediately visible.

As a second moment, it is clear that whereas the – unified – (Repressive) State Apparatus belongs entirely to the *public* domain, much the larger part of the Ideological State Apparatuses (in their apparent dispersion) is, on the contrary, part of the *private* domain. Churches, parties, trade unions, families, some schools, most newspapers, cultural ventures, etc., etc., are private.

---

8   The family obviously has other 'functions' than that of an ISA. It intervenes in the reproduction of labour-power. In different modes of production it is the unit of production and/or the unit of consumption.

9   The 'law' belongs both to the (Repressive) State Apparatus and to the system of the ISAs.

We can ignore the first observation for the moment. But someone is bound to question the second, asking me by what right I regard as Ideological *State* Apparatuses, institutions which for the most part do not possess public status, but are quite simply *private* institutions. As a conscious Marxist, Gramsci already forestalled this objection in one sentence. The distinction between the public and the private is a distinction internal to bourgeois law, and valid in the (subordinate) domains in which bourgeois law exercises its 'authority'. The domain of the state escapes it because the latter is 'above the law': the state, which is the state *of* the ruling class, is neither public nor private; on the contrary, it is the precondition for any distinction between public and private. The same thing can be said from the starting-point of our Ideological State Apparatuses. It is unimportant whether the institutions in which they are realized are 'public' or 'private'. What matters is how they function. Private institutions can perfectly well 'function' as Ideological State Apparatuses. A reasonably thorough analysis of any one of the ISAs proves it.

But now for what is essential. What distinguishes the ISAs from the (Repressive) State Apparatus is the following basic difference: the Repressive State Apparatus functions 'by violence', whereas the Ideological State Apparatuses' *function 'by ideology'*.

I can clarify matters by correcting this distinction. I shall say rather that every state apparatus, whether repressive or ideological, 'functions' both by violence and by ideology, but with one very important distinction which makes it imperative not to confuse the Ideological State Apparatuses with the (Repressive) State Apparatus.

This is the fact that the (Repressive) State Apparatus functions massively and predominantly *by repression* (including physical repression), while functioning secondarily by ideology. (There is no such thing as a purely repressive apparatus.) For example, the army and the police also function by ideology both to ensure their own cohesion and reproduction, and in the 'values' they propound externally.

In the same way but inversely, it is essential to say that for their part the Ideological State Apparatuses function massively and predominantly *by ideology*, but they also function secondarily by repression, even if ultimately, but only ultimately, this is very attenuated and concealed, even symbolic. (There is no such thing as a purely ideological apparatus.) Thus schools and churches use suitable methods of punishment, expulsion, selection, etc., to 'discipline' not only their shepherds, but also their flocks. The same is true of the family . . . The same is true of the cultural ISA (censorship, among other things), etc.

Is it necessary to add that this determination of the double 'functioning' (predominantly, secondarily) by repression and by ideology, according to whether it is a matter of the (Repressive) State Apparatus or the Ideological State Apparatuses, makes it clear that very subtle explicit or tacit combinations may be woven from the interplay of the (Repressive) State Apparatus and the Ideological State Apparatuses? Everyday life provides us with innumerable examples of this, but they must be studied in detail if we are to go further than this mere observation.

Nevertheless, this remark leads us towards an understanding of what constitutes the unity of the apparently disparate body of the ISAs. If the ISAs 'function' massively and predominantly by ideology, what unifies their diversity is precisely this functioning, insofar as the ideology by which they function is always in fact unified, despite its diversity and its contradictions, *beneath the ruling ideology*, which is the ideology of 'the ruling class'. Given the fact that the 'ruling class' in principle holds state power (openly or more often by means of alliances between classes or class fractions), and therefore has at its disposal the (Repressive) State Apparatus, we can accept the fact that this same ruling class is active in the Ideological State Apparatuses insofar as it is ultimately the ruling ideology which is realized in the Ideological State Apparatuses, precisely in its contradictions. Of course, it is a quite different thing to act by laws and decrees in the (Repressive) State Apparatus and to 'act' through the intermediary of the ruling ideology in the Ideological State Apparatuses. We must go into the details of this difference – but it cannot mask the reality of a profound identity. To my knowledge, *no class can hold state power over a long period without at the same time exercising its hegemony over and in the Ideological State Apparatuses*. I only need one example and proof of this: Lenin's anguished concern to revolutionize the educational Ideological State Apparatus (among others), simply to make it possible for the Soviet proletariat, who had seized state power, to secure the future of the dictatorship of the proletariat and the transition to socialism.[10]

This last comment puts us in a position to understand that the Ideological State Apparatuses may be not only the *stake* but also the *site* of class struggle, and often of bitter forms of class struggle. The class (or class alliance) in power cannot lay down the law in the ISAs as easily as it can in the (Repressive) State Apparatus, not only because the former ruling classes are able to retain strong positions there for a long time, but also because the resistance of the exploited classes is able to find means and

---

10 In a pathetic text written in 1937, Krupskaya relates the history of Lenin's desperate efforts and what she regards as his failure.

occasions to express itself there, either by the utilization of their contradictions, or by conquering combat positions in them in struggle.[11]

Let me run through my comments.

If the thesis I have proposed is well founded, it leads me back to the
classical Marxist theory of the state, while making it more precise in one
point. I argue that it is necessary to distinguish between state power (and
its possession by . . .) on the one hand, and the state apparatus on the
other. But I add that the state apparatus contains two bodies: the body of
institutions which represent the Repressive State Apparatus on the one
hand, and the body of institutions which represent the body of Ideological State Apparatuses on the other.

But if this is the case, the following question is bound to be asked, even in
the very summary state of my suggestions: what exactly is the extent of the
role of the Ideological State Apparatuses? What is their importance based on?
In other words: to what does the 'function' of these Ideological State Apparatuses, which do not function by repression but by ideology, correspond?

IV ON THE REPRODUCTION OF THE RELATIONS OF PRODUCTION

I can now answer the central question which I have left in suspense
for many long pages: *how is the reproduction of the relations of production
secured?* In the topographical language (base, superstructure), I can say:
for the most part,[12] it is secured by the legal-political and ideological
superstructure.

---

11   What I have said in these few brief words about the class struggle in the ISAs is
obviously far from exhausting the question of the class struggle.

To approach this question, two principles must be borne in mind:

The first principle was formulated by Marx in the Preface to *A Contribution to the Critique
of Political Economy*: 'In considering such transformations [a social revolution] a distinction
should always be made between the material transformation of the economic conditions of
production, which can be determined with the precision of natural science, and the legal,
political, religious, aesthetic or philosophic – in short, ideological forms in which men
become conscious of this conflict and fight it out.' The class struggle is thus expressed and
exercised in ideological forms, thus also in the ideological forms of the ISAs. But the class
struggle *extends far beyond* these forms, and it is because it extends beyond them that the
struggle of the exploited classes may also be exercised in the forms of the ISAs, and thus
turn the weapon of ideology against the classes in power.

This by virtue of the *second principle*: the class struggle extends beyond the ISAs because
it is rooted elsewhere than in ideology, in the infrastructure, in the relations of production,
which are relations of exploitation and constitute the basis for class relations.

12   For the most part. For the relations of production are first reproduced by the
materiality of the processes of production and circulation. But it should not be forgotten
that ideological relations are immediately present in these same processes.

But as I have argued that it is essential to go beyond this still descriptive language, I shall say: for the most part, it is secured by the exercise of state power in the state apparatuses, on the one hand the Repressive State Apparatus, on the other the Ideological State Apparatuses.

What I have just said must also be taken into account, and it can be assembled in the form of the following three features:

1) All the state apparatuses function both by repression and by ideology, with the difference that the (Repressive) State Apparatus functions massively and predominantly by repression, whereas the Ideological State Apparatuses function massively and predominantly by ideology.

2) Whereas the (Repressive) State Apparatus constitutes an organized whole whose different parts are centralized beneath a commanding unity, that of the politics of class struggle applied by the political representatives of the ruling classes in possession of state power, the Ideological State Apparatuses are multiple, distinct, 'relatively autonomous' and capable of providing an objective field to contradictions which express, in forms which may be limited or extreme, the effects of the clashes between the capitalist class struggle and the proletarian class struggle, as well as their subordinate forms.

3) Whereas the unity of the (Repressive) State Apparatus is secured by its unified and centralized organization under the leadership of the representatives of the classes in power executing the politics of the class struggle of the classes in power, the unity of the different Ideological State Apparatuses is secured, usually in contradictory forms, by the ruling ideology, the ideology of the ruling class.

Taking these features into account, it is possible to represent the reproduction of the relations of production[13] in the following way, according to a kind of 'division of labour'.

The role of the Repressive State Apparatus, insofar as it is a repressive apparatus, consists essentially in securing by force (physical or otherwise) the political conditions of the reproduction of relations of production which are in the last resort relations of exploitation. Not only does the state apparatus contribute generously to its own reproduction (the capitalist state contains political dynasties, military dynasties, etc.), but also and above all, the state apparatus secures by repression (from the most brutal physical force, to mere administrative commands and interdictions, open and tacit censorship, etc.) the political conditions for the action of the Ideological State Apparatuses.

---

13   For that part of reproduction to which the Repressive State Apparatus and the Ideological State Apparatus *contribute*.

In fact, it is the latter which largely secure the reproduction specifically of the relations of production, behind a 'shield' provided by the Repressive State Apparatus. It is here that the role of the ruling ideology is heavily concentrated, the ideology of the ruling class, which holds state power. It is the intermediation of the ruling ideology that ensures a (sometimes teeth-gritting) 'harmony' between the Repressive State Apparatus and the Ideological State Apparatuses, and between the different Ideological State Apparatuses.

We are thus led to envisage the following hypothesis, as a function precisely of the diversity of Ideological State Apparatuses in their single, because shared, role of the reproduction of the relations of production.

Indeed we have listed a relatively large number of Ideological State Apparatuses in contemporary capitalist social formations: the educational apparatus, the religious apparatus, the family apparatus, the political apparatus, the trade union apparatus, the communications apparatus, the 'cultural' apparatus, etc.

But in the social formations of that mode of production characterized by 'serfdom' (usually called the feudal mode of production), we observe that although there is a single Repressive State Apparatus which, since the earliest known ancient states, let alone the absolute monarchies, has been formally very similar to the one we know today, the number of Ideological State Apparatuses is smaller and their individual types are different. For example, we observe that during the Middle Ages, the Church (the religious Ideological State Apparatus) accumulated a number of functions which have today devolved on to several distinct Ideological State Apparatuses, new ones in relation to the past I am invoking, in particular educational and cultural functions. Alongside the Church there was the family Ideological State Apparatus, which played a considerable part, incommensurable with its role in capitalist social formations. Despite appearances, the Church and the family were not the only Ideological State Apparatuses. There was also a political Ideological State Apparatus (the Estates General, the Parlement, the different political factions and leagues, the ancestors of the modern political parties, and the whole political system of the free communes and then of the *villes*). There was also a powerful 'proto-trade union' Ideological State Apparatus, if I may venture such an anachronistic term (the powerful merchants' and bankers' guilds and the journeymen's associations, etc.). Publishing and communications, even, saw an indisputable development, as did the theatre; initially both were integral parts of the Church, then they became more and more independent of it.

In the pre-capitalist historical period which I have examined extremely broadly, it is absolutely clear that *there was one dominant Ideological State Apparatus, the Church*, which concentrated within it not only religious functions but also educational ones, and a large proportion of the functions of communications and 'culture'. It is no accident that all ideological struggle from the sixteenth to the eighteenth century, starting with the first shocks of the Reformation, was *concentrated* in an anti-clerical and anti-religious struggle; rather this is a function precisely of the dominant position of the religious Ideological State Apparatus.

The foremost objective and achievement of the French Revolution was not just to transfer state power from the feudal aristocracy to the merchant-capitalist bourgeoisie, to break part of the former Repressive State Apparatus and replace it with a new one (e.g. the national popular army) but also to attack the number-one Ideological State Apparatus: the Church. Hence the civil constitution of the clergy, the confiscation of ecclesiastical wealth, and the creation of new Ideological State Apparatuses to replace the religious Ideological State Apparatus in its dominant role.

Naturally, these things did not happen automatically: witness the Concordat, the Restoration and the long class struggle between the landed aristocracy and the industrial bourgeoisie throughout the nineteenth century for the establishment of bourgeois hegemony over the functions formerly fulfilled by the Church: above all by the schools. It can be said that the bourgeoisie relied on the new political, parliamentary-democratic, Ideological State Apparatus, installed in the earliest years of the Revolution, then restored after long and violent struggles, for a few months in 1848 and for decades after the fall of the Second Empire, in order to conduct its struggle against the Church and wrest its ideological functions away from it, in other words, to ensure not only its own political hegemony, but also the ideological hegemony indispensable to the reproduction of capitalist relations of production.

That is why I believe that I am justified in advancing the following thesis, however precarious it is. I believe that the Ideological State Apparatus which has been installed in the *dominant* position in mature capitalist social formations as a result of a violent political and ideological class struggle against the old dominant Ideological State Apparatus is the *educational ideological apparatus*.

This thesis may seem paradoxical, given that for everyone, i.e. in the ideological representation that the bourgeoisie has tried to give itself and the classes it exploits, it really seems that the dominant Ideological State Apparatus in capitalist social formations is not the schools, but the political Ideological State Apparatus, i.e. the regime of parliamentary democracy combining universal suffrage and party struggle.

However, history, even recent history, shows that the bourgeoisie has been and still is able to accommodate itself to political Ideological State Apparatuses other than parliamentary democracy: the First and Second Empires, constitutional monarchy (Louis XVIII and Charles X), parliamentary monarchy (Louis-Philippe), presidential democracy (De Gaulle), to mention only France. In England this is even clearer. The Revolution was particularly 'successful' there from the bourgeois point of view, since unlike France, where the bourgeoisie, partly because of the stupidity of the petty aristocracy, had to agree to being carried to power by peasant and plebeian '*journées révolutionnaires*', something for which it had to pay a high price, the English bourgeoisie was able to 'compromise' with the aristocracy and 'share' state power and the use of the state apparatus with it for a long time (peace among all men of good will in the ruling classes!). In Germany it is even more striking, since it was behind a political Ideological State Apparatus in which the imperial Junkers (epitomized by Bismarck), their army and their police provided it with a shield and leading personnel, that the imperialist bourgeoisie made its shattering entry into history, before 'traversing' the Weimar Republic and entrusting itself to Nazism.

Hence I believe I have good reasons for thinking that behind the scenes of its political Ideological State Apparatus, which occupies the front of the stage, what the bourgeoisie has installed as its number-one, i.e. as its dominant Ideological State Apparatus, is the educational apparatus, which has in fact replaced in its functions the previously dominant Ideological State Apparatus, the Church. One might even add: the school–family couple has replaced the Church–family couple.

Why is the educational apparatus in fact the dominant Ideological State Apparatus in capitalist social formations, and how does it function?

For the moment it must suffice to say:

1) All Ideological State Apparatuses, whatever they are, contribute to the same result: the reproduction of the relations of production, i.e. of capitalist relations of exploitation.

2) Each of them contributes towards this single result in the way proper to it. The political apparatus by subjecting individuals to the political State Ideology, the 'indirect' (parliamentary) or 'direct' (plebiscitary or fascist) 'democratic' ideology. The communications apparatus by cramming every 'citizen' with daily doses of nationalism, chauvinism, liberalism, moralism, etc., by means of the press, the radio and television. The same goes for the cultural apparatus (the role of sport in chauvinism is of the first importance), etc. The religious apparatus by recalling in sermons, the great ceremonies of birth, marriage and death, etc., that man

is only ashes, unless he loves his neighbour to the extent of turning the other cheek to whoever strikes the first one. The family apparatus . . . but there is no need to go on.

3) This concert is dominated by a single score, occasionally disturbed by contradictions (those of the remnants of former ruling classes, those of the proletarians and their organizations): the score of the ideology of the current ruling class which integrates into its music the great themes of the humanism of the great forefathers, who produced the Greek miracle even before Christianity, and afterwards the Glory of Rome, the Eternal City, and the themes of interest, particular and general, etc., nationalism, moralism and economism.

4) Nevertheless, in this concert, one Ideological State Apparatus certainly has the dominant role, although hardly anyone lends an ear to its music: it is so silent! This is the school.

It takes children from every class at infant-school age, and then for years, the years in which the child is most 'vulnerable', squeezed between the family state apparatus and the educational state apparatus, it drums into them, whether it uses new or old methods, a certain amount of 'know-how' wrapped in the ruling ideology (French, arithmetic, natural history, the sciences, literature) or simply the ruling ideology in its pure state (ethics, civic instruction, philosophy). Somewhere around the age of sixteen, a huge mass of children are ejected 'into production': these are the workers or small peasants. Another portion of scholastically adapted youth carries on: and, for better or worse, it goes somewhat further, until it falls by the wayside and fills the posts of small and middle technicians, white-collar workers, small and middle civil servants, petty bourgeois of all kinds. A last portion reaches the summit, either to fall into intellectual semi-employment, or to provide, as well as the 'intellectuals of the collective labourer', the agents of exploitation (capitalists, managers), the agents of repression (soldiers, policemen, politicians, administrators, etc.), and the professional ideologists (priests of all sorts, most of whom are convinced 'laymen').

Each mass ejected *en route* is practically provided with the ideology which suits the role it has to fulfil in class society: the role of the exploited (with a 'highly-developed' 'professional', 'ethical', 'civic', 'national' and a political consciousness); the role of the agent of exploitation (ability to give the workers orders and speak to them: 'human relations'), of the agent of repression (ability to give orders and enforce obedience 'without discussion', or ability to manipulate the demagogy of a political leader's rhetoric), or of the professional ideologist (ability to treat consciousnesses with the respect, i.e. with the contempt, blackmail and demagogy, they deserve, adapted to the accents of Morality, of Virtue, of 'Transcendence', of the Nation, of France's World Role, etc.).

Of course, many of these contrasting virtues (modesty, resignation, submissiveness on the one hand, cynicism, contempt, arrogance, confidence, self-importance, even smooth talk and cunning on the other) are also taught in the family, in the Church, in the army, in good books, in films and even in the football stadium. But no other Ideological State Apparatus has the obligatory (and not least, free) audience of the totality of the children in the capitalist social formation, eight hours a day for five or six days out of seven.

But it is by an apprenticeship in a variety of know-how wrapped up in the massive inculcation of the ideology of the ruling class that the *relations of production* in a capitalist social formation, i.e. the relations of exploited to exploiters and exploiters to exploited, are largely reproduced. The mechanisms which produce this vital result for the capitalist regime are naturally covered up and concealed by a universally reigning ideology of the school, universally reigning because it is one of the essential forms of the ruling bourgeois ideology: an ideology which represents the school as a neutral environment purged of ideology (because it is . . . lay), where teachers respectful of the 'conscience' and 'freedom' of the children who are entrusted to them (in complete confidence) by their 'parents' (who are free, too, i.e. the owners of their children) open up for them the path to the freedom, morality and responsibility of adults by their own example, by knowledge, literature and their 'liberating' virtues.

I ask the pardon of those teachers who, in dreadful conditions, attempt to turn the few weapons they can find in the history and learning they 'teach' against the ideology, the system and the practices in which they are trapped. They are a kind of hero. But they are rare and how many (the majority) do not even begin to suspect the 'work' the system (which is bigger than they are and crushes them) forces them to do, or worse, put all their heart and ingenuity into performing it with the greatest possible conscientiousness (the famous new methods!). So little do they suspect it that their own devotion contributes to the maintenance and nourishment of this ideological representation of the school, which makes the school today as 'natural', indispensable-useful and even beneficial for our contemporaries as the Church was 'natural', indispensable and generous for our ancestors a few centuries ago.

In fact, the Church has been replaced today *in its role as the dominant Ideological State Apparatus* by the school. It is coupled with the family just as the Church was once coupled with the family. We can now claim that the unprecedentedly deep crisis which is now shaking the education system of so many states across the globe, often in conjunction with a crisis (already proclaimed in the *Communist Manifesto*) shaking the family system, takes on a political meaning, given that the school (and the school–family couple) constitutes the dominant Ideological State Apparatus, the apparatus playing a determinant part in the reproduction of the relations of production of a mode of production threatened in its existence by the world class struggle.

V ON IDEOLOGY

When I put forward the concept of an Ideological State Apparatus, when I said that the ISAs 'function by ideology', I invoked a reality which needs a little discussion: ideology.

It is well known that the expression 'ideology' was invented by Cabanis, Destutt de Tracy and their friends, who assigned to it as an object the (genetic) theory of ideas. When Marx took up the term fifty years later, he gave it a quite different meaning, even in his early works. Here, ideology is the system of the ideas and representations which dominate the mind of a man or a social group. The ideologico-political struggle conducted by Marx as early as his articles in the *Rheinische Zeitung* inevitably and quickly brought him face to face with this reality and forced him to take his earliest intuitions further.

However, here we come upon a rather astonishing paradox. Everything seems to lead Marx to formulate a theory of ideology. In fact, *The German Ideology* does offer us, after the *1844 Manuscripts*, an explicit theory of ideology, but . . . it is not Marxist (we shall see why in a moment). As for *Capital*, although it does contain many hints towards a theory of ideologies (most visibly, the ideology of the vulgar economists), it does not contain that theory itself, which depends for the most part on a theory of ideology in general.

I should like to venture a first and very schematic outline of such a theory. The theses I am about to put forward are certainly not off the cuff, but they cannot be sustained and tested, i.e. confirmed or corrected, except by much thorough study and analysis.

Ideology has no history

One word first of all to expound the reason in principle which seems to me to found, or at least justify, the project of a theory of ideology *in general*, and not a theory of particular ideolog*ies*, which, whatever their form (religious, ethical, legal, political), always express *class positions*.

It is quite obvious that it is necessary to proceed towards a theory of ideologies in the two respects I have just suggested. It will then be clear that a theory of ideolog*ies* depends in the last resort on the history of social formations, and thus of the modes of production combined in social formations, and of the class struggles which develop in them. In this sense it is clear that there can be no question of a theory of ideolog*ies* in *general*, since ideolog*ies* (defined in the double respect suggested above: regional and class) have a history, whose determination in the last instance is clearly situated outside ideologies alone, although it involves them.

On the contrary, if I am able to put forward the project of a theory of ideology *in general*, and if this theory really is one of the elements on which theories of ideolog*ies* depend, that entails an apparently paradoxical proposition which I shall express in the following terms: *ideology has no history*.

As we know, this formulation appears in so many words in a passage from *The German Ideology*. Marx utters it with respect to metaphysics, which, he says, has no more history than ethics (meaning also the other forms of ideology).

In *The German Ideology*, this formulation appears in a plainly positivist context. Ideology is conceived as a pure illusion, a pure dream, i.e. as nothingness. All its reality is external to it. Ideology is thus thought as an imaginary construction whose status is exactly like the theoretical status of the dream among writers before Freud. For these writers, the dream was the purely imaginary, i.e. null, result of 'day's residues', presented in an arbitrary arrangement and order, sometimes even 'inverted', in other words, in 'disorder'. For them, the dream was the imaginary, it was empty, null and arbitrarily 'stuck together' [*bricolé*], once the eyes had closed, from the residues of the only full and positive reality, the reality of the day. This is exactly the status of philosophy and ideology (since in this book philosophy is ideology *par excellence*) in *The German Ideology*.

Ideology, then, is for Marx an imaginary assemblage [*bricolage*], a pure dream, empty and vain, constituted by the 'day's residues' from the only full and positive reality, that of the concrete history of concrete material individuals materially producing their existence. It is on this basis that ideology has no history in *The German Ideology*, since its history is outside it, where the only existing history is, the history of concrete individuals, etc. In *The German Ideology*, the thesis that ideology has no history is therefore a purely negative thesis, since it means both:

1) ideology is nothing insofar as it is a pure dream (manufactured by who knows what power: if not by the alienation of the division of labour, but that, too, is a *negative* determination);

2) ideology has no history, which emphatically does not mean that there is no history in it (on the contrary, for it is merely the pale, empty and inverted reflection of real history) but that it has no history of its *own*.

Now, while the thesis I wish to defend formally speaking adopts the terms of *The German Ideology* ('ideology has no history'), it is radically different from the positivist and historicist thesis of *The German Ideology*.

For on the one hand, I think it is possible to hold that ideolog*ies have a history of their own* (although it is determined in the last instance by the class struggle); and on the other, I think it is possible to hold that ideology *in general has no history*, not in a negative sense (its history is external to it), but in an absolutely positive sense.

This sense is a positive one if it is true that the peculiarity of ideology is that it is endowed with a structure and a functioning such as to make it a non-historical reality, i.e. an *omni-historical* reality, in the sense in which that structure and functioning are immutable, present in the same form throughout what we can call history, in the sense in which the *Communist Manifesto* defines history as the history of class struggles, i.e. the history of class societies.

To give a theoretical reference-point here, I might say that, to return to our example of the dream, in its Freudian conception this time, our proposition – ideology has no history – can and must (and in a way which has absolutely nothing arbitrary about it, but, quite the reverse, is theoretically necessary, for there is an organic link between the two propositions) be related directly to Freud's proposition that the *unconscious is eternal*, i.e. that it has no history.

If eternal means, not transcendent to all (temporal) history, but omnipresent, trans-historical and therefore immutable in form throughout the extent of history, I shall adopt Freud's expression word for word, and write *ideology is eternal*, exactly like the unconscious. And I add that I find this comparison theoretically justified by the fact that the eternity of the unconscious is not unrelated to the eternity of ideology in general.

That is why I believe I am justified, hypothetically at least, in proposing a theory of ideology *in general*, in the sense that Freud presented a theory of the unconscious *in general*.

To simplify the phrase, it is convenient, taking into account what has been said about ideologies, to use the plain term ideology to designate ideology in general, which I have just said has no history, or, what comes to the same thing, is eternal, i.e. omnipresent in its immutable form throughout history (= the history of social formations containing social classes). For the moment I shall restrict myself to 'class societies' and their history.

Ideology is a 'representation' of the imaginary relationship of individuals to their real conditions of existence

In order to approach my central thesis on the structure and functioning of ideology, I shall first present two theses, one negative, the other positive. The first concerns the object which is 'represented' in the imaginary form of ideology, the second concerns the materiality of ideology.

THESIS I: Ideology represents the imaginary relationship of individuals to their real conditions of existence.

We commonly call religious ideology, ethical ideology, legal ideology, political ideology, etc., so many 'world outlooks'. Of course, assuming that we do not live one of these ideologies as the truth (e.g. 'believe' in God, Duty, Justice, etc. . . .), we admit that the ideology we are discussing from a critical point of view, examining it as the ethnologist examines the myths of a 'primitive society', that these 'world outlooks' are largely imaginary, i.e. do not 'correspond to reality'.

However, while admitting that they do not correspond to reality, i.e. that they constitute an illusion, we admit that they do make allusion to reality, and that they need only be 'interpreted' to discover the reality of the world behind their imaginary representation of that world (ideology = *illusion/allusion*).

There are different types of interpretation, the most famous of which are the *mechanistic* type, current in the eighteenth century (God is the imaginary representation of the real King), and the '*hermeneutic*' interpretation, inaugurated by the earliest Church Fathers and revived by Feuerbach and the theologico-philosophical school which descends from him, e.g. the theologian Barth (to Feuerbach, for example, God is the essence of real Man). The essential point is that on condition that we interpret the imaginary transposition (and inversion) of ideology we arrive at the conclusion that in ideology 'men represent their real conditions of existence to themselves in an imaginary form'.

Unfortunately, this interpretation leaves one small problem unsettled: why do men 'need' this imaginary transposition of their real conditions of existence in order to 'represent to themselves' their real conditions of existence?

The first answer (that of the eighteenth century) proposes a simple solution: priests or despots are responsible. They 'forged' the Beautiful Lies so that, in the belief that they were obeying God, men would in fact obey the priests and despots, who are usually in alliance in their imposture, the priests acting in the interests of the despots or *vice versa*, according to the political positions of the 'theoreticians' concerned. There is therefore a cause for the imaginary transposition of the real conditions of existence: that cause is the existence of a small number of cynical men who base their domination and exploitation of the 'people' on a falsified representation of the world which they have imagined in order to enslave other minds by dominating their imaginations.

The second answer (that of Feuerbach, taken over word for word by Marx in his early works) is more 'profound', i.e. just as false. It, too, seeks and finds a cause for the imaginary transposition and distortion of men's real conditions of existence, in short, for the alienation in the imaginary of the representation of men's conditions of existence. This cause is no longer priests or despots, nor their active imagination and the passive imagination of their victims. This cause is the material alienation which reigns in the conditions of existence of men themselves. This is how, in *The Jewish Question* and elsewhere, Marx defends the Feuerbachian idea that men make themselves an alienated (= imaginary) representation of their conditions of existence because these conditions of existence are themselves alienating (in the *1844 Manuscripts*: because these conditions are dominated by the essence of alienated society – '*alienated labour*').

All these interpretations thus take literally the thesis which they presuppose, and on which they depend, i.e. that what is reflected in the imaginary representation of the world found in an ideology is the conditions of existence of men, i.e. their real world.

Now I can return to a thesis which I have already advanced: it is not their real conditions of existence, their real world, that 'men' 'represent to themselves' in ideology, but above all it is their relation to those conditions of existence which is represented to them there. It is this relation which is at the centre of every ideological, i.e. imaginary, representation of the real world. It is this relation that contains the 'cause' which has to explain the imaginary distortion of the ideological representation of the real world. Or rather, to leave aside the language of causality it is necessary to advance the thesis that it is the *imaginary nature of this relation* which underlies all the imaginary distortion that we can observe (if we do not live in its truth) in all ideology.

To speak in a Marxist language, if it is true that the representation of the real conditions of existence of the individuals occupying the posts of agents of production, exploitation, repression, ideologization and scientific practice does in the last analysis arise from the relations of production, and from relations deriving from the relations of production, we can say the following: all ideology represents in its necessarily imaginary distortion not the existing relations of production (and the other relations that derive from them), but above all the (imaginary) relationship of individuals to the relations of production and the relations that derive from them. What is represented in ideology is therefore not the system of the real relations which govern the existence of individuals, but the imaginary relation of those individuals to the real relations in which they live.

If this is the case, the question of the 'cause' of the imaginary distortion of the real relations in ideology disappears and must be replaced by a different question: why is the representation given to individuals of their (individual) relation to the social relations which govern their conditions of existence and their collective and individual life necessarily an imaginary relation? And what is the nature of this imaginariness? Posed in this way, the question explodes the solution by a 'clique',[14] by a group of individuals (priests or despots) who are the authors of the great ideological mystification, just as it explodes the solution by the alienated character of the real world. We shall see why later in my exposition. For the moment I shall go no further.

THESIS II: Ideology has a material existence.

I have already touched on this thesis by saying that the 'ideas' or 'representations', etc., which seem to make up ideology do not have an ideal [*idéale* or *idéelle*] or spiritual existence, but a material existence. I even suggested that the ideal [*idéale, idéelle*] and spiritual existence of 'ideas' arises exclusively in an ideology of the 'idea' and of ideology, and let me add, in an ideology of what seems to have 'founded' this conception since the emergence of the sciences, i.e. what the practitioners of the sciences represent to themselves in their spontaneous ideology as 'ideas', true or false. Of course, presented in affirmative form, this thesis is unproven. I simply ask that the reader be favourably disposed towards it, say, in the name of materialism. A long series of arguments would be necessary to prove it.

This hypothetical thesis of the not spiritual but material existence of 'ideas' or other 'representations' is indeed necessary if we are to advance in our analysis of the nature of ideology. Or rather, it is merely useful to us in order the better to reveal what every at all serious analysis of any ideology will immediately and empirically show to every observer, however critical.

While discussing the Ideological State Apparatuses and their practices,

---

14 I use this very modern term deliberately. For even in communist circles, unfortunately, it is a commonplace to 'explain' some political deviation (left or right opportunism) by the action of a 'clique'.

I said that each of them was the realization of an ideology (the unity of these different regional ideologies – religious, ethical, legal, political, aesthetic, etc. – being assured by their subjection to the ruling ideology). I now return to this thesis: an ideology always exists in an apparatus, and its practice, or practices. This existence is material.

Of course, the material existence of the ideology in an apparatus and its practices does not have the same modality as the material existence of a paving-stone or a rifle. But, at the risk of being taken for a Neo-Aristotelian (NB Marx had a very high regard for Aristotle), I shall say that 'matter is discussed in many senses', or rather that it exists in different modalities, all rooted in the last instance in 'physical' matter.

Having said this, let me move straight on and see what happens to the 'individuals' who live in ideology, i.e. in a determinate (religious, ethical, etc.) representation of the world whose imaginary distortion depends on their imaginary relation to their conditions of existence, in other words, in the last instance, to the relations of production and to class relations (ideology = an imaginary relation to real relations). I shall say that this imaginary relation is itself endowed with a material existence.

Now I observe the following.

An individual believes in God, or Duty, or Justice, etc. This belief derives (for everyone, i.e. for all those who live in an ideological representation of ideology, which reduces ideology to ideas endowed by definition with a spiritual existence) from the ideas of the individual concerned, i.e. from him as a subject with a consciousness which contains the ideas of his belief. In this way, i.e. by means of the absolutely ideological 'conceptual' device [*dispositif*] thus set up (a subject endowed with a consciousness in which he freely forms or freely recognizes ideas in which he believes), the (material) attitude of the subject concerned naturally follows.

The individual in question behaves in such and such a way, adopts such and such a practical attitude, and, what is more, participates in certain regular practices which are those of the ideological apparatus on which 'depend' the ideas which he has in all consciousness freely chosen as a subject. If he believes in God, he goes to church to attend Mass, kneels, prays, confesses, does penance (once it was material in the ordinary sense of the term) and naturally repents and so on. If he believes in Duty, he will have the corresponding attitudes, inscribed in ritual practices 'according to the correct principles'. If he believes in Justice, he will submit unconditionally to the rules of the Law, and may even protest when they are violated, sign petitions, take part in a demonstration, etc.

Throughout this schema we observe that the ideological

representation of ideology is itself forced to recognize that every 'subject' endowed with a 'consciousness' and believing in the 'ideas' that his 'consciousness' inspires in him and freely accepts, must '*act* according to his ideas', must therefore inscribe his own ideas as a free subject in the actions of his material practice. If he does not do so, 'that is wicked'.

Indeed, if he does not do what he ought to do as a function of what he believes, it is because he does something else, which, still as a function of the same idealist scheme, implies that he has other ideas in his head than those he proclaims, and that he acts according to these other ideas, as a man who is either 'inconsistent' ('no one is willingly evil'), or cynical, or perverse.

In every case, the ideology of ideology thus recognizes, despite its imaginary distortion, that the 'ideas' of a human subject exist in his actions, or ought to exist in his actions, and if that is not the case, it lends him other ideas corresponding to the actions (however perverse) that he does perform. This ideology talks of actions: I shall talk of actions inserted into *practices*. And I shall point out that these practices are governed by the *rituals* in which these practices are inscribed, within the *material existence of an ideological apparatus*, be it only a small part of that apparatus: a small mass in a small church, a funeral, a minor match at a sports' club, a school day, a political party meeting, etc.

Besides, we are indebted to Pascal's defensive 'dialectic' for the wonderful formula which will enable us to invert the order of the notional schema of ideology. Pascal says, more or less: 'Kneel down, move your lips in prayer, and you will believe.' He thus scandalously inverts the order of things, bringing, like Christ, not peace but strife, and in addition something hardly Christian (for woe to him who brings scandal into the world!) – scandal itself. A fortunate scandal which makes him stick with Jansenist defiance to a language that directly names the reality.

I will be allowed to leave Pascal to the arguments of his ideological struggle with the religious Ideological State Apparatus of his day. And I shall be expected to use a more directly Marxist vocabulary, if that is possible, for we are advancing in still poorly explored domains.

I shall therefore say that, where only a single subject (such and such an individual) is concerned, the existence of the ideas of his belief is material in that *his ideas are his material actions inserted into material practices governed by material rituals which are themselves defined by the material ideological apparatus from which derive the ideas of that subject.* Naturally, the four inscriptions of the adjective 'material' in my proposition must be affected by different modalities: the materialities of a displacement for going to mass, of kneeling down, of the gesture of the sign of the cross, or of the *mea culpa*, of a sentence, of a prayer, of an act of contrition, of a penitence, of a gaze, of a hand-shake, of an external verbal discourse or an 'internal' verbal discourse (consciousness), are not one and the same materiality. I shall leave on one side the problem of a theory of the differences between the modalities of materiality.

It remains that in this inverted presentation of things we are not dealing with an 'inversion' at all, since it is clear that certain notions have purely and simply disappeared from our presentation, whereas others on the contrary survive, and new terms appear.

Disappeared: the term *ideas*.

Survive: the terms *subject, consciousness, belief, actions*.

Appear: the terms *practices, rituals, ideological apparatus*.

It is therefore not an inversion or overturning (except in the sense in which one might say a government or a glass is overturned), but a reshuffle (of a non-ministerial type), a rather strange reshuffle, since we obtain the following result.

Ideas have disappeared as such (insofar as they are endowed with an ideal or spiritual existence), to the precise extent that it has emerged that their existence is inscribed in the actions of practices governed by rituals defined in the last instance by an ideological apparatus. It therefore appears that the subject acts insofar as he is acted by the following system (set out in the order of its real determination): ideology existing in a material ideological apparatus, prescribing material practices governed by a material ritual, which practices exist in the material actions of a subject acting in all consciousness according to his belief.

But this very presentation reveals that we have retained the following notions: subject, consciousness, belief, actions. From this series I shall immediately extract the decisive central term on which everything else depends: the notion of the *subject*.

And I shall immediately set down two conjoint theses:

1) There is no practice except by and in an ideology.

2) There is no ideology except by the subject and for subjects.

I can now come to my central thesis.

Ideology interpellates individuals as subjects

This thesis is simply a matter of making my last proposition explicit: there is no ideology except by the subject and for subjects. Meaning, there is no ideology except for concrete subjects, and this destination for ideology is only made possible by the subject: meaning *by the category of the subject* and its functioning.

By this I mean that, even if it only appears under this name (the subject) with the rise of bourgeois ideology, above all with the rise of legal ideology,[15] the category of the subject (which may function under other names: e.g., as the soul in Plato, as God, etc.) is the constitutive category of all ideology, whatever its determination (regional or class) and whatever its historical date – since ideology has no history.

I say: the category of the subject is constitutive of all ideology, but at the same time and immediately I add that *the category of the subject is only constitutive of all ideology insofar as all ideology has the function (which defines it) of 'constituting' concrete individuals as subjects.* In the interaction of this double constitution exists the functioning of all ideology, ideology being nothing but its functioning in the material forms of existence of that functioning.

In order to grasp what follows, it is essential to realize that both he who is writing these lines and the reader who reads them are themselves subjects, and therefore ideological subjects (a tautological proposition), i.e. that the author and the reader of these lines both live 'spontaneously' or 'naturally' in ideology in the sense in which I have said that 'man is an ideological animal by nature'.

That the author, insofar as he writes the lines of a discourse which claims to be scientific, is completely absent as a 'subject' from 'his' scientific discourse (for all scientific discourse is by definition a subject-less discourse, there is no 'Subject of science' except in an ideology of science) is a different question which I shall leave on one side for the moment.

As St Paul admirably put it, it is in the 'Logos', meaning in ideology, that we·'live, move and have our being'. It follows that, for you and for me, the category of the subject is a primary 'obviousness' (obviousnesses are always primary): it is clear that you and I are subjects (free, ethical, etc. . . . .). Like all obviousnesses, including those that make a word 'name a thing' or 'have a meaning' (therefore including the obviousness of the 'transparency' of language), the 'obviousness' that you and I are subjects – and that that does not cause any problems – is an ideological effect, the elementary ideological effect.[16] It is indeed a peculiarity of ideology that it imposes (without appearing to do so, since these are 'obviousnesses') obviousnesses as obviousnesses, which we cannot *fail to recognize* and before which we have the inevitable

---

15 Which borrowed the legal category of 'subject in law' to make an ideological notion: man is by nature a subject.

16 Linguists and those who appeal to linguistics for various purposes often run up against difficulties which arise because they ignore the action of the ideological effects in all discourses – including even scientific discourses.

and natural reaction of crying out (aloud or in the 'silence of consciousness'): 'That's obvious! That's right! That's true!'

At work in this reaction is the ideological *recognition* function which is one of the two functions of ideology as such (its inverse being the function of *misrecognition* [*méconnaissance*]).

To take a highly 'concrete' example, we all have friends who, when they knock on our door and we ask, through the door, the question 'Who's there?', answer (since 'it's obvious') 'It's me'. And we recognize that 'it is him' or 'her'. We open the door, and 'it's true, it really was she who was there'. To take another example, when we recognize somebody of our (previous) acquaintance [*(re)-connaissance*] in the street, we show him that we have recognized him (and have recognized that he has recognized us) by saying to him 'Hello, my friend', and shaking his hand (a material ritual practice of ideological recognition in everyday life – in France, at least; elsewhere, there are other rituals).

In this preliminary remark and these concrete illustrations, I only wish to point out that you and I are *always already* subjects, and as such constantly practice the rituals of ideological recognition, which guarantee for us that we are indeed concrete, individual, distinguishable and (naturally) irreplaceable subjects. The writing I am currently executing and the reading you are currently[17] performing are also in this respect rituals of ideological recognition, including the 'obviousness' with which the 'truth' or 'error' of my reflections may impose itself on you.

But to recognize that we are subjects and that we function in the practical rituals of the most elementary everyday life (the hand-shake, the fact of calling you by your name, the fact of knowing, even if I do not know what it is, that you 'have' a name of your own, which means that you are recognized as a unique subject, etc.) – this recognition only gives us the 'consciousness' of our incessant (eternal) practice of ideological recognition – its consciousness, i.e. its *recognition* – but in no sense does it give us the (scientific) *knowledge* of the mechanism of this recognition. Now it is this knowledge that we have to reach, if you will, while speaking in ideology, and from within ideology we have to outline a discourse which tries to break with ideology, in order to dare to be the beginning of a scientific (i.e. subject-less) discourse on ideology.

Thus in order to represent why the category of the 'subject' is constitutive of ideology, which only exists by constituting concrete subjects as

---

17 NB: this double 'currently' is one more proof of the fact that ideology is 'eternal', since these two 'currentlys' are separated by an indefinite interval; I am writing these lines on 6 April 1969, you may read them at any subsequent time.

subjects, I shall employ a special mode of exposition: 'concrete' enough to be recognized, but abstract enough to be thinkable and thought, giving rise to a knowledge.

As a first formulation I shall say: *all ideology hails or interpellates concrete individuals as concrete subjects*, by the functioning of the category of the subject. This is a proposition which entails that we distinguish for the moment between concrete individuals on the one hand and concrete subjects on the other, although at this level concrete subjects only exist insofar as they are supported by a concrete individual.

I shall then suggest that ideology 'acts' or 'functions' in such a way that it 'recruits' subjects among the individuals (it recruits them all), or 'transforms' the individuals into subjects (it transforms them all) by that very precise operation which I have called *interpellation* or hailing, and which can be imagined along the lines of the most commonplace everyday police (or other) hailing: 'Hey, you there!'[18]

Assuming that the theoretical scene I have imagined takes place in the street, the hailed individual will turn round. By this mere 180-degree physical conversion, he becomes a *subject*. Why? Because he has recognized that the hail was 'really' addressed to him, and that 'it was *really him* who was hailed' (and not someone else). Experience shows that the practical telecommunication of hailings is such that they hardly ever miss their man: verbal call or whistle, the one hailed always recognizes that it is really him who is being hailed. And yet it is a strange phenomenon, and one which cannot be explained solely by 'guilt feelings', despite the large numbers who 'have something on their consciences'.

Naturally for the convenience and clarity of my little theoretical theatre I have had to present things in the form of a sequence, with a before and an after, and thus in the form of a temporal succession. There are individuals walking along. Somewhere (usually behind them) the hail rings out: 'Hey, you there!' One individual (nine times out of ten it is the right one) turns round, believing/suspecting/knowing that it is for him, i.e. recognizing that 'it really is he' who is meant by the hailing. But in reality these things happen without any succession. The existence of ideology and the hailing or interpellation of individuals as subjects are one and the same thing.

I might add: what thus seems to take place outside ideology (to be precise, in the street), in reality takes place in ideology. What really takes place in ideology seems therefore to take place outside it. That is why those who are in ideology believe themselves by definition outside

---

18   Hailing as an everyday practice subject to a precise ritual takes a quite 'special' form in the policeman's practice of 'hailing' which concerns the hailing of 'suspects'.

ideology: one of the effects of ideology is the practical *denegation* of the ideological character of ideology by ideology: ideology never says, 'I am ideological'. It is necessary to be outside ideology, i.e. in scientific knowledge, to be able to say: I am in ideology (a quite exceptional case) or (the general case): I was in ideology. As is well known, the accusation of being in ideology only applies to others, never to oneself (unless one is really a Spinozist or a Marxist, which, in this matter, is to be exactly the same thing). Which amounts to saying that ideology *has no outside* (for itself), but at the same time *that it is nothing but outside* (for science and reality).

Spinoza explained this completely two centuries before Marx, who practiced it but without explaining it in detail. But let us leave this point, although it is heavy with consequences, consequences which are not just theoretical but also directly political, since, for example, the whole theory of criticism and self-criticism, the golden rule of the Marxist-Leninist practice of the class struggle, depends on it.

Thus ideology hails or interpellates individuals as subjects. As ideology is eternal, I must now suppress the temporal form in which I have presented the functioning of ideology, and say: ideology has always-already interpellated individuals as subjects, which amounts to making it clear that individuals are always-already interpellated by ideology as subjects, which necessarily leads us to one last proposition: *individuals are always-already subjects*. Hence individuals are 'abstract' with respect to the subjects which they always already are. This proposition might seem paradoxical.

That an individual is always-already a subject, even before he is born, is nevertheless the plain reality, accessible to everyone and not a paradox at all. Freud shows that individuals are always 'abstract' with respect to the subjects they always-already are, simply by noting the ideological ritual that surrounds the expectation of a 'birth', that 'happy event'. Everyone knows how much and in what way an unborn child is expected. Which amounts to saying, very prosaically, if we agree to drop the 'sentiments', i.e. the forms of family ideology (paternal/maternal conjugal/fraternal) in which the unborn child is expected: it is certain in advance that it will bear its father's name, and will therefore have an identity and be irreplaceable. Before its birth, the child is therefore always-already a subject, appointed as a subject in and by the specific familial ideological configuration in which it is 'expected' once it has been conceived. I hardly need add that this familial ideological configuration is, in its uniqueness, highly structured, and that it is in this implacable and more or less 'pathological' (presupposing that any meaning can be assigned to that term) structure that the former subject-to-be will have to 'find' 'its' place, i.e. 'become' the sexual subject (boy or girl) which it already is in advance. It is clear that this ideological constraint and pre-appointment, and all the rituals of rearing and then education in the family, have some relationship with what Freud studied in the forms of the pre-genital and genital 'stages' of sexuality, i.e. in the 'grip' of what Freud registered by its effects as being the unconscious. But let us leave this point, too, on one side.

Let me go one step further. What I shall now turn my attention to is the way the 'actors' in this *mise-en-scène* of interpellation, and their respective roles, are reflected in the very structure of all ideology.

An example: the Christian religious ideology

As the formal structure of all ideology is always the same, I shall restrict my analysis to a single example, one accessible to everyone, that of religious ideology, with the proviso that the same demonstration can be produced for ethical, legal, political, aesthetic ideology, etc.

Let us therefore consider the Christian religious ideology. I shall use a rhetorical figure and 'make it speak', i.e. collect into a fictional discourse what it 'says' not only in its two Testaments, its theologians and its sermons, but also in its practices, its rituals, its ceremonies and its sacraments. The Christian religious ideology says something like this:

It says: I address myself to you, a human individual called Peter (every individual is called by his name, in the passive sense, it is never he who provides his own name), in order to tell you that God exists and that you are answerable to Him. It adds: God addresses Himself to you through my voice (Scripture having collected the Word of God, tradition having transmitted it, papal infallibility fixing it for ever on 'nice' points). It says: this is who you are: you are Peter! This is your origin, you were created by God for all eternity, although you were born in the 1920th year of Our Lord! This is your place in the world! This is what you must do! By these means, if you observe the 'law of love' you will be saved, you, Peter, and will become part of the Glorious Body of Christ!, etc. . . .

Now this is quite a familiar and banal discourse, but at the same time quite a surprising one.

Surprising because if we consider that religious ideology is indeed addressed to individuals,[19] in order to 'transform them into subjects', by interpellating the individual, Peter, in order to make him a subject, free to obey or disobey the appeal, i.e. God's commandments; if it calls these

---

19 Although we know that the individual is always already a subject, we go on using this term, convenient because of the contrasting effect it produces.

individuals by their names, thus recognizing that they are always-already interpellated as subjects with a personal identity (to the extent that Pascal's Christ says: 'It is for you that I have shed this drop of my blood!'); if it interpellates them in such a way that the subject responds: '*Yes, it really is me!*'; if it obtains from them the *recognition* that they really do occupy the place it designates for them as theirs in the world, a fixed residence: 'It really is me, I am here, a worker, a boss or a soldier!' in this vale of tears; if it obtains from them the recognition of a destination (eternal life or damnation) according to the respect or contempt they show to 'God's Commandments', Law become Love; if everything does happen in this way (in the practices of the well-known rituals of baptism, confirmation, communion, confession and extreme unction, etc. . . .), we should note that all this 'procedure' to set up Christian religious subjects is dominated by a strange phenomenon: the fact that there can only be such a multitude of possible religious subjects on the absolute condition that there is a Unique, Absolute, *Other Subject*, i.e. God.

It is convenient to designate this new and remarkable Subject by writing Subject with a capital S to distinguish it from ordinary subjects, with a small s.

It then emerges that the interpellation of individuals as subjects presupposes the 'existence' of a unique and central other Subject, in whose name the religious ideology interpellates all individuals as subjects. All this is clearly[20] written in what is rightly called the Scriptures. 'And it came to pass at that time that God the Lord (Yahweh) spoke to Moses in the cloud. And the Lord cried to Moses, "Moses!" And Moses replied "It is (really) I! I am Moses thy servant, speak and I shall listen!" And the Lord spoke to Moses and said to him, "*I am that I am*".'

God thus defines Himself as the Subject *par excellence*, He who is through Himself and for Himself ('I am that I am'), and He who interpellates His subject, the individual subjected to Him by his very interpellation, i.e. the individual named Moses. And Moses, interpellated-called by his name, having recognized that it 'really' was he who was called by God, recognizes that he is a subject, a subject *of* God, a subject subjected to God, *a subject through the Subject and subjected to the Subject*. The proof: he obeys Him, and makes his people obey God's Commandments.

God is thus the Subject, and Moses and the innumerable subjects of God's people, the Subject's interlocutors-interpellates: His *mirrors*, His *reflections*. Were not men made *in the image* of God? As all theological reflection proves, whereas He 'could' perfectly well have done without

---

20 I am quoting in a combined way, not to the letter but 'in spirit and truth'.

men, God needs them, the Subject needs the subjects, just as men need God, the subjects need the Subject. Better: God needs men, the great Subject needs subjects, even in the terrible inversion of his image in them (when the subjects wallow in debauchery, i.e. sin).

Better: God duplicates Himself and sends his Son to the Earth, as a mere subject 'forsaken' by Him (the long complaint of the Garden of Olives which ends in the Crucifixion), subject but Subject, man but God, to do what prepares the way for the final Redemption, the Resurrection of Christ. God thus needs to 'make Himself' a man, the Subject needs to become a subject, as if to show empirically, visibly to the eye, tangibly to the hands (see St Thomas) of the subjects, that, if they are subjects, subjected to the Subject, that is solely in order that finally, on Judgement Day, they will re-enter the Lord's Bosom, like Christ, i.e. re-enter the Subject.[21]

Let us decipher into theoretical language this wonderful necessity for the duplication of the *Subject into subjects* and of *the Subject itself into a subject-Subject*.

We observe that the structure of all ideology, interpellating individuals as subjects in the name of a Unique and Absolute Subject, is *speculary*, i.e. a mirror-structure, and *doubly* speculary: this mirror duplication is constitutive of ideology and ensures its functioning. This means that all ideology is *centred*, that the Absolute Subject occupies the unique place of the Centre, and interpellates around it the infinity of individuals into subjects in a double mirror-connexion such that it *subjects* the subjects to the Subject, while giving them in the Subject in which each subject can contemplate its own image (present and future) the *guarantee* that this really concerns them and Him, and that since everything takes place in the Family (the Holy Family: the Family is in essence Holy), 'God will *recognize* His own in it', i.e. those who have recognized God, and have recognized themselves in Him, will be saved.

Let me summarize what we have discovered about ideology in general. The duplicate mirror-structure of ideology ensures simultaneously:

1) the interpellation of 'individuals' as subjects;

2) their subjection to the Subject;

3) the mutual recognition of subjects and Subject, the subjects' recognition of each other, and finally the subject's recognition of himself;[22]

---

21 The dogma of the Trinity is precisely the theory of the duplication of the Subject (the Father) into a subject (the Son) and of their mirror-connexion (the Holy Spirit).

22 Hegel is (unknowingly) an admirable 'theoretician' of ideology insofar as he is a 'theoretician' of Universal Recognition who unfortunately ends up in the ideology of Absolute Knowledge. Feuerbach is an astonishing 'theoretician' of the mirror connexion, who unfortunately ends up in the ideology of the Human Essence. To find the material

4) the absolute guarantee that everything really is so, and that on condition that the subjects recognize what they are and behave accordingly, everything will be all right: Amen − '*So be it*'.

Result: caught in this quadruple system of interpellation as subjects, of subjection to the Subject, of universal recognition and of absolute guarantee, the subjects 'work', they 'work by themselves' in the vast majority of cases, with the exception of the 'bad subjects' who on occasion provoke the intervention of one of the detachments of the (Repressive) State Apparatus. But the vast majority of (good) subjects work all right 'all by themselves', i.e. by ideology (whose concrete forms are realized in the Ideological State Apparatuses). They are inserted into practices governed by the rituals of the ISAs. They 'recognize' the existing state of affairs (*das Bestehende*), that 'it really is true that it is so and not otherwise', and that they must be obedient to God, to their conscience, to the priest, to De Gaulle, to the boss, to the engineer, that thou shalt 'love thy neighbour as thyself', etc. Their concrete, material behaviour is simply the inscription in life of the admirable words of the prayer: '*Amen − So be it*'.

Yes, the subjects 'work by themselves'. The whole mystery of this effect lies in the first two moments of the quadruple system I have just discussed, or, if you prefer, in the ambiguity of the term *subject*. In the ordinary use of the term, subject in fact means: 1) a free subjectivity, a centre of initiatives, author of and responsible for its actions; 2) a subjected being, who submits to a higher authority, and is therefore stripped of all freedom except that of freely accepting his submission. This last note gives us the meaning of this ambiguity, which is merely a reflection of the effect which produces it: the individual *is interpellated as a (free) subject in order that he shall submit freely to the commandments of the Subject, i.e. in order that he shall (freely) accept his subjection*, i.e. in order that he shall make the gestures and actions of his subjection 'all by himself'. *There are no subjects except by and for their subjection*. That is why they 'work all by themselves'.

'*So be it . . .*' This phrase which registers the effect to be obtained proves that it is not 'naturally' so ('naturally': outside the prayer, i.e. outside the ideological intervention). This phrase proves that it *has* to be so if things are to be what they must be, and let us let the words slip: if the reproduction of the relations of production is to be assured, even in the processes of production and circulation, every day, in the 'consciousness', i.e. in the attitudes of the individual-subjects occupying the posts which the socio-technical division of labour assigns to them in

with which to construct a theory of the guarantee, we must turn to Spinoza.

production, exploitation, repression, ideologization, scientific practice, etc. Indeed, what is really in question in this mechanism of the mirror recognition of the Subject and of the individuals interpellated as subjects, and of the guarantee given by the Subject to the subjects if they freely accept their subjection to the Subject's 'commandments'? The reality in question in this mechanism, the reality which is necessarily *ignored* [*méconnue*] in the very forms of recognition (ideology = misrecognition/ ignorance), is indeed, in the last resort, the reproduction of the relations of production and of the relations deriving from them.

January–April 1969

P.S. If these few schematic theses allow me to illuminate certain aspects of the functioning of the superstructure and its mode of intervention in the base, they are obviously *abstract* and necessarily leave several important problems unanswered, which should be mentioned:

1) The problem of the *total process* of the realization of the reproduction of the relations of production.

As an element of this process, the ISAs *contribute* to this reproduction. But the point of view of their contribution alone is still an abstract one.

It is only within the processes of production and circulation that this reproduction is *realized*. It is realized by the mechanisms of those processes, in which the training of the workers is 'completed', their posts assigned them, etc. It is in the internal mechanisms of these processes that the effect of the different ideologies is felt (above all the effect of legal–ethical ideology).

But this point of view is still an abstract one. For in a class society the relations of production are relations of exploitation, and therefore relations between antagonistic classes. The reproduction of the relations of production, the ultimate aim of the ruling class, cannot therefore be a merely technical operation training and distributing individuals for the different posts in the 'technical division' of labour. In fact there is no 'technical division' of labour except in the ideology of the ruling class: every 'technical' division, every 'technical' organization of labour, is the form and mask of a *social* (= class) division and organization of labour. The reproduction of the relations of production can therefore only be a class undertaking. It is realized through a class struggle which counterposes the ruling class and the exploited class.

The *total process* of the realization of the reproduction of the relations of production is therefore still abstract, insofar as it has not adopted the point of view of this class struggle. To adopt the point of view of reproduction is therefore in the last instance to adopt the point of view of the class struggle.

2) The problem of the class nature of the ideolog*ies* existing in a social formation.

The 'mechanism' of ideology *in general* is one thing. We have seen that it can be reduced to a few principles expressed in a few words (as 'poor' as those which, according to Marx, define production *in general*, or in Freud, define *the* unconscious *in general*). If there is any truth in it, this mechanism must be *abstract* with respect to every real ideological formation.

I have suggested that the ideologies were *realized* in institutions, in their rituals and their practices, in the ISAs. We have seen that on this basis they contribute to that form of class struggle, vital for the ruling class, the reproduction of the relations of production. But the point of view itself, however real, is still an abstract one.

In fact, the state and its apparatuses only have meaning from the point of view of the class struggle, as an apparatus of class struggle ensuring class oppression and guaranteeing the conditions of exploitation and its reproduction. But there is no class struggle without antagonistic classes. Whoever says class struggle of the ruling class says resistance, revolt and class struggle of the ruled class.

That is why the ISAs are not the realization of ideology *in general*, nor even the conflict-free realization of the ideology of the ruling class. The ideology of the ruling class does not become the ruling ideology by the grace of God, nor even by virtue of the seizure of state power alone. It is by the installation of the ISAs in which this ideology is realized and realizes itself that it becomes the ruling ideology. But this installation is not achieved all by itself; on the contrary, it is the stake in a very bitter and continuous class struggle: first against the former ruling classes and their positions in the old and new ISAs, then against the exploited class.

But this point of view of the class struggle in the ISAs is still an abstract one. In fact, the class struggle in the ISAs is indeed an aspect of the class struggle, sometimes an important and symptomatic one: e.g. the anti-religious struggle in the eighteenth century, or the 'crisis' of the educational ISA in every capitalist country today. But the class struggle in the ISAs is only one aspect of a class struggle which goes beyond the ISAs. The ideology that a class in power makes the ruling ideology in its ISAs is indeed 'realized' in those ISAs, but it goes beyond them, for it comes from elsewhere. Similarly, the ideology that a ruled class manages to defend in and against such ISAs goes beyond them, for it comes from elsewhere.

It is only from the point of view of the classes, i.e. of the class struggle, that it is possible to explain the ideolog*ies* existing in a social formation.

Not only is it from this starting-point that it is possible to explain the realization of the ruling ideology in the ISAs and of the forms of class struggle for which the ISAs are the seat and the stake. But it is also and above all from this starting-point that it is possible to understand the provenance of the ideologies which are realized in the ISAs and confront one another there. For if it is true that the ISAs represent the *form* in which the ideology of the ruling class must *necessarily* be realized, and the form in which the ideology of the ruled class must *necessarily* be measured and confronted, ideologies are not 'born' in the ISAs, but from the social classes at grips in the class struggle: from their conditions of existence, their practices, their experience of the struggle, etc.

April 1970

Index